THE HIDDEN PLACES OF

YORKSHIRE

INCLUDING THE YORKSHIRE DALES, MOORS AND COAST

By Barbara Vesey

© Travel Publishing Ltd.

Regional Hidden Places

Cornwall
Devon
Dorset, Hants & Isle of Wight
East Anglia
Lake District & Cumbria
Northumberland & Durham
Peak District and Derbyshire
Yorkshire

National Hidden Places

England
Ireland
Scotland
Wales

Hidden Inns

East Anglia
Heart of England
South
South East
West Country

Country Pubs and Inns

Cornwall
Devon
Sussex
Wales
Yorkshire

Country Living Rural Guides

East Anglia
Heart of England
Ireland
North East of England
North West of England
Scotland
South
South East
Wales
West Country

Other Guides

Off the Motorway

Published by: Travel Publishing Ltd, 7a Apollo House, Calleva Park, Aldermaston, Berks, RG7 8TN

ISBN 1-904-434-52-5

© Travel Publishing Ltd

First published 1990, second edition 1993, third edition 1995, fourth edition 1998, fifth edition 2000, sixth edition 2002, seventh edition 2004, eighth edition 2006

Printing by: Scotprint, Haddington

Maps by: © Maps in Minutes ™ (2005)
© Crown Copyright, Ordnance Survey 2005

Editor: Peter Long

Cover Design: Lines and Words, Aldermaston

Cover Photograph: Attermire Scars, ne Settle
© www.picturesofbritain.co.uk

Text Photographs: © www.picturesofbritain.co.uk
and © Bob Brooks, West-super-Mare

Foreword

This is the 8th edition of the *Hidden Places of Yorkshire* which has been fully updated. In this respect we would like to thank the many Tourist Information Centres in Yorkshire for helping us update the editorial content. Regular readers will note that the pages of the guide have been extensively redesigned to allow more information to be presented on the many places to visit in **Yorkshire**. In addition, although you will still find details of places of interest and advertisers of places to stay, eat and drink included under each village, town or city, these are now cross referenced to more detailed information contained in a separate, easy-to-use section of the book. This section is also available as a free supplement from the local Tourist Information Offices.

The county of Yorkshire is full of scenic, historical and cultural diversity. In the northwest are the picturesque Dales with their varied scenery of peat moorland, green pastureland and scattered woods intersected by the numerous brooks, streams and rivers. To the northeast are the imposing Yorkshire Moors, the rich agricultural Vale of York, the chalky hills of the Wolds and the dramatic storm-tossed coastline. In the south are the industrial and commercial cities and towns, which have made such a major contribution to our industrial and cultural heritage

The **Hidden Places** series is a collection of easy to use local and national travel guides taking you on a relaxed but informative tour of Britain and Ireland. Our books contain a wealth of interesting information on the history, the countryside, the towns and villages and the more established places of interest. But they also promote the more secluded and little known visitor attractions and places to stay, eat and drink many of which are easy to miss unless you know exactly where you are going.

We include hotels, inns, restaurants, public houses, teashops, various types of accommodation, historic houses, museums, gardens, and many other attractions all of which are comprehensively indexed. Most places are accompanied by an attractive photograph and are easily located by using the map at the beginning of each chapter. We do not award merit marks or rankings but concentrate on describing the more interesting, unusual or unique features of each place with the aim of making the reader's stay in the local area an enjoyable and stimulating experience.

Whether you are visiting Yorkshire for business or pleasure or are a local inhabitant, we do hope that you enjoy reading and using this book. We are always interested in what readers think of places covered (or not covered) in our guides so please do not hesitate to use the reader reaction forms provided to give us your considered comments. We also welcome any general comments which will help us improve the guides themselves. Finally if you are planning to visit any other corner of the British Isles we would like to refer you to the order form for other **Hidden Places** titles to be found at the rear of the book and to the Travel Publishing website at www.travelpublishing.co.uk.

Travel Publishing

Contents

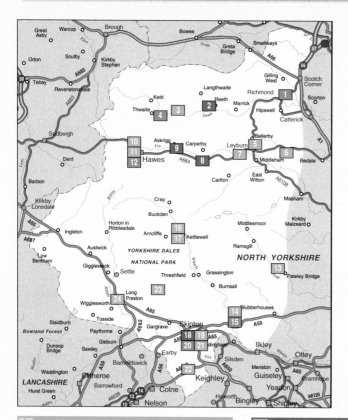

🍴 FOOD & DRINK

🛏 ACCOMMODATION

🏛 PLACES OF INTEREST

The Yorkshire Dales

The Yorkshire Dales make up one of the 11 National Parks in England and Wales. An area rich in farmland, high moorland and deep valleys, the predominant limestone found here gives rise to many of the area's interesting geological features – such as those found around Malham, the waterfalls at Aysgarth and Hardraw and White Scar Cave – while there is also an abundance of potholes and disappearing rivers that characterise the area. Considered by many to be the most appealing and beautiful region in the country, the Yorkshire Dales have drawn increasing numbers of visitors since the arrival of the railways in the 1800s. Many settlements date back to the Bronze and Iron Ages. With the large industrial areas of Yorkshire, and with Lancashire close to hand, the Dales are easily accessible – and with so much open countryside, visitors are able to avoid the more popular attractions and enjoy the beauty of the region in solitude.

The largest of the northern Dales, Swaledale is also one of the grandest and it has a rugged beauty that is in contrast to the pretty and busier Wensleydale to the south. It is this dale's sheep, the Swaledale, with their characteristic black faces, white muzzles and grey speckled legs, which have been adopted as the symbol for the National Park. The valley of the River Ure, Wensleydale, is, perhaps, the one that most people associate with the Yorkshire Dales. One of the longer dales, it is a place of green pastureland grazed by flocks of Wensleydale sheep, lines of drystone walls and, of course, this is where the famous cheese is made. Further south again, is Wharfedale, a spectacular valley

that is home to one of the National Park's most famous features, the Strid, where the River Wharfe charges through a narrow gorge just to the north of Bolton Abbey. To the east lies Nidderdale, a charming valley that was dubbed 'Little Switzerland' by the Victorians as its upper reaches are steep and wooded with the River Nidd flowing through narrow gorges. To the west is Ribbledale that is overlooked by the famous Three Peaks of Whernside, Ingleborough and Pen-ghent, and that is also home to a spectacular stretch of the famous Settle-Carlisle Railway. Finally, there is Airedale, the valley of the River Aire, where, near the river's source, can be found the extraordinary limestone landscape around Malham Tarn. Further downstream lies Skipton, an ancient market town and 'Gateway to the Dales' that is often many people's first experience of this glorious region of Britain.

The Yorkshire Dales provide the perfect setting for walking with at least 1,000 miles of public footpaths and ancient trackways, along with miles of bridleways. The Pennine Way, Britain's first long-distance footpath, is some 270 miles in length and particularly inviting for ramblers in part or as a whole. Meanwhile, the much shorter Dales Way, from Leeds to Lake Windermere in Cumbria, takes in old textile villages and the towns of West Yorkshire before heading through the western section of the Dales and on into Lancashire. There is also the Trans Pennine Trail that not only runs right across the country from east to west but also has a variety of extra, small diversions for those wishing to undertake shorter walks.

SWALEDALE

Swaledale sheep will be a familiar sight to anyone who spends time in the Dales. Recognised by their black faces, white muzzle and grey speckled legs, the Swaledale sheep were introduced to the area in the 1920s. Each flock knows its own territory – they are said to be 'heafed' to the moor. The sheep have to cope with extremely wild weather and their hardiness is typified by the warmth and durability of their wool. No surprise to find that the ram has been adopted as the emblem of the Yorkshire Dales National Park.

For many, Swaledale is the loveliest of the Yorkshire Dales. From historic Richmond it runs westwards through countryside that ranges from the dramatic lower dale with its steep-sided wooded hills to austere upper reaches – a terrain where your nearest neighbour could be several miles away. Its rugged beauty makes quite a contrast to pretty and busier Wensleydale just to the south. There are several other noticeable differences: the villages in Swaledale all have harsher, Nordic sounding names, the dale is much less populated, and the rivers and becks are more fast flowing mountain streams.

At one time Swaledale was a hive of activity and enjoyed a prosperous century and more when the lead-mining industry flourished here. The valley of the River Swale still bears many of the scars left behind since the mining declined and the dale once again became a remote and under-populated place. The attractive market town of Richmond, first settled by the Romans, has for many years been the major focal point of this northerly region of Yorkshire. With several interesting museums, a fine Norman castle and excellent shopping facilities, Richmond is still the key town in the northern dales.

There are several side dales to Swaledale: the small, thriving market town of Reeth lies at the junction of Arkengarthdale and the valley of the River Swale. First settled by Norsemen who preferred wild and remote countryside, the valley of Arkle Beck was not considered important enough to gain an entry in the *Domesday Book*. There is much evidence of the old lead-mining days although the dale is now chiefly populated by hardy Swaledale sheep. At the head of this rather bleak and barren dale lies England's highest inn, Tan Hill. Though only a short section of the River Tees flows through Yorkshire, the section of Teesdale around Piercebridge is particularly charming and well worth a visit.

RICHMOND

4 miles SW of Scotch Corner on the A6108

The former county of Richmondshire (which still

Swaledale

survives as a parliamentary constituency) once occupied a third of the North Riding of Yorkshire. Alan Rufus, the 1st Earl of Richmond, built the original **Richmond Castle** in 1071 and the site, 100 feet up on a rocky promontory with the River Swale passing below, is imposing and well chosen. The keep rises to 109 feet with walls 11 feet thick, while the other side is afforded an impregnable defence by means of the cliff and the river. Richmond Castle was the first Norman castle in the country to be built, right from the foundations, in stone. Additions were made over subsequent years but it reached its final form in the 14th century. Since then it has fallen into ruin though a considerable amount of the original Norman stonework remains intact.

Richmond Castle

With such an inspiring setting, it is hardly surprising that there is a legend suggesting that King Arthur himself is buried here, reputedly in a cave beneath the castle. The story goes that a simple potter called Thompson stumbled across an underground passage which led to a chamber where he discovered the king and his knights lying in an enchanted sleep, surrounded by priceless treasures. A voice warned him not to disturb the sleepers and he fled. Predictably, he was unable to locate the passage again. Another legend associated with the castle tells how a drummer boy was sent down the passageway. Beating his drum as he walked, the boy's progress was followed by the soldiers on the surface until, suddenly, the drumming stopped. Though the passageway was searched the boy was never seen again but, it is said, his drumming can still be heard.

During the Middle Ages, the markets of Richmond gave the town much of its prosperity and its influence spread across Yorkshire to Lancashire. Also, like many North Yorkshire towns and villages, the textile industry played an important role in the continuation of the town's wealth and, for some time, Richmond became famous for its knitted stockings.

The **Green Howards Museum**, the regimental museum of the North Riding's infantry, is based in the old Trinity Church in the centre of the cobbled market square. The regiment dates back to 1688, when it was founded, and the displays and collections illustrate its

In 1315, Edward II granted Richmond the right to protect the town by a stone wall after Scottish raiders had caused considerable damage in the surrounding area. By the 16th century, the walls were in a state of disrepair and little survives today. Two road bridges cross the River Swale in the town. The older of the two, Green Bridge, was erected in 1789 to the designs of John Carr after the existing bridge had been swept away by flood water. Its picturesque setting is enhanced by the massive cliff crowned by Richmond Castle that towers above it.

I RICHMONDSHIRE MUSEUM

Richmond

The museum tells the history of Richmond and its people and contains several interesting reconstructions.

 see page 200

About a mile east of the town lies Easby Abbey, a delightful monastic ruin which looks down to the River Swale. Founded in 1155 by Roald, Constable of Richmond Castle, its order of monks were of more modest leanings than the Cistercians, and the building certainly possesses none of the grandiose lines of Rievaulx and Fountains, although the riverside setting is a common feature. The Abbey's most notable feature is its replica of the Easby Cross, an Anglo-Saxon cross dating from the 9th century and the extensive ruins can be reached by a pleasant riverside walk that is well sign-posted.

history with war relics, weapons, uniforms, medals, and regimental silver. Also housed in the museum is the town's silver. The church itself was founded in 1135 and, though it has been altered and rebuilt on more than one occasion, the original Norman tower and some other masonry have survived.

One of the grandest buildings in the town is the **Culloden Tower**, just off the town green. It was erected in 1747 by the Yorke family, one of whose members had fought at the Battle of Culloden the previous year. Unlike most follies, the interior of the three storey tower is elaborately decorated in the rococo style and since it is now in the care of the Landmark Trust it is possible to stay there.

It is not surprising that a town steeped in history should have several museums. The **Richmondshire Museum** traces the history of this old place and its county. There is also a reconstruction of James Herriot's veterinary surgery taken from the popular television series as well as other period costumes and displays.

Richmond is also home to England's oldest theatre, the **Georgian Theatre Royal**, which originally formed part of a circuit that included Northallerton, Ripon, and Harrogate. Built in 1788 by the actor and manager Samuel Butler, it had at that time an audience capacity of 400. The connection with the theatrical Butler family ended in 1830 and from then until 1848 it was used, infrequently, by

travelling companies. After the mid-19th century and right up until the 1960s, the theatre saw a variety of uses, as a wine cellar and a corn chandler's among others, and it did not re-open as a theatre until 1963 and only then after much restoration work had been carried out. The **Georgian Theatre Royal Museum** was also opened and it contains a unique collection of original playbills as well as the oldest and largest complete set of painted scenery in Britain.

AROUND RICHMOND

HUDSWELL

2 miles W of Richmond off the A6136

This ancient village, which was well established by the time it was recorded in the *Domesday Book*, stands high above the River Swale and over the years the village has gravitated to a more sheltered spot. The present St Michael's Church was built in the late 19th century on the site of an older building and the view from the churchyard is considered to be one of the finest in Richmondshire.

The walk from the village down to the river leads through pleasant woodland and also takes in some 365 steps. About half way down, below a path leading off to an old lime kiln, can be found **King Arthur's Oven**, a horizontal crack in the limestone which, it is claimed, has connections with Richmond Castle and the legend of King Arthur.

KIRBY HILL

4 miles NW of Richmond off the A66

This quiet hamlet lies midway between London and Edinburgh on the old Great North Road and in the days of the stagecoach it was a busy stopping place. The cellar of the Blue Bell Inn still retains the rings to which prisoners travelling between the two capitals were tethered overnight.

RAVENSWORTH

5 miles NW of Richmond on minor road off the A66

Lying in the small and little-known dale of Holmedale, the Methodist chapel here, built in 1822, is the oldest chapel on the Richmond circuit. To the southeast of the village are the remains of the Fitzhughs' Norman castle which is believed to have been in existence in 1180. However, the present ruins suggest that the demolished building was of a 14th-century construction. The castle is privately owned with no public access.

EAST LAYTON

4 miles NW of Scotch Corner off the B6274

The summer of 1999 saw the opening of a major new visitor attraction in North Yorkshire. **Miniature World** offers families and school groups a wonderful day out, giving them the opportunity of meeting a wide range of small animals (including rare breeds), enjoying pony rides, honing their orienteering skills and much more. Miniature World is open by appointment only. Gill and Stephen Sims, who created this unique project, like to ensure that each visit is individually tailored to suit the party.

FORCETT

6 miles N of Scotch Corner on the B6274

The mainly Norman village Church of St Cuthbert underwent a drastic restoration programme in 1859 and the interior is now chiefly Victorian. Nearby Forcett Park, which is privately owned, is a particularly outstanding example of an early Georgian house, complete with stables, lodges, and a fine dovecote. The dovecote and the splendid east gate can be seen from the road leading to the park from the village.

REETH

11 miles W of Richmond on the B6270

Considered the capital of Upper Swaledale, this small town is poised at the junction of the River Swale and its main tributary, Arkle Beck. The local lead-mining industry, which was begun by the Romans, served the town well for many years, until competition from abroad gradually caused its decline and Reeth became chiefly an agricultural centre. Noted in the *Domesday Book*, while everything else in the area was written off as untaxable wasteland, Reeth prospered and it is still today a much-visited place.

Along the top of the green is High Row, with its inns and shops and outstanding Georgian architecture, reflecting the affluence of the town in the 18th century

Until the end of the 19th century a total of four fairs were held in Reeth annually, as well as a weekly market. Today, the annual agricultural show in September is still a magnet for farmers from the entire length of the dale and beyond.

2 THE BURGOYNE HOTEL

Reeth

Gracious and elegant hotel on the B6270 west of Richmond, 30 minutes from Scotch Corner and the A66. First-class facilities.

 see page 200

•

Running northwestwards from Reeth, Arkengarthdale is a small and remote valley, mostly treeless moorland with scarcely a human habitation in sight. It was first settled by Norsemen and their presence is still reflected in the dale's place names – Booze, Eskeleth, and Wham. Overlooked completely during the Domesday survey, when it was considered of no value, the dale experienced a period of prosperity in the 18th and 19th centuries from lead-mining. Ruins of the old industrial buildings are scattered around the valley, as yet overlooked by the heritage industry.

•

when the trade in wool and lead was booming.

The newly refurbished **Swaledale Folk Museum**, housed in what was once the old Methodist Sunday School, is the home for exhibits of local farming methods, crafts, and mining skills, as well as displays on local pastimes, the impact of Wesleyan Methodism, and the exodus of the population to the industrial areas of the south Pennines and America when the lead mines closed.

This little town is noted for its variety of craft shops. There's a cluster of them at the **Reeth Craft Workshops** near the green. Here you'll find a cabinet maker, a furniture maker, a guitar maker, a pottery shop, a clock maker and restorer, a sculptor, a silversmith, a photographer and Stef's Models where visitors can see the production of beautifully crafted animal models. Paintings are also on sale here.

GRINTON

1 mile S of Reeth on the B6270

Just to the south of Reeth lies the quiet village of Grinton whose parish **Church of St Andrew** served the whole of the dale for centuries. The building dates back to the 13th and 15th centuries, though there are still some Norman remains as well as a Leper's Squint (a small hole through which those afflicted by the disease could follow the service within). For those people living in the upper reaches of Swaledale who died, there was a long journey down the track to Grinton which became known as the **Corpse Way**.

HEALAUGH

2 miles W of Reeth on the B6270

In the 12th century an Augustinian Priory was founded here but none of the remaining fragments date from earlier than the 15th century. However, the village Church of St Helen and St John, which dates from around 1150, not only has outstanding views over the dale to the Pennines but also has a bullet hole which, it is alleged, was made by a Cromwellian trooper on his way to Marsden Moor.

LANGTHWAITE

3 miles NW of Reeth off the B6270

Langthwaite, the main village of Arkengarthdale, will seem familiar to many who have never been here before as its bridge featured in the title sequence of the popular television series *All Creatures Great and Small*. Just outside this beautiful place stands the cryptically named CB Hotel – named after Charles Bathurst, an 18th-century lord of the manor who was responsible for the development of the lead-mining industry in the dale. His grandfather, Dr John Bathurst, physician to Oliver Cromwell, had purchased the land here in 1659 with the exploitation of its mineral wealth in mind.

LOW ROW

4 miles W of Reeth on the B6270

In medieval times the track along the hillside above Low Row formed part of the Corpse Way along which relays of bearers would carry the deceased in a large wicker basket on journeys that could take two days to complete. Along their route, you can still see the large stone slabs where they rested their burden. Even more convenient was the 'Dead Barn' above Low Row where the carriers could deposit the body and scramble downhill for a convivial evening at the Punch Bowl Inn.

Located on the edge of the village, **Hazel Brow Organic Farm & Visitor Centre** provides a popular family day out. Set in glorious Swaledale scenery the 200-acre traditional family-run farm offers children the opportunity of bottle feeding lambs, riding a pony or helping to feed the calves, sheep and pigs. The farm also has a tea room, children's play area and gift shop, and hosts various demonstrations of farming activities throughout the year.

GUNNERSIDE

6 miles W of Reeth on the B6270

This charming Dales village in the heart of Swaledale was, until the late 19th century, a thriving lead-mining village. Gunnerside became known as the Klondyke of Swaledale and, although the boom centred around lead rather than gold, the Old Gang Mines are the most famous in Yorkshire. The paths and trackways here are mainly those trodden by the many successions of miners travelling to their work and the valley's sides still show the signs of the mine workings. In the village, one

can visit tearooms that offer such delights as 'Lead Miners' Bait' and the delicious 'Gunnerside Cheese Cake' made from a recipe handed down from mining days.

After the closure of the mines, many families left the village to find work elsewhere in northern England while others emigrated to America and even as far afield as Australia. For many years afterwards one of the village's most important days was Midsummer Sunday when those who had left would, if able, return and catch up with their families and friends.

Gunnerside's most impressive building is its **Methodist Chapel,** a classically elegant building, wonderfully light and airy. The indefatigable John Wesley visited Gunnerside in 1761 and found the

Just west of Low Row, a road to the left attracts many visitors with its signpost pointing to 'Crackpot'. All you will find is a perfectly sensible-looking cluster of working farmhouses. Crackpot simply means a place where crows (crack) congregate around a deep hole in the hills (a pot).

Gunnerside

9

3 THE KING'S HEAD

Gunnerside

Superb pub with real ales and chef-prepared food, found on the B6270 west of Reeth.

 see page 201

4 SWALEDALE WOOLLENS

Muker in Swaledale

Reached via the B6270, one of Yorkshire's premier attractions for over 30 years.

 see page 200

local congregation 'earnest, loving and simple people'.

What makes **The Old Working Smithy & Museum** rather special is the fact that nothing has been bought in – all the artefacts on show are from the smithy itself, indeed many of them were actually made here. The smithy was established in 1795 and over the years little has been thrown away. Cartwheels, cobblers' tools, horseshoes, fireside implements and a miner's 'tub' (railway wagon) from a lead mine are just some of the vintage articles on show. This is still a working smithy. Stephen Calvert is the 6th generation of his family to pursue the trade of blacksmith and he still uses the original forge and hand bellows to create a wide range of wrought ironwork.

Gunnerside's picturesque hump-backed bridge over the Swale is reputed to be haunted by a headless ghost. Oddly, no gruesome tale has grown up around this unfortunate spirit.

IVELET

7 miles W of Reeth off the B6270

Just a few hundred yards off the B6270, the 14th-century **Packhorse bridge** at Ivelet is regarded as one of the finest in Yorkshire. It's a very picturesque spot and you can also join a delightful riverside walk here.

MUKER

8 miles W of Reeth on the B6270

An old stone bridge leads into this engaging village which consists of a collection of beige-coloured stone cottages overlooked by the **Church of St Mary** which dates back to the time of Elizabeth I – one of the very few to be built in England during her reign. Most church builders until that time had spared no expense in glorifying the house of God. At Muker they were more economical: the church roof was covered in thatch, its floor in rushes. No seating was provided. Despite such penny-pinching measures, the new church of 1580 was warmly welcomed since it brought to an end the tedious journey for bereaved relatives along the Corpse Way to the dale's mother church at Grinton, some eight miles further to the east.

On the gravestones in the churchyard local family names, such as Harker, Alderson, and Fawcett feature prominently as they do among the villagers still living here.

Close by the church is a quaint little building identified as the Literary Institute from whence you may hear the strains of a brass band rehearsing. In Victorian times, most of the Dales villages had their own brass band – Muker's is the only survivor and is in great demand at various events throughout the year.

Swaledale cuisine is equally durable: specialities on offer in the local tearooms include Swaledale Curd Tart, Yorkshire Rarebit, and Deep Apple Pie with Wensleydale cheese. And the main crafts still revolve around the wool provided by the hardy Swaledale sheep, in great demand by carpet manufacturers and for jumpers worn by fell walkers, climbers, and anyone else trying to defeat the British weather.

THWAITE

10 miles W of Reeth on the B6270

Surrounded by dramatic countryside which includes Kisdon Hill, Great Shunnor, High Seat, and Lovely Seat, this is a tiny village of ancient origins. Like so many places in the area the name comes from the Nordic language, in this case *thveit*, meaning a clearing in the wood. The woodlands which once provided shelter and fuel for the Viking settlers have long since gone.

To the southwest of the village lies **Buttertubs Pass**, one of the highest and most forbidding mountain passes in the country. The Buttertubs themselves are a curious natural feature of closely packed vertical stone stacks rising from some unseen, underground base to the level of the road. A local Victorian guide to the Buttertubs, perhaps aware that the view from above was not all that impressive, solemnly assured his client that 'some of the Buttertubs had no bottom, and some were deeper than that'. No one is quite sure where the Buttertubs name came from. The most plausible explanation is that farmers used its deep-chilled shelves as a convenient refrigerator for the butter they couldn't sell immediately. Unusually, these potholes

are not linked by a series of passages as most are, but are free-standing and bear only a slight resemblance to the objects after which they are named. The narrow road from Thwaite across the Buttertubs Pass is not for the faint-hearted driver. Only a flimsy post and wire fence separates the road from a sheer drop of Alpine proportions. In any case, it's much more satisfying to cross the pass from the other direction, from Hawes: from the south, as you crest the summit you will be rewarded with a stupendous view of Swaledale stretching for miles.

KELD

10 miles W of Reeth on the B6270

The little cluster of stone buildings that make up this village stand beside the early stages of the River Swale. The place is alive with the

The Buttertubs, Thwaite

• *The good people of Muker devised means of making savings. For many years, the thrifty mourners of the parish shared a communal coffin. Year after year the same coffin would bear the departed to the churchyard where the shrouded body was removed, placed in the grave and the coffin retrieved for use at the next funeral. It wasn't until 1735 that the vicar decreed that everyone buried in his parish deserved the dignity of a personal coffin.* •

For really serious walkers, Keld is the most important crossroads in northern England. Here the south-to-north Pennine Way and the east-to-west Coast-to-Coast long-distance walks intersect.

sound of rushing water and it comes as no surprise that the word *keld* is Nordic for spring. For lovers of green woodlands and breathtaking waterfalls, this village is definitely well worth a visit and it has also managed to retain an impression of being untouched by modern life.

Wain Wath Force, with rugged Cotterby Scar providing a fine backdrop, can be found alongside the Birkdale road. Catrake Force, with its stepped formation, can be reached from the cottages on the left at the bottom of the street in the village. Though on private land the falls and, beside them, the entrance to an old lead mine can still be seen. For less adventurous pedestrians Kisdon Force, the most impressive waterfall in Swaledale, can be reached by a gentle stroll of less than a mile from the village along a well-trodden path.

TAN HILL

10 miles NW of Reeth off the B6270

Standing at the head of Arkengarthdale on the border with County Durham, 1,732 feet above sea level, is England's highest pub, the **Tan Hill Inn**. Why on earth should there be a pub here, in one of the most remote and barren stretches of the north Pennines, frequently cut off and in total isolation during the winter? A century ago, the inn's patrons didn't need to ask. Most of them were workers from the Tan Hill coal mines; others were drivers waiting for their horse-drawn carts to be filled with coal. The coal mines

have long since closed but an open coal fire still burns in the inn 365 days a year and some 50,000 visitors a year still find their way to Tan Hill. Many of them are walkers who stagger in from one of the most gruelling stretches of the Pennine Way Walk and, clutching a pint of Theakston's 'Old Peculier', collapse on the nearest settle.

During the long winters when the moorland roads have disappeared under 12-feet deep snowdrifts and, despite cellar walls three feet thick, the pub's beer-pumps have frozen, trade tends to fall off a bit. It revives spectacularly on the last Thursday in May. This is when the **Tan Hill Sheep Fair** takes place and, if only for a day, Tan Hill Inn becomes the centre of agricultural Yorkshire. 'It's the Royal Show for Swaledale Sheep is Tan Hill,' said one proud farmer scrutinising his flock, 'and I've got some princes and princesses here.' In cash terms the value of the prizes awarded at the Fair is negligible – just a few pounds for even a first class rosette. But at the auction that follows it's a different story. In 1990 one particularly prized Tupp Hogg (a young ram) was sold for £30,000.

WENSLEYDALE

Wensleydale, perhaps above all the others, is the dale most people associate with the Yorkshire Dales. Charles Kingsley once described it as 'the richest spot in all England ... a beautiful oasis in the mountains'. At some 40 miles long it is certainly the longest dale and it is also softer and greener than many of its neighbours. The pasture land, grazed by flocks of Wensleydale sheep, is only broken by the long lines of dry stone walls and the dale is, of course, famous for its cheese whose fortunes have recently been given an additional boost by Wallace and Gromit who have declared it to be their favourite!

Wensleydale is the only major dale not to be named after its river, the Ure, although until fairly recent years most locals still referred to the area as Yoredale, or Uredale. The dale's name comes from the once important town of Wensley where the lucrative trade in cheese began in the 13th century. Wensley prospered for many years until 1563 when the Black Death annihilated most of its people and Leyburn became the trading centre of the lower dale. Wensleydale is also recorded in the 12th century as Wandelesleydale – 'Waendel's woodland clearing in the valley'. Waendel has disappeared into the mists of time but undoubtedly his clearing was somewhere near this attractive little village.

At the western end of the dale is Hawes, derived from the Norse word *hals* meaning neck and, indeed, the town does lies on a neck of land between two hills. Home of the Dales Countryside Museum and the Wensleydale Creamery, Hawes is an ideal starting point for exploring the dale. It is widely believed that the medieval monks of Jervaulx Abbey were

River Ure, Wensleydale

responsible for introducing the manufacture of cheese to the dale some 700 years ago (they were of French origin). It was first made from ewe's milk but by the 1600s the milk of shorthorn cows was used instead since the sheep were becoming increasingly important for their wool and mutton. Originally just a summer occupation and mainly the task of the farmer's wife, the production of Wensleydale cheese was put on a commercial footing when the first cheese factory was established at Gayle Beck, near Hawes, in 1897.

As it flows down the dale, the Ure is fed by a series of smaller rivers and becks, many of which have their own charming dale. Among the better-known are Coverdale, the home of some of England's finest racehorse stables,

•

Using Hawes as a base, visitors can also follow the Turner Trail which takes in the scenic sights that so impressed JMW Turner when he visited Wensleydale and neighbouring Swaledale in 1816.

•

13

•

Wensleydale, along with Swaledale and the area around Thirsk, are commonly referred to as Herriot Country *since it was this region of fells and friendly villages that provided many locations for the BBC series* **All Creatures Great and Small.** *Based on the working life of the real life vet, Alf Wight (1916-95), the stories recount the working life of Dalespeople between the 1930s and 1960s with humour and affection.*

•

5 THE GOLDEN LION HOTEL

Leyburn

Superb traditional inn with a good reputation for excellent food, drink and accommodation, in the heart of Leyburn overlooking the Market Square.

 〓 see page 202

and peaceful Bishopdale with its ancient farmhouses. Remote Cotterdale, with its striking waterfall, and the narrow valley of the River Waldern are also well worth exploring.

LEYBURN

The main market town and trading centre of mid-Wensleydale, Leyburn is an attractive town with a broad marketplace lined by handsome late-Georgian and Victorian stone buildings. Friday is market day when the little town is even busier than usual. There's an interesting mix of traditional family-run shops and surprisingly large supermarkets behind deceptively small frontages. Leyburn also boasts the only cinema, The Elite, to be found in the Dales.

The town has several interesting connections with famous people. Lord Nelson's surgeon, Peter Goldsmith, once lived in the Secret Garden House on Grove Square (and is buried in Wensley church, just a mile up the road). Flight Lieutenant Alan Broadley DSO, DFC, DFM, of Dam Busters fame, is named on the War Memorial in the main square, and just a few yards away is the birthplace of the 'Sweet Lass' of Richmond Hill. Many believe that the popular song refers to Richmond Hill in Surrey rather than Richmond, North Yorkshire. Not so. Frances I'Anson was born in her grandfather's house on Leyburn High Street and his initials,

WIA, can still be seen above the door of what is now an interior decorator's shop. It was her husband-to-be, Leonard McNally, who composed the immortal song.

A fairly recent addition to Leyburn's attractions is **Beech End Model Village** in Commercial Square. Unique among model villages, this one is indoors. The scenery is finely detailed and there's plenty of hands-on fun to be had controlling the working models.

On the eastern edge of the town is Leyburn Station. Until recently you would have had a long wait here for a train – the last passenger train left some 50 years earlier. But an energetic group of railway enthusiasts have laboured for years to get the line re-opened and on July 4th, 2003 their efforts were finally successful. The **Wensleydale Railway** now offers regular services to Bedale and Leeming Bar, a 12-mile route through pretty countryside. Normally, the train is driven by a vintage diesel locomotive but there are special steam train days. The Wensleydale Railway Company hopes to extend the service to the main line station at Northallerton and, even more ambitious, to extend westwards to meet up with the Settle and Carlisle railway.

The Shawl, to the west of the town, is a mile-long limestone scarp along which runs a footpath offering lovely panoramic views of the dale. A popular legend suggests that it gained its unusual name when Mary, Queen of Scots dropped her shawl here during her unsuccessful attempt to escape from Bolton Castle. However, a more likely explanation is that Shawl is a corruption of the name given to the ancient settlement here.

Leyburn Business Park is home to **The Violin Making Workshop.** Little has changed in the art of violin making over the centuries and the traditional tools and methods used by such master craftsmen as Stradivari are still employed today. Repairs and commissions are undertaken.

Close by, at **The Teapottery**, you can see other craftspeople at work – in this case creating a whole range of witty and unusual teapots, anything from a grand piano to a bathtub complete with yellow duck. The finished pots can be purchased in the showroom where there's also a tea room where your tea is served, naturally, in one of the astonishing teapots produced here.

Within the same business park are Tennant's of Yorkshire, the only major provincial auction house in England which holds regular auctions throughout the year, and the Little Chocolate Shop where visitors can watch hand-made chocolates being crafted and purchase the end product.

About two miles east of Leyburn, off the A684, the **Longwool Sheepshop** at Cross Lanes Farm in Garriston is a treat for anyone who appreciates good knitwear. Garments can be specially knitted to the customer's requirements. You can see the raw material grazing in the surrounding fields – rare Wensleydale longwool

sheep. The Sheepshop also stocks an extensive range of hand knitting yarns and patterns for the enthusiast.

AROUND LEYBURN

CONSTABLE BURTON

4 miles E of Leyburn on the A684

Surrounded by walled and wooded parkland **Constable Burton Hall** is famous for its gardens (open March to October) and in particular its spacious, romantic terraces. The house itself is not open to the public but its stately Georgian architecture provides a magnificent backdrop to the fine gardens, noble trees and colourful borders.

SPENNITHORNE

2 miles SE of Leyburn off the A684

This pleasant little village dates back many years. The present Church of St Michael and All Angels stands on the site of a Saxon church although the only remains of the ancient building to be seen are two ornamental stones set into the walls of the chancels and a Saxon monument in the vestry.

Two of Spennithorne's earlier residents are worth mentioning. John Hutchinson was born here in 1675 and went on to become steward to the 6th Duke of Somerset – and a rather controversial philosopher. He vehemently disagreed with Sir Isaac Newton's theory of gravity and was equally ardent in asserting that the earth was neither flat, nor a sphere,

6 THE QUEEN'S HEAD

Finghall

Superb country inn set in picturesque surroundings with first-class cuisine, real ales and excellent accommodation.

see page 203

•

Middleham is often referred to as the 'Newmarket of the North', a term you'll understand when you see the strings of thoroughbred racehorses clip-clopping through the town on their way to training runs on Low Moor. It was the monks of Jervaulx Abbey who founded this key industry. By the late 18th century races were being run across the moorland and the first stables established. Since then, the stables have produced a succession of classic race winners with one local trainer, Neville Crump, having three Grand National winners to his credit within the space of 12 years.

•

but a cube. Though there are no records mentioning that Hutchinson was ever considered as of unsound mind, another resident of Spennithorne, Richard Hatfield, was officially declared insane after he fired a gun at George III.

MIDDLEHAM

2 miles SE of Leyburn on the A6108

Middleham is an enchanting little town which, despite having a population of fewer than 800, boasts its own Mayor, Corporation and quaint Town Hall. It is also the site of one of Yorkshire's most historic castles, 12 of England's most successful racing stables and not just one, but two, marketplaces. It is almost totally unspoilt, with a wealth of handsome Georgian houses and hostelries huddled together in perfect architectural harmony.

Rising high above the town are the magnificent ruins of **Middleham Castle** (English Heritage), a once-mighty fortress whose most glorious days came in the 15th century when most of northern England was ruled from here by the Neville family. The castle's most famous resident was the 'evil' Richard III who was sent here as a lad of 13 to be trained in the 'arts of nobilitie'. Whatever crimes he committed later down in London, Richard was popular locally, ensuring the town's prosperity by granting it a fair and a twice-yearly market. The people of Middleham had good reason to mourn his death at the Battle of Bosworth in 1485.

EAST WITTON

4 miles SE of Leyburn on the A6108

An attractive village set beside the confluence of the rivers Cover and Ure, East Witton was almost entirely rebuilt after a great fire in 1796. The new buildings included the well-proportioned Church of St John although the old churchyard with its many interesting gravestones remains. Some two decades after that conflagration the village was struck by another calamity. In 1820, 20 miners perished in a coal mine accident at Witton Fell. They were all buried together in one grave in the new churchyard.

Just to the west of the village is **Jervaulx Abbey**, one of the great Cistercian sister houses to Fountains Abbey. The

Middleham Castle

name Jervaulx is a French derivation of Yore (or Ure), and Vale, just as Rievaulx is of Rye Vale. Before the Dissolution, the monks of Jervaulx Abbey owned huge tracts of Wensleydale and this now-solitary spot was once a busy trading and administrative centre. Despite its ruination, Jervaulx is among the most evocative of Yorkshire's many fine abbeys. The grounds have been transformed into beautiful gardens with the crumbling walls providing interesting backdrops for the sculptured trees and colourful plants and shrubs.

COVERHAM

4 miles S of Leyburn off the A6108

Lying beside the River Cover in little-visited Coverdale, this village is perhaps best known for the remains of **Coverham Abbey** (private). Built in the late 1200s, only some decorated arches remain, along with a Norman gateway. The nearby 17th-century manor house, Braithwaite Hall (National Trust), as well as other surrounding buildings, have clearly used the Abbey's stones in their construction – in some of the walls effigies from the old building can clearly be seen. The Hall can be visited by prior arrangement.

Also in the village is the delightful walled Forbidden Garden, which includes a grotto with an underground labyrinth of chambers and passages. There is a shop and refreshment room; admission is by pre-booked tickets only. The garden is open daily from April until October and on Sundays until Christmas.

WENSLEY

1 mile W of Leyburn on the A684

This peaceful little village beside the River Ure was once the main settlement in mid-Wensleydale and such was its importance it gave its name to the dale. However, in 1563, the town was struck by plague and those who could fled up the hill to Leyburn which was thought to be a healthier place.

The stately **Church of the Holy Trinity** is one of only two surviving medieval structures in Wensley (the other is the graceful bridge nearby) and it is thought to have been built on the site of an earlier Saxon church. Inside can be seen the unusual Bolton family pews which are actually a pair of opera boxes that were brought here from London during the 1700s when a theatre was being refurbished.

The Bolton family still live at nearby Bolton Hall, a massive 18th-century house which is closed to the public although its splendid gardens are occasionally open during the summer months.

'Purveyors to the Military, Colonies, Overseas Missions, Churches and the Cinematograph Industries' runs the proud claim in the brochure for **White Rose Candles Workshop**. 'Patronised by the Nobility and Gentry' it continues; 'Cathedrals supplied include Ripon and Norwich'. One of Wensleydale's most popular attractions, the workshop is housed

7 THE THREE HORSESHOES INN

Wensley

Ales from the inn's own brewery, great food and a warm welcome, found adjacent to the A684 near Leyburn.

see page 206

About a mile to the west of Wensley, on the Tupgill Park Estate, The Forbidden Corner is an unusual attraction. Strange and exotic buildings are scattered around the park, some of them underground, and visitors are given a list but must discover these fantastic constructions by themselves. 'In parts you might find your heart's delight,' says the brochure, 'In others you'll tremble with fear.' There's also a shop, refreshment room, and toilets which are all accessible to the disabled but some parts of the garden are only reached by way of steps. Admission is by pre-booked tickets only which can be obtained at Leyburn Tourist Information Office.

17

To the north of the River Ure, and reached by footpath from Castle Bolton, is the isolated Apedale, named after its original owner, Api. Now a deserted valley with heather-clad moorland and wonderful views, Apedale still shows signs of former industry and activity when it was a busy lead-mining area.

in a 19th-century water mill – the water wheel still exists and mills have been recorded on this site since 1203.

WEST WITTON
4 miles W of Leyburn on the A684

Recorded in the *Domesday Book* as 'Witun', this village was then the largest in Wensleydale and exceptional in having stone rather than wooden houses. West Witton is well known for its annual feast of St Bartholomew, patron saint of the parish church. The festival takes place on August 24th when an effigy of a man, known as the Bartle, is carried through the village. According to legend, Bartle was an 18th-century swine that was hunted over the surrounding fells before being captured and killed. The culmination of the three days of celebration is the burning of the effigy at Grassgill End.

CARLTON-IN-COVERDALE
4 miles SW of Leyburn on minor road off the A684

Carlton is Coverdale's principal village – with a population of less than 100. Nevertheless it has its own pub and is a wonderfully peaceful base for walking, hiking, fishing or touring the Dales National Park.

REDMIRE
4 miles W of Leyburn off the A684

Throughout its long history this village is thought to have occupied several sites in the vicinity. However, Redmire has been at its present location for many years and, on the village green, stands an old oak tree, supported by props, which is estimated to be at least 300 years old. When John Wesley preached in the village during his two visits in 1744 and 1774 it is believed that he stood in the shade of this very tree.

CASTLE BOLTON
5 miles W of Leyburn off the A684

Bolton Castle has dominated mid-Wensleydale for more than six centuries and is one of the major tourist attractions of the area. In 1379 the lord of the manor, Richard le Scrope, Lord Chancellor of England in the reign of Richard II, was granted permission to fortify his manor house and, using stone from a nearby quarry and oak beams from Lake District forests, the building was completed some 18 years later. Today, this luxurious fortified manor house is still occupied by a direct descendant of the 1st Lord Scrope and it remains an impressive sight with its four-square towers acting as a local landmark. The halls and galleries are remarkably well-preserved as are some of the private apartments used by Mary, Queen of Scots when she was a reluctant visitor here between 1568-69. Indeed, modern day visitors can take tea in the grand room where she spent many melancholy days.

Vivid tableaux help bring history to life – the castle chaplain, the miller at work, the blacksmith at his forge – and there are regular living history events during the summer. If you climb to the battlements you will be rewarded with some breathtaking views along the dale.

The owner, Lord Bolton, has recently restored two of the castle gardens as they would have been in medieval times – a Herb Garden and a Walled Garden.

THORALBY

8 miles W of Leyburn off the A684

Situated on the north slope of Bishopdale, opposite its sister village Newbiggin, Thoralby was once a centre for lead-mining and although lead is no longer extracted here the mine can still be found on maps of the area. A side dale of Wensleydale, Bishopdale was once covered by a glacial lake that has given rise to its distinctive wide valley base. Here can be found many of Wensleydale's oldest houses.

NEWBIGGIN-IN-BISHOPDALE

9 miles SW of Leyburn on the B6160

As might be supposed, the name of this Bishopdale village means 'new buildings' and it is indeed a relatively new settlement having been first mentioned in 1230! There is only one road along Bishopdale, a beautiful unspoilt valley with hay meadows, stone barns, traditional Dales long houses and a fine old coaching inn.

WEST BURTON

7 miles SW of Leyburn off the B6160

One of the most picturesque villages in Wensleydale, West

Bolton Castle

Burton developed around its large central green where a busy weekly market used to take place. A distinctive feature of the green is its market 'cross'- actually a modestly sized pyramid erected here in 1820. Just to the east of the village a path leads across a small packhorse bridge to **Mill Force**, perhaps the most photogenic of the Wensleydale waterfalls.

Cat lovers will enjoy the wide variety of felines on display at the **Cat Pottery**, overlooking the village green. This original collection of cats in ceramics and metallic or granite resin includes life-size stone cats for house or garden.

West Burton lies at the bottom of Walden, a narrow, steep-sided valley that provides a complete contrast to neighbouring Bishopdale. Secluded and with a minimal scattering of houses and farms, Walden was one of the last places in Yorkshire where wild red deer were seen.

19

Market Cross, Carperby

8 PALMER FLATT

Aysgarth

Superb hotel in the heart of Wensleydale: a tranquil and impressive place within easy reach of the many sights and attractions of the region.

  see page 204

CARPERBY

7 miles W of Leyburn off the A684

This ancient village reflects its typical Danish layout with its long straggling street and small green at one end. In some of the nearby fields, grassy terraces indicate the old ploughed strips left by both pre-Norman Conquest and medieval farming methods. One of the first villages to have a market (the charter was granted in 1305), Carperby's market cross dates from 1674 and it was from here that George Fox, the founder of the Quaker Movement, preached in the 17th century.

AYSGARTH

7 miles W of Leyburn on the A684

The village is famous for the spectacular **Aysgarth Falls** where the River Ure thunders through a rocky gorge and drops some 200 feet over three huge slabs of limestone which divide this wonderful natural feature into the

Upper, Middle and Lower Falls. So cinematic are they that they were deemed to be the perfect location for the battle between Robin Hood and Little John in Kevin Costner's film *Robin Hood, Prince of Thieves*.

Close to the falls stands the **Church of St Andrew**, home of the Jervaulx Treasures – a vicar's stall that is made from the beautifully carved bench ends salvaged from Jervaulx Abbey. During the Middle Ages, Aysgarth enjoyed the distinction of being the largest parish in England though the parish has since been subdivided into more manageable areas. But it still has the largest churchyard in England.

The Dales National Park has a Visitor Information Centre here, with a spacious car park and café located close to the Church and Falls.

ASKRIGG

10½ miles W of Leyburn off the A684

Recorded in the *Domesday Book* as 'Ascric', this once-important market town became better known to TV viewers as Darrowby, a major location for the long-running series *All Creatures Great and Small*. The 18th-century Kings Arms Hotel often featured as 'The Drovers Arms', and Cringley House doubled as 'Skeldale House', the fictional home of the TV vets.

During the 18th century Askrigg was a thriving town with several prosperous industries. Cotton was spun in a nearby mill, dyeing and brewing took place here and it was also a centre for hand-knitting. However, the town is particularly famous for clock-making, introduced by John Ogden in 1681. The village has been popular with tourists since the days of Turner and Wordsworth when the chief attractions here were the two waterfalls, Whitfield Force and Mill Gill. Despite its olde worlde atmosphere Askrigg was one of the first places in the dales to be supplied with electricity. That was in 1908 when the local miller harnessed the power of Mill Gill Beck.

Askrigg

Askrigg is bountifully supplied with footpaths radiating out to other villages, river crossings and farmsteads. One of the most scenic takes little more than an hour and takes in two impressive waterfalls, Whitfield Gill Force and Mill Gill Force. The route is waymarked from Mill Lane alongside the church.

BAINBRIDGE

11½ miles W of Leyburn on the A684

Back in the Middle Ages this area of Upper Wensleydale was a hunting forest, known as the Forest and Manor of Bainbridge and the village itself was established around the 12th century as a home for the foresters. One of their duties was to show travellers the way through the forest. If anyone was still out by nightfall a horn was blown to guide them home. The custom is still continued between the Feast of Holy Rood (September 27th) and Shrove Tuesday when the present horn is blown at 9 p.m.

Ancient stocks are still in place on the spacious village green and on the eastern edge of the village, the River Bain rushes over a small waterfall as it makes its way down from Semer Water.

Just to the east of Bainbridge is **Brough Hill** (private) where the Romans built a succession of forts known collectively as *Virosidum*. First excavated in the late 1920s, they now appear as overgrown grassy hummocks. Much easier to see is the Roman road that strikes southwestwards from Bainbridge, part of the trans-Pennine route to Lancaster. It passes close to the isolated lake of **Semer Water**, one of Yorkshire's only two natural lakes. (The other is Lake Gormire, near Thirsk.) Semer Water stretches half a mile in length and teems with wild fowl. To the north the lake is drained by the River Bain which, at little more than two miles long, is the shortest river in England.

An enduring legend claims that

9   THE WHITE ROSE HOTEL

Askrigg

Superb hotel in the heart of the Yorkshire Dales National Park. Bar and restaurant open to non-residents.

see page 205

10 WILSON'S

Hawes

Tasty homemade dishes in attractive family-run establishment in the heart of charming market town of Hawes. Open 10.30–5.

 see page 206

11 BECKINDALES CONTINENTAL CAFE

Hawes

Spacious, bright and welcoming café with full range of hot and cold meals, snacks and tempting cakes.

 see page 206

12 DALES COUNTRYSIDE MUSEUM

Hawes

Award winning museum where the past of the Yorkshire Dales is brought to life.

 see page 207

a town lies beneath the depths of Semer Water, cast under water by a curse. A poor traveller once sought shelter in the town but was turned away by the affluent inhabitants. The next day he stood on the hill above the town, pronounced a curse, and a great flood engulfed the town immediately. There's an intriguing postscript to this tale. During a severe drought the level of the lake dropped to reveal the remains of a Bronze Age town.

GAYLE

15½ miles W of Leyburn off the A684

Archaeological finds have proved there's been a settlement here since prehistoric times; by the late 18th century a mill was here beside the Duerly Beck, originally to support cotton spinning but then changing to wool to supply local hand-knitters. In 1870 the old waterwheel was replaced by a turbine. This, in turn, gave the village electric street lights as early as 1917.

HAWES

15½ miles W of Leyburn off the A684

At 850 feet above sea level, Hawes is the highest market town in Yorkshire. The present town expanded greatly in the 1870s after the arrival of the railways but there's still plenty of evidence of the earlier settlement in street names relating to ancient trades: Dyer's Garth, Hatter's Yard and Printer's Square. Now the commercial and market centre of

the upper dale, Hawes offers a good range of shopping, accommodation and visitor attractions.

Housed in the former railway station, the **Dales Countryside Museum** tells the story of how man's activities have helped to shape the Dales' landscape. Providing fascinating historical details on domestic life, the lead-mining industry, hand-knitting and other trades as well as archaeological material, the museum covers many aspects of Dales' life from as far back as 10,000 BC.

One of those local industries was rope-making and at **The Hawes Ropeworkers**, adjacent to the museum, visitors can still see it in operation, with experienced ropers twisting cotton and man-made fibres to make halters, hawsers, picture cords, dog leads, clothes lines and other 'rope' items. The gift shop here stocks a comprehensive range of rope-related items along with an extensive choice of other souvenirs of the dale.

Wensleydale's most famous product (after its sheep), is its soft, mild cheese, and at the **Wensleydale Cheese Experience** not only can you sample this delicacy but also learn about its history through a series of interesting displays. With a museum, viewing gallery of the production area, cheese shop, gift shop and licensed restaurant, there's plenty here for the cheese lover to enjoy.

HARDRAW

15½ miles W of Leyburn off the A684

Located in a natural amphitheatre of limestone crags, **Hardraw Force** is the highest, unbroken waterfall in England above ground, a breathtaking cascade 98 feet high. The top ledge of hard rock projects so far beyond the softer stone beneath that it used to be possible to walk behind the falling water as JMW Turner and Wordsworth did. Sadly, for safety reasons this is no longer possible. The waterfall shows at its best after heavy rain as, generally, the quantity of water tumbling over the rocks is not great. On two separate occasions, in 1739 and 1881, the falls froze solid into a 100-feet icicle.

The amphitheatre here provides superb acoustics, a feature which has been put to great effect in the annual brass band competitions which began here in 1885 and have recently resumed. Access to Hardraw Force is through the Green Dragon pub where a small fee is payable. The inn itself is pretty venerable with records of a hostelry on this site since at least the mid-13th century. At that time the land here was a grange belonging to the monks of Fountains Abbey who grazed their sheep nearby.

COTTERDALE

18 miles W of Leyburn off the A684

The small valley of Cotter Beck lies below the vast bulk of Great Shunner Fell which separates the head of Wensleydale from Swaledale. **Cotter Force**, although smaller than Hardraw, is extremely attractive though often neglected in favour of its more famous neighbour.

NIDDERDALE

This typical Yorkshire dale with its dry stone walls, green fields, and pretty stone villages was christened 'Little Switzerland' by the Victorians. Indeed, the upper reaches of the valley of the River Nidd are steep and wooded, with the river running through gorges, and with a covering of snow in winter it is easy to see the

In the 1870s, the French stuntman Blondin astounded spectators when, not content with crossing the falls at Hardraw Force on a tightrope, he paused halfway to cook an omelette.

Nidderdale

The dry stone walls that are such a feature of the countryside in the Yorkshire Dales originated from the new demand for the scientific management of the land by enclosure following the Agricultural Revolution in the 18th century. The arrow-straight dividing walls sprang up high on the hillsides and the enclosures are still easily recognised by their geometric shapes. The walls are constructed by packing small stones on top of a firm foundation and tying these together with 'troughs' – stones spanning the width of the wall. Their mortarless construction remains a fascinating feature and the clumsy, irregular shaped stones require extremely skilful selection and placement.

13   THE WILLOW

Pateley Bridge

Morning coffee, afternoon tea, lunch and dinner expertly prepared and presented at this charming 18th-century cottage which also offers two bedrooms.

 see page 207

resemblance. It is this natural beauty that draws many people to the dale and there are also several remarkable features that are well worth exploring.

The history of the dale is similar to that of its neighbours. The Romans and Norsemen both settled here and there are also reminders that the dale was populated in prehistoric times. It was the all powerful Cistercian monks of Fountains and Byland Abbeys who began the business-like cultivation of the countryside to provide grazing for cattle and sheep and the space to grow food. This great farming tradition has survived and, though prosperity came and went with the lead-mining, a few of the textile mills established in the golden age of the Industrial Revolution can still be found.

Best explored from Pateley Bridge, keen walkers will delight in the wide variety of landscape that can be covered within a reasonable amount of time. High up on the moorland, famed for its brilliant colour in late summer, there are several reservoirs, built to provide water for the growing population and industry in Bradford. This area is a must for bird watchers as there are excellent opportunities for spotting a number of species of duck as well as brent geese and whooper swans. Further down the valley, in the rich woodland, wildlife again abounds and the well-signposted footpaths help visitors reach the most spectacular sights.

PATELEY BRIDGE

Considered one of the prettiest towns in the Dales, Pateley Bridge straggles up the hillside from its elegant 18th-century bridge over the Nidd. Considering its compact size, the town is remarkably well connected by roads which have been here since the monastic orders established trade routes through the town for transporting their goods. A street market, whose charter was granted in the 14th century, has however, been abandoned for some time although sheep fairs and agricultural shows still take place here.

Pateley Bridge is more than just a market centre – the nearby lead mines, spinning and hand-loom weaving also provided employment for the local community. The construction of the turnpike road to Ripon in 1751, followed by the opening of a road to Knaresborough in 1756, gave the town a further economic boost. In the early 19th century, the brothers George and John Metcalfe moved their flax-spinning endeavour to nearby Glasshouses, where the business expanded rapidly. The lead mines, too, were expanding, due to the introduction of new machinery, and the town saw a real boom. The arrival of the railway in 1862 maintained this flourishing economy, making the transportation of heavy goods cheaper and the carriage of perishable foods quicker.

Much of the Pateley Bridge seen today was built in those prosperous years. A town of quaint and pretty buildings, the oldest is St Mary's Church, a lovely ruin dating from 1320 from which there are some fine panoramic views. Another excellent vista can be viewed from the aptly named **Panorama Walk**, part of the main medieval route from Ripon to Skipton. The **Nidderdale Museum**, a winner of the National Heritage Museum of the Year, is housed in one of the town's original Victorian workhouses and presents a fascinating record of local folk history. The exhibits include a complete cobbler's shop, general store, Victorian parlour, kitchen and schoolroom, chemist's, haberdasher's, joiner's shop, solicitor's office as well as an agricultural, transport and industrial display.

Just to the northwest of the town, up the river, is **Foster Beak Watermill**, a former flax mill that dates from the 18th century.

AROUND PATELEY BRIDGE

WILSILL

1 mile E of Pateley Bridge on the B6165

About two miles east of Wilsill are **Brimham Rocks** (National Trust), an extraordinary natural sculpture park. Formed into fantastic shapes by years of erosion, these great millstone grit boulders lie atop a steep hill amidst some 400 acres of heathland. Some of the shapes really do resemble their names –

the 'Dancing Bear' in particular, but perhaps the most awe-inspiring is 'Idol Rock', a huge boulder weighing several tons which rests on a base just a foot in diameter.

The National Trust has provided large scale maps showing suggested itineraries and the positions and names of the major formations.

SUMMERBRIDGE

3½ miles SE of Pateley Bridge on the B6165

In 1825 Summerbridge was just a small settlement with a bridge and a

The bridge at Pateley is a long established crossing which was used by the monks of Fountains Abbey. The original ford was replaced by a wooden bridge in the 16th century and the present stone structure dates from the 18th century.

Brimham Rocks

Ramsgill is situated at the head of Gouthwaite Reservoir, built in the early 20th century by Bradford Corporation to satisfy the demand from the rapidly expanding town. Gouthwaite, along with the other two reservoirs in the Dale (Scar House and Angram), is now a popular and important site for wildfowl.

corn mill. By the end of that year, however, New York Mill had been built. By the mid-1800s this large flax mill had helped the village to flourish, and another five mills, a rope works and a foundry were all in operation.

BEWERLEY

1 mile SW of Pateley Bridge on the B6265

Recorded as *Bevrelie* (a clearing inhabited by badgers) in the *Domesday Book*, this is Nidderdale's oldest settlement. It was also the site of the earliest and most important of Fountains Abbey's many granges. Not only were they farming here but lead was being extracted from the nearby moor. The recently restored Chapel, built here by one of the last abbots, Marmaduke Huby, acted for many years as the village school.

In the 17th century the Yorke family moved to the embellished hall at Bewerley following their purchase of the former lands of Byland Abbey in Nidderdale. During the subsequent years, the family laid out the parkland as well as rebuilding some of the village and, though the estate was sold in the 1920s and the hall demolished, the park remains and plays host to the annual Nidderdale Show. The name of the village's most influential family, however, is not lost to the village as Yorke's Folly, two stone stoops, still stand on the hillside overlooking Bewerley.

RAMSGILL

5 miles NW of Pateley Bridge off the B6265

This pleasant village, clustered

around its well kept green, was the birthplace of Eugene Aram in 1704. The son of a gardener at Newby Hall, Aram was arrested in 1758 in Kings Lynn for the murder of Daniel Clark in Knaresborough 13 years before. The trial took place in York and Aram caused a stir by conducting his own defence. However, he was convicted and later executed before his body was taken to Knaresborough where it was hung from a gibbet. The gruesome story has been the centre of many tales and songs including a very romantic version by Sir Bulwer Lytton.

LOFTHOUSE

7 miles NW of Pateley Bridge off the B6265

This is a small dales' village lying in the upper valley of the River Nidd and, unlike neighbouring Wharfedale, the stone walls and rocky outcrops are of millstone grit though the valley bottom consists of limestone. As a result, only in excessive weather is there water under the bridge here as, in normal conditions, the river drops down two sumps: Manchester Hole and Goydon Pot. The monks of Fountains Abbey certainly had a grange here but it is also probable that the village was first settled by Norsemen.

Nearby **How Stean Gorge**, in the heart of Nidderdale, is often called Yorkshire's Little Switzerland and for good reason. This spectacular limestone gorge, which is up to 80 feet deep in places, through which the Stean Beck flows is a popular tourist attraction.

A narrow path with footbridges guide the visitor along the gorge where the waters rush over the large boulders below. However, there are also many sheltered areas of calm water where fish hide under the rocks. As well as taking a stroll up this fascinating path, visitors can also step inside Tom Taylor's Cave and, along the walk, marvel at the wide variety of plant life that grows in this steep ravine.

MIDDLESMOOR

8 miles NW of Pateley Bridge off the B6265

This tucked away village of stone built cottages and houses lies at the head of Upper Nidderdale and is reached by a single, winding road. The existence of ancient settlers can be seen in the present 19th-century Church of St Chad where an early 10th- or 11th-century preaching cross, bearing the inscription *Cross of St Ceadda* can be seen.

WHARFEDALE

The valley of the River Wharfe, **Wharfedale,** is the longest of the Yorkshire Dales following the river from its origins on **Cam Fell** for over 70 miles to Cawood, where it joins the River Ouse. At its source, almost 2,000 feet above sea level, the river is nothing more than a moorland stream and, even in mid-Wharfedale, it is little more than a mountain river, broad, shallow, and peat brown in colour. The Romans named a local Goddess, *Verbeia,* after the river, and those who visit will understand why as the goddess

was known for her treachery as well as her beauty. Wharfedale is one of the most spectacular and most varied of the Yorkshire dales, and no one who sees the river charging through the narrow gorge at The Strid, near Bolton Abbey, will deny that the power of the river is to be respected.

For many years, Wharfedale has been the place to which those working in the grim industrial towns of Yorkshire visited for clean air and solitude. Today, it is probably the most popular of all Yorkshire's dales and there is certainly a lot on offer to those who visit here. The chief towns of the dale are little more than villages and they have retained much of their charm despite the various invasions of industry and tourism. Perhaps, this is because they were first invaded some 10,000 years ago by the hunter-gatherers of the mesolithic age.

There is much to see in Wharfedale and, in keeping with much of the Yorkshire Dales National Park, there is a variety of landscape to discover. From the high moorland and fell to the deep, eroded limestone gorges the landscape varies almost, it seems, with every turn of the River Wharfe.

GRASSINGTON

One of the best loved villages within the Yorkshire Dales National Park, Grassington in many ways typifies the dales' settlement with its characteristic market square.

Wharfedale has, over the years, inspired many of Britain's poets, writers, and painters. Both Coleridge and Wordsworth were taken with its beauty and, in the case of Wordsworth, with the local stories and legends. Ruskin enthused about its contrasts and Turner painted several scenes that also capture something of the dale's history and mystery.

•

Throughout the year, there were many festivals and holidays observed by the dales people and one, the Feast Sports, still takes place here at the Upper Wharfedale Folk Museum in Grassington on a Saturday in October. Among the many traditional events which are carried out there is the tea cake eating race, where children have to eat a tea cake, and race to the other end of the field. The winner is the first child to then whistle a tune.

•

Known as the capital of Upper Wharfedale, the historically important valley roads meet here and the ancient monastic route from Malham to Fountains Abbey passes through the village.

Grassington's origins are rooted in ancient history; there was certainly a Bronze Age settlement here, the remains of an Iron Age village have been found, a Celtic field system lies on nearby **Lea Green**, and the village was mentioned in the *Domesday Book*. However, the settlement seen today is Anglian and, having passed through various families, is now part of the estate of the Dukes of Devonshire. With its narrow streets lined with attractive Georgian buildings, Grassington is a delightful place to wander around.

The **Upper Wharfedale Folk Museum** is housed in two 18th-century lead miners' cottages. Containing many exhibits and displays relating to the lives of those who have lived in the dale, the museum is open (afternoons only) at the weekend during the winter and daily throughout the summer.

AROUND GRASSINGTON

HEBDEN

3 miles E of Grassington on the B6265

From this quiet hamlet it is only a short distance to the wonderful 500,000-year-old cave at **Stump Cross Caverns**. The large show cave holds a fantastic collection of stalactites and stalagmites which

make it one of the most visited underground attractions in the area. During excavations, the remains of animals were found here and they can be seen on display at the visitor centre where there is also a gift shop and tea room.

THORPE

2 miles SE of Grassington off the B6160

This small hamlet, the full name of which is Thorpe-sub-Montem (meaning 'below the hill'), lies in a secluded hollow between drumlins – long, low alluvial mounds. As well as taking advantage of its hidden position, ideal for secreting valuables and family members here during Scots' raids, the village was also known for its cobblers. Their fame was such that the monks of Fountains Abbey were among their regular customers. However, the influence of the monks did not prevent the high spirited cobblers from stealing nearby Burnsall's maypole and planting it on their own village green. The maypole did, eventually, return to its home village but not until the villagers of Burnsall had organised a rescue party.

BURNSALL

2 miles S of Grassington on the B6160

The village is very dramatically situated on a bend in the River Wharfe with the slopes of Burnsall Fell as a backdrop. Of ancient origins it is thought that, prior to the 8th century, Wilfrid Bishop of York, founded a wooden church, on the site of which now stands the village's 12th-century church. The only remains of Wilfrid's building is the font which can still be seen at the back of **St Wilfrid's Church**. The churchyard is entered via a unique lychgate and here can be seen two hogback tombstones and various other fragments which date back to the times of the Anglo-Saxons and the Danes.

However, it is not this sturdy dales' church which draws visitors to Burnsall but its bridge. Today, this typical dales' bridge of five stone arches is the start of the annual Classic Fell Race which takes place on a Saturday towards the end of August. Over the years, the flood waters of the River Wharfe have washed away the arches on several occasions but the villagers have always replaced them as this is the only crossing point for three miles in each direction.

APPLETREEWICK

4 miles SE of Grassington off the B6160

This peaceful village, which is known locally as Aptrick, lies between the banks of the River Wharfe and the bleak moorland and is overlooked by the craggy expanse of **Simon's Seat**, one of Wharfedale's best-loved hilltops. Dating back to monastic times, lead has been mined on the surrounding moorland for many centuries and the northern slopes were the property of the monks of nearby Bolton Priory. The village was also the home of William Craven, a Lord Mayor

of London, who returned to spend much of his amassed wealth on improvements and additions to Appletreewick's fine old buildings. Known as the Dick Whittington of the Dale, William Craven was born in 1548 and he moved to London when he became apprenticed to a mercer (a dealer in textiles and fine fabrics).

The nearby gorge of **Trollers Gill** is said to be haunted by a fearsome ghost dog, with huge eyes and a shaggy coat, that drags a clanking chain. A local story, recorded in 1881, tells how a man, somewhat foolishly, went to the gorge in the middle of the night. He failed to return and his body, on which there were marks not made by a human, was later found by shepherds.

A little further down river is the stately ruin of **Barden Tower**, a former residence of Lord Henry Clifford, owner of Skipton Castle. It was built in the 15th century but allowed to fall into decay and, despite repair in 1657, it is once

•

Just to the north of Appletreewick lie Parcevall Hall Gardens, a wonderful woodland garden which includes many varieties of unusual plants and shrubs. Though the 16-acre gardens are high above sea level (which provides the visitor with splendid views), many of the plants still flourish in these beautiful surroundings. The gardens, which are open between Easter and October, have a special quality of peace and tranquillity – appropriately enough since the lovely old Hall is now a Bradford Diocesan Retreat and Conference Centre.

•

Barden Tower

29

14 THE BUFFERS COFFEE SHOP

Storiths, Bolton Abbey

Home-made refreshments amid fantastic model railway collection with full sets and accessories available to buy.

🍴 see page 207

15 BOLTON ABBEY

Bolton Abbey, Skipton

Visitors flock to the Yorkshire Estate of the Duke and Duchess of Devonshire, to enjoy the magnificent scenery and superb facilities.

 see page 208

more a ruin. Nearby is the attractive Barden Bridge, a 17th-century arch now designated as an ancient monument.

BOLTON ABBEY

7 miles S of Grassington on the B6160

The village is actually a collection of small hamlets which have all been part of the estate of the Dukes of Devonshire since 1748. **Bolton Abbey** itself lies on the banks of the River Wharfe while the hamlets of Storiths, Hazelwood, Deerstones, and Halton East lie higher up.

The main attraction in the village is the substantial ruin of **Bolton Priory**, an Augustinian house that was founded in 1155 by monks from Embsay. In an idyllic situation on the banks of the River Wharfe, the ruins are well preserved while the nave of the priory church, first built in 1220, is now incorporated into the parish church.

After the Dissolution of the Monasteries the priory was sold to the 2nd Earl of Cumberland, Henry Clifford and it has since passed into the hands of the Dukes of Devonshire, the Cavendish family. The 14th-century priory gatehouse, Bolton Hall, is the present duke's shooting lodge. Visitors walking to the priory ruins from the village pass through a hole in the wall which frames one of the most splendid views of the romantic ruins. An attractive option when visiting the priory is to travel on the Embsay and Bolton Abbey Steam Railway whose station is about half a mile away, reached by a pleasant riverside footpath.

In and around this beautiful village there are some 80 miles of footpaths and nature trails, skirting the riverbanks and climbing up onto the high moorland. Upstream from the priory lies one of the most visited natural features in Wharfedale, a point where the wide river suddenly narrows into a confined channel of black rock through which the water thunders. This spectacular gorge is known as **The Strid** because, over the centuries, many heroic (or foolhardy) types have attempted to leap across it as a test of bravery.

LINTON

1 mile SW of Grassington off the B6160

This delightful and unspoilt village, that is more correctly called Linton-in-Craven, has grown up around its village green through which runs a small beck. This flat area of land was once a lake and around its edge was grown flax which the villagers spun into linen. The village is also

14th Century Packhorse Bridge, Linton

the home of the **Church of St Michael and All Angels**, a wonderful building that is a fine example of rural medieval architecture. Probably built on the site of a pagan shrine, the church lies some way from the village centre though its handsome bell-cote is a suitable landmark. Among the 14th-century roof bosses can be seen the Green Man, an ancient fertility symbol of a man's head protruding through foliage, which was adopted by the Christian church.

Spanning Linton beck is a graceful 14th-century packhorse bridge that was repaired by Dame Elizabeth Redmayne in the late 17th century. During the repair work, Dame Elizabeth had a narrow parapet added to the bridge to prevent carts from crossing because, so it is said, the local farmers refused to contribute to the cost of the repairs.

CRACOE

3 miles SW of Grassington on the B6265

The village contains several 17th-century houses that are typical examples of the building style of the day. Constructed from stone quarried on nearby Cracoe and Rylstone Fell, the cavity between the three feet thick walls was filled with rubble. Above the village, on top of the fell, is a cairn built in memory of local men who died during the First World War. Construction of the cairn began in the early 1920s but the professional masons experienced great difficulty as high winds tore down their work over night. Eventually, a local man was hired for the task and, instead of coming down from the fell each night, he pitched his tent close to the cairn and remained on-site until it was completed.

RYLSTONE

4 miles SW of Grassington on the B6265

On Rylstone Fell, above this Pennine village, stands **Rylstone Cross** which was, originally, a large stone that looked rather like a man. In 1885, a wooden cross was erected on top of the stone to commemorate peace with France and the initials DD and TB, carved on the back of the cross, refer to the Duke of Devonshire and his land agent, Mr T Broughton.

THRESHFIELD

1 mile W of Grassington on the B6160

Across the river from Grassington, Threshfield has at its heart a small village green called the Park, complete with the original village stocks and surrounded by charming 17th-century houses. Perhaps the most striking building is the Free Grammar School built in 1674. According to local people its porch is haunted by a fairy known as Old Pam the Fiddler. Threshfield was once famed for the production of *besoms* (birch brooms) but the last family to make them, the Ibbotsons, died out in the 1920s.

CONISTONE

2½ miles NW of Grassington off the B6160

This ancient settlement, whose name suggests that it once belonged to a king, is clustered

• *At the beginning of the 19th century, when Wordsworth was touring the area, he heard a local legend which became the basis for his poem The White Doe of Rylstone, published in 1815. The story, set in the 16th century, concerns the local Norton family and, in particular, Francis who gave his sister Emily a white doe before he went off to battle. Francis survived the conflict but he was murdered in Norton Tower on his return. Emily was struck down with grief and she was comforted by the same white doe, returned from the wild, and it also accompanied her on her visits to her brother's grave. Long after Emily's death, a white doe could still be seen lying on Francis's grave.* •

around its maypole and village green. The village Church of St Mary is thought to have been founded in Saxon times and there are certainly two well-preserved Norman arches to be seen. The land surrounding Conistone is unusually flat and it was once the bottom of a lake formed by the melt water from the glacier that carved out Kilnsey Crag.

KILNSEY

3 miles NW of Grassington on the B6160

This small hamlet, on the opposite bank of the River Wharfe from Conistone, is a great place from which many anglers fly fish and the Kilnsey Angling Club has its home in the village pub. This quiet and peaceful place is overlooked by the now uninhabited Old Hall which was originally built as a grange for the monks of Fountains Abbey.

Kilnsey Park and Trout Farm is a popular place for family outings. Under-12s can enjoy their first experience of trout fishing, with all the tackle provided. Pony trekking is available, there's an estate shop selling dales' produce and fresh Kilnsey trout, restaurant and children's adventure centre, and visitors can also wander around the farm. Fly fishing, for those who like to indulge, is available in two well-stocked lakes.

The striking outline of **Kilnsey Crag** is unmistakable as one side of this limestone hill was gouged out by a passing glacier during the Ice Age. One of the most spectacular natural features in the dales, the crag has a huge 'lip' or overhang which presents an irresistible challenge to adventurous climbers.

KETTLEWELL

Surrounded by the beautiful countryside of Upper Wharfedale, Kettlewell is a popular centre for tourists and walkers. At the meeting point of several old packhorse routes, which now serve as footpaths and bridleways, the village was a busy market centre and, at one time, the home of 13 public houses which catered to the needs of the crowds. The market charter, granted in the 13th century, is evidence that Kettlewell was once a more important place than it is today and the various local religious houses of Bolton Priory, Coverham Abbey, and Fountains Abbey all owned land in the area.

Today, however, Kettlewell is a

Kettlewell

conservation area, a charming place of chiefly 17th- and 18th-century houses and cottages. Its original 13th-century waterfall, later converted into a textile mill, has gone though evidence of a local lead-mining industry remains. The late-19th-century Church of St Mary attracts many visitors to its attractive churchyard and lychgate built on the site of a 12th-century building.

AROUND KETTLEWELL

STARBOTTON

2 miles N of Kettlewell on the B6160

This quiet little Wharfedale village was the scene in 1686 of a disastrous flood when a huge head of water descended from the surrounding fells and swept away many of the houses and cottages. The damage was such that a national appeal was started and aid, in the form of money, was sent from as far afield as Cambridgeshire.

BUCKDEN

4 miles N of Kettlewell on the B6160

Marking the beginning of Wharfedale proper, Buckden is the first full-sized village of the dale and proudly boasts that it is also home to Wharfedale's first shop. Unusually for this area, the village was not settled by the Anglo-Saxons but, later, by the Normans and it was the headquarters of the officers hunting in the forest of Langstrothdale. As the forest was cleared to make way for agriculture, Buckden became an important market town serving a large part of the surrounding area. Wool was one of the important sources of income for the dalesfolk and the local inn here still has some of the old weighing equipment from the days when the trade was conducted on the premises. The village is an excellent starting point for those wanting to climb Buckden Pike (2,302 feet), which lies to the east. The route to the summit takes in not only superb views but also several waterfalls.

Designated in Norman times as one of the feudal hunting forests, **Langstrothdale Chase** was governed by the strict forest laws. Just to the south of the village, which lies on the edge of the Chase, can be seen an old stone cross which was used to mark the forest boundary. Buckden's name means the 'valley of the bucks' but its last deer was hunted and killed here in the 17th century.

HUBBERHOLME

5 miles N of Kettlewell off the B6160

This small village was originally two places: Hubberholme proper and Kirkgill, which takes its name from the nearby Church of St Michael and All Angels that was, at one time, a forest chapel. Each year, on New Year's Day, the villagers gather at the local pub for the **Hubberholme Parliament**. For that night, the public bar becomes the House of Commons, where the farmers congregate, while the room where the vicar and churchwardens

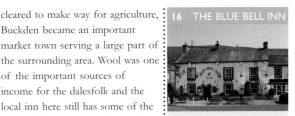

16 THE BLUE BELL INN

Kettlewell

Traditional 17th-century coaching inn with ales from local Skipton brewery, six ensuite bedrooms and home-cooked food at lunch and dinner daily.

see page 208

17 THE KINGS HEAD

Kettlewell

Hearty and freshly prepared food, real ales and comfortable accommodation in characterful Georgian inn.

see page 209

•

Near Arncliffe village bridge, over the River Skirfare, stands a house, Bridge End, *that was once the home of the Hammond family. While staying with the Hammonds, author Charles Kingsley was so taken with the village and Littondale that he incorporated the house and his hostess in his famous work* The Water Babies.

•

meet is the House of Lords. Bidding then takes place between the farmers for the rent of a field behind the church and, encouraged by the vicar, the highest bidder gains the lease for the coming year.

LITTON

5 miles NW of Kettlewell off the B6160

This pretty village lends it name to the dale, **Littondale**, which is actually the valley of the River Skirfare. Once part of a Norman hunting forest, the dale was originally called Amerdale (meaning 'deep fork') and this ancient name is preserved in Amerdale Dub, where the River Skirfare joins the River Wharfe near Kilnsey.

YOCKENTHWAITE

6 miles NW of Kettlewell off the B6160

The unusual name of this small village is Viking in origin and, though once a prosperous place, Yockenthwaite is now a collection of old stone farms. On the surrounding fells lies a well-preserved Bronze Age stone circle and **Giant's Grave**, the remains of an Iron Age settlement.

ARNCLIFFE

3 miles W of Kettlewell off the B6160

Situated in Littondale, the village name dates back to Saxon times when the valley was referred to as Amerdale. This is a quiet, tranquil dale and life has remained the same here for many years in this small village. Many of the buildings around the central village green are listed and, in its early years, the

long running TV series *Emmerdale* was filmed here. Strongly recommended is a visit to the Falcon Inn where almost nothing has changed in half a century.

AIREDALE

The 'Gateway to the Dales', Skipton has long been a starting-point for any tour of the Yorkshire Dales and, though still a bustling centre for Airedale and its neighbour Malhamdale, the town's old industries have given way, to a large degree, to tourism. The source of the River Aire lies in Malhamdale, just to the north of Malham, and it flows through both dales before finally joining the River Ouse. For some of its length, in Airedale, the river lies side-by-side with the Leeds and Liverpool Canal. The construction of a navigable waterway, linking the two great industrial areas of Lancashire and Yorkshire, changed the lives of many living in the dales and certainly played a major part in establishing the textile mills in the area.

However, the importance of farming has never been lost and market day is a key event in the daily lives of the dalesfolk. As well as the sheep, other constant features of the countryside are the dry stone walls- a familiar sight to all those visiting the Yorkshire Dales.

Of the many and varied attractions in Airedale and the area surrounding Skipton, the most impressive feature is the beautiful limestone formations found to the north of Malham. The spectacular and enormous curved cliff of Malham Cove, created by glacial action during the last Ice Age, the limestone pavements above the cove, the deep gorge of Gordale Scar, and the remote natural lake, Malham Tarn, are all well worth a visit.

This dramatic scenic area has been designated a Site of Special Scientific Interest and, as well as the wonderful formations themselves, the area supports a wide range of animals, birds, and plant life. As there is a variety of terrain, from bleak, bracken strewn moorland to coniferous plantations, there is also a wide variety of flora and fauna. Birdwatchers, particularly, will delight in the opportunity to catch sight of red grouse and short-eared owls on the moors while also having the chance to view the many wading birds which populate the lakes and reservoirs of the area.

1090 and the powerful stone structure seen today was devised in 1310 by Robert de Clifford, the 1st Earl of Skipton. The Cliffords were a fighting breed and, throughout the Middle Ages, wherever there was trouble a member of the family was sure to be found. The 8th Lord Clifford, Thomas, and his son John were both killed while fighting for the House of Lancaster during the War of the Roses. Later, George Clifford, Champion to Queen Elizabeth I and a renowned sailor, fought against the Spanish Armada and, as well as participating in many voyages of his own, he also lent a ship to Sir Walter Raleigh.

One of the most complete and well-preserved medieval castles in England, it is thanks to Lady Anne Clifford that visitors to Skipton can marvel at its buildings. Following the ravages of the Civil War, from which the castle did not escape, Lady Anne undertook a comprehensive restoration programme and, though little of the original Norman stonework

18 SKIPTON PARK GUEST'OTEL

Skipton
4-star accommodation in impressive late-Victorian guest house/hotel; ideal touring base for the Dales.

see *page 210*

SKIPTON

Often called the 'Gateway to the Dales', Skipton's origins can be traced to the 7th century when Anglian farmers christened it Sheeptown. Featuring in the *Domesday Book*, the Normans decided to build a castle here to guard the entrance to Airedale and Skipton became a garrison town. **Skipton Castle**, home of the Cliffords, was begun in

Skipton Castle

remains, much of the work of the 1st Lord Clifford still stands.

As well as an enormous banqueting hall, a series of kitchens still remain with some of their original fittings, and a beautiful Tudor courtyard. There is also a rather unusually decorated room whose walls are lined with shells that were collected by George Clifford in the 19th century while he was travelling in the South Seas. However, the most striking feature of the castle is the impressive 14th-century gateway, which is visible from the High Street, and carries the Clifford family motto *Desormais* meaning 'Henceforth'.

Adjacent to the castle, at the top of the High Street, lies the parish **Church of the Holy Trinity** which was originally built in the 12th century and replaced in the 1300s. There is a wealth of interest inside the building which has been topped by a beautiful oak roof since the 15th century. It is possible to spend much time discovering the centuries of artefacts in the church and the various tombs and memorials are just as interesting and include the many tombs of the Clifford family. The church suffered damage during the Civil War and, again, Lady Anne Clifford came to the rescue, restoring the interior and rebuilding the steeple in 1655. Inside the church, among the many tombstones, is that of the Longfellow family, which included the uncle of the American poet, Henry Wadsworth Longfellow. As well as the fine castle and church,

the Normans also established Skipton as a market town and it received its first charter in 1204. The market today is still thriving and is very much an important part of daily life in the area.

For many years Skipton remained a market town, then, with the development of the factory system in the 19th century, the nature of the town began to change. Textile mills were built and cottages and terraced houses were constructed for the influx of mill workers. However, not all were happy with the changes that the Industrial Revolution brought about and, in 1842, a group of men, women, and children set out from the Pennine cotton towns and villages to protest at the mechanisation taking place. By the time the group had reached nearby Broughton, their number had grown to 3,000 and the Skipton magistrates urged them to turn back and return home. But the protesters continued, surging on Skipton, and the worried magistrates sent for military help. Moving from mill to mill, the mob stopped the looms and created panic among the townspeople. Special constables were quickly sworn in to help contain the situation and the Riot Act was read from the town hall steps. Though the mob retreated to nearby Anne Hill, they refused to disperse and the soldiers were ordered to charge. During the ensuing violence, one soldier was killed and a magistrate blinded but the mob, bar six of the leaders who were arrested, fled as the first shots were fired.

The **Leeds and Liverpool Canal**, which flows through the town, provided a cheap form of transport as well as linking Skipton with the major industrial centres of Yorkshire and Lancashire. The first of three trans-Pennine routes, the 127-mile canal has 91 locks along the full length as well as two tunnels, one of which is over a mile long. Today, the canal basin, behind the town centre, is busy with pleasure craft and boat journeys can be taken along a section in the direction of Gargrave. The towpath was also restored at the same time as the canal and there are a number of pleasant walks which includes a stretch along the cul-de-sac Spring Branch beside the castle walls.

A walk around the town is also worth while and there are many interesting buildings to be found here. One, in particular, is the Town Hall which is now also the home of the **Craven Museum**. Dedicated to the surrounding area, there are many interesting displays relating to the geological and archaeological treasures that have been found locally, including a piece of Bronze Age cloth which is considered the oldest textile fragment in the country. Closer to the present day, there are displays of furniture illustrating the fine craftsmanship that went into even the most mundane household item and also farming exhibits which reflect the changing lives of many of the people who lived off the surrounding countryside.

Almost opposite the Town Hall, on the High Street, are the premises of the **Craven Herald**, a newspaper that was established in 1874 although the publication was produced for a short time in the 1850s. The building is fortunate in having retained its late-Victorian shop front, as well as the passageway to one side, and it was first occupied by William Chippendale in the late 18th century. A trader in textiles, Chippendale made his money by buying then selling on the cloth woven by the farmers in their own homes. Close to the newspaper's offices is the **Public Library** which opened in 1910 and was funded by Andrew Carnegie. A large, ornate building, it is in contrast to the town's older buildings and stands as a reminder to the change in character which Skipton underwent in the late 19th century.

It seems fitting that, in a town which over many years has been dedicated to trade and commerce, Thomas Spencer, co-founder of Marks and Spencer, should have been born here in 1851. Skipton, too, was the home of Sir Winston Churchill's physician, Lord Moran, who grew up here as the son of the local doctor.

As with many historic market towns, Skipton has its fair share of inns and public houses which provided farmers with refreshment during the busy markets. The **Black Horse Inn** is one such pub and its date stone of 1676 is well worth a second look as it is carved with symbols of the butcher's trade: axes, animal heads, and twisted

Before the days of the canal, travelling by road, particularly in winter, was often a hazardous business. One local tale tells how, on Christmas Eve, during a bad snow storm, a young waggoner set out from the town for Blubberhouses. Though an inn-keeper tried to dissuade him, the young man carried on into the night – thinking only of his betrothed, Ruth. He soon lost his way in a snow drift and chilled by the fierce northerly winds, he fell to the ground in a comatose state. Safe in her cottage, Ruth suddenly awoke and ran out of the house crying that her John was lost. Two men hurried after her and by the time they had caught up with Ruth she was digging out John with her bare hands. He was none the worse for his misadventure and the couple married on New Year's Day.

•

Well before the days of railways, Embsay was home to an Augustinian priory, founded in 1130. However, for some reason the monks found life difficult here and, in 1145, they crossed Embsay Moor and moved to what is now Bolton Abbey.

•

22 THE DOG AND GUN INN

Malsis

Outstanding inn located in hamlet off the A606/A56 a few miles southwest of Skipton.

 see page 212

fleeces. Originally called The King's Head, the inn was built by, not surprisingly, a butcher, Robert Goodgion. In the 19th century it served as a headquarters to Lord Ribblesdale's cavalry when they held their annual training in the town.

AROUND SKIPTON

EMBSAY

1 mile N of Skipton off the A59

The village is home to the **Embsay Steam Railway** which is based at the small country station. As well as taking a scenic steam train journey to the end of the line, a couple of miles away, there are over 20 locomotives, both steam and diesel, on display together with railway carriages. Special events are arranged throughout the year and opening times vary though the trains run every Sunday.

Those choosing to walk over the moor to the north of the village should take care as the area is peppered with old coal pits and disused shafts. However, the view from **Embsay Crag** (1,217 feet high) is well worth the effort of climbing.

KILDWICK

3 miles S of Skipton off the A629

This picturesque little village, on the north bank of the River Aire, is approached over a bridge that was built in the early 14th century by the canons of Bolton Priory. The village **Church of St Andrew** was also rebuilt around the 14th and 15th centuries, though the choir

was extended to its unusually long length sometime later which gives the church its local name of Lang Kirk o'Craven.

The River Aire is not the only waterway which passes through the village as it also lies on the banks of the Leeds and Liverpool Canal. Once a hive of industry with many spinning and weaving mills in the village and the surrounding area producing wool and silk yarn and cloth, the decline of the textile industry has caused many of the mills to close though some have now been converted to provide interesting accommodation or as offices for small business units. The canal, which until the 1930s was still in commercial use, is now the preserve of pleasure craft and Kildwick is a popular overnight mooring.

LOTHERSDALE

4 miles SW of Skipton off the A629

A dramatic stretch of the Pennine Way passes through this village set in a deep valley in the heart of the moors. Charlotte Brontë knew the village well and in *Jane Eyre* the house she calls Gateshead is modelled on Lothersdale's Stonegappe, up on the hillside near the church.

ELSLACK

4 miles SW of Skipton off the A56

Overlooking the village is the 1,274-ft high Pinhaw Beacon from which there are some fine panoramic views over the heather covered moorland. During the Napoleonic Wars in the early 19th century, when there was great fear of an invasion from France, the beacon, one in a countrywide chain of communication beacons, was manned 24 hours a day. Unfortunately, during a raging blizzard on a January night in 1805, the lookout, Robert Wilkinson, died and was buried on the moor. His body was later exhumed and his grave can be seen in the parish churchyard to the northeast of the village.

THORNTON-IN-CRAVEN

5 miles SW of Skipton on the A56

This attractive village stands on the Pennine Way and from here there are magnificent views of Airedale and, towards, the west, Pendle Forest in Lancashire. Now a quiet place, during the Civil War the manor house was ruined by Royalist soldiers shortly after Cromwell had stayed here to attend a local wedding. The present house is situated opposite the original site. Past parish records associated with the 12th-century Church of St Mary are lost as they were accidentally burnt by the local rector.

EARBY

6 miles SW of Skipton on the A56

Though the Yorkshire Dales are thought of as a once thriving textile producer, lead-mining, for many centuries, was also a key industry. Housed in an old grammar school, that was founded in 1591 by Robert Windle, is the **Museum of Yorkshire Dales Lead Mining** which was opened in 1971. The

large collection, as well as the substantial documentation and indexing, has been put together by several local interest groups who began their work in 1945 when the Earby Mines Research Group was formed within the Earby Pothole Club. The museum, which has limited opening times, has many excellent displays including mine tubs, photographs, mine plans, small implements, mining machinery, and miners' personal belongings.

BROUGHTON

4 miles W of Skipton on the A59

The Tempest family has been associated with this farming community for the past 800 years and their family home, **Broughton Hall** dates back to 1597, with additions made in the 18th and 19th centuries. The estate covers 3,000 acres and is now also home to a business park where many small businesses thrive. Those who visit on the last Sunday in June will also be witness to the Broughton Hall Game Fair, a well-attended event which covers all manner of country sports and pursuits. The building itself may seem familiar since it, as well as the grounds, have been used frequently by film crews as an historic location.

GARGRAVE

5 miles NW of Skipton on the A65

This picturesque small village in Upper Airedale was once a thriving market town and it also became a busy transport centre after the Leeds and Liverpool Canal was

Site of a Roman Villa, Kirk Sink, nr. Gargrave

and Cliffe Castle Museums; the site itself has since been re-covered.

CONISTON COLD

7 miles NW of Skipton on the A65

Lying midway between Skipton and Settle, this small village lies on the old route to the Lake District. Like most places situated on once busy routes, the village had its share of coaching inns and one in particular was the Punch Bowl Inn (until recently it acted as the post office) which has an unusual circular indentation on the front outside wall. In days gone by the inn's patrons would stand a few yards from the wall and try to kick a ball to this mark.

AIRTON

8 miles NW of Skipton off the A65

This charming Airedale village is well known to long-distance walkers as it lies on the Pennine Way. Though small, there are a couple of buildings of interest including a corn mill (now converted into flats) that was first recorded in 1198. As sheep farming took over from corn, the mill, like so many in the southern dales, turned to cotton spinning though, with the advent of steam powered machinery, the industry moved to nearby Skipton.

At the beginning of the 18th century Airton became a Quaker community and the **Meeting House**, which was built on land

built. Lead from the nearby mines was loaded on to the barges at the five wharves here, while other goods were unloaded ready for distribution to the surrounding area. The village too played a part in the textile boom and there were two cotton mills in the village. Now no longer in commercial use, like the canal, some of the mills have been turned into residential accommodation while the canal is very much alive with pleasure boats.

The remains of Celtic crosses found within the village Church of St Andrew indicate that, although the present building is chiefly Victorian, there has been a church here for centuries. The original church was destroyed by the Scots during a raid in 1318. To the south of the village, at **Kirk Sink**, is the site of a Roman villa that was excavated in the 1970s. Relics recovered from the building can be seen in Skipton

donated by the well-known Quaker weavers William and Alice Ellis, can still be seen by the village green. Another legacy of the village's Quaker community is the absence of a public house as the drinking of alcohol was strictly forbidden by the Friends.

Also found on the village green is a 17th-century Squatter's Cottage – so-called because, according to the law, any person building a house and having smoke rising from the chimney within 24 hours was granted the freehold of the property including the land within a stone's throw of the front door.

MALHAM

11 miles NW of Skipton off the A65

Malham village was originally two settlements, Malham East and Malham West, which were separated by the beck. Each came under the influence of a different religious house: Bolton Priory and Fountains Abbey respectively. United after the Dissolution of the Monasteries, the focal point of Malham became the village green where the annual sheep fairs were held. This pretty village of farms and cottages is one of the most visited places in the Yorkshire Dales though it is not the charming stone built dwellings which visitors come to admire but the spectacular limestone scenery which lies just to the north. However, the two ancient stone bridges in the village centre are also worth a second glance. The New Bridge, which is also known as the Monks' Bridge,

was built in the 17th century while the Wash-Dub Bridge dates from the 16th century and is of a clapper design (limestone slabs placed on stone supports).

To the north of the village lies the ancient glacial grandeur of **Malham Cove**. Access is from the Langcliffe road beyond the last buildings of the village, down a path alongside the beck that leads through a scattering of trees. The 300-ft limestone amphitheatre is the most spectacular section of the mid-Craven fault and, as recently as the 1700s, a massive waterfall that was higher than Niagara Falls cascaded over its edge. A steep path leads to the limestone pavement at the top, with its characteristic clints and grykes, where water has carved a distinctive natural sculpture through the weaknesses in the limestone.

From here it is not too far to reach the equally inspiring **Gordale Scar**, a huge gorge carved by glacial melt water with an impressive waterfall leaping, in two stages, from a fissure in its face. Further on still is another waterfall known as Janet's Foss. Beside the waterfall is a cave which Janet, a friendly fairy, is reputed to inhabit. Three miles north of the scar is **Malham Tarn**, a glacial lake which by way of an underground stream is the source of the River Aire, and Malham Tarn House, where such famous names as Ruskin, Darwin, and Charles Kingsley (author of *The Water Babies*) received inspiration.

23   THE LISTER ARMS HOTEL

Malham

Great atmosphere at this traditional inn with real ales, tasty food (lunchtimes only) and superior accommodation.

❙❙ ╠═┥ see page 213

RIBBLESDALE AND THE THREE PEAKS

The River Ribble, the source of which lies high up on bleak moorland to the northeast of Ingleton, flows through several ancient settlements before leaving the county of Yorkshire and flowing on into the mill town country of Lancashire. On opposite banks of the river, lie Settle and Giggleswick, which are overlooked by the towering white limestone cliffs of Castleberg Crag and Langcliffe Scar, parts of the mid-Craven fault.

Further north from these two market towns lies one of the most popular tourist centres in the dales,

Ingleton, and high above the village are the famous **Three Peaks** of Ingleborough, Pen-y-ghent, and Whernside. The surrounding countryside is dominated by caves, potholes, and waterfalls and it is ideal country for all those who enjoy the outdoors.

The layer of limestone which lies across this whole area was laid down around 400 million years ago, when the shells of dead sea creatures along with mud accumulated at the bottom of the warm sea that covered a huge area of northern England. Much later, the layer of sandstone, known as millstone grit, was formed over the top. Much is talked about the **Craven Fault** and, though it was formed by a series of mighty earthquakes, this all happened well over 30 million years ago so visitors need not worry about visiting the area. However, the line of the fault, where the land to the northwest was lifted up and the land to the southeast slipped down, is all too evident today. It was the action of water, seeping into the limestone, which froze during the Ice Age that has created the many caves and potholes of the area. Erosion, though this time on the surface, near Malham and elsewhere, formed the magnificent limestone pavements while the Three Peaks, as they are capped by millstone grit, have stood the test of time and still stand proud.

Pen-y-Ghent, Ribblesdale

42

This is farming country and the traditional agricultural methods, along with the abundance of limestone, have given this region its own distinctive appeal. The high fells, composed of grits and sandstone, support heather moorlands and here can be found the only bird unique to Britain, the red grouse, and several birds of prey. Meanwhile, the limestone areas support a much more varied plant life, though the woodlands are chiefly of ash. In these shaded places, among the wild garlic and lily of the valley, visitors might be lucky enough to come across roe deer, badgers, and foxes.

SETTLE

This small market town, which received its charter in 1249, still retains its thriving weekly market on Tuesdays. A busy stopping place in the days of the stagecoach, when travellers journeying between York and Lancaster and Kendal called here, Settle is now a popular place for visitors, walkers, and cyclists who stop in the town to take full advantage of the wide range of inns and hotels.

Settle itself is dominated by one of the huge viaducts from the **Settle-Carlisle Railway** as well as the towering limestone cliffs of **Castleberg Crag** which offers spectacular views over the town. It can be reached by following the recently opened Tot Lord Woodland Trail.

Settle's architecture is very distinctive, in the main being Victorian sandstone buildings that all look as if they are born of the railway culture. Buildings of note include the arcaded Shambles, originally butchers' slaughter houses, the French-style Town Hall and the Victorian Music Hall. The town's oldest building is the 17th-century **Preston's Folly,** described as an extravaganza of mullioned windows and Tudor masonry. It is named after the man who created this anomalous fancy and impoverished himself in the process.

Apart from the grander structures on the main streets, there are charming little side streets, lined with Georgian and Jacobean cottages, and criss-crossed with quirky little alleyways and ginnels with hidden courtyards and workshops of a time gone by.

Just outside the town, housed in an old cotton mill dating from the 1820s, is the **Watershed Mill Visitor Centre.** This charming place, on the banks of the River Ribble, offers a unique shopping experience.

The features of the surrounding countryside are equally interesting and, in particular, there is the fascinating **Victoria Cave.** Discovered in 1838 by Michael Horner, the cave has yielded finds of Roman relics, Stone Age artefacts, and even 120,000 year old mammoth bones. Unfortunately, the instability of the rock in the area has caused the cave and the surrounding land to be closed to the public.

•

Settle is probably best known because of the famous Settle-Carlisle Railway, a proudly preserved memento of the glorious age of steam although the regular daily services are now provided by diesel locomotives. The 72-mile line is still flanked by charming little signal boxes and stations that are a real tourist magnet. This attractive railway was built in the midst of great controversy and even greater cost, in both money and lives, earning it the dubious title of 'the line that should never have been built'. There is a churchyard at St Leonard's in Chapel-le-Dale where over 100 of the workers and miners, who laboured under the most adverse conditions, lie buried. Today, the trains still thunder over the 21 viaducts, through the 14 tunnels, and over the numerous bridges for which they gave their lives.

•

For particularly energetic visitors to Horton, there is the demanding Three Peaks Challenge which is organised by the Pen-y-ghent Café. The 24-mile hike takes in not only Pen-y-ghent but the other two peaks, Ingleborough and Whernside, and those completing the trek within 12 hours qualify for membership of the Three Peaks of Yorkshire Club. Less energetic walkers will be glad to hear that the café not only supplies well-earned refreshments but also has copious local information and runs a highly efficient safety service.

AROUND SETTLE

LANGCLIFFE

1 mile N of Settle on the B6479

As its name suggests, Langcliffe lies in the shelter of the long cliff of the Craven fault where the millstone grit sandstone meets the silver grey of the limestone. Although the majority of the houses and cottages surrounding the central village green are built from the limestone, some sandstone has also been used which gives this pretty village an added charm. The Victorian urn on the top of the **Langcliffe Fountain** was replaced by a stone cross, after the First World War, in memory of those villagers who died in the conflict.

STAINFORTH

1 mile N of Settle on the B6479

This sheltered sheep farming village owes its existence to the Cistercian

monks who brought those animals to this area. The monks were also responsible for building the 14th-century stone packhorse bridge which carries the road over the local beck, a tributary of the River Ribble. Although the village is certainly old, there are few buildings which date beyond the days of the Civil War: during those turbulent times, much of Stainforth was destroyed.

Catrigg Force, found along a track known as Goat Scar Lane, is a fine waterfall which drops some 60 feet into a wooded pool, while to the west is **Stainforth Force** flowing over a series of rock shelves.

HORTON IN RIBBLESDALE

6 miles N of Settle on the B6479

First mentioned in the *Domesday Book*, the village, whose name means literally the settlement on the muddy land or marsh, was probably in existence long before the 11th century. The oldest building here is the 12th-century **St Oswald's Church** which still shows signs of its Norman origins in the chevron designs over the south door. Inside, peculiarly, all the pillars lean to the south and, in the west window, there is an ancient piece of stained glass showing Thomas à Becket wearing his bishop's mitre.

This village is the ideal place from which to explore the limestone landscapes and green hills of Upper

Stainforth Force

Ribblesdale. To the east lies **Pen-y-ghent** (2,273 feet high), one of the famous Three Peaks.

The whole of this area has been designated as being of Special Scientific Interest, mainly due to the need to conserve the swiftly eroding hillsides and paths. This is an ancient landscape, well worth the efforts to preserve its ash woodlands, primitive earthworks, and rare birdlife such as peregrine falcon, ring ouzel, curlew and golden plover. There are also a great many caves in the area, which add to the sense of romance and adventure one feels in this place.

There are several listed buildings in the area including Lodge Hall, which was formerly known as Ingman Lodge. Before the 20th century, a judge would travel around the countryside on horseback stopping to try cases rather than villagers commuting to major towns for their trials. Here, if anyone was found guilty of a capital crime, they were brought to Ingman Lodge to be hanged.

LONG PRESTON

3 miles S of Settle on the A65

Hard to imagine today but this pleasant village which straddles the main road was once larger than Leeds. Close to the pretty Church of St Mary's, which dates back in part to the 12th century, the remains of a Roman encampment have been discovered. The other interesting building in Long Preston is Cromwell House which, so the legend goes, once gave refuge to the Puritan leader.

RATHMELL

2 miles S of Settle off the A65

From this small village, set beside the River Ribble, there are many footpaths along the riverbanks, through the nearby woods, and up to Whelpstone Crag. An old farming community, the oldest farm here is dated 1689 and a little row of farm cottages called Cottage Fold are from around the same period.

Rathmell is also home to the **Horses Health Farm & Visitor Centre** which was established in 1991 to provide a unique centre for the treatment of horses and ponies, and to put an edge of the fitness of performance animals. Within the centre are a hydrotherapy pool, solarium, an all-weather arena for schooling and a farrier's forge. The Visitor Centre was opened in 1998 in response to public interest in the work done here. Visitors can watch horses swimming in the pool and enjoying the solarium treatment, and cheer on the Racing Miniature Shetlands. The centre is only open on limited occasions - check before travelling.

GIGGLESWICK

1 mile W of Settle off the A65

This ancient village, which lies below the limestone scar that is part of the Craven fault, is home to several interesting places including the 15th century **Church of St Alkelda** and the well-known **Giggleswick School**. Alkelda is thought to have been a Saxon saint

24 THE BOAR'S HEAD HOTEL

Long Preston

Large and impressive 16th-century public house serving great food and drink, adjacent to the A65 three miles south of Settle. Four ensuite guest bedrooms.

 see page 213

45

Just to the north of Giggleswick can be found the famous Ebbing and Flowing Well, one of many in the area which owe their unusual names to the porous nature of the limestone of the area which causes there sometimes to be water here and sometimes not.

•

The most peculiar feature of the area surrounding Clapham has to be the Norber Boulders: a series of black boulders that stand on limestone pedestals which, despite their contrived appearance, are a completely natural feature. They are also known locally as the Norber Erratics because they are anomalous – the grey silurian slate they are composed of usually occurs beneath limestone rather than on top. The mystery of their existence is explained by the fact that these huge rocks were originally deposited by glacial action at the end of the last Ice Age. Another distinctive local feature is the clapper bridge, a medieval structure made from large slabs of rock that span the local becks.

•

who was strangled for her faith while the school, founded by James Carr, was granted a Royal Charter in 1553 by Edward VI. The school's fame stems from its observatory which was used by the Astronomer Royal in 1927 to observe an eclipse of the sun. The school's chapel, the copper dome of which is a well-known local landmark, was built to commemorate the Diamond Jubilee of Queen Victoria by Walter Morrison, a school governor who lived at Malham Tarn House.

On the edge of town is the **Yorkshire Dales Falconry & Conservation Centre,** home to a wide variety of Birds of Prey from around the world. The centre has been careful to re-create their natural habitats, transporting 350 tons of limestone boulders to provide cliff-faced aviaries. The star attraction is Andy, the Andean condor, with a wingspan of 10 feet 6 inches. Along with other vultures, eagles and hawks, Andy takes part in the regular free-flying demonstrations. The centre has full educational facilities, an adventure playground, tea rooms and shops.

FEIZOR

3 miles NW of Settle off the A65

The village dates back to monastic times when it lay on the route from Kilnsey to the Lake District which was much used by the monks of Fountains Abbey. Although both Fountains Abbey and Sawley Abbey had possessions in the area, there are few reminders of those times

today. However, the **Yorkshire Dales Falconry and Conservation Centre** does bring visitors to this village. With demonstration flights held throughout the day, when the centre's wide range of birds of prey are seen flying free, and much else on offer it does make an interesting and unusual day out.

AUSTWICK

4 miles NW of Settle off the A65

This ancient village of stone cottages and crofts, dry stone walls, abandoned quarries, and patchwork hills was originally a Norse settlement: the name is Nordic for Eastern Settlement. The mostly 17th-century buildings, with their elaborately decorated stone lintels, flank what remains of the village green where the ancient cross stands as a reminder of when this was the head of a dozen neighbouring manors and the home of an annual cattle fair.

CLAPHAM

6 miles NW of Settle off the A65

By far the largest building in the village is **Ingleborough Hall**, once the home of the Farrer family and now a centre for outdoor education. One member of the family, Reginald Farrer, was an internationally renowned botanist and he was responsible for introducing many new plant species into the country. Many examples of his finds still exist in the older gardens of the village and in the hall's grounds and there is a particularly pleasant walk, the **Reginald Farrer Nature Trail**, which leads from Clapham to nearby Ingleborough Cave.

Though the whereabouts of **Ingleborough Cave** was known for centuries, it was not until the 19th century that its exploration was begun. One of the explorers, geologist Adam Sedgwick, is quoted as saying, 'we were forced to use our abdominal muscles as sledges and our mouths as candlesticks', which gives an excellent indication of the conditions the early pot-holers had to endure. However, their work proved very much worth while and the system is extremely extensive. Those visiting the caves today see only a small part of the five miles of caverns and tunnels though, fortunately, this easily accessible portion is spectacular. As well as exotic cave formations and illuminated pools there is **Eldon Hall Cavern**, home to a vast mushroom bed.

This is an area that has a great abundance of natural waterfalls but the waterfall seen near the village church is one of the very few which owes its existence to man. In the 1830s the Farrer family created a large lake, covering some seven acres of land, and the waterfall is the lake's overflow. As well as providing water for the village, a turbine was placed at the bottom of the waterfall and, with the help of the electrical power, Clapham was one of the first villages in the country to have street lighting. This is perhaps not as surprising as it might seem as

Michael Faraday, the distinguished 19th-century scientist, was the son of the village blacksmith.

KEASDEN

4 miles S of Ingleton off the A65

Today, Keasden is a scattered farming community that is easily missed but evidence from the 17th-century church records tell a different story. At that time there were some 40 farms here (now there are around 15) as well as many associated trades and craftsmen. The name Keasden comes from the Old English for 'cheese valley' and some of the farms still retain the vast stone weights of the cheese presses though, unfortunately, the recipe for the local cheese has been lost.

NEWBY

7 miles NW of Settle off the A65

This tiny hamlet was originally situated about a mile south of its present position because, in the 17th century, the Great Plague decimated the village's population. The survivors moved away and rebuilt Newby and many of the buildings date from this time.

The village came under the direction of the monks of Furness Abbey and the remains of their walled garden can still be seen. By the Victorian era, Newby had become a thriving weaving community. However, the cottage industry was soon overtaken by the new factory systems and, by 1871, the village had once again returned to peace and quiet.

•

Overlooked by Ingleborough, close to the village of Clapham is the giant pothole known as Gaping Gill. Some 340 feet deep, the hole is part of the same underground limestone cave system as Ingleborough Cave and the main chamber is similar in size to York Minster. Twice a year, the public can gain access via a bosun's chair on a winch that is operated by local caving clubs.

•

Discovered in 1865 by Joseph Carr, the Ingleton Waterfalls, which were not immediately made accessible to the public, have been delighting visitors since 1885. Along the four miles of scenic walks, the stretch of waterfalls includes those with such interesting names as Pecca Twin Falls, Holly Bush Spout, Thornton Force, and Baxengill Gorge.

INGLETON

10 miles NW of Settle off the A65

Mentioned in the *Domesday Book* – the name means 'beacon town' – Ingleton is certainly one of the most visited villages in the dales. As a gateway to the Three Peaks, it is also popular with walkers. From as long ago as the late 1700s, Ingleton has been famous for the numerous caves and other splendid scenery that lie within a short distance though some are harder to find and even harder to reach. The coming of the railway, which gave those working in the towns easy and cheap access to the countryside, greatly increased the numbers of visitors looking for clean, country air. Though Ingleton is no longer served by trains, the village is still dominated by the railway viaduct that spans the River Greta. The river, which is formed here by the meeting of the Rivers Twiss and Doe, is famous for its salmon leaps.

Many thousands of years old, **White Scar Caves** were only discovered in 1923, by an adventurous student named Christopher Long. Though he saw only by the light of a torch, standing alone in the vast underground cave now known as Battlefield Cavern must have been an awesome experience. It stretches for more than 330 feet, soaring in places to 100 feet high, with thousands of oddly-shaped stalactites dripping from its roof. The 80-minute guided tour covers one mile and passes cascading waterfalls and curious cave

formations such as the Devil's Tongue, the Arum Lily and the remarkably lifelike Judge's Head. The temperature inside the cave stays constant all year round at a cool 8°c (46°f) so don't forget to bring something warm.

Ingleborough which, at 2,375 feet, is the middle summit of the **Three Peaks**. For over 2,000 years, the peak has been used as a beacon and a fortress and, as a result, it is perhaps the most interesting. A distinctive feature of the horizon for miles around as it is made of several layers of rock of differing hardnesses, there are several paths to the summit most of which begin their journey in Ingleton. As well as the fine views, on a clear day, there are also several interesting features on top of the peak. The most recent of these are the remains of a tower that was built by a local mill owner, Mr Hornby Roughsedge. Though the intended use of the building is not known, its short history is well-documented. A grand opening was arranged on the summit and the celebrations, probably helped by a supply of ale, got a little out of hand when a group of men began tearing down the structure.

At the highest point is a triangulation point while, close by, a cross-shaped shelter has been built which offers protection from the elements whatever their direction. The shelter acts as a reminder that the weather can change quickly in this area and a walk to the summit, however nice the day is at lower levels, should not be undertaken without careful thought as to suitable clothing.

To the east, on the edge of the summit plateau, are the remains of several ancient hut circles and, beyond, the remains of a wall. The Romans are known to have used Ingleborough as a signal station but the wall may have been built by the Brigantes whose settlement on the mountain was called *Rigodunum*.

LOW BENTHAM

3 miles S of Ingleton on the B6480

Lying close to the county border with Lancashire and on the slopes of the Pennines, this village is pleasantly situated in the valley of the River Wenning, a tributary of the River Lune. Like many Pennine villages in the late 17th and early 18th centuries, Low Bentham was taken over by the textile industry and there was a linen mill here. After a time, the mill changed hands, and also direction, taking on the specialised task of spinning silk before that, too, ceased in the 1960s as a result of the increasing use of man-made fibres.

The growth in textiles in the area coincided with an increase in Quakerism within the parish and, in 1680, a meeting house was set up in the village. Established as a place of non-conformist worship, the village was also well known as a place of Wesleyan Methodism by 1800.

THORNTON IN LONSDALE

1 mile NW of Ingleton off the A65

This small village of a few houses, an inn, and an interesting church dates back to at least the 12th century and is probably much older.

CHAPEL-LE-DALE

6 miles N of Ingleton on the B6255

Whernside, to the north of the village, is the highest of the **Three Peaks**, at 2,418 feet, and also the least popular of the mountains – consequently there are few paths to the summit. Just below the top are a number of tarns. Here, in 1917, it was noticed that they were frequented by black-headed gulls. Those walking to the top of the peak today will also see the birds, a reminder that the northwest coast is not so far away.

RIBBLEHEAD

10 miles N of Settle on the B6479

Lying close to the source of the River Ribble is the impressive structure, the **Ribblehead Viaduct**, which was built to carry the Settle-Carlisle Railway. Opened in 1876, after taking five years to construct, its 24 arches span the dark moorland and it is overlooked by Whernside. A bleak and exposed site, the viaduct is often battered by strong winds which on occasion can literally stop a train in its tracks. The **Ribblehead Station & Visitor Centre**, housed in former station buildings, presents an interpretive display showing the history of the line with special emphasis on the Ribblehead locality.

•

The 13th-century Church of St Oswald in Thornton in Lonsdale was unfortunately burnt almost to the ground in 1933 and only the tower remains of the original building. The rest of the church was rebuilt to resemble the extensive restoration work that was undertaken here in 1870. On an outside wall of the tower is an unusual carving, of a rose, a thistle, and a shamrock, which is believed to commemorate the union of England and Wales with Scotland and Ireland in 1801.

•

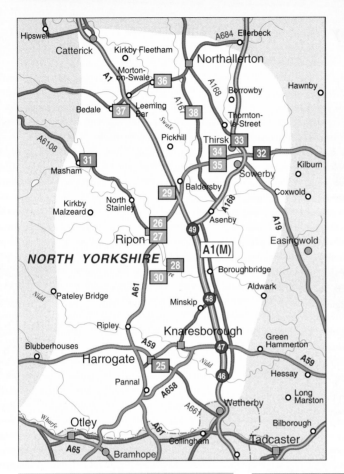

FOOD & DRINK

ACCOMMODATION

PLACES OF INTEREST

Yorkshire Spa Towns

The Vale of York – or Plain, as it's sometimes called – is rich, agricultural land that stretches some 60 miles northwards from York almost to the Tees. Although flat itself, there are almost always hills in view: the Hambleton and Cleveland Hills to the east, the Dales and the Pennines to the west. In between lies this fertile corridor of rich farmland and low-lying meadows, a vast plain bisected by the Great North Road linking London and Edinburgh. For most of its life, the Great North Road has been a rocky, pot-holed and swampy obstacle course. The best stretches, by far, were those where it ran along the meticulously engineered course the Romans had built centuries earlier. It took more than 1,800 years for the English to realise themselves the importance of constructing viable, all-weather roads. Throughout this area the skyline is dotted with the spires and towers of churches that were built in those relatively prosperous times. The two towns of Harrogate and Knaresborough dominate the lower section of Nidderdale and though, today, Harrogate is the larger, for centuries Knaresborough was the more important of the two. Older than its neighbour, Knaresborough was inhabited long before the days of the Romans and, along with its Norman castle, it is now best known as being the home of England's most famous prophetess, Mother Shipton and the Petrifying Well that stands beside her birthplace. A small village until the 17th century, Harrogate developed into one of the country's foremost spa towns following the discovery of a chalybeate well in the late 16th century. As the fame of its healing waters spread, along with the fashion for seeking cures

for any number of ailments increased, so Harrogate grew into the elegant and genteel town that remains today. The key features here are the Georgian and Victorian architecture along with the wide tree-lined boulevards and the numerous gardens.

Ripon has been a cathedral city since Victorian times, and also boasts a peaceful and gracious air. Though the city tried to exploit the fashion for 'taking the waters', it did not have its own healing springs and so water had to be pumped in from Aldfield, near Fountains Abbey. Many Edwardian spa buildings remain in Ripon, along with some fine Art Nouveau features and their surrounding gardens. Ripon is also home to one of the country's most beautiful racecourses; throughout the summer season there are race meetings here on what is known as Yorkshire's Garden Racecourse. Nearby, at Thirsk, is another of the country's delightful racecourses, although the town is best known as having been the home of the real-life James Herriot, Alf Wight.

Although ancient monuments abound in this area – such as the Devil's Arrows near Boroughbridge – and many of the settlements have Roman roots, it is the magnificent ruin of Fountains Abbey for which this region is best known. Set beside the River Skell, this was one of the wealthiest Cistercian houses in the country in medieval times and, today, the remains are Yorkshire's only World Heritage Site. However, there are other places of interest to see close by, including the fine stately home of Newby Hall, the Northern Horticultural Society's Harlow Carr Botanical Gardens and the breweries at Masham.

HARROGATE

One of England's most attractive towns and a frequent winner of Britain in Bloom, Harrogate features acres of gardens that offer an array of colour throughout the year, open spaces, and broad tree lined boulevards. However, until the 17th century Harrogate – or 'Haregate' as it was then called – was just a collection of cottages close to the thriving market town of Knaresborough. It was William Slingsby, of Bilton Hall near Knaresborough, who, while out walking his dog, discovered a spring bubbling up out of the rock that was to found the fortunes of the town. Tasting the waters, Slingsby found them to be similar to those he had tasted at the fashionable wells of Spaw, in Belgium. Expert opinion was sought and, in 1596, Dr Timothy Bright confirmed the spring to be a chalybeate well and the waters to have medicinal powers – curing a wide variety of illness and ailments from gout to vertigo.

Slingsby's well became known as **Tewit Well**, after the local name for peewits, and it can still be seen today, covered by a dome on pillars. Other wells were also found in the area, St John's Well in 1631 and the **Old Sulphur Well** which went on to become the most famous of Harrogate's springs. Though this spring had been known locally for years, it was not until 1656 that the sulphurous, vile-smelling waters, nicknamed 'the Stinking Spaw', began to attract attention.

During the mid-17th century bathing in the heated sulphurous waters became fashionable as well as a cure for various ailments and lodging houses were built around the sulphur well in Low Harrogate. Bathing took place in the evening and, each morning, the patients would drink a glass of the water with their breakfasts. The cupola seen over the well was erected in 1804.

In order to serve the growing number of people arriving at Harrogate seeking a cure for their

Pump Room Museum, Harrogate

ailments, the Queen's Head Hotel was built and it is probably the oldest inn here as it dates from before 1687. When stagecoaches began to arrive in the 18th century the inn moved with the times and became the first at the spa to serve the needs of the coaches.

By the late 1700s it was one of the largest hotels in the fast growing town and, though the hotel changed its name to the Queen's Hotel in 1828 and underwent extensive renovation and remodelling in the mid-19th century, it did not survive the decline of the spa and, in 1951, it became the offices for the Regional Hospital Board. Many other hotels were built including the Crown Inn, next to the Old Sulphur Well, which became a coaching inn in 1772 and hosted a visit by Lord Byron in 1806. However, one of the town's most famous hotels, The Majestic, a turn-of-the-century red brick building, does survive and it was the place where Elgar stayed while visiting Harrogate.

The **Royal Pump Room Museum** was built in 1842 to enclose the Old Sulphur Well and this major watering place for spa visitors has been painstakingly restored to illustrate all the aspects of Harrogate's history. Beneath the building the sulphur water still rises to the surface and can be sampled.

There will be few Harrogate residents who have not heard of Betty Lupton, the almost legendary 'Queen of the Wells' who, for over 50 years, dispensed the spa waters, dishing out cupfuls to paying

visitors, who were then encouraged to walk off the dubious effects of the medicine by taking a trip around the Bogs Fields, known today as **Valley Gardens**. She conducted her business in the ostentatiously named **Royal Baths Assembly Rooms** which, in their heyday, were full of rich visitors sampling the waters. Today, the buildings have been restored to house the **Turkish Baths** where visitors can enjoy a sauna, beauty treatment and massage. The baths are open to the public daily. The **Mercer Art Gallery** is housed in the oldest of the town's surviving spa buildings, originally built in 1806. The Promenade Room has been restored to its former glory and displays a superb collection of fine art along with the Kent Bequest – an archaeological collection that includes finds from both ancient Greece and Egypt.

By the late 18th century Harrogate had become one of Europe's most fashionable spa towns and it was not only serving the needs of those with acute and chronic ailments but also members of 'good society'. Fuelled by competition from spa towns abroad, Harrogate sought to provide not only medical care for the sick but also to appeal to the needs of the fashionable. In 1858, Charles Dickens visited the town and described it as 'the queerest place, with the strangest people in it leading the oddest lives of dancing, newspaper reading, and table d'hôte.' Though its status as a spa town has declined, it is still a

25 MERCER ART GALLERY

Harrogate

The Mercer Art Gallery is home to the district's superb collection of fine art.

 see page 214

Perhaps the most well-known tale associated with Harrogate is the disappearance of Agatha Christie in 1926. In a set of circumstances reminiscent of one of her novels, Agatha went missing in the December of that year, possibly as a result of marital difficulties. Her crashed car was discovered near a chalk pit near her home but the novelist was nowhere to be found and one of the largest police manhunts was put into operation. Agatha had, in fact, travelled to Harrogate, after abandoning her car, and booked into the Old Swan Hotel under the name of her husband's mistress, Theresa Neele. After 10 days she was spotted and her husband came to collect her, putting her disappearance down to loss of memory. However, this did not dispel rumours that the marriage was in trouble or that the surprising event was nothing more than a publicity stunt. Whatever the truth, two years later the couple divorced and Colonel Christie married his long-time mistress Theresa.

fashionable place, a sought after conference location, home of the annual Northern Antiques Fair, and a town with much to offer the visitor.

As well as a spa, Harrogate developed into a centre for shopping for the well-to-do and the many old-fashioned shops are typified by Montpellier Parade, a crescent of shops surrounded by trees and flowerbeds. Another attractive aspect of the town is **The Stray**, which is unique to Harrogate and virtually encircles the town centre. The 215 acres of open space are protected by ancient law to ensure that the residents of, and visitors to, the town always have access for sports, events, and walking. The spacious lawns are at their most picturesque during the spring when edged with crocus and daffodils. Originally part of the Forest of Knaresborough the land was, fortunately, not enclosed under the 1770 Act of Parliament. The large gritstone pillar, beside The Stray, marks the boundary of the Leeds and Ripon turnpike. On The Stray stands the Commemorative Oak Tree, planted in 1902 by Samson Fox to commemorate the ox roasting that took place here as part of the celebrations for Queen Victoria's Jubilee in 1887 and the end of the Boer War in 1902.

One of Harrogate's major visitor attractions is the **RHS Harlow Carr Botanical Gardens,** just over a mile from the town centre. Established in 1948 by the Northern Horticultural Society and now covering some 58 acres, the

gardens feature all manner of plants in a wide variety of landscapes which allows members of the public to see how they perform in the unsympathetic conditions of northern England. The society, as well as having their study centre here, has also opened a fascinating **Museum of Gardening**.

A major summer event is the **Great Yorkshire Show,** a three day event that includes top class show-jumping, displays and demonstrations of various kinds, some 10,000 animals, miles of shopping, a flower show and much, much more.

AROUND HARROGATE

HAMPSTHWAITE

4 miles NW of Harrogate off the A59

This picturesque Nidderdale village lies on an ancient Roman way between Ilkley and Aldborough and traces of Roman tin mining have been found in the area. The village Church of St Thomas has remnants of a Saxon building in the tower and, in the churchyard, is buried Peter Barker. Known as 'Blind Peter', Barker was a local character very much in the tradition of Jack Metcalfe and he did not let his disability hinder him: he was a skilled cabinet-maker, glazier and musician. The mysterious portrait of the bearded man hanging in the church, painted by the local vicar's daughter, may well be of Blind Peter.

ALDBOROUGH

4 miles NW of Harrogate off the A59

The ancient Roman town of Isurium Brigantum, or Aldborough, as it is known today, was once the home of the 9th Legion, who wrested it from the Celtic Brigantian tribe. The modern-day focal point of the village is the tall maypole on the village green, around which traditional dances take place each May. At one end of the green is a raised platform which is all that remains of the Old Court House and it bears an inscription recalling that up to 150 years ago the election of members of Parliament was announced here. Below are some well-preserved stocks that are, in fact, only replicas of the originals. The **Aldborough Roman Museum** houses relics of the town's past. This was once a thriving Roman city of vital strategic importance and near the museum are some of the original walls and tessellated pavements of that city.

Roman City Walls, Aldborough

BECKWITHSHAW

3 miles SW of Harrogate on the B6161

This village, as its name suggests, was once bounded by a stream and woodland though, sadly, most of the trees are now gone. It was once part of the great Forest of Knaresborough and a local legend tells how John O'Gaunt promised John Haverah, a cripple, as much land as he could hop around between sunrise and sunset. By throwing his crutch the last few yards, just as the sun was setting, John Haverah managed to secure himself seven square miles, the remainder of which is today called Haverah Park.

KNARESBOROUGH

3 miles NE of Harrogate on the A59

This ancient town of pantiled cottages and Georgian houses is precariously balanced on a hillside by the River Nidd. A stately railway viaduct, 90 feet high and 338 feet long, completed in 1851, spans the gorge. There are many unusual and attractive features in the town, among them a maze of steep stepped narrow streets leading down to the river and numerous alleyways. In addition to boating on the river, there are many enjoyable riverside walks.

The town is dominated by the ruins of **Knaresborough Castle**, built high on a crag overlooking the River Nidd by Serlo de Burgh, who had fought alongside William the Conqueror at Hastings. Throughout

- *The Church of St Andrew in Aldborough was built in 1330 on the site of a Norman church that was burnt down by the Scots in 1318. This in turn had been built on the site of an ancient Temple of Mercury. Modern archaeologists no doubt reel in horror at the thought that parts of the present church were built with stones from the Temple's walls. One ancient relic that is still preserved in the church's grounds is an Anglo-Saxon sundial known as the Ulph Stone.*

In Knaresborough Market Square, visitors should also keep an eye out for Ye Oldest Chemists' Shoppe in England which was first recorded in 1720 although the building is probably a hundred years older. The old chemist's drawers, each marked with the scientific name of its contents, are still in place but the pungent potions have been replaced by a wide selection of quality confectionery.

the Middle Ages, the castle was a favourite with the court and it was to Knaresborough that the murderers of Thomas à Becket fled in 1170. Queen Philippa, wife of Edward III, also enjoyed staying at Knaresborough and she and her family spent many summers here. However, following the Civil War, during which the town and its castle had remained loyal to the king, Cromwell ordered the castle's destruction.

Also in the town is the Old Courthouse Museum which tells the history of the town and houses a rare Tudor Courtroom. The nearby Bebra Gardens are named after Knaresborough's twin town in Germany and its attractive flower beds are complemented by luxurious lawns and a paddling pool.

Knaresborough boasts not only the oldest chemist's shop but also the oldest tourist attraction in the UK, **Mother Shipton's Cave**, which opened in 1630. It was the birthplace of the famous

prophetess and its Petrifying Well has fascinated visitors for generations. The effects that the well's lime-rich water has on objects are truly amazing and an array of paraphernalia, from old boots to bunches of grapes, are on view – seemingly turned to stone. It is little wonder that these were considered magical properties by the superstitious over the centuries or that the well was associated with witchcraft and various other interesting tales.

The foremost tale concerns Mother Shipton, who was said to have been born in the cavern situated by the well on 6th July 1488 and who has the reputation of being England's most famous fortune-teller. The story says that she was born in the midst of a terrible storm and was soon found to have a strange ability to see the future. As she grew older her prophetic visions became more widely known and feared throughout England. However, the most singular feature about Mother Shipton has to be that she died peacefully in her bed, as opposed to being burnt at the stake as most witches were at that time.

She had been threatened with burning by, among others, Cardinal Wolsey, when she had warned him on a visit to York that he might see the city again but never enter. True to her prediction Wolsey never did enter York, for he was arrested on a charge of treason at Cawood. Among her many other prophesies she reputedly foretold

Mother Shipton's Cave

the invasion and defeat of the Spanish Armada in 1588 and Samuel Pepys recorded that it was Mother Shipton who prophesied the disastrous Great Fire of London in 1666.

While in Knaresborough, it is well worth taking the opportunity to visit the **House in the Rock** hewn out of solid rock by Thomas Hill, an eccentric weaver, between 1770 and 1786. It was Hill's son who renamed the house Fort Montagu and flew a flag and fired a gun salute on special occasions. On the banks of the River Nidd there is also **St Robert's Cave** which is an ancient hermitage. St Robert was the son of a mayor of York who, at the time of his death in 1218, was so beloved that the people of Knaresborough would not allow the monks of Fountains Abbey to bury him. Instead they kept his bones and finally interred him in a place near the altar in the **Chapel of Our Lady of the Crag**. It is guarded by the statue of a larger than life-size figure of a knight in the act of drawing his sword.

In the tradition of this town's reputation for exceptional and odd characters is 'Blind Jack of Knaresborough'. Jack Metcalfe was born in 1717 and lost his sight at the age of six, but went on to achieve fame as a roadmaker. He was a remarkable person who never allowed his blindness to bar him from any normal activities – he rode, climbed trees, swam, and was often employed to guide travellers through the wild Forest of Knaresborough. He was a talented

fiddle player and one of his more roguish exploits was his elopement with Dolly Benson, the daughter of the innkeeper of the Royal Oak in Harrogate, on the night before she was due to marry another man. His most memorable achievement however, was the laying of roads over the surrounding bogs and marshes which he achieved by laying a foundation of bundles of heather, a technique that had never been used before.

Another of Knaresborough's attractive amenities is **Conyngham Hall**, a majestic old house enclosed within a loop of the River Nidd. Once the home of Lord Macintosh, the Halifax toffee magnate, the Hall itself is not open to the public but its landscaped grounds, stretching down to the river, are and provide tennis, putting and other activities.

SPOFFORTH

4½ miles SE of Harrogate on the A661

This ancient village, situated on the tiny River Crimple, is home to the splendid Palladian mansion, **Stockeld Park**, built between 1758 and 1763 by Paine. Containing some excellent furniture and a fine picture collection, the house is surrounded by extensive parkland which offers garden walks. Though privately owned, the house is open

Statue of Knight in our Lady of the Crag

- A mile or so to the south of Knaresborough, *Plumpton Rocks* provide an ideal picnic spot. There's an idyllic lake surrounded by dramatic millstone grit rocks and woodland paths that were laid out in the 18th century. It has been declared a garden of special historic interest by English Heritage and is open every weekend, on public holidays and daily from March to October.

-

Visitors strolling around Ripley cannot fail to notice the Hotel de Ville – the Town Hall. Sir William Amcotts Ingilby was responsible for this curiosity when, in 1827, he began to remodel the entire village on one that he had seen in Alsace-Lorraine. The original thatched cottages were replaced with those seen today and now Ripley is a conservation area with every pre-1980 dwelling being a Grade II listed building.

by appointment.

Spofforth Castle (English Heritage) is another place of note, an historic building whose sight stirs the imagination, despite its ruined state. The powerful Percy family originally built the castle here in the 16th century to replace the manor house which had been repeatedly laid to waste. The castle itself is now a crumbling ruin after it was destroyed during the Civil War. According to some accounts, the castle was the birthplace of Harry Hotspur.

GOLDSBOROUGH

5 miles E of Harrogate off the A59

This rather special village was an estate village from the time of the Norman Conquest until the 1950s when it was sold by the Earl of Harewood to pay enormous death duties. The charming 12th-century **Church of St Mary** has some interesting features including a Norman doorhead and an effigy of a knight. It is also a 'green man church' and the image of the Celtic god of fertility, with his oak-leafed head, is well hidden on one of the many Goldsborough family tombs. In 1859, while the church was being restored, a lead casket was discovered containing Viking jewellery and coins. In the 1920s, Mary, the daughter of George V and Queen Mary, lived in the village after her marriage and her eldest son, George, was christened in the church.

BIRSTWITH

5 miles NW of Harrogate off the B6165

Evidence in the form of a

Neolithic axe-head suggests that this one-time estate village in the valley of the River Nidd was a Stone Age settlement in what was to become known as the Forest of Knaresborough. Along with both quarrying and coal-mining, Birstwith also had a cotton mill beside the river – though all that now remains is the weir that was created to ensure a good head of water for the mill-race. One notable visitor to this village was Charlotte Brontë, who stayed with the Greenwood family at Swarcliffe Hall for about six months in the 1840s, when she was governess to the children. The Hall is now a private boys' school.

RIPLEY

3 miles N of Harrogate off the A61

In the outer walls of the parish church, built around 1400, are holes said to have been caused by musket balls from Cromwell's firing squad who executed Royalist prisoners here after the battle of Marston Moor. Inside, there is a fine Rood Screen dating from the reign of King Stephen, a mid-14th-century tomb chest, and the stone base of an **Old Weeping Cross** (where one was expected to kneel in the stone grooves and weep for penance) survives in the churchyard.

Ripley, still very much an estate village, is a quiet and pretty place, with cobbled streets, a castle, a wonderful hotel, and an interesting history. A knighthood was granted to Thomas Ingilby in the 1300s for killing a wild boar in

Old Weeping Cross, Ripley

on a sofa with two pistols pointing at his head, declared the next morning, 'It was well that he behaved in so peaceable a manner; had it been otherwise, he would not have left the house alive.' Cromwell, his pride severely damaged by a woman ordered the immediate execution of his Royalist prisoners and left Trooper Jane regretting staying her hand during the previous night.

BURNT YATES

2 miles W of Ripley on the B6165

Knaresborough Forest that was charging at King Edward III.

Magnificent **Ripley Castle** has been home to the Ingilby family for nearly 700 years. The castle is open to the public and is set in an outstanding Capability Brown landscape, with lakes, a deer park, and an avenue of tall beeches over which the attractive towers only just seem to peek. Its tranquillity belies the events that took place here after the battle at Marston Moor, when Cromwell, exhausted after his day's slaughter, camped his Roundheads here and chose to rest in the castle.

The Ingilbys, however, were Royalist and his intrusion was met with as much ill-will as possible; they offered neither food nor a bed. Jane Ingilby, aptly named 'Trooper Jane' due to her fighting skills, was the house's occupant and, having forced the self-styled Lord Protector of England to sleep

Located at one of the highest points in Nidderdale, Burnt Yates enjoys some fine views of the surrounding hills and moors. Its tiny village school of 1750 still stands. Its original endowment provided for 30 poor boys to be taught the three Rs and for an equivalent number of poor girls to learns the skills of needlework and spinning.

RIPON

This attractive cathedral city, on the banks of the Rivers Ure, Skell, and Laver, dates from the 7th century when Alfrich, King of Northumbria granted an area of land here, surrounding a new monastery, to the Church. Later that century, in AD 672, St Wilfrid built a church on the high ground between the three rivers but, at the time of the demise of the

Ripon Cathedral

Fountains Abbey and, traditionally, the people of Ripon follow this ancient route on Boxing Day.

A striking survival of the Saxon cathedral is the 1,300-year-old Crypt. At its northeast corner is a narrow passage known as The Needle. According to the 17th-century antiquary Thomas Fuller, women whose chastity was suspect were made to pass through it. If they were unable to do so, their reputations were irretrievably tarnished. 'They pricked their credit', Fuller wrote 'who could not thread the Needle'.

The Crypt is all that remains of St Wilfrid's church but the magnificent **Cathedral of St Peter and St Wilfrid**, which now stands on the site, is certainly well worth visiting. Begun in the mid-12th century by Archbishop Roger of York, it was originally designed as a simple cruciform church; the west front was added in the mid-13th century and the east choir in 1286. Rebuilding work was begun in the 16th century but the disruption of the Dissolution of the Monasteries caused the work to be abandoned and it was only the intervention of James I in the early 1600s that saved the building from ruin. Then established as a collegiate church, the diocese of Ripon was formed in 1836 and the church made a cathedral. Often referred to as the Cathedral of the Dales, the building, though one of the tallest cathedrals in England, is also the smallest. Discovered in 1976 close to the cathedral, the Ripon Jewel is the only surviving trace of

---

26 THE LAMB AND FLAG

Ripon

Just minutes from Ripon's many charming sights and attractions, convivial and welcoming Georgian pub. Home-made food served at lunchtime.

¶ see page 214

Northern Kingdom in the mid-10th century, the monastery and church were destroyed, though the Saxon crypt survives to this day. By the time of the Norman Conquest, Ripon was a prosperous agricultural settlement under ecclesiastical rule and it was at this time that a second St Wilfrid's Church was erected on the site of the Saxon building. On Christmas Day 1132, monks from York worshipped here while they were making a journey to found

the magnificence that was characteristic of the cathedral's early history. A small gold roundel inlaid with gemstones, the jewel's design suggests that it was made to embellish a relic casket or cross ordered by St Wilfrid.

Throughout the Middle Ages, the town prospered: its market charter had been granted by King Alfred in the 9th century and, at one time, Ripon produced more woollen cloth than Halifax and Leeds. The collapse of the woollen industry saw a rise in spur manufacture in the 16th century and their fame was such that Ripon spurs were referred to in the old proverb: 'As true steel as a Ripon rowel.' As well as having three rivers, Ripon also had a canal. Built between 1767 and 1773 to improve the navigation of the River Ure: John Smeaton, builder of the Eddystone Lighthouse, was the designer. However, by 1820 the company running the canal had fallen into debt and it was little used after that time.

Fortunately, for today's visitor, the Industrial Revolution, and all its associated implications, by-passed Ripon and it was not until the early 20th century that the town flourished, though briefly, as a spa. However, many ancient customs and festivals have survived down the centuries. Perhaps the most famous is the sounding of the 'Wakeman's Horn' each night at 9 p.m. in the marketplace. Dating back to the 9th century, the Wakeman was originally appointed to patrol the town after the nightly curfew had been blown and, in many ways, this was the first form of security patrol. The Wakeman was selected each year from the town's 12 aldermen and those choosing not to take office were fined heavily. Today, this old custom is revived in the Mayor-making Ceremony when the elected mayor shows great reluctance to take office and hides from his colleagues.

As might be expected, any walk around this ancient town reveals, in its buildings, its interesting and varied past. The heart of the town is the Market Place and here stands a tall obelisk which was erected in 1702 to replace the market cross. Restored in 1781, at its summit are a horn and a rowel spur, symbolizing Ripon's crafts and customs. Situated at the edge of the square are the picturesque, half-timbered 14th-century **Wakeman's House** and the attractive Georgian **Town Hall**.

The Spa Baths building, opened in 1905 by the Princess of Battenberg, is a reminder of Ripon's attempt to become a fashionable spa resort. With no spring of its own, the town had to pipe in sulphur mineral water from Aldfield near Fountains Abbey. However, the scheme failed, though the building, which now houses the city's swimming pool, is a fine example of art nouveau architecture and the **Ripon Spa Gardens** with its 18-hole putting course, flat green bowling, nine hole crazy golf, tennis courts, bandstand and café, is still a pleasant place for a stroll.

To the southeast of the city is one of the area's finest stately homes, Newby Hall. Built in the 18th century and designed by Robert Adam, much of the house is open to the public including the splendid Billiard Room with its fine portrait of Frederick Grantham Vyner. An ancestor of the family who have lived here from the mid-19th century, Frederick was murdered by Greek bandits after being kidnapped. The house is perhaps most famous for its superb tapestries and there is also a fine collection of Chippendale furniture.

It is, though, the award-winning Newby Hall Gardens that draw most people to the house. Extensive and well designed, it was the present owner's father who transformed a nine hole golf course into the 25 acres of award-winning gardens that offer something for everyone whatever the time of year. Also found here is a wonderful Woodland Discovery Walk, a miniature railway, plenty of other attractions specially designed for children, a plant stall, shop and restaurant.

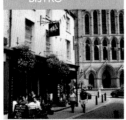

27 DISH'S CAFÉ BAR & BISTRO

Ripon

Fresh and contemporary place with the best in good, honest, home-made food. Open 9.30 to 5, evenings by prior booking.

 see page 215

28 NEWBY HALL AND GARDENS

Ripon

A renowned Adam House with spectacular treasures and antiques, standing in 25 acres of beautiful landscaped gardens.

 see page 215

29 THE GEORGE AND DRAGON INN

Melmerby

Superb inn with real ales, excellent home-cooked food and 3 ensuite bedrooms, in quiet village off the A1/A61 near Ripon and Thirsk.

 see page 216

62

Near to the cathedral is Ripon's old **Courthouse** that was built in 1830 on the site of an earlier (17th-century) Common Hall, used for the Quarter Sessions and the Court Military. Adjacent to this fine Georgian courthouse is a Tudor building that was part of the Archbishop of York's summer palace.

Also not far from the cathedral is the House of Correction, built in 1686 which served as the local prison between 1816 and 1878 and then became the police station until the late 1950s. This austere building is now home to the **Prison and Police Museum**, established in 1984, which depicts the history of the police force as well as giving visitors a real insight into the life of a prisoner in Victorian times. Almost as unfortunate as those prisoners were the inmates of **Ripon Workhouse**, the city's newest museum. The restored vagrants' wards of 1877 provide a chilling insight into the treatment of paupers in Yorkshire workhouses and the displays include a 'Victorian Hard Times Gallery'.

Horse racing at Ripon dates back to 1713 and the present course opened in 1900. Meetings are held between April and August and the course is widely regarded as one of the most beautiful in the country.

AROUND RIPON

WATH

4 miles N of Ripon off the A1

The stately home of **Norton Conyers** has been owned by the Graham family since 1624 though, undoubtedly, the house's main claim to fame is the visit made by Charlotte Brontë. During her stay here the novelist heard the story of Mad Mary, supposedly a Lady Graham. Apparently Lady Graham had been locked up in an attic room, now tantalisingly inaccessible to the public, and Charlotte eventually based the character of Mrs Rochester in her novel *Jane Eyre* on this unfortunate woman. Visitors to the hall will also see the famous painting of Sir Bellingham Graham on his bay horse, as Master of the Quorn hunt. It is rumoured that ownership of the painting was once decided on the throwing of a pair of dice. Other family pictures, furniture and costumes are on display and there's a lovely 18th-century walled garden within the grounds.

SKELTON

3 miles SE of Ripon off the B6265

This charming little village has some surviving cottages, dating from 1540, which are built from small handmade bricks with pantiled roofs. A ferry used to cross the River Ure, at this point, to Bishop Monkton and, in 1869, it was the scene of a notorious hunting accident. Members of the York and Ainsty Hunt boarded the ferry in order to follow a fox that had swum across the river. Half way across the horses panicked, capsizing the boat, and the boatman, along with five hunt members, were drowned. Also here is Newby Hall, a beautiful Adams style house with award-winning gardens.

BOROUGHBRIDGE

7 miles SE of Ripon on the B6265

This attractive and historic town dates from the reign of William the Conqueror though it was once on a main thoroughfare used by both the Celts of Brigantia and, later, the Romans. The bridge over the River Ure, from which the village takes its name, was built in 1562 and it formed part of an important road link between Edinburgh and London. Busy throughout the coaching days with traffic passing from the West Riding of Yorkshire to the North, Boroughbridge has now returned to its former unassuming role of a small wayside town now bypassed by the A1(M) which takes most of the 21st century traffic from its streets.

The great **Devil's Arrows**, three massive Bronze Age monoliths, stand like guardians close to the new road and form

Yorkshire's most famous ancient monument: thought to date from around 2000 BC, the tallest is 30 feet high. The monoliths stand in a line running north-south and are fashioned from millstone grit which has been seriously fluted by weathering. A local legend, however, attributes the great stones to the Devil suggesting that they were, actually, crossbow bolts that he fired at nearby Aldborough which, at the time, was a Christian settlement.

STUDLEY ROGER

2 miles SW of Ripon off the B6265

The magnificent **Studley Royal Gardens** were created in the early 18th century before they were merged with nearby Fountains Abbey in 1768. Started by John Aislabie, Chancellor of the Exchequer and founder of the South Sea Company that spectacularly went bust in 1720, the landscaping took some 14 years. It then took a further 10 years to

30 THE MASONS ARMS

Bishop Monkton, Harrogate
Real ales and great food in picture-postcard village setting a few miles south of Ripon off the A61.

🍴 *see page 216*

Devil's Arrows, Boroughbridge

63

It is commonly thought that one of Fountain Abbey's friars, renowned for his strength and skill as an archer, challenged Robin Hood to a sword fight. Forced to concede, the friar joined the Merry Men of Sherwood and became known as Friar Tuck.

complete the construction of the buildings and follies found within the gardens. With a network of paths and the River Skell flowing through the grounds, it is well worth exploring these superb gardens.

A National Trust property, like the adjoining gardens, **Fountains Abbey** is the pride of all the ecclesiastical ruins in Yorkshire and the only World Heritage Site in Yorkshire. The Abbey was one of the wealthiest of the Cistercian houses and its remains are the most complete of any Cistercian abbey in Britain. Founded in 1132, with the help of Archbishop Thurstan of York, the first buildings housed just 12 monks of the order and, over the centuries its size increased, even spreading across the River Skell itself. The Abbey reached its peak in the 15th century with the grandiose designs of Abbot Marmaduke Huby, whose beautiful tower still stands as a reminder of just how rich and powerful Fountains became. In fact, the abbey was run on such businesslike lines that, at its height, as well as owning extensive lands throughout Yorkshire, it had an income of about £1,000 a year, then a very substantial sum indeed.

The Dissolution hit the abbey as it did all the powerful religious houses. The abbot was hanged, the monks scattered, and its treasures taken off or destroyed. The stonework, however, was left largely intact, possibly due to its remote location. In 1579, Sir Stephen Proctor pulled down some

outbuildings, in order to construct **Fountains Hall**, a magnificent Elizabethan mansion which still stands in the Abbey's grounds and part of which is open to the public.

NORTH STAINLEY

4½ miles NW of Ripon on the A6108

Just over 100 years ago, in 1895, excavations in a field just outside the village revealed the site of a Roman villa called Castle Dykes though all that can be seen now are the grassed outlines of the foundations and the moat. However, the discovery does prove that there has been a settlement here for many centuries. The monks of Fountains Abbey also knew North Stainley. Slenningford Grange is thought to have been one of their many properties and a fishpond, dating from medieval times, is still in existence.

Just to the south of the village lies the **Lightwater Valley Theme Park** set in 175 acres of scenic grounds. The Park boasts 'Ultimate' – the biggest roller-coaster in the world (authenticated by the *Guinness Book of Records*), the Rat Ride, Falls of Terror, and the Viper to name just a few and there are also plenty of more appropriate activities for younger children. Also within the grounds is Lightwater Village which offers a wide variety of retail and factory shops, a garden centre, restaurant and coffee shop.

KIRKBY MALZEARD

6 miles NW of Ripon off the A6108

Dating back to the 11th century, the **Church of St Andrew** is noted for its associations with witchcraft. Apparently, the northeastern corner of the churchyard was favoured by practitioners of the black arts for conducting their strange rituals and charms. Black magic aside, the church has been pealing its bells for over 400 years and records show that in 1591 one of the bells was recast – the process taking place inside the church building.

This traditional Yorkshire village is also one of the few places in the country that can boast its own Sword Dance. Certainly a pagan ritual, thought to date back to prehistoric times, the performance of the dance is supposed to make the grass grow tall and to wake the earth from her winter's sleep.

Many of the farms around the village are dairy farms and at Kirby Malzeard Dairy they still produce the traditionally made Coverdale cheese. Very much a local speciality, it is one of the few remaining Dales' cheeses still made though, at one time, each dale had its own particular variety.

Marmion Tower, West Tanfield

WEST TANFIELD
6 miles NW of Ripon on the A6108

This attractive village on the banks of the River Ure is home to a remarkable Tudor gatehouse known as the **Marmion Tower**. Overlooking the river and with a beautiful oriel window, the tower is open to the public.

For many years, West Tanfield was associated with the powerful Marmion family and the 14th-century Church of St Nicholas

contains many effigies belonging to the family.

Though the purpose of the **Thornborough Circles**, which lie just outside the village, remains a mystery, these late Neolithic or early Bronze Age oval earthworks are very impressive, especially from the air.

GREWELTHORPE
6½ miles NW of Ripon off the A6108

It was long thought that the

65

31 THEAKSTON BREWERY & VISITOR CENTRE

Masham

A guided tour will take you through the brewing process at the famous Theakston Brewery.

 see page 217

Romans had a camp to the north of this leafy village and the discovery in the early 1900s of the complete skeleton of a Roman soldier confirmed the story. The remains were reburied in the churchyard at Kirkby Malzeard but the soldier's sandals are on view in the York Museum.

North of the village are the beautiful **Hackfall Woods** through which the River Ure flows. During the 19th century the Victorians developed the woodland, creating waterfalls and transforming the 18th-century follies that had been built here into splendid vantage points. Following a period of neglect which began with the sale of the woodland in the 1930s, the Hackfall Woods are now in the care of the Woodland Trust and the area is being gradually restored to its 19th-century condition.

ILTON

9½ miles NW of Ripon off the A6108

This village is close to one of the area's most interesting and unusual features – the **Druid's Temple**. Though the name suggests that this was an ancient meeting place for pagan worshippers, the charming folly was built in the 1820s by William Danby of the nearby Swinton Estate. Resembling a miniature Stonehenge, the folly was inspired by a similar temple Danby saw on his travels in Europe and his building project was intended to provide work for local unemployed people. It is considered one of the best Druidic follies in the country. From Ilton village it can be reached

by following part of the long-distance footpath known as the Ripon Rowel Walk.

MASHAM

9 miles NW of Ripon on the A6108

Set beside the River Ure, Masham (pronounced *Massam*) is a very picturesque place with a huge marketplace at its heart. The ancient Church of St Mary stands in one corner, a school founded in 1760 in another, while at the centre is the market cross surrounded by trees and flowers. The size of the marketplace reflects Masham's historical importance as a market town and its position, between the sheep-covered hills and the corn growing lowlands, certainly helped to support its flourishing trade. The sheep fairs held in the town in the 18th and 19th centuries were among the largest in the country and in September the **Masham Sheep Fair** revives those heady days, giving visitors the chance of seeing many rare breeds of sheep and goats as well as witnessing events such as dog agility and sheep racing.

The town is famed for its beer, boasting two celebrated breweries – Theakston's and Black Sheep. **Theakston's Brewery**, noted for its Old Peculier brew, was founded in 1827 by two brothers, Thomas and Robert. Adjoining the brewery today is a modern visitor centre which illustrates the process of brewing and the art of cooperage. Those taking the tour (which must be pre-booked) should be aware that there are two flights of steep steps along the route and the tour is not suitable for children under 10. Interestingly, the name of the famous brew derives from the fact that Masham in medieval times had its own Peculier Court (meaning special rather than odd) – an ecclesiastical body with wide-ranging powers.

WELL

8 miles NW of Ripon off the B6267

This pretty village takes its name from St Michael's Well which was already being venerated long before the Romans came here and one of them built a spacious villa near the well. Part of the tessellated pavement of that villa is now on display in the parish church, which is itself a venerable building with foundations that date back to Norman times. The church's greatest treasure is a font cover dating from 1325, one of the oldest in the country. It was a gift to the church from Ralph Neville, Lord of Middleham, who also founded the line of almshouses near the church which were rebuilt by his descendants in 1758.

SNAPE

9½ miles NW of Ripon off the B6268

This quiet and unspoilt village, where the original timber-framed cottages stand side by side with their more modern neighbours, is still dominated by its castle as it has been for centuries. Reached via an avenue of lime trees, **Snape Castle** has a famous, if somewhat

complicated, royal connection as it was the home of Lord Latimer of Snape (a member of the Neville family), the first husband of Catherine Parr, Henry VIII's last wife. The Nevilles owned the castle for over 700 years and its beautiful chapel, still used by the villagers, saw the marriages of many Latimers and Nevilles.

Set in over 1,000 acres of parkland, **Thorp Perrow Arboretum** is unique to Britain, if not Europe, in that it was the creation of one man, Colonel Sir Leonard Ropner (1895-1977). Sir Leonard travelled all over the world collecting rare and unusual species for Thorp Perrow and today the hundreds of trees he enthusiastically collected are in their prime. The arboretum was initially Sir Leonard's private hobby but after his death his son, Sir John Ropner, decided to open the 85-acre garden to the public and the arboretum is now one of the area's prime attractions. A treasure trove

•

The Black Sheep Brewery is also well worth a visit. It is owned by another Theakston, Paul, who is the 5th generation of this famous brewing family. The vessels, plants and methods employed here are from a bygone era and currently produce five different ales, including a Monty Python ale which was specially commissioned to celebrate the 30th anniversary of the cult comedy series. The brewery also offers a guided tour and visitors get the chance to sample the traditionally made ales. In addition to the working brewery, the old Maltings building is home to a 'sheepy' shop and a popular bistro.

•

Snape Castle

32 DIVAN HOTEL

Thirsk

Spacious, modern and elegant hotel renowned for its food, drink and accommodation.

  see page 217

33 THE WORLD OF JAMES HERRIOT

Thirsk

A popular attraction, celebrating the life of the famous vet, and where you can visit his house, restored to how it was in the 40s and 50s.

 see page 218

•

On the edge of Thirsk, housed in a mid-Victorian maltings, Treske specialises in producing bespoke furniture made from solid hardwoods and designer upholstery fabrics. Among Treske's most notable commissions are some 400 chairs for the OBE chapel in St Paul's Cathedral, bedroom furniture for the College of St George's, Windsor Castle, and period replica furniture for the monks' cells at Mount Grace Priory. The showrooms are open daily and group tours of the workshop are available by prior arrangement.

•

of specimen trees, woodland walks, nature trail, tree trails, a large lake, picnic area and children's play area, the arboretum also embraces the Milbank Pinetum, planted by Lady Augusta Milbank in the mid-19th century, and the medieval Spring Wood dating back to the 16th century. Thorp Perrow provides interest all year round but perhaps the most popular time is the spring when you can witness one of the finest and most extensive plantings of daffodils in the north of England, among them some old and unusual varieties. In addition to the fascinating collection of trees, visitors will also find an information centre, a tea room and a plant sales area. An additional attraction at Thorp Perrow, opened in the spring of 2000, is **The Falcons of Thorp Perrow**, a bird-of-prey, captive-breeding and conservation centre which has been created within a large, formerly derelict walled garden. There are more than 75 birds from all continents of the world and regular flying demonstrations three times a day, weather permitting.

THIRSK

Thirsk has become famous as the home of veterinary surgeon Alf Wight, better known as James Herriot, author of *All Creatures Great and Small*, who died in 1995. In his immensely popular books, Thirsk is clearly recognisable as 'Darrowby'. The Easter of 1999 saw the opening in Thirsk of a £1.4m tribute to the celebrated vet.

The World of James Herriot is housed in the original surgery in Kirkgate and offers visitors a trip back in time to the 1940s, exploring the life and times of the world's most famous country vet. There's also the opportunity to take part in a TV production, and a Visible Farm exhibit where you can explore farm animals inside and out!

Just across the road from the surgery is the birthplace of another famous son of Thirsk. The building is now the town's museum and a plaque outside records that Thomas Lord was born here in 1755: 30 years later he was to create the famous cricket ground in Marylebone that took his name. A more recent celebrity whose home was in Thirsk was Bill Foggitt (died Sep 2004, aged 91), renowned for his weather forecasts based on precise observations of nature.

This pleasant small town of mellow brick houses has a sprawling Market Place and the magnificent 15th-century **St Mary's Church** which is generally regarded as the finest parish church in North Yorkshire. It was here that the real life 'James Herriot' married his wife, Helen. Cod Beck, a tributary of the River Swale, wanders through the town, providing some delightful – and well-signposted riverside walks.

Thirsk appeared in the *Domesday Book* not long after William the Conqueror had granted the Manor of Thirsk to one of his barons, Robert de Mowbray. The Mowbrays became a powerful family in the area, a fact reflected in the naming of the area to the north and west of Thirsk as the Vale of Mowbray. In the early 1100s the family received permission to hold a market at Thirsk but then blotted their copybook by rebelling against Henry II in 1173. The rebellion failed and their castle at Thirsk was burnt to the ground. Not a trace of it remains. The market however is still thriving, held twice-weekly on Mondays and Saturdays. An old market by-law used to stipulate that no butcher be allowed to kill a bull for sale in the market until the beast had been baited by the town dogs. That by-law was abandoned in the early 1800s and the bull-ring to which the animal was tethered has also disappeared.

Sion Hill Hall, about four miles northwest of Thirsk, is celebrated as the 'last of the great country houses'. Its light, airy and well-proportioned rooms, all facing south, are typical of the work of the celebrated Yorkshire architect, Walter Brierley – the 'Lutyens of the North'. He completed the building in 1913 for Percy Stancliffe and his wife Ethel, the wealthy daughter of a whisky distiller. The rooms haven't altered one bit since they were built, but the furniture and furnishings certainly have. In 1962, the Hall was bought by Herbert Mawer, a compulsive but highly discerning collector of antiques. During the 20 years he lived at Sion Hill, Herbert continued to add to what was already probably the best collection of Georgian, Victorian and Edwardian artefacts in the north of

England. Furniture, paintings, porcelain, clocks (all working), ephemera, crowd the 20 richly furnished rooms and make Sion Hill a delight to visit. A recent addition to the many sumptuous displays is a charming exhibition of dolls from the early 1900s.

In the Hall's Victorian Walled Garden is another major visitor attraction – **Falconry UK's Bird of Prey and Conservation Centre.** More than 80 birds from 34 different species have their home here: owls, hawks, falcons, buzzards, vultures and eagles from all around the world. At regular intervals throughout the day these fierce-eyed, sharp-beaked predators behave in a remarkably docile and co-operative way as they take part in fascinating flying demonstrations.

AROUND THIRSK

SOWERBY

1 mile S of Thirsk on the B1448

Georgian houses stand beneath a majestic avenue of lime trees, an old packhorse bridge crosses Cod Beck, footpaths lead across fields and the quiet stream provides a peaceful refuge. All-in-all an attractive village.

SUTTON-UNDER-WHITESTONECLIFF

3 miles E of Thirsk on the A170

Boasting the longest place-name in England, Sutton is more famous for the precipitous cliff that towers above it, **Sutton Bank.** For one of the grandest landscape views in

> • Near Thirsk is Thirsk Racecourse, known to devotees of the turf as the 'Country Racecourse'. There are around 12 race meetings each year, all well attended by visitors keen to experience this intrinsic feature of Yorkshire life. Travelling through the areas between the Dales and the North York Moors, one is constantly reminded of the great tradition of horse-breeding that the county is famous for. The tradition runs deep: even the long flat straight stretch of main railway line between York and Darlington is known as the 'racecourse'. •

69

34 THE VALE OF YORK

Carlton Miniott, Thirsk

Fresh food, real ales and pristine and comfortable accommodation in a relaxed and welcoming atmosphere perfect for exploring the Dales and North Yorkshire.

 see page 218

35 THE DOG & GUN

Carlton Miniott

Oak beams, open fires and traditional comforts, real ales and great food two miles southwest of Thirsk off the A61.

 see page 219

England, go to the top of Sutton Bank and look across the vast expanse of the Vale of York to the Pennine hills far away to the west. The real-life James Herriot called it the 'finest view in England'. He knew this area well since his large veterinary practice covered the farms from here right over to the Dales. A continuation of the Cleveland Hills, the Hambleton Hills themselves lead into the Howardian Hills: together they form the mighty southwest flank of the North York Moors.

There's a National Park Information Centre at the summit of Sutton Bank and a well-marked Nature Trail leads steeply down to, and around, **Lake Gormire,** an Ice Age lake trapped here by a landslip. Gormire is one of Yorkshire's only two natural lakes, the other being Semerwater in Wensleydale. Gormire is set in a large basin with no river running from it: any overflow disappears down a 'swallow hole' and emerges beneath White Mare Cliffs.

Sutton Bank used to be a graveyard for caravans because of its steep (1 in 3) climb and sharp bends. On one July Saturday in 1977, some 30 vehicles broke down on the ascent and five breakdown vehicles spent all day retrieving them. Caravans are now banned from this route. Sutton Bank may be tough on cars but its sheer-sided cliffs create powerful thermals making this a favoured spot for gliders and bright-winged hang-gliders.

BOLTBY

5 miles NE of Thirsk, off the A170

Boltby is an engaging village tucked away at the foot of the Hambleton Hills, close to where the oddly-named Gurt of Beck tumbles down the hillside and, depending on how much rain has fallen on the moors, passes either under or over a little humpback bridge. On the plain below is Nevison House, reputed to be the home of the 17th-century highwayman, William Nevison, 'Swift Nick' as Charles II dubbed him. Some historians claim that it was Swift Nick, not Dick Turpin, who made the legendary ride on Black Bess from London to York to establish an alibi.

NORTHALLERTON

The county town of North Yorkshire, Northallerton has the broad High Street, almost half a mile long, typical of the county's market towns. (Wednesday and Saturday are the market days here.) In stage coach days the town was an important stop on the route from Newcastle to London and several old coaching inns still stand along the High Street. The most ancient is The Old Fleece, a favoured drinking haunt of Charles Dickens during his several visits to the town. It's a truly Dickensian place with great oak beams and a charming olde-worlde atmosphere. The Old Fleece recalls the great days of the stage coach which came to an abrupt end with the arrival of the railway. One day in 1847, a coach called the Wellington made the whole of the 290-mile journey from Newcastle to London, via Northallerton, completely empty. The era of this romantic – if uncomfortable and extremely expensive – mode of transport was over.

Northallerton has many old buildings of interest, including an ancient Grammar School whose history goes back to at least 1322. The school was rebuilt in 1776 at the northern end of the High Street – a building that is now a solicitors' office. By the end of the 19th century the school had 'no great reputation' and by 1902 only 13 pupils were registered. Things went from bad to worse the next year when the headmaster was convicted of being drunk and disorderly. Fortunately, the school, now Northallerton College and in new buildings, has recovered its reputation for academic excellence.

The town also boasts a grand medieval church, a 15th-century almshouse and, of more recent provenance, a majestic County Hall built in 1906 and designed by the famous Yorkshire architect Walter Brierley. The oldest private house in Northallerton is Porch House which bears a carved inscription with the date 1584. According to tradition, Charles I came here as a guest in 1640 and returned seven years later as a prisoner.

Two miles north of the town of Northallerton, a stone obelisk beside the A167 commemorates the Battle of the Standard, fought here in 1138. It was one of the countless conflicts fought between the English and the Scots, and also one of the bloodiest with more than 12,000 of the Scots, led by King David, perishing under a rain of English arrows. The battle took its name from the unusual standard raised by the English: the mast of a ship mounted on a wagon and, crowning its top, a pyx containing the consecrated Host.

AROUND NORTHALLERTON

DANBY WISKE

4 miles NW of Northallerton off the A167 or B6271

This pleasant little village takes its name from the Danby family, once great landowners with huge properties across North Yorkshire, and the little River Wiske. It has a moated former rectory and a village green overlooked by a traditional hostelry.

CATTERICK VILLAGE

9 miles NW of Northallerton off the A1

This is an ancient settlement with an attractive village green and a nearby race-course which, every Sunday, hosts the largest street market in England.

Ever since the time of the Romans, when the settlement was known as *Cataractonium*, Catterick has been associated with the armed forces. Located on the Roman highway between London and Hadrian's Wall, the garrison was also close to the place where Paulinus, Bishop of York baptised 10,000 Christians in the River Swale. Today, the army garrison (the largest in

•

Catterick's connections with Nelson are not immediately obvious but it was Alexander Scott, vicar of Catterick in 1816, who was at Nelson's side when he died at Trafalgar. Also, the Admiral's sister-in-law, Lady Tyrconnel, lived at nearby Kiplin Hall, a beautiful Jacobean country home famed for its wonderful interior plasterwork and medieval fishponds. The hall also contains many mementoes of Nelson and Lady Hamilton and, on display in the Blue Room, is a folding library chair from the Admiral's cabin on HMS Victory. The hall also has a strong American connection since it was built by the 1st Lord Baltimore, who was instrumental in founding the state of Maryland, whose capital city bears his name.

•

36 THE WELLINGTON HEIFER

Ainderby Steeple, Northallerton

Impressive family-run inn with real ales, home-cooked food at lunch and dinner, and cosy accommodation.

  see page 220

Europe) is some three miles to the west. RAF Leeming lies just south of the village.

MOULTON

11 miles NW of Northallerton off the A1

This small village is home to two fine 17th-century manor houses that were built by members of the Smithson family. The Manor House, in the village centre, was originally built in the late-16th century and was improved greatly in the mid-17th century. Just to the south lies **Moulton Hall**, built by George Smithson following his marriage to Eleanor Fairfax in 1654. Similar in size to the original Smithson family home and somewhat resembling it, Moulton Hall is now in the hands of the National Trust.

MIDDLETON TYAS

12 miles NW of Northallerton off the A1

Situated in a sheltered position yet close to the Great North Road, the position of the village church, away

from the village centre and at the end of a long avenue of trees seems strange. However, when the Church of St Michael was built it served not only Middleton Tyas but also Moulton and Kneeton (the latter no longer in existence), between which Middleton lay. During the 18th century, the village saw a period of prosperity when copper was found and mined from the fields near the church. Several grand houses were built including East Hall, which belonged to Leonard Hartley, who founded the industry, though his son, George, had a grander house on the outskirts of Middleton that was designed by John Carr of York.

ALDBROUGH

14 miles NW of Northallerton off the B6275

To the west of the village lies the enormous complex of earthworks known as **Stanwick Camp**. The series of banks and ditches were excavated in the 1950s and their discovery also revealed that the constructions had been carried out in the 1st century. The site, open to the public, is now owned by English Heritage.

PIERCEBRIDGE

17 miles NW of Northallerton on the A67

This picturesque village in upper Teesdale was once an important Roman fort – part of a chain of forts linking the northern headquarters at York with Hadrian's Wall. (Another

Stanwick Camp, Aldbrough

fort in the chain can be found to the south, at Catterick.) The Romans are thought to have originally chosen Piercebridge as a suitable river crossing back in AD 70, when Cerialis attacked the British camp at Stanwick. The remains of the fort, which are visible today, can be dated from coin evidence to around AD 270. The site is always open, though the finds from the excavations are housed in the Bowes Museum at Barnard Castle.

The attractive River Tees forms part of the northern boundary of North Yorkshire, and though Teesdale is not, strictly, a Yorkshire dale, it is well worth visiting. In its upper reaches the river is noted for its waterfalls, and the narrow valley soon widens to give attractive meadow land.

BEDALE

7½ miles SW of Northallerton on the A684

This pleasant little market town with its many fine Georgian buildings and old coaching inns developed around the point where the Saxon track from Ripon joined the route from Northallerton to Wensleydale. Traders met here and in 1251 Henry III granted a charter for a weekly market every Tuesday which still flourishes today. The market cross still stands at the top of Emgate, a narrow street leading from the river to the marketplace. As commercial activity increased, water power was harnessed from the Bedale Beck for the processing of wool. Skinners and tanners worked down by the ford and the

town was a lively hub of cottage industry.

The curving main street leads to the beautiful parish **Church of St Gregory** at the northern end. Recorded in the *Domesday Book* and incorporating architectural styles from the 12th to the 14th centuries, the building has a fine fortified tower and a striking medieval wall-painting of a left-handed St George. Just inside the churchyard is an old building dating from the mid-1600s which served as a school in the 18th century.

Across the road from the church is **Bedale Hall,** a Palladian-style mansion with a superb ballroom. The Hall houses the library and local museum. The north front of the building is a particularly fine example of the Georgian architecture which gives Bedale its special character. Another building of interest is the 18th-century Leech House beside the beck, so called because it was once used by the local chemist to store his leeches.

A popular family attraction located just west of the town is **The Big Sheep and Little Cow Farm**. There are guided tours which include bottle feeding the lambs, bathing George the pig, holding poultry and going into the fields to meet a menagerie of other animals. You don't have to take the tour – you can relax next to the old mill and sample the delicious Oakwoods Speciality Ice Cream which is produced on the farm from the milk of ewes grazed on the old water meadows next to the

37 THE WAGGON AND HORSES

Bedale

Real ales, tasty food and spacious, charming accommodation in welcoming traditional inn.

 see page 221

38 OTTERINGTON SHORTHORN

South Otterington, Northallerton

Locally sourced and delicious food at lunch and dinner, four pristine and comfortable guest bedrooms.

 see page 221

watermill. Pony rides are available, there's an all weather children's play area and a picnic area.

CRAKEHALL

8½ miles SW of Northallerton on the A684

Crakehall has a huge village green with a small church and a huge former rectory overlooking it. Part of the green serves as the village's cricket pitch and is in regular use during the summer.

Sometime around AD 1090 the *Domesday Book* commissioners arrived in Crakehall and noted details of a mill on the beck that runs through this picturesque village. More than 900 years later there's still a mill on the very same spot. The present **Crakehall Water Mill** building dates from the 1600s; its mighty machinery from the 18th

and 19th centuries. The Mill was still working until 2003 but at the time of writing it is up for sale and currently closed.

OSMOTHERLEY

5 miles NE of Northallerton off the A19

Long-distance walkers will be familiar with this attractive moorland village since it is the western starting point for the Lyke Wake Walk, which winds for more than 40 miles over the moors to Ravenscar on the coast. At the centre of the village is a heavily carved cross and, next to it, a low stone table which was probably once a market stall and also served John Wesley as a pulpit.

About a mile northeast of the village, **Mount Grace Priory** (English Heritage & National Trust) is quite unique among Yorkshire's ecclesiastical treasures. The 14th-century building set in tranquil surroundings was bought in 1904 by Sir Lothian Bell who decided to rebuild one of the well-preserved cells, a violation of the building's 'integrity' that would provoke howls of outrage from purists if it were proposed today. When English Heritage inherited the Carthusian Priory, however, it decided to go still further by reconstructing other outbuildings and filling them with replica furniture and artefacts to create a vivid impression of what life was like in a 14th-century

Crakehall Mill

Osmotherley

Housed in a former Methodist chapel in Crakehall and dating back to 1840, the Museum of Badges and Battledress is a private collection displaying uniforms, equipment, cap badges, formation signs, trade badges and photographs of all branches of the Armed Forces. The exhibits include more than 60 mannequins dressed in various uniforms along with military equipment and ephemera dating from 1900 to the present day. The museum is open from Easter to September inclusive but guided tours are available at any time by prior arrangement.

monastic house. The Carthusians were an upper-class order whose members dedicated themselves to solitude – even their meals were served through an angled hatch so they would not see the servant who brought them. Most visitors find themselves fascinated by Mount Grace's sanitary arrangements which were ingeniously designed to take full advantage of a nearby spring and the sloping site on which the Priory is built. Along with discovering what life was like for a monk in this almost hermit-like order, visitors can also wander around the remains of the Great Cloister and outer court, and see the new monks' herb garden designed specifically to aid contemplation and spiritual renewal. Mount Grace Priory is open all year though times are limited in the winter months.

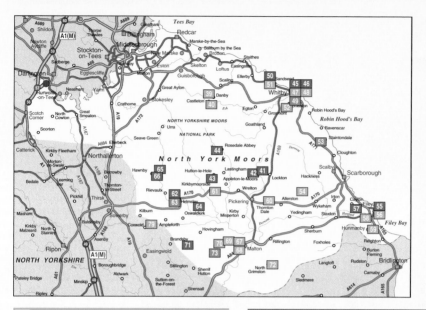

🍴 FOOD & DRINK

🛏 ACCOMMODATION

🏛 PLACES OF INTEREST

North York Moors, Heritage Coast and Vale of Pickering

Some 40 miles across and about 20 miles deep, the North York Moors National Park encompasses a remarkable diversity of scenery. There are great rolling swathes of moorland rising to 1,400 feet above sea level, stark and inhospitable in winter, still wild and romantic in summer, and softened only in early Autumn when they are mantled by a purple haze of flowering heather. Almost one-fifth of the area is woodland, most of it managed by Forest Enterprise which has established many picnic sites and forest drives. Settlements are few and far between: indeed, there may have been more people living here in the Bronze Age (1500-500 BC) than there are now to judge by the more than 3,000 'howes', or burial mounds, that have been discovered.

Also scattered across these uplands is a remarkable collection of medieval stone crosses. There are more than 30 of them and one, the Lilla Cross, is reckoned to be the oldest Christian monument in northern England. Perhaps the finest example is **Ralph Cross**, high on Westerdale Moor. It stands nine feet tall at almost precisely the geographical centre of the moors and has been adopted by the North York Moors National Park as its emblem.

Wild as they look, the moors are actually cultivated land, or perhaps 'managed by fire' is the better term. Each year, gamekeepers burn off patches of the old heather in carefully limited areas called swiddens or swizzens. The new growth that soon appears is a crucial resource for the red grouse which live only in heather moorland, eat little else but heather and find these young green shoots particularly appetising.

Just as the Yorkshire Dales have large areas of moorland, so the North York Moors have many dales – Eskdale, Ryedale, Farndale, more

than 100 of them in all. They cut deep into the great upland tracts and are as picturesque, soft and pastoral as anywhere in Yorkshire. To the west lies the mighty bulk of the Cleveland Hills; to the east the rugged cliffs of the Heritage Coast. This is marvellously unspoilt countryside, a happy state of affairs that has come about as a result of the Moors being designated a National Park in 1952, a status which severely restricts any development that would adversely affect either its natural or man-made beauty.

Between Saltburn and Filey lies some of the most striking coastal scenery in the country. Along this stretch of the Heritage Coast you'll find the highest cliffs in the country, a shoreline fretted with rocky coves, with miles of golden sandy beaches, a scattering of picture postcard fishing villages and, at its heart, the historic port of Whitby dramatically set around the mouth of the River Esk.

This glorious seaboard was designated as a Heritage Coast in 1979 in recognition of its beauty and its long history. From its small ports, fishermen have for centuries sailed out in their distinctive cobles to harvest the sea; from Whitby, sturdy whaling ships set off on their dangerous and now, thankfully, abandoned trade. It was at Whitby that one of England's greatest mariners, Captain Cook, learnt his seafaring skills and it was from here that he departed in the tiny bark, *Endeavour*, a mere 370 tons, on his astonishing journeys of exploration.

Further down the coast are the popular resorts of Scarborough (where visitors were frolicking naked in the sea as early as 1735), and Filey, both of them offering long stretches of sandy beach and a huge variety of holiday entertainments.

77

39 THE MOORS TEA ROOM

Danby

Excellent tea room adjacent to the Moors Visitor Centre in Danby. Open daily 10-5 (April to November; 11-4 at other times).

 see page 222

ESKDALE

Eskdale is the largest, and one of the loveliest, of the dales within the National Park. It is unusual in that it runs east-west, the Esk being the only moorland river that doesn't find its way to the Humber. Instead, the river winds tortuously through the dale to join the sea beneath the picturesque cliffs at Whitby. Along the way, many smaller dales branch off to the north and south – Fryup, Danby, Glaisdale – while even narrower ones can only be explored on foot. The Esk is famed for its salmon fishing, but permits are required. These can be obtained from the local branches of the National Rivers Authority. Walkers will appreciate the Esk Valley walk, a group of 10 linking walks which traverse the length of the valley.

DANBY

12 miles W of Whitby off the A174

A visit to **The Moors Centre** at

Danby Lodge provides an excellent introduction to the North York Moors National Park. The Centre is housed in a former shooting lodge and set in 13 acres of riverside, meadow, woodland, formal gardens and picnic areas. Visitors can either wander on their own along the waymarked woodland walks and nature trails or join one of the frequent guided walks. Inside the Lodge various exhibits interpret the natural and local history of the moors, there's a bookshop stocked with a wide range of books, maps and guides, and a tea room serving refreshments. The centre is open all year round except for January.

Downstream from The Moors Centre is a superb 14th-century packhorse bridge, one of three to be found in Eskdale. This one is known as **Duck Bridge** but the name has nothing to do with aquatic birds. It was originally called Castle Bridge but re-named after an 18th-century benefactor, George Duck, a wealthy mason who paid for the bridge to be repaired. To the south of Duck Bridge are the remains of Danby Castle, now a private farmhouse and not open to the public. Built in the 14th century, and originally much larger, it was once the home of Catherine Parr, the sixth wife of Henry VIII. In Elizabethan times, the justices met here and the Danby Court Leet and Baron, which administers the common land and rights of way over the 11,000 acres of

Duck Bridge, Eskdale

78

the Danby Estate, still meets here every year in the throne room. One of the court's responsibilities is issuing licences for the gathering of sphagnum moss, a material once used for stuffing mattresses but now more commonly required for flower arranging.

For most of the latter half of the 19th century Danby's vicar was Canon JC Atkinson, who married three times, fathered 13 children and authored one of the most fascinating books ever written about rural England in Victorian times. His *Forty Years in a Moorland Parish* is still in print and well worth seeking out.

River Esk, Lealholm

CASTLETON

14 miles W of Whitby off the A171

Spread across the hillside above the River Esk, Castleton is a charming village which at one time was the largest settlement in Eskdale. It still has a station on the scenic Esk Valley railway that runs between Whitby and Middlesbrough and a well-used cricket field in a lovely setting on the valley floor. The village's amber-coloured Church of St Michael and St George was built in memory of the men who fell during the First World War; inside there is some fine work by Robert Thompson, the famous 'Mouseman of Kilburn'. The benches, organ screen and panelling at each side of the altar all bear his distinctive 'signature' of a crouching mouse.

LEALHOLM

9 miles W of Whitby off the A171

From The Moors Centre at Danby a scenic minor road winds along the Esk Valley and brings you to the attractive village of Lealholm, its houses clustering around a 250-year-old bridge over the Esk. A short walk leads to some picturesque stepping stones across the river. The village was one of Canon Atkinson's favourite places – 'Elsewhere , you have to go in search of beautiful views,' he wrote, 'here, they come and offer themselves to be looked at.'

On one of the stone houses, now a tea room and restaurant, a carved inscription reads, 'Loyal Order of Ancient Shepherds' together with the date 1873 in Roman numerals. The Loyal Order ran their lodge on the lines of a men-only London club but their annual procession through the

40 CASTLETON TEA ROOMS

Castleton, Whitby

Everything is home-made at this superb and welcoming tea room, including the all-day breakfasts, tasty lunches and delicious afternoon teas.

 see *page 223*

The village of Grosmont is dominated by the massive Church of St Hedda built in 1866. It has a dazzling roof painted blue with gold stars and the altar incorporates some distinguished Belgian terracotta work. Appropriately, St Hedda's is a Roman Catholic church since it was at Egton Bridge that the martyr Nicholas Postgate was born in 1596. He was ordained as a priest in France but returned to the moors to minister to those still loyal to the outlawed Catholic faith. He travelled disguised as a jobbing gardener and eluded capture for many years but was finally betrayed for a reward of £20. He was 81 years old when he was hung, drawn and quartered at York. A sad story to be associated with such a delightful village.

village and the subsequent festivities were one of the highlights of the autumn. In recent years, Lealholm has become very popular with naturalists who come to study the wealth of trees, ferns, flowers and rare plants in the deep, dramatic ravine known as **Crunkley Gill**. Sadly, the ravine is privately owned and not open to the public.

GLAISDALE

8 miles W of Whitby off the A171

From Lealholm a country lane leads to Glaisdale, another picturesque village set at the foot of a narrow dale beside the River Esk with Arncliffe Woods a short walk away. The ancient stone bridge here was built around 1620 by Thomas Ferris, Mayor of Hull. As an impoverished young man he had lived in Glaisdale and fell in love with Agnes Richardson, the squire's daughter. To see Agnes, he had to wade or swim across the river and he swore that if he prospered in life he would build a bridge here. Fortunately, he joined a ship which sailed against the Spanish Armada and captured a galleon laden with gold. Tom returned to Glaisdale a rich man, married Agnes and later honoured his promise by building what has always been called the **Beggar's Bridge**.

EGTON BRIDGE

7 miles W of Whitby off the A171

This little village tucked around a bend in the River Esk plays host each year to the famous **Gooseberry Show**. Established in

1800, the show is held on the first Tuesday in August. It attracts entrants from all over the world who bring prize specimens in an attempt to beat the current record of 2.18oz for a single berry.

GROSMONT

6 miles SW of Whitby off the A169 or A171

Grosmont is the northern terminus of the **North Yorkshire Moors Railway**, the nation's most popular heritage railway, and houses the vintage steam locomotives that ply the 18-mile-long route. The station itself has been restored to the British Railways style of the 1960s and contains a tea room and a two shops with a wide variety of rail-related and other items on sale. In high season as many as eight trains a day in each direction are in service and there are many special events throughout the year. And if you have ever harboured the dream of driving a train, the NYMR offers a range of courses, from one day to a full week, enabling you to realise the fantasy.

CENTRAL MOORS

The area around Goathland provides some of the wildest scenery in the National Park. Murk Mire Moor, Black Rigg, Howl Moor – the very names conjure up the rigours of these upland tracts where heather reigns supreme. Even those who know the moors well treat its sudden mists and savage storms with respect. The historian of the area, Joseph Ford, recollected hearing as a child of an itinerant trader who travelled the moorland paths selling bottle corks to farmers' wives. During one particularly severe winter it was remarked that he had not paid his usual calls. The following autumn a skeleton was found on Wintergill Moor: the unfortunate victim was only 'identified by the scattered bottle corks lying nearby'. As Ford noted, 'the story was not unusual'.

It's a very different picture in the narrow dales that cleave their way down to the rivers. The sheltered villages here are as pretty as any in the better known western dales.

GOATHLAND

7 miles SW of Whitby off the A169

Goathland today is perhaps best known as 'Aidensfield' – the main location for the television series *Heartbeat*. Mostyn's Garage & Funeral Services (actually the Goathland Garage); The Aidensfield Arms (The Goathland Hotel) and the Aidensfield Stores all attract thousands of visitors each year, as does **Goathland Station** on the North Yorkshire Moors Railway whose vintage steam locomotives have often featured in the series. The station also served as Hogsmeade Station in the film *Harry Potter and the Philosopher's Stone*.

This attractive village 500 feet up on the moors, where old stone houses are scattered randomly around spacious sheep-groomed greens, was popular long before

television. Earlier visitors mostly came in order to see **Mallyan Spout**, a 70-ft high waterfall locked into a crescent of rocks and trees. They were also interested in Goathland's rugged church and the odd memorial in its graveyard to William Jefferson and his wife. The couple died in 1923 within a few days of each other, at the ages of 80 and 79, and chose to have their final resting place marked by an enormous anchor.

In the award-winning **Goathland Exhibition Centre** you'll find a full explanation of the curious tradition of the Plough Stots Service, performed at Goathland every January. It's an ancient ritual for greeting the new year which originated with the Norsemen who settled here more than a thousand years ago. 'Stots' is the Scandinavian word for the bullocks which were used to drag a plough through the village, followed by dancers brandishing 30-inch swords. This pagan rite is still faithfully observed but with the difference that nowadays Goathland's young men have replaced the 'stots' in the plough harness.

The Exhibition Centre can also provide you with information about the many walks in the area and guide you to one of the oldest thoroughfares in the country, **Wade's Way**. If you believe the legend, it was built by a giant of that name, but it is actually a remarkably well-preserved stretch of Roman road. A popular walk is the **Rail Trail**, a three-and-a-half

Wade's Way, Goathland

placed on top of simple bogies and pulled by horses. At Beck Hole, however, there was a 1-in-15 incline up to Goathland so the carriages had to be hauled by a complicated system of ropes and water-filled tanks. (Charles Dickens was an early passenger on this route and wrote a hair-raising description of his journey.) The precipitous incline caused many accidents so, in 1865, a 'Deviation Line' was blasted through solid rock. The gradient is still one of the steepest in the country at 1 in 49, but it opened up this route to steam trains. The original 1 in 15 incline is now a footpath, so modern walkers will understand the effort needed to get themselves to the summit, let alone a fully laden carriage.

Every year, this little village plays host to the **World Quoits Championship**. The game, which appears to have originated in Eskdale, involves throwing a small iron hoop over an iron pin set about 25 feet away. Appropriately enough, one of the houses on the green has a quoit serving as a door knocker.

On the hillside, a mile or so to the west of Beck Hole, is the curiously-named **Randy Mere**, the last place in England where leeches were gathered commercially. An elderly resident of Goathland in 1945 recalled how as a young man he had waded into the lake and emerged in minutes with the slug-like creatures firmly attached to his skin. For those interested in repeating his exploit, the leeches are still there.

mile route along the track bed of the original railway line between Goathland and Grosmont, and a return by steam train.

BECK HOLE

8 miles SW of Whitby off the A169

A mile or so up the dale from Goathland is the pretty little hamlet of Beck Hole. When the North Yorkshire Moors Railway was constructed in the 1830s (designed by no less an engineer than George Stephenson himself), the trains were made up of stage coaches were made up of stage coaches

LOCKTON

15 miles SW of Whitby off the A169

About three miles north of Lockton, the **Hole of Horcum** is a huge natural amphitheatre which, so the story goes, was scooped out of Levisham Moor by the giant Wade. It is now a popular centre for hang gliders. Lockton village itself is set high above a deep ravine, boasts one of the few duck ponds to have survived in the National Park, and offers some fine walks.

LEVISHAM

15 miles SW of Whitby off the A169

Just to the west of the village, in the scenic valley of Newton Dale, lies Levisham Station, one of several that lie on the route of the North Yorkshire Moors Railway. This stop is the ideal location for walking with a wide variety of wildlife and flowers within a short distance of the station.

NEWTON UPON RAWCLIFFE

4 miles N of Pickering off the A169

A delightful unspoilt village on the southern fringe of the North York Moors National Park, with old stone cottages and farms clustered round the village green and duck pond. A haven of peace in delightful countryside, miles of forest and moor offer wonderful walking and touring.

APPLETON-LE-MOORS

5 miles NW of Pickering off the A170

Located just inside the southern boundary of the Moors National Park, Appleton-le-Moors is noted for its fine church whose tower and spire provide a landmark for miles around. It was built in Victorian times to a design by J L Pearson, the architect of Truro Cathedral, and it reflects the same Gothic style as the Cornish cathedral.

CROPTON

4 miles NW of Pickering off the A170

This tiny village, records hold, has been brewing ales from as far back as 1613 even though home-brewing was illegal in the 17th century. Despite a lapse in the intervening decades, brewing returned to the village when, in 1984, the cellars of the village pub were converted to accommodate Cropton Brewery, a micro-brewery with visitors' centre, guided tours and regional dishes.

HUTTON-LE-HOLE

10 miles NW of Pickering off the A170

Long regarded as one of Yorkshire's prettiest villages, Hutton-le-Hole has a character all of its own. 'It is all up and down,' wrote Arthur Mee, visiting half a century ago, 'with a hurrying stream winding among houses scattered here and there, standing at all angles'. Fifty years on, little has changed.

Facing the green is the **Ryedale Folk Museum**, an imaginative celebration of 4,000 years of life in North Yorkshire. Among the 13 historic buildings is a complete Elizabethan Manor House rescued from nearby Harome and reconstructed here; a

41 RECTORY FARM HOUSE

Levisham, Pickering

18th-century Yorkshire farmhouse offering B&B, alongside two charming self-catering cottages in restored barn and granary.

see page 223

42 MANOR FARM COTTAGES

Newton upon Rawcliffe, Pickering

Three pristine and spacious, characterful self-catering cottages in pretty, unspoilt village.

see page 224

43 THE BARN HOTEL & TEA ROOMS

Hutton-le-Hole

Home-made dishes at licensed tearooms and superb accommodation on the edge of the North York Moors National Park, perfect as a touring base.

see page 224

44 THE ORANGE TREE

Rosedale

Relax and unwind at this superb guest house with excellent accommodation, delicious meals, sauna, hot tub and a range of relaxation treatments.

 see page 225

medieval crofter's cottage with a thatched, hipped roof, peat fire and garth; and the old village shop and post office fitted out as it would have looked just after Elizabeth II's coronation in 1953. Other exhibits include workshops of traditional crafts such as tinsmiths, coopers and wheelwrights, and an Edwardian photographic studio. The National Park has an Information Centre here and throughout the year there are special events such as a Rare Breeds Day and re-enactments of Civil War battles by the Sealed Knot.

Anyone interested in unusual churches should make the short trip from Hutton-le-Hole to **St Mary's Church, Lastingham**, about three miles to the east. The building of a monastery here in the 7th century was recorded by no less an authority than the Venerable Bede, who visited Lastingham not long after it was completed. That monastery was rebuilt in 1078 with

a massively impressive crypt that is still in place – a claustrophobic space with heavy Norman arches rising from squat round pillars. The church above is equally atmospheric, lit only by a small window at one end.

GILLAMOOR
10 miles NW of Pickering off the A170

This pleasant little village is well worth a visit to see its very rare, and very elegant four-faced sundial erected in 1800, and to enjoy the famous **Surprise View**. This is a ravishing panoramic vista of Farndale with the River Dove flowing through the valley far below and white dusty roads climbing the hillside to the heather-covered moors beyond.

Also of interest is the nearby village church which was once the church at Bransdale about six miles away. In the late 1700s, Bransdale Church was in good repair but little used; Gillamoor's was dilapidated but the villagers wanted a place of worship. This was achieved by commissioning a single stonemason, James Smith, to remove Bransdale church stone by stone and re-erect it at Gillamoor.

ROSEDALE ABBEY
11 miles NW of Pickering off the A170

To the east of Farndale is another lovely dale, Rosedale, a nine-mile-long steep-sided valley through which runs the River Seven. The largest settlement in the dale is Rosedale Abbey which takes its

Surprise View, Gillamore

name from the small nunnery founded here in 1158. Nothing of the old Abbey has survived although some of its stones were recycled to build the village houses. A peaceful village now, Rosedale was once crowded with workers employed in iron-ore mines on the moors. It was said that, such was the shortage of lodgings during the 1870s, 'the beds were never cold' as workers from different shifts took turns to sleep in them. The great chimney of the smelting furnace was once a striking landmark on the summit of the moor, but in 1972 it was found to be unsafe and demolished. Its former presence is still recalled at Chimney Bank where a steep and twisting road, with gradients of 1 in 3, leads up to the moor. High on these moors stands **Ralph Cross**, nine feet tall and one of more than 30 such stone crosses dotted across the moors. It was erected in medieval times as a waymark for travellers and when the North York Moors National Park was established in 1952, the Park authorities adopted Ralph Cross as its emblem.

CHURCH HOUSES

17 miles NW of Pickering off the A170

A few miles north of Hutton-le-Hole, the moorland road comes to Lowna, set beside the River Dove in one of the Moors most famous beauty spots, **Farndale**. In spring, some six miles of the river banks are smothered in thousands of wild daffodils, a short-stemmed variety whose colours shade from a pale

buttercup yellow to a rich orange-gold. According to local tradition, the bulbs were cultivated by monks who used the petals in their medical concoctions. Yorkshire folk often refer to daffodils as Lenten Lilies because of the time of year in which they bloom. The flowers, once mercilessly plundered by visitors, are now protected by law with 2,000 acres of Farndale designated as a local nature reserve.

Ralph Cross, Rosedale

GREAT AYTON

This appealing village, set around the River Leven, is an essential stopping point for anyone following the Captain Cook Country Tour, a 70-mile circular trip taking in all the major locations associated with the great seafarer. Cook's family moved to Great Ayton when he was eight years old and he attended the little school which is now the **Captain Cook Schoolroom Museum**, open daily from April to October. The building dates back to 1785 and was built as a school and poorhouse on the site of the original charity school that was built in 1704 by Michael Postgate, a wealthy local landowner. It was at the Postgate School that James received his early education paid for by Thomas Skottowe, his father's employer.

85

The Great Ayton of today is very different from the village that Cook would have known. Now a pleasant place with two spacious greens, with the River Leven flowing through it, this conservation area was, in the 18th and 19th centuries, home to much industrial activity including weaving, tanning, brewing and tile-making. Situated in a secluded position on Low Green is the 12th-century Church of All Saints, still medieval in structure though the original tower and western portion of the nave were demolished in the late 19th century to make room for burials.

The museum first opened in the 1920s and the exhibits here relate to Cook's life and to the 18th-century village in which he lived. The family had moved to Great Ayton in 1736, but in 1745 James moved to Staithes before finally becoming an apprentice seaman in Whitby. James Cook joined the Royal Navy in 1755 and first surveyed the coast of Canada before being appointed 1st Lieutenant in 1768 and being given command of his most famous ship, *Endeavour.* After locating Tahiti and New Zealand in 1769, Cook went on to Australia in 1770 and, following further voyages in the Pacific, was killed by native Hawaiians in 1779.

On High Green a statue commissioned by Hambleton District Council and sculpted by Nicholas Dimbleby portrays Cook at the age of 18 when he left the village for Staithes.

The house in Easby Lane where the Cook family lived is sadly no longer here. In 1934 it was transported to Australia brick by brick, together with the climbing plants that covered them, and re-erected in Fitzroy Park, Melbourne. A cairn of stones is all that remains to mark the site. A much more impressive monument is the 60-foot obelisk to Cook's memory erected on Easby Moor above the village by Robert Campion, a Whitby banker, in 1827. It can only be reached by a steepish climb on foot but it is well worth making the effort: from the base of the monument there are stupendous views over the Moors, the Vale of Mowbray and across to the oddly shaped hill called Roseberry Topping. The loftiest of the Cleveland Hills and sometimes called the Matterhorn of Yorkshire, Roseberry's summit towers 1,000 feet above Great Ayton.

AROUND GREAT AYTON

GUISBOROUGH

5 miles NE of Great Ayton on the A171

The stark ruins of **Guisborough Priory** (English Heritage) stand on an elevated site overlooked by the Cleveland Hills. Founded by a great landowner in the region, Robert de Brus II, in 1119 the monastery became one of the most powerful in Yorkshire. It was extended in 1200 but almost a century later the whole complex was destroyed by fire. Rebuilding took several generations and was not completed until the late 1300s. A contemporary remarked that the

Guisborough Priory

Prior kept 'a most pompous house' and that some 500 households were dependent in some way on the priory. In 1540 the priory's estate was sold to a Thomas Chaloner who cannibalised much of the fabric to grace ornamental gardens at his mansion nearby. That mansion has since disappeared. Of the priory itself, the great arch of the east end is the most striking survival, an outstanding example of Gothic architecture. The priory grounds are a popular venue for picnics.

INGLEBY GREENHOW

3 miles S of Great Ayton off the B1257

Located on the very edge of the National Park, Ingleby Greenhow enjoys a favoured position, protected from east winds by the great mass of Ingleby Moor. The beckside church looks small and unimposing from the outside, but inside there is a wealth of rugged Norman arches and pillars, the stonework carved with fanciful figures of grotesque men and animals.

STOKESLEY

3 miles SW of Great Ayton on the A172

This pleasing market town lies beneath the northern edge of the moors, its peace only troubled on market day which has taken place here every Friday since its charter was granted in 1223. Nikolaus Pevsner called Stokesley 'one of the most attractive small towns in the county'. There are rows of elegant Georgian and Regency houses reached by little bridges

over the River Leven which flows through the town, and an old water wheel which marks the entrance to the town.

In the Middle Ages, Stokesley was owned by the Balliol family, one of whose scions is remembered as the founder of the Oxford college of that name.

CARLTON IN CLEVELAND

5 miles SE of Great Ayton off the A172

A pleasing little village just inside the National Park, Carlton has a haunted Manor House and a church which was destroyed by fire in 1881 just weeks after its rector had spent years helping to re-build it an the earlier one had been demolished.

WHITBY

From Sandsend, the A174 skirts the shore and then passes between open fields and a breezy cliff-top golf course before entering one of North Yorkshire's most historic and attractive towns. Whitby is famed as one of the earliest and most important centres of Christianity in England; as Captain James Cook's home port, and as the place where, according to Bram Stoker's famous novel, Count Dracula in the form of a large dog loped ashore from a crewless ship that had drifted into the harbour. The classic 1931 film version of the story, starring Bela Lugosi, was filmed in the original locations at Whitby and there were several reports of holidaymakers being startled by coming across the Count, cloaked and fanged, as he

•

A later incumbent in the church in Carlton in Cleveland, Canon John Kyle, fervently maintained the 18th-century traditions of the 'squarson' – a parson who was also the village squire. Canon Kyle took the latter of these two roles much more seriously, riding to hounds, running three farms, boxing with the local lads, and also running the village pub, the Fox and Hounds. The Archbishop of York was not pleased that one of his ministers owned a drinking house but the canon pointed out that his proprietorship allowed him to close the pub on Sundays.

•

87

45 THE WHITE HORSE AND GRIFFIN HOTEL

Whitby

Superb establishment with a proud history of providing first-class food and accommodation.

 see *page 225*

46 THE GALLERY GUEST HOUSE

Whitby

Pristine and welcoming mid-Victorian guest house, a real home from home in the centre of Whitby.

 see *page 226*

rested between takes. The **Dracula Experience** on Marine Parade gives a lively rendition of the enduring tale with the help of live actors and electronic special effects.

High on the cliff that towers above the old town stand the imposing and romantic ruins of **Whitby Abbey** (English Heritage). In AD 664, many of the most eminent prelates of the Christian Church were summoned here to attend the Synod of Whitby. They were charged with settling once and for all a festering dispute that had riven Christendom for generations: the precise date on which Easter should be celebrated. The complicated formula they devised to solve this problem is still in use today. Just across from the abbey, a recently opened Visitor Centre combines the best of modern technology with displays of artefacts in tracing the long history of the site.

A short walk from the Abbey is **St Mary's Church**, a unique building 'not unlike a house outside and very much like a ship inside.' Indeed, the fascinating interior with its clutter of box-pews built in the 1600s and rented by families whose names were put on the sides, iron pillars and long galleries, was reputedly fashioned by Whitby seamen during the course of the 18th century. The three-decker pulpit is from the same period; the huge ear trumpets for a rector's deaf wife were put in place about 50 years later. Outside, a carved sandstone cross commemorates Brother Caedmon whose 7th-century poem, *The Song of Creation*, is the earliest known poem in English.

St Mary's stands atop the cliff: the old town clusters around the harbour mouth far below. Linking them are the famous 199 steps that wind up the hillside: many a churchgoer or visitor has been grateful for the frequent seats thoughtfully provided along the way.

The old port of Whitby developed on the slim shelf of land that runs along the east bank of the River Esk, an intricate muddle of narrow, cobbled streets and

Grape Lane, Whitby

shoulder-width alleys. Grape Lane is typical, a cramped little street where ancient houses lean wearily against each other. Young James Cook lived here during his apprenticeship: the handsome house in Grape Lane where he lodged is now the **Captain Cook Memorial Museum.** The rich collection includes period rooms, models, maps and manuscripts, ships' plans, furniture, artefacts from Cook's voyages, and many original drawings, prints and paintings, including one of Cook's notorious contemporary, Captain Bligh of the *Bounty*.

By the early 19th century, old Whitby was full to bursting and a new town began to burgeon on the West bank of the River Esk. The new Whitby, or 'West Cliff', was carefully planned with the nascent industry of tourism in mind. There was a quayside walk or 'promenade', a bandstand, luxury hotels, and a Royal Crescent of upmarket dwellings reminiscent of Buxton or Cheltenham but with the added advantage of enjoying a sea air universally acknowledged as 'invariably beneficial to the health of the most injured constitution'.

In a dominating position on West Cliff, a bronze statue of Captain Cook gazes out over the harbour he knew so well. Nearby the huge jawbone of a whale, raised as an arch, recalls those other great Whitby seafarers, the whalers. Between 1753 and 1833, Whitby was the capital of the whaling industry, bringing home 2,761 whales in 80 years. Much of that

success was due to the skills of the great whaling captains William Scoresby and his son, also named William. The elder William was celebrated for his great daring and navigational skills, as well as for the invention of the crow's nest, or masthead lookout. His son was driven by a restless, enquiring mind and occupied himself with various experiments during the long days at sea in the icy Arctic waters. He is most noted for his discoveries of the forms of snow crystals and the invention of the 'Greenland' magnet which made ships' compasses more reliable. The whaling industry is now, thankfully, long dead, but fortunately the fishing industry is not, as many of Whitby's restaurants bear witness, being famous for their seafood menus.

A popular souvenir of the town is jet stone, a lustrous black stone which enjoyed an enormous vogue in Victorian times. After the death of Prince Albert, jewellery in jet was the only ornament the Queen would allow herself to wear. The Court and the middle classes naturally followed her example and for several decades Whitby prospered greatly from the trade in jet. By 1914, workable deposits of the stone were virtually exhausted and a new generation shunned its gloomy association with death. Recent years have seen a revival of interest in the glossy stone and several shops have extensive displays of jet ornaments and jewellery. The original **Victorian Jet Works**, established in 1867, are open daily and visitors can see the

47 THE KHYBER RESTAURANT

Whitby

Overlooking the harbour, a pristine, spacious and airy place with a great menu of fresh fish, steaks, snacks, sandwiches and salads, all freshly prepared to order.

 see page 226

48 THE BOTTOM HOUSE

Whitby

Large and convivial pub with food, open all day every day for ale. Excellent home cooking 12-5 p.m. (to 7 in summer).

 see page 226

49 WHITBY MUSEUM

Whitby

An outstanding variety of bygones and artefacts are on display at the Whitby Museum

 see page 226

One of Whitby's unique attractions is The Sutcliffe Gallery in Flowergate. The Gallery celebrates the great photographer Frank Meadow Sutcliffe who was born in Whitby in 1853. His studies of local people, places and events powerfully evoke the Whitby of late-Victorian and Edwardian times in photographs that are both beautifully composed and technically immaculate. Few visitors to the Gallery can resist the temptation to purchase at least one of the nostalgic prints on sale.

craftspeople at work as well as purchase jet from a wide range of interesting and contemporary jewellery designs. Whitby often features in the TV series, *Heartbeat*.

On the southeastern edge of the town the **Whitby Museum and Pannett Art Gallery** stands in the attractive setting of Pannett Park. The museum contains a nationally-important collection of Whitby jet jewellery, relics of Captain Cook and the lands he visited, displays on whaling and many other items from Whitby's past.

The **Whitby Archives Heritage Centre**, which is open all year, holds an exhibition of local photographs and, along with its local history research facilities, has a shop and heritage gallery. Meanwhile, the **Museum of Victorian Whitby** has a re-creation of a 19th-century lane in the town complete with interiors and shop windows along with miniature rooms and settings.

AROUND WHITBY

SALTBURN-BY-THE-SEA

10 miles E of Middlesbrough on the A174

The charming seaside resort of Saltburn lies at the northern end of the Heritage Coast. It was custom-built in Victorian times and designed for affluent middle-class visitors – so much so that in the early years excursion trains were barred from calling there. Created in the 1860s by the Quaker entrepreneur Henry Pease, Saltburn is set on a cliff, high above a long sandy beach. To

transport visitors from the elegant little town to the promenade and pier below, an ingenious water-balanced **Tramway** was constructed. It is still in use, the oldest such tramway to have survived in Britain. Saltburn's Victorian heritage is celebrated in mid-August each year with a full programme of events, many of them with the participants clad in appropriate costume. It seems appropriate, too, that such an olde world town should be well-known for its many shops selling antiques and collectables.

Saltburn's genteel image in Victorian times was a far cry from its notoriety in the late 18th century when it was one of the North East's busiest centres for smuggling. The 'King of the Smugglers', John Andrew, had his base here and during a long and profitable career was never apprehended. His story, and that of his partners in villainy, is colourfully recalled at **The Saltburn Smugglers Heritage Centre** near the Ship Inn of which Andrew was landlord.

From the sea front, a miniature railway will take you to the splendid **Italian Gardens** – another Victorian contribution to the town. Here you can take tea on the lawn and explore the **Woodlands Centre** set between the formal pleasure gardens and the wild natural woodlands beyond.

STAITHES

9 miles NW of Whitby off the A174

Visitors to this much-photographed fishing port leave their cars at the park in the modern village at the top of the cliff and then walk down the steep road to the old wharf. Take care – one of these narrow, stepped alleys is called Slippery Hill, for reasons that can become painfully clear. The old stone chapels and rather austere houses testify to the days when Staithes was a stronghold of Methodism.

The little port is proud of its associations with Captain James Cook. He came here, not as a famous mariner, but as a 17-year-old assistant in Mr William Sanderson's haberdashery shop. James didn't stay long, leaving in 1746 to begin his naval apprenticeship in Whitby with Thomas Scottowe, a friend of Sanderson.

Staithes is still a working port with one of the few fleets in England still catching crabs and lobsters. Moored in the harbour and along the river are the fishermen's distinctive boats. Known as cobles, they have an ancestry that goes back to Viking times. Nearby is a small sandy beach, popular with families (and artists), and a rocky shoreline extending north and south pitted with thousands of rock pools hiding starfish and anemones. The rocks here are also rich in fossils and you may even find ingots of 'fools gold' – actually iron pyrites and virtually worthless.

A little further up the coast rises Boulby cliff, at 666 feet (202m) the highest point on the east coast of England.

RUNSWICK BAY

6 miles NW of Whitby, off the A174

A little further down the coast, Runswick Bay is another picturesque fishing village with attractive cottages clinging to the steep sides of the cliff. This perilous position proved disastrous in 1682 when the cliff face collapsed during a violent storm and the whole of Runswick, with the exception of a single cottage, tumbled into the sea. A disaster fund was set up and a new village established.

GOLDSBOROUGH

5 miles NW of Whitby off the A174

Just outside this small village are the remains of one of five signal stations built by the Romans in the 4th century when Saxon pirates were continually raiding the coastal towns. The stations were all built to a similar design with a timber or stone watchtower surrounded by a wide ditch.

•

At Runswick, as in most of Yorkshire's remote communities, superstition was once widespread. Even at the beginning of the 20th century, many still believed in witches and almost everyone would avert their gaze or cross the road to avoid someone afflicted with the 'Evil Eye'. In the late 1800s, the Revd Cooper, Vicar of Filey, visited the village and came across a 'perfectly horrible superstition'. Apparently, it was considered unlucky to save a drowning man. The Vicar was told of 'men nearly dragged ashore, and then, by the advice of the elders, abandoned to their fate lest ill-fortune should result from saving them'.

•

Old Wharf, Staithes

50 ESTBEK HOUSE

Sandsend, nr Whitby
Situated in a pretty coastal
village near Whitby, **Estbek
House** offers a combination
of Georgian elegance and
modern amenities, with fine
food, high-quality wines and
superb bedrooms.

 see page 227

51 BRIDGE COTTAGE CAFÉ TEA ROOMS

Sandsend, Whitby
Beautiful 16th-century
cottage housing excellent tea
rooms and café with fresh
food. Breakfast, lunch and
afternoon tea.

see page 228

LYTHE
4 miles NW of Whitby off the A174

Perched on a hill top, Lythe is a
small cluster of houses with a
sturdy little church which is well
worth a visit. Just south of the
village is **Mulgrave Castle**,
hereditary home of the Marquis of
Normanby. The Castle grounds,
which are open to the public,
contain the ruins of Foss Castle
built shortly after the Norman
Conquest. Charles Dickens once
spent a holiday at Mulgrave Castle
and 'danced on its lawns in ecstasy
at its beauty'. It's not known
whether the great author witnessed
the ancient custom of 'Firing the
Stiddy'. This celebrates notable
events in the Normanby family and
begins with dragging the anvil from
the blacksmith's shop, upturning it,
and placing a charge of gunpowder
on its base. A fearless villager then
approaches with a 20-ft long metal
bar, its tip red hot, and detonates
the powder.

In the 1850s, Mulgrave Castle
was leased by an exiled Indian
Maharajah, Duleep Singh. He
enjoyed going hawking on the
moors in full oriental dress and the
story is often told of how he had
the first road between Sandsend
and Whitby constructed because his
elephants disliked walking along the
beach. Much as one would like to
believe this tale, no one has yet
proved it to be true.

SANDSEND
2 miles NW of Whitby on the A174

From Runswick Bay, the A174
drops down the notoriously steep

Lythe Bank to Sandsend, a pretty
village that grew up alongside the
Mulgrave Beck as it runs into the
sea at 'sands' end' – the
northern tip of the long sandy
beach that stretches some two-and-
a-half miles from here to Whitby.

The Romans had a cement
works nearby, later generations
mined the surrounding hills for the
elusive jet stone and for alum, and
the Victorians built a scenic railway
along the coast. The railway track
was dismantled in the 1950s but
sections of the route now form
part of the Sandsend Trail, a
pleasant and leisurely two-and-a-
half hour walk around the village
which is made particularly
interesting if you follow it with the
National Park's booklet describing
the route.

ROBIN HOOD'S BAY
5 miles S of Whitby off the A171

Artists never tire of painting this
'Clovelly of the North', a
picturesque huddle of red-roofed
houses clinging to the steep face of
the cliff. Bay Town, as locals call
the village, was a thriving fishing
port throughout the 18th and 19th
centuries. By 1920 however there
were only two fishing families left
in the Bay, mainly because the
harbour was so dilapidated, and the
industry died out. Today, small
boats are once again harvesting the
prolific crab grounds that lie along
this stretch of the coast.

Because of the natural isolation
of the bay, smuggling was quite as
important as fishing to the local
economy. The houses and inns in

the Bay were said to have connecting cellars and cupboards, and it was claimed that 'a bale of silk could pass from the bottom of the village to the top without seeing daylight.' These were the days when press gangs from the Royal Navy were active in the area since recruits with a knowledge of the sea were highly prized. Apparently, these mariners were also highly prized by local women: they smartly despatched the press gangs by means of pans and rolling pins.

Shipwrecks in the Bay were frequent, with many a mighty vessel tossed onto its reefs by North Sea storms. On one memorable occasion in the winter of 1881, a large brig called *The Visitor* was driven onto the rocks. The seas were too rough for the lifeboat at Whitby to be launched there so it was dragged eight miles through the snow and let down the cliffside by ropes. Six men were rescued. The same wild seas threatened the village itself, every storm eroding a little more of the chalk cliff to which it clings. Fortunately, Robin Hood's Bay is now protected by a sturdy sea wall.

Detailed information about the village and the Bay is on display at the **Old Coastguard Station** on The Dock. This National Trust property also houses the National Park Visitor and Education Centre. Also worth a visit are the **Robin Hood's Bay Museum**, and **Music in Miniature**, a unique exhibition of 50 dioramas at a scale of 1:12 created by a local craftswoman.

SLEIGHTS
3 miles SW of Whitby on the A169

This village is home to the River Gardens and Perry's Plants, an historic Victorian tea garden on the banks of the River Esk with an international reputation for hardy plants. Open daily from March to October.

RAVENSCAR
10 miles N of Scarborough off the A171

The coastline around Ravenscar is particularly dramatic and, fortunately, most of it is under the protection of the National Trust. There are some splendid cliff-top walks and outstanding views across Robin Hood's Bay. Ravenscar

Robin Hoods Bay

The most extraordinary building in Robin Hood's Bay is undoubtedly Fyling Hall Pigsty. It was built in the 1880s by Squire Barry of Fyling Hall in the classical style although the pillars supporting the portico are of wood rather than marble. Here the Squire's two favourite pigs could enjoy plenty of space and a superb view over the Bay. The building is now managed by the Landmark Trust who rent it out to holidaymakers.

52   THE WILSON ARMS

Sneaton

In a handsome village just a short drive from the coast, spacious and recently refurbished Grade II 18th-century inn with food, drink and accommodation.

see page 228

53 STAINTONDALE SHIRE HORSE FARM

Staintondale

A fantastic day out for all the family, where you can meet horses and ponies from the largest to the smallest, and see them performing in live shows.

 see page 229

is the eastern terminus of the 42-mile hike across the moors to Osmotherley known as the **Lyke Wake Walk**.

During the late 19th century there was an unsucceful attempt to turn this scattered village, then known as Peak, into a small town and, although the roads were built, little of the land that was made available to potential buyers was ever developed. Thus, it retains a tranquil air and, along with the small church and a couple of village shops, the only building of any size here is the Raven Hall Hotel. Local legend has it that King George III visited here when it was a private house, while recovering from one of his recurring bouts of mental illness.

About three miles south of Ravenscar, at Staintondale, are two very different animal centres. At the **Staintondale Shire Horse Farm** visitors can enjoy a 'hands-on' experience with these noble creatures, watch a video of the horses working and follow a scenic route around the area. Cart rides are also usually available. There's also a café, souvenir shop, picnic area and a play area with a variety of small farm animals to entertain the children.

At nearby **Wellington Lodge Llama Trekking**, a variety of treks with llamas is on offer, ranging from a three or four-hour journey to a whole day with a three-course meal included in the price. The llamas have many years of trekking experience and are sure-footed and friendly. They carry heavy loads of food, drink, stools and extra

clothing, leaving you free to admire the splendid surroundings. Handlers and specialist guides accompany walkers.

HACKNESS

5 miles NW of Scarborough off the A170 or A171

For generations the Forge Valley has attracted sightseers – especially in autumn when the steep wooded banks of the ravine present a dazzling display of colours. There are several splendid walks along this lovely two-mile stretch of the River Derwent, a valley which takes its name from the ancient iron workings of which today not a trace remains. Nothing has survived either of the monastery established at Hackness in AD 681 by the first Abbess of Whitby although some of its stones were used in the building of St Peter's Church, founded in 1060. Inside the church is a fragment of an Anglo-Saxon cross with inscriptions in English, Latin and runic characters. The grandest building in the village is Hackness Hall (private), a Georgian mansion that is the home of Lord Derwent.

CLOUGHTON

4 miles N of Scarborough on the A171

Cloughton village lies less than a mile from the coast and the rocky inlet of Cloughton Wyke. Here, in 1932, a huge whale was cast, or threw itself, ashore. Press photographers and postcard publishers rushed to the scene and paid the smallest local children they could find to pose beside the stranded Leviathan. For a while,

Cloughton village was busy with a steady stream of sightseers. Their numbers quickly diminished as the six tons of blubber began to rot. In Cloughton itself, residents came to dread an east wind: it reached them only after washing over the vast hulk lying on the rocks. It's surely the worst thing that has ever happened to this pleasant little village, set around a sharp kink in the A171, where the breezes now – depending on the direction of the wind – either bring a fresh tang of ozone from the sea or a soft perfume of heather from the moors.

Farrer in 1626 and popularised in a book published by a certain Dr Wittie who named the site Scarborough Spaw. Anne Brontë came here in the hope that the spa town's invigorating air would improve her health, a hope that was not fulfilled. She died at the age of 29 and her grave lies in St Mary's churchyard at the foot of the castle. **Scarborough Castle** itself can be precisely dated to the decade between 1158 and 1168 and

SCARBOROUGH

With its two splendid bays and dramatic cliff-top castle, Scarborough was targeted by the early railway tycoons as the natural candidate for Yorkshire's first seaside resort. The railway arrived in 1846, followed by the construction of luxury hotels, elegant promenades and spacious gardens, all of which confirmed the town's claim to the title 'Queen of Watering Places'. The 'quality', people like the eccentric Earls of Londesborough, established palatial summer residences here, and an excellent train service brought thousands of excursionists from the industrial cities of the West Riding.

Even before the advent of the railway, Scarborough had been well-known to a select few. They travelled to what was then a remote little town to sample the spring water discovered by Mrs Tomyzin

Scarborough Castle

95

Scarborough

the area around Foreshore Road. Another tradition maintained by local people around this time is the sounding of the Pancake Bell, a custom started by the wives of the town to alert their menfolk in the fields and in the harbour that they were about to begin cooking the pancakes.

As befits such a long-established resort, Scarborough offers a vast variety of entertainment. If you tire of the two sandy beaches, there's **Peasholm Park** to explore with its glorious gardens and regular events, among them the unique sea battle in miniature on the lake. Or you could seek out the intellectual attractions of the **Rotunda Museum** (closed for 2006) on Vernon Road, 'the finest Georgian museum in Britain', which includes among its exhibits a genuine ducking stool for 'witches'; the art collections at the **Scarborough Art Gallery**; or the futuristic world of holograms at Corrigans Arcade on Foreshore Road. **The Stephen Joseph Theatre in the Round** is well known for staging the premiere performances of comedies written by its resident director, the prolific playwright Sir Alan Ayckbourn. And at Scalby Mills, on the northern edge of the town, **Sea-Life Marine Sanctuary** offers the chance of close encounters with a huge variety of marine creatures from shrimps to sharks, octopi to eels.

Also worth visiting is the **Wood End Museum of Natural History** on The Crescent, once the

surviving records show that construction costs totalled £650. The castle was built on the site of a Roman fort and signal station and its gaunt remains stand high on Castle Rock Headland, dominating the two sweeping bays. The spectacular ruins often provide a splendid backdrop for staged battles commemorating the invasions of the Danes, Saxons and the later incursions of Napoleon's troops. The surrounding cliffs are also well worth exploring – just follow the final part of the famous Cleveland Way.

If you happen to be visiting the resort on Shrove Tuesday, be prepared for the unusual sight of respectable citizens exercising their ancient right to skip along the highways. This unexpected traffic hazard is now mostly confined to

home of the eccentric Sitwell family. There are permanent displays of their books and photographs, as well as changing exhibitions of local wildlife. The double-storeyed conservatory and the aquarium here are particularly interesting.

AROUND SCARBOROUGH

CAYTON

3 miles S of Scarborough on the B1261

Cayton is one of only 31 'Thankful Villages' in England. They were so named after the First World War because all of their men came back safely from that horrific conflict. Cayton had all the more reason to

Filey Parish Church

be grateful since 43 of its men returned – more than to any other of the Thankful Villages.

An unusual attraction here is the **Stained Glass Centre** where Valerie Green and her team produce stained glass and leaded lights for churches, hotels, restaurants, public houses and homes throughout the country. Visitors can watch the craftspeople at work, browse in the showroom and examine the exhibition of stained glass.

FILEY

7 miles S of Scarborough on the A1039

With its six-mile crescent of safe, sandy beach, Filey was one of the first Yorkshire resorts to benefit from the early 19th-century craze for sea bathing. Filey's popularity continued throughout Victorian times but the little town always prided itself on being rather more select than its brasher neighbour just up the coast, Scarborough. Inevitably, modern times have brought the usual scattering of amusement arcades, fast food outlets and, from 1939 to 1983, a Butlin's Holiday Camp capable of accommodating 10,000 visitors. But Filey has suffered less than most seaside towns and with its many public parks and

54 THE ANVIL INN

Sawdon, Scarborough

Superb restored traditional blacksmith's forge open every session Tues - Sun. Lunchtime and evening menu of delicious food.

 see page 229

55 HALLAM GUEST HOUSE

Filey

Spacious and welcoming guesthouse near the seafront, offering comfortable accommodation (B&B or D,B&B).

 see page 229

56 VICTORIA COURT BAR AND RESTAURANT

Filey

Overlooking the seashore, fine family-run establishment with chef-prepared food and a good selection of drinks to suit every taste.

 see page 230

97

gardens still retains a winning, rather genteel atmosphere.

Until the Local Government reforms of 1974, the boundary between the East and North Ridings cut right through Filey. The town lay in the East Riding, the parish church and graveyard in the North. This curious arrangement gave rise to some typically pawky Yorkshire humour. If, as a resident of Filey town, you admitted that you were feeling poorly, the response might well be, 'Aye, then tha'll straightly be off t'North Riding' – in other words, the graveyard.

Filey's parish church, the oldest parts of which date back to the 12th century, is appropriately dedicated to St Oswald, patron saint of fishermen, and the Fishermen's Window here commemorates men from the town who died at sea. At the **Filey Folk Museum**, housed in a lovely old building dating back to 1696, you can explore the town's long history, while the **Edwardian Festival**, held every June, re-creates the pleasures of an earlier, more innocent age.

Just to the north of the town, the rocky promontory known as **Filey Brigg** strikes out into the sea, a massive mile-long breakwater protecting the town from the worst of the North Sea's winter storms. From the Brigg, there are grand views southwards along the six-mile-long bay to the cliffs that rise up to Flamborough Head and Scarborough Castle. Despite the fact that there is no harbour at Filey, it was once quite a busy fishing port and one can still occasionally see a few cobles – direct descendants of the Viking longships that arrived here more than a millennium ago – beached on the slipways.

Filey Brigg is the southern starting point for the oddly-named **Cleveland Way**, odd because only a few miles of the 110-mile footpath actually pass through Cleveland. The path follows the coast as far north as Saltburn-by-the-Sea then turns south to Roseberry Topping and the Cleveland Hills, finally ending up at Helmsley.

HUNMANBY

3m SW of Filey between the A165 and A1039

Here's a question worthy of Trivial Pursuit: 'On which vehicle was the wing mirror first used?' Your answer is almost certainly wrong unless you know about the grave of a 1st century British charioteer uncovered at Hunmanby in 1907. Along with his bones, those of his horses, and fragments of the chariot wheels was a rectangular strip of shiny metal: archaeologists are convinced that this was fixed to the side of the chariot as a mirror so that the driver could see the competitors behind him.

Another curiosity in Hunmanby is the village lock-up with two cells and tiny windows designed for human miscreants, and next to it a circular stone pinfold intended for straying cattle.

THE VALE OF PICKERING

Not all that long ago, the Vale of Pickering was the Lake of Pickering, an immense stretch of water far larger than any English lake today, about 32 miles long and four to eight miles wide. As the Ice Age retreated, the waters gradually drained away leaving a low-lying plain of good arable soil based on Kimmeridge clay. Much of it remained marshy however and at Star Carr, near Seamer, archaeologists have uncovered a late Stone Age lake community, dating back some 7,500 years, where the houses were built on stilts above the water. Sadly, the remains of this fascinating excavation lie on private land and are not open to the public. It is only in comparatively recent times that the Vale has been properly drained, which explains why most of the towns and villages lie around its edge in a rough kind of horseshoe formation.

For much of its length, the Vale is watered by the River Derwent, which was also powerfully affected by the changes that occurred during the Ice Age. Originally it entered the sea near Scarborough but an Ice Age glacier blocked that outlet. The Derwent still flows to within a mile-and-a-half of Scarborough, but now turns abruptly and makes a 90-mile detour through the vale and then southwards to join the River Ouse near Howden.

The main traffic artery through the vale is the Thirsk to Scarborough road, the A170, which in summer peak periods can become very congested. But you only have to turn off this busy thoroughfare to find yourself in quiet country lanes leading to sleepy market towns and unspoilt villages. To the north rise the intricate folds of the North York Moors: to the south, the Yorkshire Wolds roll gently away towards Beverley, Hull and the River Humber. Our exploration of the vale begins at the eastern end of this broad, low-lying corridor, at East Ayton near Scarborough, and follows it westwards to the lower slopes of the Hambleton Hills.

PICKERING

This busy little town developed around the important crossroads where the Malton to Whitby, and the Thirsk to Scarborough roads intersect. It's the largest of the four market towns in Ryedale and possibly the oldest, claiming to date from 270 BC when (so it's said) it was founded by a King of the Brigantes called Peredurus. William the Conqueror's attempts to dominate the area are recalled by Pickering's ruined Castle (English Heritage), and the many inns and posting houses reflect the town's prosperity during the stage coach era.

The parish church of **St Peter and St Paul** is well worth visiting for its remarkable 15th-century murals. During the glum days of

•

Lying at the heart of the fertile Vale of Pickering, Pickering town's reputation was originally based on its famous pigs and horses. Vast quantities of pork were transported across the moors to Whitby, salted and used as shipboard rations. The famous Cleveland Bay horses, with their jet-black manes and tails, were extensively bred in the area. (In Eskdale, a little further north, they still are). These sweet-natured, sturdy and tireless animals have always been in great demand. During the 19th century, their equable temperament made them ideal for pulling Hansom cabs and street-cars, and nowadays they are often seen in more dignified events such as State Processions.

•

99

Ruined Castle, Pickering

●

If you catch a whiff of sulphurous smoke in Pickering, then you must be close to the station. Pickering is the southern terminus of the North Yorkshire Moors Railway and here you can board a steam-drawn train for an 18-mile journey along one of the oldest and most dramatically scenic railways in the country. Thanks to a grant from the Heritage Lottery Fund, the Booking and Parcels Office has been restored to how it was in 1937. The station's refreshment room is now a tea room and there's a shop with a wide range of gifts, books and videos.

●

Puritanism, these lively paintings were denounced as idolatrous and plastered over. They stayed forgotten for some 200 years but were rediscovered when the church was being restored in 1851. Unfortunately, the vicar at that time shared the Puritans' sentiments and, despite opposition from his parishioners and even from his bishop, had them smothered again under whitewash. A more liberal successor to the Vicar had the murals restored once again in 1878 and they now give one a vivid idea of how cheerful, colourful and entertaining many English churches were before the unforgivable vandalism of the Puritan years. These superb paintings, sharp, vigorous and well-observed, happily embrace scenes from the Bible, old legends and actual history: a real insight into the medieval mind that had no difficulty in accepting both the story of St George slaying the dragon and the martyrdom of St

Thomas à Becket as equally real, and inspiring, events.

Also not to be missed in Pickering is the **Beck Isle Museum** housed in a gracious Regency mansion. Its 27 display areas are crammed with a 'magnificent assortment of items curious, mysterious, marvellous and commonplace from the last 200 years'. There are intriguing re-creations of typical Victorian domestic rooms, shops, workshops and even a pub. The comprehensive collection of photographs by Sydney Smith presents a remarkable picture of the Ryedale area as it was between 1909 and the 1950s. The exhibition is made even more interesting by its acquisition of the very cameras and other photographic equipment used by Sydney Smith.

Collectors of antiques can really indulge themselves at the **Pickering Antique Centre** where 32 dealers display their wares in 3,500 square feet of showrooms.

Just up the road, at the **Pickering Trout Lake,** you can hire a rod and tackle and attempt to beat the record for the largest fish ever caught here – it currently stands at a mighty 25lb 4oz (11.45 kg).

AROUND PICKERING

EAST AYTON

13 miles E of Pickering on the A170

Victorian visitors to Scarborough, occasionally tiring of its urban attractions, welcomed excursions to

100

beauty spots such as the **Forge Valley** near East Ayton. Aeons ago, a sharp-edged glacier excavated the valley; then centuries of natural growth softened its hills, clothed them with over-arching trees and, quite by chance, created one of the loveliest woodland walks in England. For a steady walker, going say four miles an hour, the round trip walk from East Ayton to the old forge from which the valley derives its name – along one side of the river returning on the other, takes about 2.5 hours. A short diversion will lead you to the ruins of **Ayton Castle** at the edge of the road near the junction of the A170 and B1261. Dating from around 1400, this is one of the most southerly of the hundreds of pele towers built in those turbulent times as a protection against invading Scottish marauders. In more peaceful days, many of these towers had a more comfortable mansion added but their defensive origins are still clearly recognisable.

BROMPTON-BY-SAWDON

10 miles E of Pickering on the A170

It was in the medieval church of this small village, on an autumn day in 1802, that William Wordsworth was married to Mary Hutchinson whose family lived at nearby Gallows Hill Farm. 'A perfect woman', he wrote of Mary, 'nobly planned/To warn, to comfort, and command;/And yet a spirit still, and bright/With something of an angelic light'. Mary's home, now the Wordsworth Gallery, plays host to an exhibition on the poets

Wordsworth and Coleridge, while the medieval barn is now filled with designer gifts, ladies clothes and licensed tea rooms. The gallery is open Tuesday to Saturday all year round.

Wydale Hall (private) was the home of the Squire of Brompton, Sir George Cayley (1773-1857), a pioneer aviator who achieved successful flights with small gliders although it was his coachman who was actually dragooned into being the pilot. Sir George is also credited with inventing the caterpillar tractor.

EBBERSTON

7 miles E of Pickering on the A170

About a mile to the west of Ebberston, in 1718, Mr William Thompson, MP for Scarborough, built for himself what is possibly the smallest stately home in England, **Ebberston Hall.** From the front, the house appears to be just one storey high, with a pillared doorway approached by a grand flight of stone steps flanked by a moderately sized room on each side. In fact, behind this modest front, there's also an extensive basement – 'deceptively spacious' as the estate agents say. Ebberston Hall can be viewed from the road or churchyard as it is now a private house.

THORNTON-LE-DALE

2 miles E of Pickering on the A170

As long ago as 1907, a *Yorkshire Post* poll of its readers acclaimed Thornton-le-Dale as the most beautiful village in Yorkshire. Despite stiff competition for that title, most visitors still find

60   THE NEW INN

Thornton-le-Dale

Superb food and accommodation in the North York Moors National Park at this traditional 17th-century coaching inn.

¶ ⊨ see *page 231*

About three miles north of Thornton-le-Dale, the Dalby Visitor Centre is the starting point for the Dalby Forest Drive (toll payable), a nine-mile circuit through what was once the royal hunting Forest of Pickering. The Visitor Centre can provide plentiful details of the various facilities available – waymarked walks, cycle routes, picnic/barbecue sites, children's play areas, an orienteering course and wildlife observation hide, and much more.

61 THE BLACK SWAN

Kirkbymoorside

A place to head for excellent food in relaxed and friendly surroundings. Real ales and a range of tempting light bites, main courses and sweets.

 see page 232

themselves in agreement.

If further proof were needed, just off the A170 near the parish church of All Saints you'll find one of the most photographed houses in Britain. The thatched cottage, set beside a sparkling beck, appears regularly on chocolate boxes, jigsaws and calendars. On the nearby village green there's an ancient cross and a set of wooden stocks and, across the road, are Lady Lumley's Almshouses, 12 dwellings built in 1670 and still serving their original purpose. The North York Moors National Park actually creates a special loop in its boundary to include this picture-postcard village which, somewhat confusingly, is also frequently shown on maps as 'Thornton Dale'.

KIRBY MISPERTON

3 miles S of Pickering, off the A169

The 375 acres of wooded parkland surrounding Kirby Misperton Hall provide the setting for **Flamingo Land,** a zoo and fun park that is home to more than 1,000 birds, animals and reptiles. Red-necked wallabies, meerkats, Bactrian camels, lynx, tigers, rheas, scimitar-horned oryx, bison, sea lions, baboons and guanacos (a South American relative of the camel) are just some of the many exotic creatures in residence. Beyond doubt, the most spectacular sight is that of the flock of pink flamingos gathered around the lake fringed with willow trees. With more than 100 different attractions, including a fun fair with some truly scary rides, an adventure playground and

a real working farm, it's no surprise to learn that Flamingo Land is the 4th most visited theme park in the country.

SINNINGTON

4m W of Pickering off the A170

At Sinnington the River Seven drops down from the moors and the valley of Rosedale into the more open country of the Vale of Pickering. The stream passes through this tiny village, running alongside a broad green in the centre of which stands a graceful old packhorse bridge. At one time this medieval bridge must have served a useful purpose but whatever old watercourse once flowed beneath it has long since disappeared – thus the bridge is known as the 'dry' bridge.

An excellent walk begins and ends at Sinnington. Covering some 7½ miles (12.1km), though it can also be done in parts, it starts at the village's fascinating Saxon and Norman church and leads along woodland paths and farm tracks towards Cropton, Rosedale and Lastingham to Lower Askew, then back through Appleton-le-Moors to the starting point. Details available from North York Moors National Park (tel. 01439 770173).

KIRKBYMOORSIDE

7m W of Pickering on the A170

Set quietly off the main road, this agreeable market town of fine Georgian houses, narrow twisting lanes, family-owned shops and a cobbled marketplace, straggles up the hillside. After you pass the last house on the hill, you enter the great open spaces of the North York Moors National Park, 553 square miles of outstanding natural beauty which, since they were accorded the status of a National Park in 1952, have been protected from insensitive encroachments. Within the park you don't have to worry about traffic lights – there aren't any. But you may well have to step down firmly on your brakes to avoid sheep crossing the road at their own leisurely and disdainful pace.

Of the several old coaching inns in Kirkbymoorside, the timbered Black Swan is believed to be the most venerable – the intricately carved entrance porch bears the date 1692.

It was in another ancient inn, the King Head's Hotel, that one of the 17th century's most reviled politicians expired. In what is now Buckingham House, but was then part of the adjoining hotel, George Villiers, 2nd Duke of Buckingham died. The duke had been a favourite of Charles II and a member of the notorious 'Cabal' of the king's five most powerful ministers who colluded with him in trying to frustrate the democratic instincts of the elected Parliament. Each letter of the word 'Cabal' represented the initial of one of its five members – Buckingham being the 'B'. The duke had come to Kirkbymoorside to take part in a hunt through the nearby Forest of Pickering. In the heat of the chase he was thrown from his horse and mortally wounded. The duke's

retainers carried him to the King's Head Inn where he died later that day. In the parish register for 1687 the passing of a once-mighty politician merited only a laconic, phonetic entry: *Died: April 17th George Viluas: Lord Dooke of Bookingham.*

HELMSLEY

13m W of Pickering on the A170

One of North Yorkshire's most popular and attractive towns, with lots of specialty shops and a market every Friday, Helmsley lies on the banks of the River Rye on the edge of the North York Moors National Park. The spacious cobbled market square is typical of the area but the Gothic memorial to the 2nd Earl of Feversham that stands there is not. This astonishingly ornate construction was designed by Sir Giles Gilbert Scott and looks like a smaller version of his famous memorial to Sir Walter Scott in Edinburgh.

The Earls of Feversham lived at **Duncombe Park** whose extensive grounds sweep up to within a few yards of the Market Place. Most of the original mansion, designed by Vanbrugh, was gutted by a disastrous fire in 1879: only the north wing remained habitable and that in its turn was ruined by a second fire in 1895. The Fevershams lavished a fortune on rebuilding the grand old house, largely to the original design, but the financial burden eventually forced them to lease the house and grounds as a preparatory school for girls. Happily, the Fevershams were

62   THE FEATHERS HOTEL

Helmsley

A superb hotel offering good quality food, drink and accommodation.

 see page 233

63   DUNCOMBE PARK

Helmsley

A baroque mansion, built in 1713, with principal rooms restored in late 19th century style and set amid superb parkland and landscaped gardens.

 see page 234

64   THE PHEASANT AT HAROME

Harome

Luxury and comfort at small and gracious country house hotel. Drinks and excellent meals also available to non-residents.

 see page 234

Rievaulx Abbey

With the castle as its backdrop, **Helmsley Walled Garden** offers five acres of lovely gardens containing many unusual varieties of flowers, vegetables and herbs. Originally established in the 1700s, by the late 1900s the garden had become a wilderness but has now been completely restored and work is currently under way to bring the Victorian glasshouses back into service. Plants, cut and dried flowers, vegetables and herbs are on sale; there's a café, shop and picnic area.

Just to the west of Helmsley rise the indescribably beautiful remains of **Rievaulx Abbey** (English Heritage), standing among wooded hills beside the River Rye – 'the most beautiful monastic site in Europe.' JMW Turner was enchanted by this idyllic landscape; Dorothy Wordsworth, 'spellbound'. Founded in 1131, Rievaulx was the first Cistercian abbey in Yorkshire and, with some 700 people – monks, lay brothers, servants – eventually living within its walls, became one of the largest. Like Kirkham Abbey a few years earlier, Rievaulx was endowed by Walter l'Espec, Lord of Helmsley, still mourning the loss of his only son in a riding accident. The Abbey was soon a major landowner in the county, earning a healthy income from farming and at one time owning more than 14,000 sheep.

able to return to their ancestral home in 1985 and the beautifully restored house with its 35 acres of lovely gardens and a further 400 acres of superbly landscaped grounds are now open to the public.

Before they were ennobled, the Fevershams' family name was Duncombe and it was Sir Thomas Duncombe, a wealthy London goldsmith, who established the family seat here when he bought **Helmsley Castle** (English Heritage) and its estate in 1687. Founded in the early 1100s, seriously knocked about during the Civil War, the castle was in a dilapidated state but its previous owner, the Duke of Buckingham, had continued to live there in some squalor and discomfort. Sir Thomas quickly decided to build a more suitable residence nearby, abandoning the ruins to lovers of the romantic and picturesque.

The Abbey also had its own fishery at Teesmouth, and iron-ore mines at Bilsdale and near Wakefield.

Looking down on the extensive remains of the Abbey is **Rievaulx Terrace** (National Trust), a breathtaking example of landscape gardening completed in 1758. The cunningly contrived avenues draw your eyes to incomparable views of the Abbey itself, to vistas along the Rye Valley and to the rolling contours of the hills beyond. At each end of the terrace is a classical temple, one of which is elaborately furnished and decorated as a dining room.

NUNNINGTON

11 miles SW of Pickering off the B1257

Nunnington Hall (National Trust) is a late 17th-century manor house in a beautiful setting beside the River Rye with a picturesque packhorse bridge within its grounds. Inside, there is a magnificent panelled hall, fine tapestries and china, and the famous Carlisle collection of miniature rooms exquisitely furnished in different period styles to one-eighth life size.

HAWNBY

16 miles W of Pickering, off the A170

Hawnby was home of the first community of Methodists in Ryedale. This caused a great scandal within the established church, and the Methodist rebels were taken before the magistrates and charged with disorderly conduct as 'lewd fellows of the baser sort'. That is why, to this day, the village of Hawnby is in two distinct parts: the original village is halfway up the hill,while down at the bottom by the bridge is the settlement the early Methodists built. Within a few years their original houses had been replaced by the ones that stand there now. The village's two chapels also no longer exist – one stands in ruins at Snilesworth on the edge of the moor; the other has been converted into business premises.

The village is close to many hiking trails including the **Cleveland Way** and **Mark Reid's Inn Way**; cycling enthusiasts will enjoy the challenging terrain with trails such as National Cycle Route 65, which passes through the village, and the MTB trails in Boltby Forest. Trout fishing is permitted on Arden Great Lake for a small fee. Other activities such as hang gliding, clay pigeon shooting, 4x4 off-road driving are available locally.

MALTON

Malton has been the historic centre of Ryedale ever since the Romans came. They built a large fort and called it Derventio after the river Derwent beside which it stands. For many years, archaeologists were puzzled by the large scale of the fort, a mystery resolved in 1970 when a building dedication was uncovered which revealed that the fort housed a cavalry regiment, the Ala Picentiana – the extra space was needed to accommodate their horses. Many fine relics from the site, showing the sophisticated lifestyles of the Roman centurions

65 LASKILL GRANGE

Hawnby

Impressive traditional farmhouse (B&B accommodation) and superb self-catering cottages in 600 acres of scenic countryside.

🛏 see page 235

66 THE HAWNBY HOTEL

Hawnby

Excellent food and accommodation in a peaceful village in the heart of the North Yorkshire Moors National Park.

🛏 🍴 see page 236

67 THE HIDDEN MONKEY TEA ROOMS

Malton

Charming tea rooms in the heart of the Market Place in Malton, with home-cooked hot and cold dishes and a range of mouthwatering home-made cakes.

🍴 see page 236

105

68 THE KING'S HEAD

Malton

Large and welcoming pub open all day with a good range of keg ales and hearty food served 12-7.

🍴 *see page 236*

•

New in 2006 is the walled garden at Scampston Hall a few miles northeast of Malton off the A64. Designed by Piet Oudolf, who was awarded a Gold Veitch Memorial Medal by the RHS in 2002, in recognition of services given in the advancement of the science and practice of horticulture, the 4.5-acre garden is a series of hedged enclosures with a dazzling display of modern and colourful planting. A grass pyramid makes for an observation mount from where you can see this marvellous creation in all its glory. The site also offers a selection of plants for sale and an excellent restaurant.

•

and civilians, can be seen in the Malton Museum, along with items from the Iron Age settlement that preceded the Roman garrison.

The River Derwent was vitally important to Malton. The river rises in the moors near Scarborough, then runs inland through the Vale of Pickering bringing an essential element for what was once a major industry in Malton – brewing. In the 19th century, there were nine breweries here, now only the Malton Brewery Company survives. It operates in a converted stable block behind Suddabys Crown Hotel in Wheelgate and welcomes visitors, but telephone them first on 01653 697580.

Charles Dickens stayed in the area with his friend, Charles Smithson, a solicitor, and is believed to have modelled Scrooge's Counting House in *A Christmas Carol* on Smithson's office in Chancery Lane.

Old Malton is located just to the north of the Roman Fort, an interesting and historic area on the edge of open countryside. Nearby villages such as Settrington and their secluded country lanes are home to many famous racehorse stables: if you are up and about early enough you will see the horses out on their daily exercises. In the centre of Old Malton stands a beautiful fragment of **St Mary's Priory**, incorporating a particularly fine Norman doorway. The Priory

St Mary's Priory, Malton

was built around 1155 by the only monastic order in Christendom to have originated entirely in England – the Gilbertines. The order was founded in 1148 by a Lincolnshire parish priest, St Gilbert of Sempringham.

Parts of the parish church are quite as old as the Priory but one of its most interesting features is relatively modern, the work of the 'Mouseman of Kilburn', Robert Thompson. A gifted woodcarver and furniture maker, Thompson 'signed' all his pieces with a discreetly placed carving of a mouse. There's one on the stout oak door of the church and, inside, the stalls are carved elaborately with all manner of wondrous beasts along with historical and mythical scenes.

A mile or so north of Old Malton is **Eden Camp**, a theme

museum dedicated to re-creating the dramatic experiences of ordinary people living through the Second World War. This unique museum is housed in some 30 huts of a genuine prisoner of war camp, built in 1942. Sound, lighting effects, smells, even smoke generators are deployed to make you feel that you are actually there, taking part. Visitors can find out what it was like to live through an air raid, to be a prisoner of war or a sailor in a U-boat under attack. Among the many other exhibits are displays on Fashion in the '40s, Children at War, and even one on Rationing. In 1941, one discovers, the cheese ration was down to 1oz (28 grams) a week!

AROUND MALTON

AMOTHERBY

3 miles W of Malton off the B1257

With 264 residents living in around 100 houses in the year 2000, Amotherby is a small village with mainly stone housing bordering the long main street which continues onto Kirkbymoorside. The church of St Helens is situated at the end of a street off to the right about 100 yards from the cross roads. The cemetery surrounds the church and spills out into the fields to the north of the church. The Old Vicarage is on the right, 50 yards from the crossroads and boasting an impressive array of trees. Only one farm now exists in the village but it is surrounded with arable farmland on all sides. The graveyard is in the process of being

renovated. 'Aimundrebi', as it was known, was in the land of Hugh, Son of Baldrick, and belonged to the Manor of Hovingham. It is on the edge of an Area of Outstanding Natural Beauty with the River Rye supporting an abundance of wildlife.

APPLETON-LE-STREET

4 miles W of Malton off the B1257

Appleton's Grade I listed Saxon church escaped 'improvement' by the Victorians, so contains much original stonework and has one of the finest Anglo-Saxon towers in the North of England. Inside, effigies date from the 13th and 14th centuries and some interior woodwork dates from 1636. Outside, a statue of the Virgin and Child, defaced at the time of the Reformation, can be seen in a niche above the porch. Set high above the

Saxon Church, Appleton-le-Street

69 THE QUEEN'S HEAD

Amotherby

Superb traditional English pub serving real ales, with a renowned Cantonese restaurant, beer garden and more in picturesque Ryedale.

🍴 *see page 237*

70 THE CRESSWELL ARMS

Appleton-le-Street

Traditional stonebuilt inn with excellent food, drink and accommodation in peaceful rural village just west of Malton.

🍴 🛏 *see page 238*

71 CHURCH FARM

Scackleton

Guests return again and again to this charming family-run farmhouse B&B in a peaceful hamlet in the rolling Howardian Hills.

 see page 239

72 THE MIDDLETON ARMS

North Grimston

18th-century coaching inn in peaceful village a few miles southeast of Malton. Food daily, real ales, quality accommodation.

 see page 239

village, All Saints commands magnificent views over the Vale of Pickering. Access is via a footpath from the main road, or follow the lane down the side of the Cresswell Arms pub and turn right, following signposts to the church. Car parking is available in the designated area of the churchyard, which is managed as a conservation churchyard.

HOVINGHAM

8 miles W of Malton on the B1257

'Hall, church and village gather round like a happy family', wrote Arthur Mee describing Hovingham some 60 years ago. Today the idyllic scene remains unspoilt, a lovely place boasting no fewer than three village greens. Overlooking one of them is a Victorian school, still in use and boasting an elegant oriel window.

Nearby Hovingham Hall, an imposing Georgian mansion, was built in 1760 for Sir Thomas Worsley, Surveyor General to George III, and almost exactly 200 years later, on June 8th 1961, his descendant Katherine Worsley returned here for a royal reception following her marriage to the Duke of Kent. The Worsley family still live at the Hall so it is only open to visitors for a short time in summer, but you can see its unusual entrance which leads directly off the village green. The huge archway opens, not as you would expect, into a drive leading to the Hall but to a vast riding school and stables through which visitors have to pass. Within the Hall's grounds is the

village's cricket pitch, enjoying what is surely the most picturesque setting for the game.

EAST HESLERTON

7 miles NE of Malton on the A64

This little village is distinguished by one of the many churches gifted by Sir Tatton Sykes of Sledmere House in the mid-1800s. Designed in 13th-century style the church has a fine west portico, a vaulted chancel and an iron screen of very fine workmanship. The north tower has an octagonal belfry and spire, and statues of the four Latin Doctors (Ambrose, Augustine, Gregory and Jerome) originally sculpted for Bristol Cathedral.

NORTH GRIMSTON

5 miles SE of Malton on the B1248

The village church of St Nicholas has a magnificent Saxon font and fascinating corbel table complete with sheela-na-gig.

KIRKHAM

5 miles SW of Malton off the A64

In a lovely, peaceful setting beside the River Derwent, stand the remains of **Kirkham Priory**. According to legend, the priory was founded in 1125 by Walter l'Espec after his only son was thrown from his horse and killed at this very spot. (A few years later, Walter was to found another great abbey at Rievaulx). Visitors to Kirkham pass through a noble, exquisitely decorated gatehouse but one of the most memorable sights at the Priory, perhaps because it is so unexpected, is the sumptuous lavatorium in the ruined cloister. Here the monks washed their hands at two bays with lavishly moulded arches supported by slender pillars, each bay adorned with tracery.

WELBURN

5 miles SW of Malton off the A64

This typical Ryedale stone village has an ancient history and, nearby, various Roman remains have been unearthed over the centuries. Found in the delightful and peaceful setting beside the River Derwent, just a couple miles are the remains of Kirkham Priory, while just north, lying in the folds of the Howardian Hills, is the glorious Castle Howard.

CASTLE HOWARD

5 miles SW of Malton off the A64

Lying in the folds of the Howardian Hills about five miles southwest of Malton stands one of the most glorious stately homes in Britain, **Castle Howard**. Well known to TV viewers as the Brideshead of *Brideshead Revisited*, Castle Howard has astonished visitors ever since it was completed in the early 1700s.

Even that world-weary 18th-century socialite Horace Walpole was stirred to enthusiasm: 'Nobody had informed me,' he wrote, 'that at one view I should see a palace, a town, a fortified city, temples on high places ... the noblest lawn in the world fenced by half the horizon and a mausoleum that would tempt one to be buried alive: in short, I have seen gigantic places before, but never a sublime one.'

Kirkham Priory

Winner of York Tourism Bureau's 'Out of Town Attraction of the Year' award, this magnificent 18th-century house with its extensive collections and breathtaking grounds, featuring temples, lakes and fountains, includes various places to stop and enjoy refreshments and also a plant centre and tree nursey. A varied programme of events takes place throughout the year, including the Proms Spectacular and Archaeology Weekends.

Perhaps the most astonishing fact of all concerns the architect of Castle Howard, Sir John Vanbrugh. Vanbrugh had been a soldier and a playwright but until he began this sublime building had never yet overseen the placing of one block of masonry on another.

Castle Howard is open daily between February and November. A land-train is available to transport visitors from the car park to the house, and there is disabled access to many parts.

73   CASTLE HOWARD

Castle Howard, Nr Malton

A major tourist attraction. A magnificent 18th century house with extensive collections and superb grounds,

 see page 240

York and the Yorkshire Wolds

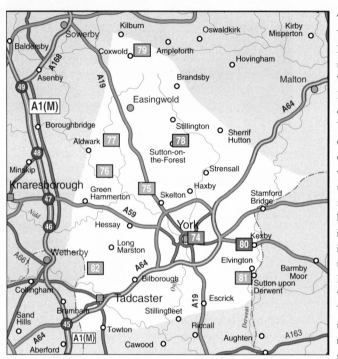

This region of North Yorkshire, between the North York Moors and the East Riding, between West Yorkshire and the Heritage Coast, is dominated by the city of York. The first settlement of any note here was created by the Romans, who named their garrison town 'Eboracum', and, from then on, York has been an important and influential force not only in Yorkshire but also in the rest of the country. Known to the Saxons as 'Eoferwic' and the Vikings as 'Jorvik', it was the creation of the magnificent Minster, started in the early 13th century that saw the city truly begin to develop. A major trading centre and, at one time, the second largest city in the country, York is also remembered as the heart of the railway network in the north of England. Not surprisingly, there is plenty to see here and, along with the numerous imaginative museums and galleries, visitors will want to walk around its medieval streets and soak up the atmosphere that encompasses architectural styles from at least the last 700 years.

▌ FOOD & DRINK

⊟ ACCOMMODATION

🏛 PLACES OF INTEREST

YORK

'The history of York is the history of England,' said the Duke of York, later to become George VI. A bold claim but well justified. For almost 2,000 years the city has been at the centre of great events and, better than any other city in England, it has preserved the evidence of each era of its glorious past.

One of the grandest cityscapes in the country opens up as you walk along the old city walls towards **York Minster,** a sublime expression of medieval faith. The Minster stands on the site of an even older building, the headquarters of the Roman legions. The Imperial troops arrived here in AD 71 when the governor, Quintus Petilius Cerealis, chose this strategic position astride the Rivers Ouse and Foss as his base for a campaign against the pesky tribe of the Brigantes. The settlement was named Eboracum. From this garrison, Hadrian directed the construction of his great wall and a later general, Constantine, was proclaimed Emperor here. The legions finally left the city around AD 410, but the evidence of their three-and-a-half centuries of occupation is manifest all around York in buildings like the **Multangular Tower,** in rich artefacts treasured in the city's museums and even in a pub: at the **Roman Bath Inn** you can see the remains of steam baths used by the garrison residents.

Little is known of York during the Dark Ages but by the 8th century the city had been colonised by the Anglo-Saxons, who named it Eoferwic, and it was already an important Christian and academic centre. The Vikings put an end to that when they invaded in the 9th century and changed the name once again, this time to Jorvik. The story of York during those years of Danish rule is imaginatively told in the many displays at the **Jorvik Centre** in Coppergate, celebrating a 1,000-year-old story. This world-famous centre transports visitors back in time to experience the sights, sounds and – perhaps most famously – the smells of 10th-century York. Visitors are shown that, in AD 975, York was a bustling commercial centre where 10,000 people lived and worked. Travelling in state-of-the-art 'time

74 JORVIK VIKING CENTRE

York

The world famous JORVIK gives a fascinating insight into the Viking age and York as it would have appeared in AD 975.

🏛 *see page 240*

Multangular Tower, York

capsules', visitors are carried past and through two-storey dwellings, enjoying views over back gardens and rooftops, and even glimpsing the Viking Age equivalent of today's Minster. Journeying through representations of real-life Viking Age Britain, you pass through a bustling market thronged with Danes bartering for chickens, corn and other provisions and wares, penetrate dark smoky houses, cross a busy wharf where goods,

transported along the rivers Ouse and Foss, are being off-loaded. Both fun and educational, 20 years after it first opened, Jorvik still retains its status as one of the world's iconic attractions, and its many superb features make it an enduring favourite with children and adults alike.

After the Norman Conquest, the city suffered badly during the Harrowing of the North when William the Conqueror mounted a brutal campaign against his rebellious northern subjects. Vast tracts of Yorkshire and Northumberland were laid waste and some historians reckon that it took more than 100 years for the area to recover from this wholesale devastation.

In later Norman times, however, York entered one of its most glorious periods. The Minster, the largest Gothic cathedral in Northern Europe, was begun around 1230 and the work was on such a scale that it would not be completed until two-and-a-half centuries later. Its stained glass windows – there are more than 100 of them – cast a celestial light over the many treasures within. A guided tour of the Great Tower gives dizzying views across the city; a visit to the crypt reveals some of the relics from the Roman fortress that stood here nearly 2,000 years ago.

This superb building has survived three major fires. The first occurred in 1829 and was started by a madman, Jonathan

The Shambles, York

Martin. Believing that God wanted him to destroy the church, he started a fire using prayer and hymn books. The fire was not discovered until the following morning by which time the east end of the Minster had been severely damaged. A second blaze, in 1840, was caused by a workman leaving a candle burning. As a result of his carelessness, the central part of the nave was destroyed. The most recent conflagration was in July 1984, shortly after a controversial Bishop of Durham had been installed. Some attributed the fire to God's wrath at the Bishop's appointment; the more prosaic view was that it had been caused by lightning. The subsequent restoration has allowed modern masons and craftsmen to demonstrate that they possess skills just as impressive as those of their medieval forebears.

The Merchant Adventurer's Hall

The network of medieval streets around the Minster is one of the city's major delights. Narrow lanes are criss-crossed by even narrower footpaths – ginnels, snickets or 'snickelways', which have survived as public rights of way despite being built over, above and around. Narrowest of all the snickelways is Pope's Head Alley, more than 100 feet long but only 31 inches wide. The alley became known as Introduction Lane – if you wanted to know someone better, you simply timed your walk along the lane so as to meet the other party half-way. Whip-ma-Whop-ma-Gate, allegedly, is where felons used to be 'whipped and whopped'. Probably most famous of these ancient streets is **The Shambles**. Its name comes from 'Fleshammels', the street of butchers and slaughter houses. The houses here were deliberately built to keep the street out of direct sunlight, thus protecting the carcasses which were hung outside the houses on hooks. Many of the hooks are still in place.

•

In Leeman Road, York is the National Railway Museum, the largest of its kind in the world. This fascinating museum (free entry) covers some 200 years of railway history, from Stephenson's Rocket to the Channel Tunnel. Among the thousands of exhibits demonstrating the technical and social impact of the Iron Horse are The Flying Scotsman. Gresley's record-breaking locomotive, Mallard, Queen Victoria's royal carriage, and displays demonstrating the workings of the railway system. There's an extensive library and reading room (booking advised), and the Brief Encounter restaurant is themed on the classic movie.

•

During these years, York was the second largest city in England and it was then that the town walls and their 'bars', or gates, were built. The trade guilds were also at their most powerful and in Fossgate one of them built the lovely black and white timbered **Merchant Adventurers Hall.** The Merchant Adventurers controlled the lucrative trade in 'all goods bought and sold foreign' and they spared no expense in building the Great Hall where they conducted their affairs beneath a complex timbered roof displaying many colourful banners of York's medieval guilds. To this period, too, belong the **York Mystery Plays**, first performed in 1397 and subsequently every four years.

During Tudor times, York's importance steadily declined but re-emerged in the 18th century as a fashionable social centre. Many elegant Georgian houses, of which **Fairfax House** in Castlegate is perhaps the most splendid, were built at this time and they add another attractive architectural dimension to the city. Fairfax House was built in the early 1700s and elegantly remodelled by John Carr half a century later. The gracious old house has had an unfortunate history. It passed through a succession of private owners and by 1909 was divided between three building societies and the York City Club. The final indignity came in 1919 when the city council permitted a cinema to be built alongside and its superb first floor rooms to be converted into a dance

hall. The York Civic Trust was able to purchase the house in 1981 and has restored this splendid old mansion to its former state of grace. The original furnishings have long since been dispersed but in their place are the marvellous pieces from the Noel Terry collection of fine furniture and clocks which includes many rare and unusual pieces.

The 19th century saw York take on a completely different role as the hub of the railway system in the north. At the heart of this transformation was the charismatic entrepreneur George Hudson, founder of what became the Great Northern Railway. Part visionary, part crook, Hudson's wheeler-dealing eventually led to his disgrace but even then the citizens of York twice elected him as Lord Mayor and he has a street named after him. It was thanks to Hudson that York's magnificent railway station, with its great curving roof of glass, was built, a tourist attraction in its own right.

Another aspect of railway history is on view at the **York Model Railway**, next door to the station, which has almost one third of a mile of track and up to 14 trains running at any one time.

A city with such a long and colourful history naturally boasts some fine museums. Set in botanical gardens close to the Minster and beside the River Ouse, the **Yorkshire Museum & Gardens** has an outstanding collection of Roman, Viking and medieval artefacts, including the exquisite Middleham Jewel which was uncovered close to Middleham

Castle. Made of finely engraved gold and adorned with a brilliant sapphire it is one of the most dazzling pieces to have been discovered from that period.

At the **York Castle Museum** visitors can venture into the prison cell of notorious highwayman Dick Turpin; stroll along Victorian and Edwardian streets complete with fully equipped shops, hostelries and houses; or browse among the more than 100,000 items on display. One of the country's most popular museums of everyday life, its exhibits range from crafts and costumes to automobiles and machine guns, from mod cons and medicines to toys and technology.

Insights into medieval daily life are provided at **Barley Hall,** a superbly restored late medieval townhouse which in Tudor times was the home of William Snawsell, a goldsmith who became Lord Mayor of York. Visitors can try out the furniture, handle all the pottery, glass and metal wares, and even try on some medieval costumes.

In a beautifully restored church close to the Shambles is the **Archaeological Research Centre**, an award-winning hands-on exploration of archaeology for visitors of all ages. Here you can meet practising archaeologists who will demonstrate how to sort and identify genuine finds or to try out ancient crafts. For the more technically minded, there's a series of interactive computer displays which illustrate how modern technology helps to discover and interpret the past.

It's impossible here to list all York's museums, galleries and fine buildings, but you will find a wealth of additional information at the Tourist Information Centre close to one of the historic old gateways to the city, **Bootham Bar**.

NORTH AND EAST OF YORK

STAMFORD BRIDGE

7 miles NE of York on the A166

Everyone knows that 1066 was the year of the Battle of Hastings but, just a few days before that battle, King Harold had clashed at Stamford Bridge with his half-brother Tostig and Hardrada, King of Norway who between them had mustered some 60,000 men. On a rise near the corn mill is a stone commemorating the event with an inscription in English and Danish. Up until 1878, a Sunday in September was designated 'Spear Day Feast' in commemoration of the battle. On this day, boat-shaped pies were made bearing the impression of the fatal spear, in memory of the Saxon soldier in his boat who slew the single Norseman defending the wooden bridge. Harold's troops were triumphant but immediately after this victory they marched southwards to Hastings and a much more famous defeat.

MURTON

3 miles E of York off the A64

Although a small village, Murton is an important, modern livestock centre and it is also home to the

•

Very popular with those who have an interest in the more macabre aspects of York's long history is the Original Ghostwalk of York which starts at the King's Arms pub on Ouse Bridge and sets off at 8pm every evening. At the last count, York was reckoned to have some 140 resident ghosts within its walls – on this guided walk you visit some of their haunts and hear dark tales, grim accounts of murder, torture, and intrigue. Prepare to have your blood chilled.

•

115

75 THE DAWNAY ARMS

Shipton by Beningborough, York

Excellent food and a range of drinks in relaxed and tasteful surroundings, in one of the best village inns in the Vale of York.

 see page 241

76 THE COLLEGE ARMS

Linton-on-Ouse, York

Traditional ales and the superb 'Saffron Spice' restaurant serving expertly prepared Indian cuisine.

 see page 242

77 THE BLUE BELL COUNTRY INN

Alne

Elegant and gracious traditional country pub and restaurant 11 miles NW of York off the A19.

 see page 243

116

Yorkshire Museum of Farming, found at Murton Park. As well as wandering around the fields and pens, visitors can also see reconstructions of a Roman fort, a Danelaw village from the Dark Ages and Celtic Roundhouses along with bumping into Romans, Viking and Saxons. Other attractions at the park include the Derwent Valley Light Railway, a children's play area and a café fashioned on a farmhouse kitchen.

BISHOP WILTON

8½ miles E of York off the A166

A small and unspoilt village between Stamford Bridge to the west and Pocklington to the south, in Saxon times Bishop Wilton was a country retreat for the bishops of York. The Saxons – whose bishops gave the village its name – began the lovely village church, which has a fine Norman chancel arch and doorway. The remarkable black-and-white marble flooring is copied from the Vatican. The village is a good centre for walking and touring, within easy reach of both York and the coast.

NEWTON-ON-OUSE

7 miles NW of York off the A19

About a mile to the south of Newton on Ouse is **Beningbrough Hall** (National Trust), a baroque masterpiece from the early 18th century with seven acres of gardens, wilderness play area, pike ponds and scenic walks. There's also a fully-operational Victorian laundry which demonstrates the painstaking

drudgery of a 19th-century washing day. A major attraction here is the permanent exhibition of more than 100 portraits on loan from the National Portrait Gallery. Other exhibitions are often held at the Hall – for these there is usually an additional charge.

EASINGWOLD

This agreeable market town was once surrounded by the Forest of Galtres, a vast hunting preserve of Norman kings. It lies at the foot of the Howardian Hills, an Area of Outstanding Natural Beauty covering 77 acres of woods, farmland and historic parkland. Easingwold's prosperity dates back to the 18th century when it flourished as a major stage coach post – at that period the town could offer a choice of some 26 public houses and inns. Until the recent construction of a bypass the old town was clogged with traffic but it is now a pleasure again to wander around the marketplace with its impressive **Market Cross** and, nearby, the outline of the old bull-baiting ring set in the cobbles. Easingwold used to enjoy the distinction of having its own private railway, a two-and-a-half mile stretch of track along which it took all of 10 minutes to reach the main east coast line at Alne. Older residents fondly remember the ancient, tall-chimneyed steam locomotive that plied this route until its deeply regretted closure to passenger traffic in 1948.

A little to the south of

Easingwold, on the B1363, is **Sutton Park,** a noble early 18th-century mansion, built in 1730 by Thomas Atkinson and containing some fine examples of Sheraton and Chippendale furniture, and much admired decorative plasterwork by the Italian maestro in this craft, Cortese. The ubiquitous Capability Brown designed the lovely gardens and parkland in which you'll find a Georgian ice-house, well-signposted woodland walks and a nature trail. There's also a gift shop and a café.

AROUND EASINGWOLD

STILLINGTON

4 miles E of Easingwold on the B1363

In 1758, one of the great works of English literature almost perished in the fireplace of Stillington Hall. The parson of Coxwold had been invited to dinner and when the meal ended was asked to read from a book he had just completed. The guests had all wined and dined well and were soon dozing off. Incensed by their inattention the parson threw the pages of his manuscript onto the fire. Fortunately his host, the Squire of Stillington, rescued them from the flames and Laurence Sterne's immortal *Tristram Shandy* was saved for posterity.

HUSTHWAITE

4 miles N of Easingwold off the A19

Old stone houses mingle with mellow Victorian and Edwardian brick and overlooking the village

green, where three lanes meet, the Church of St Nicholas still retains its original Norman doorway. Just outside the village, on the road to Coxwold, there's a stunning view across to the Hambleton Hills and the White Horse of Kilburn.

COXWOLD

5 miles N of Easingwold off the A19 or A170

Coxwold enjoys a particularly lovely setting in the narrow valley that runs between the Hambleton and Howardian Hills. At the western end of the village stands the 500-year-old **Shandy Hall,** home of Laurence Sterne, vicar of Coxwold in the 1760s. Sterne was the author of *Tristram Shandy*, that wonderfully bizarre novel which opened a vein of English surreal comedy leading directly to The Goons and the Monty Python team. The architecture of the Hall, Tudor in origin, includes some appropriately eccentric features – strangely-shaped balustrades on the wooden staircases, a Heath Robinson kind of contraption in the bedroom powder-closet by which Sterne could draw up pails of water for his ablutions, and a tiny, eye-shaped window in the huge chimney stack opening from the study to the right of the entrance. A more conventional attraction is the priceless collection of Sterne's books and manuscripts.

The Revd Sterne much preferred the cosmopolitan diversions of London to the rustic pleasures of his Yorkshire parish and rarely officiated at the imposing **Church of St Michael** nearby

78 SUTTON PARK

Sutton-on-the-Forest

This lived-in stately home is crammed with beautiful 18th century furniture, paintings and porcelain, whilst the stunning gardens are also a big attraction.

 see page 244

with its striking octagonal tower, three-decker pulpit and Fauconberg family tombs. A curiosity here is a floor brass in the nave recording the death of Sir John Manston in 1464. A space was left for his wife Elizabeth's name to be added at a later date. The space is still blank. Outside, against the wall of the nave, is Sterne's original tombstone, moved here from London's Bayswater when the churchyard there was deconsecrated in 1969.

Just to the south of Coxwold is **Newburgh Priory,** founded in 1145 as an Augustinian monastery

and now a mostly Georgian country house with fine interiors and a beautiful water garden. Since 1538, the Priory has been the home of the Fauconberg family. An old tradition asserts that Oliver Cromwell's body is interred here. Cromwell's daughter, Mary, was married to Lord Fauconberg and when Charles II had her father's corpse hanged at Tyburn and his head struck off, Lady Fauconberg claimed the decapitated body, brought it to Newburgh and, it is said, buried the remains under the floorboards of an attic room. The supposed tomb has never been opened, the Fauconbergs even resisting a royal appeal from Edward VII when, as Prince of Wales, he was a guest at the Priory. The house, which is still the home of the Earls of Fauconberg, and its extensive grounds are open to the public during the spring and summer months.

From Coxwold, follow the minor road northeastwards towards Ampleforth. After about two miles, you will see the lovely, cream-coloured ruins of **Byland Abbey** (English Heritage). The Cistercians began building their vast compound in 1177 and it grew to become the largest Cistercian church in Britain. Much of the damage to its fabric was caused by Scottish soldiers after the Battle of Byland in 1322. The English king, Edward II had been staying at the Abbey but fled after his defeat, abandoning vital stores and priceless treasures. In a frenzy of looting, the Scots made off with everything the king had

Newburgh Priory, Coxwold

118

Byland Abbey, Coxwold

79   WOMBWELL ARMS

Wass

Privately-owned Free House with superb fresh homecooked food and comfortable and tasteful accommodation, just off the A170 southwest of Helmsley.

see page 244

left and ransacked the Abbey for good measure. The ruined west front of the Abbey, although only the lower arc of its great rose window is still in place, gives a vivid impression of how glorious this building once was.

WASS

6 miles N of Easingwold off the A170

The village of Wass nestles comfortably in a small south-facing valley on the edge of the North Yorkshire Moors. This small community of about 100 people comprises two parts: the village itself and, a short distance away, the impressive ruins of Byland Abbey.

AMPLEFORTH

6 miles N of Easingwold off the A170

Set on the southern slopes of the Hambleton Hills, Ampleforth is perhaps best known for its Roman Catholic public school, Ampleforth College, established by the Benedictine community that came

here in 1809, fleeing from persecution in post-revolutionary France. The monks built an austere-looking Abbey in the Romanesque style among whose treasures are an altar stone rescued from Byland Abbey and finely crafted woodwork by the 'Mouseman of Kilburn', Robert Thompson.

KILBURN

6 miles N of Easingwold off the A170

Kilburn was the home of one of the most famous of modern Yorkshire craftsmen, Robert Thompson – the **'Mouseman of Kilburn'**. Robert's father was a carpenter but he apprenticed his son to an engineer. At the age of 20 however, inspired by seeing the medieval wood carvings in Ripon Cathedral, Robert returned to Kilburn and begged his father to train him as a carpenter. An early commission from Ampleforth Abbey to carve a cross settled his

80   IVY HOUSE FARM

Kexby, York

Charming and pristine bed-and-breakfast accommodation set in 132 acres of farmland. Three guest bedrooms, hearty and delicious food.

see page 246

81   ST VINCENT ARMS

Sutton upon Derwent, York

CAMRA Pub of the Year 2002 and 2006, friendly family-run pub with nine real ales, great food and excellent atmosphere.

see page 245

Kilburn White Horse

village church – there's one perched on the traceried pulpit, another clinging to a desk in the sanctuary, and a third sitting cheekily on the lectern.

From the northern end of the village a winding lane leads to the famous **White Horse,** inspired by the prehistoric White Horse hill-carving at Uffingham in Berkshire. John Hodgson, Kilburn's village schoolmaster, enthused his pupils and villagers into creating this splendid folly in 1857. It is 314 feet long and 228 feet high and visible from as far away as Harrogate and Otley. Unlike its prehistoric predecessor in Berkshire, where the chalk hillside keeps it naturally white, Kilburn's 'White' horse is scraped from grey limestone which needs to be regularly groomed with lime-washing and a liberal spreading of chalk chippings.

destiny: from then until his death in 1955 Robert's beautifully crafted ecclesiastical and domestic furniture was in constant demand. His work can be seen in more than 700 churches, including Westminster Abbey and York Minster. Each piece bears his 'signature' – a tiny carved mouse placed in some inconspicuous corner of the work. According to a family story, Robert adopted this symbol when one of his assistants happened to use the phrase 'as poor as a church mouse'. (Signing one's work wasn't an entirely new tradition: the 17th-century woodcarver Grinling Gibbons' personal stamp was a pod of peas). Robert Thompson's two grandsons have continued his work and their grandfather's former home is now both a memorial to his genius and a showroom for their own creations.

You can see several of the Mouseman's creations in Kilburn

SOUTH AND WEST OF YORK

ELVINGTON

7 miles SE of York off the B1228

During the Second World War RAF Elvington was the base for British, Canadian and French bomber crews flying missions to occupied

Europe. With virtually all its original buildings still intact, the base now provides an authentic setting for the **Yorkshire Air Museum** and is the largest Second World War Bomber Command Station open to the public in the UK. In addition to examining the many exhibits tracing the history of aviation, including a unique Halifax bomber, visitors can visit the control tower, browse among the historic military vehicle collection, watch engineers restoring vintage planes – and enjoy home-cooked food in the NAAFI restaurant. The museum hosts many special events throughout the year and offers conference and corporate event facilities.

LONG MARSTON
7 miles W of York off the B1224

Lying on the edge of the Vale of York and sheltered by a hill, this village is an ancient agricultural community. However, in July 1644, its tranquillity was shattered by the battle of Marston Moor, one of the most important encounters of the Civil War and one which the Royalists lost. The night before the battle, Oliver Cromwell and his chief officers stayed at Long Marston Hall and the bedroom they used is still called The Cromwell Room.

Each year the anniversary of the battle is commemorated by the members of the Sealed Knot and, it is said, that the ghosts of those who fell in battle haunt the site. Certainly, local farmers still occasionally unearth cannonballs

used in the battle when they are out ploughing the fields.

Less than 100 years later, Long Marston Hall saw the birth, in 1707, of the mother of General James Wolfe, the famous English soldier who scaled the Heights of Abraham to relieve the siege of Quebec.

TADCASTER
9m SW of York off the A64

The lovely magnesian limestone used in so many fine Yorkshire

Battle of Marston Moor Memorial

82 THE WHITE SWAN INN

Wighill, Tadcaster

Fresh food, a choice of ales and genuine Yorkshire hospitality at a venerable inn a few miles northwest of Tadcaster.

 see *page 247*

churches came from the quarries established here in Roman times. Their name for Tadcaster was simply 'Calcaria' – limestone. By 1341 however, brewing had become the town's major industry, using water from River Wharfe. Three major breweries are still based in Tadcaster: Samuel Smiths, established in 1758 and the oldest in Yorkshire; John Smith's, whose bitter is the best-selling ale in Britain; and Coors Tower Brewery. The distinctive brewery buildings dominate the town's skyline and provide the basis of its prosperity. Guided tours of the breweries are available by prior booking.

Also worth visiting is **The Ark**, the oldest building in Tadcaster dating back to the 1490s. During its long history, The Ark has served as a meeting place, a post office, an inn, a butcher's shop, and a museum. It now houses the Town Council offices and is open to the public in office hours. This appealing half-timbered building takes its name from the two carved heads on the first floor beams. They are thought to represent Noah and his wife, hence the name. Tadcaster also offers some attractive riverside walks, one of which takes you across the 'Virgin Viaduct' over the River Wharfe. Built in 1849 by the great railway entrepreneur George Hudson, the viaduct was intended to be part of a direct line from Leeds to York. Before the tracks were laid however Hudson was convicted of fraud on a stupendous scale and this route was never completed.

About four miles southwest of Tadcaster is **Hazelwood Castle,** now a superb hotel and conference centre. But for more than eight centuries it was the home of the Vavasour family who built it with the lovely white limestone from their quarry at Thevesdale – the same quarry that provided the stone for York Minster and King's College Chapel, Cambridge. The well-maintained gardens and nature trail are open every afternoon (tea room and shop open on Sundays only), and guided tours of the Castle with its superb Great Hall and 13th-century Chapel, can be arranged by telephoning 01937 832738.

BOSTON SPA

11m SW of York on the A659

Set beside the broad-flowing River Wharfe, this attractive little town enjoyed many years of prosperity after a Mr John Shires discovered a mineral spring here in 1744. The spa activities have long since ceased. There's a pleasant riverside walk which can be continued along the track of a dismantled railway as far as Tadcaster in one direction, Wetherby in the other. The town's impressive 19th-century church is notable for its stately tower and the 36 stone angels supporting the nave and aisles.

WETHERBY

11m SW of York on the A661

Situated on the Great North Road, at a point midway between Edinburgh and London, Wetherby was renowned for its coaching inns, of which the two most famous were The Angel and The Swan & Talbot. It is rumoured that serving positions at these inns were considered so lucrative that employees had to pay for the privilege of employment in them!

The town has remained unspoilt and has a quaint appearance with a central marketplace that was first granted to the Knights Templar. Many of the houses in the town are Georgian, Regency, or early Victorian. Apart from its shops, galleries, old pubs, and cafés, there is also a popular racecourse nearby. Another feature is the renowned 18th-century bridge with a long weir which once provided power for Wetherby's corn mill and possibly dates from medieval times.

The bridge once carried traffic along the Great North Road; the A1 now by-passes the town.

About five miles south of Wetherby, **Bramham Park** is noted for its magnificent gardens, 66 acres of them, and its pleasure grounds which cover a further 100 acres. They are the only example of a formal, early 18th-century landscape in Britain. Temples, ornamental ponds, cascades, a two-mile long avenue of beech trees and one of the best wildflower gardens in the country are just some of the attractions. In early June, the park hosts the Bramham Horse Trials. The house itself, an attractive Queen Anne building, is open to groups of six or more by appointment only.

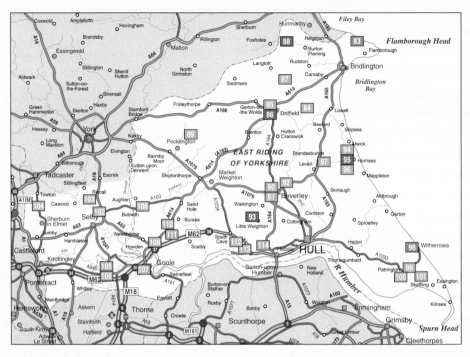

East Yorkshire

'Fold upon fold of encircling hills, piled rich and golden' – such was the author Winifred Holtby's fond memory of the Wolds landscape. She was born in 1898 in Rudston on the northern edge of the Wolds, a village dominated by the prehistoric Rudston Monolith. This colossal block of stone, a daunting symbol of some misty pagan belief, stands challengingly close to Rudston's Christian parish church. Twenty-five feet (7.6m) high, it is the tallest standing stone in Britain. Winifred Holtby left the village and became a leading figure in London literary circles, editor of the influential magazine *Time and Tide*, but in her own books it was those 'rich and golden hills' that still enthralled her. In her most successful novel, *South Riding*, the fictional Riding is unmistakably recognisable as the Wolds among whose gently rolling acres she had spent her childhood.

The Wolds are a great crescent of chalk hills that sweep round from the coast near Flamborough Head to the outskirts of Hull. There were settlers here some 10,000 years ago – but never very many. In the early 1700s, Daniel Defoe described the area as 'very thin of towns and people' and also noted the 'great number of sheep'. Little has changed: the Wolds remain an unspoilt tract of scattered farmsteads and somnolent villages with one of the lowest population densities in the country. Artists remark on the striking quality of the light and air, and on the long views that open up, perhaps across undulating hills to the twin towers of Beverley Minster or to the great towers of the Minster at York. The Wolds never rise above 800 feet but the open landscape makes them particularly vulnerable to winter snowstorms: children have been marooned in their schools, the dipping and twisting country roads, even in recent years, have been blocked for weeks at a time.

The southeastern corner of Yorkshire tends to be overlooked by many visitors. If only they knew what they were missing. Beverley is one of the most beguiling of Yorkshire towns and its Minster one of the greatest glories of Gothic architecture. Its parish church, built by a medieval guild, rivals the Minster in its grandeur and in its colourful interior. The whole town has the indefinable dignity you might expect from a community that was a capital of the East Riding in former days when Hull, just six miles to the south, was still a rather scruffy little port.

To the east and south of Beverley lies the old Land of Holderness, its character quite different from anywhere else in Yorkshire. A wide plain, it stretches to the coast where for aeons the land has been fighting an incessant, and losing, battle against the onslaught of North Sea billows. The whole length of the Holderness coast is being eroded at an average rate of three inches a year, but in some locations up to three feet or more gets gnawed away. At its southernmost tip, Spurn Point curls around the mouth of the Humber estuary, a cruelly exposed tip of land whose contours get re-arranged after every winter storm. The coastal towns and villages have a bleached and scoured look to them, perhaps a little forbidding at first. It doesn't take long however for visitors to succumb to the appeal of this region of wide vistas, secluded villages and lonely shores.

Selby is the most southerly of the eight districts that make up the vast, sprawling county of North Yorkshire. Here, the level plains of the Vale of York stretch for miles – rich, agricultural land watered by the four great Yorkshire rivers, Ouse, Wharfe, Derwent and Aire, and by the Selby Canal. It is ideal country for walking and cycling, or for exploring the waterways on which a wide variety of rivercraft is available for hire.

125

BRIDLINGTON

A corner of Bridlington Priory churchyard recalls one of the most tragic days in the town's history. During a fearsome gale in January 1871, a whole fleet of ships foundered along the coast. Bridlington's lifeboat was launched but within minutes it was 'smashed to matchwood': most of its crew perished. Twenty bodies were washed ashore and later buried in the Priory churchyard: it was estimated that 10 times as many souls found a watery grave. This awesome tragedy is still recalled each year with a solemn service of remembrance when the lifeboat is drawn through the town.

Bridlington lies at the northern tip of the crescent of hills that form the Wolds. The old town lies a mile inland from the bustling seaside resort with its manifold visitor amusements and attractions that has been understandably popular since early Victorian times. The attractions of a vast, 10-mile stretch of sandy beach distract most visitors from the less obvious beauties of **Bridlington Priory** in the old town. The Priory was once one of the wealthiest in England but it was ruthlessly pillaged during the Reformation. Externally it is somewhat unprepossessing, but step inside and the majestic 13th-century nave is unforgettably impressive.

Queen Henrietta Maria's visit to Bridlington was certainly quite exciting. In February 1643, she landed here on a Dutch ship laden with arms and aid for her beleaguered husband, Charles I. Parliamentary naval vessels were in hot pursuit and having failed to capture their quarry, bombarded the town. Their cannon balls actually hit the Queen's lodging. Henrietta was forced to take cover in a ditch where, as she reported in a letter to her husband, 'the balls sang merrily over our heads, and a sergeant was killed not 20 paces from me.' At this point Her Majesty deemed it prudent to retreat to the safety of Boynton Hall, three miles inland and well beyond the range of the Parliamentary cannons.

These stirring events, and many others in the long history of Bridlington and its people, are vividly brought to life with the help of evocative old paintings, photographs and artefacts in the **Bayle Museum**. Quite apart from its fascinating exhibits the museum is well worth visiting for its setting inside the old gatehouse to the town, built around 1390.

Penny arcades were once an indispensable feature of seaside resorts. At the **Old Penny Memories Museum** you can see 'What the Butler Saw', have your fortune told, test your strength on the Minigrip, discover your matrimonial prospects, pit your skills against a pinball machine, and enjoy a host of other entertainments on the extensive collection of antique slot machines – and all for just one old penny each. There's also a sixties café with lots of colourful memorabilia of the period.

A more recent attraction, opened at Easter 1999, is **Beside the Seaside**, an all-weather venue

The Gatehouse, Bridlington

where visitors can take a promenade through Bridlington's heyday as a resort, sampling the sights, sounds and characters of a seaside town. Film shows and period amusements such as antique coin-in-the-slot games and a Punch & Judy Show, displays reconstructing a 1950s boarding house as well as the town's maritime history – the museum provides a satisfying experience for both the nostalgic and those with a general curiosity about the town's past.

On the northern outskirts of Bridlington is **Sewerby Hall**, a monumental mansion built on the cusp of the Queen Anne and early Georgian years, between 1714 and 1720. Set in 50 acres of garden and parkland (where there's also a small zoo), the house was first opened to the public in 1936 by Amy Johnson, the dashing, Yorkshire-born pilot who had captured the public imagination by her daring solo flights to South Africa and Australia. The Museum of East Yorkshire here houses some fascinating memorabilia of Amy's pioneering feats along with displays of motor vehicles, archaeological finds and some remarkable paintings among which is perhaps the most famous portrait of Queen Henrietta Maria, wife of Charles I. Queen Henrietta loved this romantic image of herself as a young, carefree woman, but during the dark days of the Civil War she felt compelled to sell it to raise

Bridlington

funds for the doomed Royalist cause which ended with her husband's execution. After passing through several hands, this haunting portrait of a queen touched by tragedy found its last resting place at Sewerby Hall.

Close by is **Bondville Miniature Village**, one of the finest model villages in the country. The display includes more than 1,000 hand-made and painted characters, over 200 individual and unique villages, and carefully crafted scenes of everyday life, all set in a beautifully landscaped one acre site. The Village is naturally popular with children who are fascinated by features such as the steam train crossing the tiny river and passing the harbour with its fishing boats and cruisers.

127

AROUND BRIDLINGTON

FLAMBOROUGH

4 miles NE of Bridlington on the B1255.

At **Flamborough Head,** sea and land are locked in an unremitting battle. At the North Landing, huge, foam-spumed waves roll in between gigantic cliffs, slowly but remorselessly washing away the shoreline. Paradoxically, the outcome of this elemental conflict is to produce one of the most picturesque locations on the Yorkshire coast, much visited and much photographed.

Flamborough has a long and lively maritime history, not least for being the site of one of the most stubborn naval battles in British history, which took place off Flamborough Head between the American squadron led by John Paul Jones and two British ships of war. Taking place during the War of Independence in 1777, watchers on the coast were transfixed by this intense battle that eventually led to the defeat of the British, when British Captain Pearson surrendered his sword to John Paul Jones.

Victorian travel writers, in their time, also came to appreciate and honour Flamborough, not just for its dramatic setting but also for its people. They were so clannish and believed in such strange superstitions. No boat would ever set sail on a Sunday; wool could not be wound in lamplight; anyone who mentioned a hare or pig while baiting the fishing lines was inviting doom. No fisherman would leave harbour unless he was wearing a navy-blue jersey, knitted by his wife in a cable, diamond mesh peculiar to the village and still worn today. Every year the villagers would slash their way through Flamborough in a sword-dancing frenzy introduced here in the 8th century by the Vikings. Eventually, local fishermen grew weary of this primitive role so although the sword dance still takes place it is now performed by boys from the primary school, wearing white trousers, red caps and the traditional navy-blue jerseys.

Flamborough's parish church contains two particularly interesting monuments. One is the tomb of Sir Marmaduke Constable which shows him with his chest cut open to reveal his heart being devoured by a toad. The knight's death in 1518 had been caused, the story goes, by his swallowing the toad which had been

Flamborough Head

Danes Dyke, Flamborough

Just to the north of Flamborough is Danes Dyke, a huge rampart four miles long designed to cut off the headland from hostile invaders. The Danes had nothing to do with it, the dyke was in place long before they arrived. Sometime during the Bronze or Stone Age, early Britons constructed this extraordinary defensive ditch. A mile and a quarter of its southern length is open to the public as a Nature Trail.

drowsing in Sir Marmaduke's lunchtime pint of ale. The creature then devoured his heart. The other notable monument is a statue of St Oswald, patron saint of fishermen. This fishing connection is renewed every year, on the second Sunday in October, by a service dedicated to the **Harvest of the Sea,** when the area's seafarers gather together in a church decorated with crab pots and fishing nets.

Flamborough Head's first, and England's oldest surviving lighthouse, is the octagonal chalk tower on the landward side of the present lighthouse. Built in 1674, its beacon was a basket of burning coal. The lighthouse that is still in use was built in 1806. Originally signalling four white flashes, developments over the years have included a fog horn in 1859 and, in more recent years, a signal of radio bleeps. Until it was automated in 1995, it was the last manned lighthouse on the east coast.

BEMPTON

3 miles N of Bridlington on the B1229

Bempton Cliffs, 400 feet high, mark the northernmost tip of the great belt of chalk that runs diagonally across England from the Isle of Wight to Flamborough Head. The sheer cliffs at Bempton provide an ideal nesting place for huge colonies of fulmars, guillemots, puffins and Britain's largest seabird, the gannet, with a wingspan six feet wide. In Victorian times, a popular holiday sport was to shoot the birds from boats. Above them, crowds gathered to watch gangs of 'climmers' make a hair-raising descent by rope down the cliffs to gather the birds' eggs. Most were sold for food, but many went to egg collectors. The climmers also massacred kittiwakes in their thousands: kittiwake feathers were highly prized as accessories for hats and for stuffing mattresses. The first Bird

83   RSPB'S BEMPTON CLIFFS NATURE RESERVE

Bempton Cliffs
Part of England's largest seabird colony, visitors can watch the birds here, among which are puffins and gannets

🏛 *see page 246*

Protection Act of 1869 was specifically designed to protect the kittiwakes at Bempton. A ban on collecting eggs here didn't come into force until 1954. Bempton Cliffs are now an RSPB bird sanctuary, a refuge during the April to August breeding season for more than 200,000 seabirds making this the largest colony in England. The RSPB provides safe viewpoints allowing close-up watching and there's also a visitor centre, shop and refreshments.

BARMSTON

5 miles S of Bridlington off the A165

The road leading from Barmston village to the sands is just over half a mile long: in Viking times it stretched twice as far. The whole of this coast is being eroded at an average rate of three inches every year, and as much as three feet a year in the most vulnerable locations. Fortunately, that still leaves plenty of time to visit Barmston's village pub before it tumbles into the sea!

CARNABY

2 miles SW of Bridlington on the A614

Leaving Bridlington on the A166 will shortly bring you to **John Bull – World of Rock** which has become a premier tourist attraction in this part of East Yorkshire and really is a great day out. Whether you are young or old, you will be fascinated as you discover the history and delights of rock making. The older generation will particularly revel in the smell of the old-fashioned way of making toffee and the interesting bygone displays. Animation and taped conversation accompany you as you explore the establishment which is described as a total sensory experience. You can even try your hand at making a personalised stick of rock.

BURTON AGNES

5 miles SW of Bridlington on the A166

The overwhelming attraction in this unspoilt village is the sublime Elizabethan mansion, Burton Agnes Hall, but visitors should not ignore **Burton Agnes Manor House** (English Heritage), a rare example of a Norman house: a building of great historical importance but burdened with a grimly functional architecture, almost 800 years old, that chills one's soul. As Lloyd Grossman might say, 'How could anyone live in a house like this?'

Burton Agnes Hall is much more appealing. An outstanding Elizabethan house, built between 1598 and 1610 and little altered, Burton Agnes is particularly famous for its splendid Jacobean

Burton Agnes Hall

gatehouse, wondrously decorated ceilings and overmantels carved in oak, plaster and alabaster. It also has a valuable collection of paintings and furniture from between the 17th and 19th centuries – including a portrait of Oliver Cromwell 'warts and all' – and a large collection of Impressionist paintings. The gardens are extensive with more than 2,000 plants, a maze and giant board games in the Coloured Gardens. Other visitor facilities include an ice cream parlour, a dried-flower and herb shop, a children's animal corner, and an artists' studio. A very popular addition is the plant sales where numerous uncommon varieties can be obtained. The Impressionist Café, open throughout the Hall's season, seats 64 inside and, in good weather, 56 outside. Non-smoking, but licensed and offering only the very best in home cooking, the café serves some particularly delicious scones.

HARPHAM

4½ miles NE of Great Driffield off the A614

To the south of this village, where the manor once stood, lies Drummers Well, which gained its interesting name during the 14th century. Then, the Lord of the Manor, in the midst of holding an archery day, accidentally pushed his drummer boy into the well, where he subsequently drowned. The boy's mother, who was also the local wise woman, on hearing the news proclaimed that from then on the sound of drumming from the

well would precede the death of any member of the lord's family.

RUDSTON

8 miles NE of Great Driffield on the B1253

This village takes its name from the giant Monolith or 'rood stone' which stands in the village churchyard. At some 26 feet high, it is reputed to be the tallest in Britain, and local legends say that the monolith was a hugh gritstone spear thrown by the Devil, who was angered when a church was built on what was a sacred pagan site. However, it is far more likely that the giant stone was dragged here from Cayton Bay, some 10 miles away, or that it may be a relic from the Ice Age.

FOSTON ON THE WOLDS

7 miles SW of Bridlington off the B1249 or A165

If you can't tell a Gloucester Old Spot from a Saddleback, or a Belted Galloway from a Belgian Blue, then take a trip to **Cruckley Animal Farm** where all will become clear. This working farm supports many different varieties of cattle, sheep, pigs, poultry and horses. Some of the animals are endangered – Greyfaced Dartmoor and Whitefaced Woodland Sheep, for example, and the farm also safeguards all seven breeds of rare British pigs.

The farm has been approved by the Rare Breeds Survival Trust since 1994 and is the only farm in East Yorkshire to achieve this accolade. Enormously popular with children, this 60-acre working

84   THE CHESTNUT HORSE

Great Kelk

Excellent food and ales at hidden gem found in picturesque hamlet off the A165 or A614.

see page 248

85 THE BUCK HOTEL

Driffield

Large and attractive inn in the centre of Driffield. Great lunches, range of drinks and comfortable accommodation.

 see page 248

86 THE BELL IN DRIFFIELD

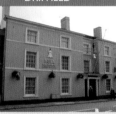

Driffield

Outstanding inn with luxury accommodation, first-class food and superb amenities including gym, sauna, pool, saunarium and more.

 see page 249

87 THE BAY HORSE INN

Kilham

Impressive inn with a good range of drinks, weekend meals and first-class service and hospitality, just a few miles from Driffield.

 see page 248

farm is home to more than 50 varieties of farm animals. There are daily milking demonstrations, seasonal events such as sheep-clipping and harvesting, and a children's paddock with hand-reared small animals where the undoubted star is Cecil the Vietnamese pot-bellied pig. Cruckley Farm is open daily from the end of April until early October and is clearly signposted.

GREAT DRIFFIELD

Located on the edge of the Wolds, Great Driffield is a busy little market town at the heart of an important corn growing area. A cattle market is held here every Thursday; a general market on both Thursday and Saturday, and the annual agricultural show has been going strong since 1854. All Saints Parish Church, dating back to the 12th century, has one of the highest towers in the county and some lovely stained glass windows portraying local nobility.

Great Driffield was once the capital of the Saxon Kingdom of Dear, a vast domain extending over the whole of Northumbria and Yorkshire. It was a King of Dear who, for administrative convenience, divided the southern part of his realm into three parts, 'thriddings', a word which gradually evolved into the famous 'Ridings' of Yorkshire.

Driffield has expanded westwards to meet up with its smaller neighbour, Little Driffield.

A tablet in the church here claims that, in the Saxon monastery that stood on this site, Aldred, King of Northumbria was buried in AD 705 after being wounded in a battle against the Danes.

AROUND GREAT DRIFFIELD

KIRKBURN

3 miles SW of Driffield on the A614

The architectural guru Nikolaus Pevsner considered **St Mary's Church** in Kirkburn to be one of the two best Norman parish churches in the East Riding. Dating from 1119, the church has an unusual tower staircase, a richly carved and decorated Victorian screen, and a spectacular early Norman font covered with carved symbolic figures.

SLEDMERE

7 miles NW of Driffield on the B1252/B1253

Sledmere House is a noble Georgian mansion built by the Sykes family in the 1750s when this area was still a wilderness infested with packs of marauding wolves. Inside, there is fine furniture by Chippendale and Sheraton, and decorated plasterwork by Joseph Rose. The copy of a naked, and well-endowed, Apollo Belvedere in the landing alcove must have caused many a maidenly blush in Victorian times, and the Turkish Room – inspired by the Sultan's salon in Istanbul's Valideh Mosque – is a dazzling example of oriental opulence. Outside, the gardens and the 220 acres of parkland were landscaped by Capability Brown.

The Sykes family set a shining example to other landowners in the Wolds by agricultural improvements that transformed a 'blank and barren tract of land' into one of the most productive and best cultivated districts in the county. They founded the famous Sledmere Stud, and the second Sir Tatton Sykes spent nearly two million pounds on building and restoring churches in the area. Sledmere House itself was ravaged by fire in 1911. Sir Tatton was enjoying his favourite lunchtime dessert of rice pudding when a servant rushed in with news of the fire and urged him to leave the house. 'First, I must finish my pudding, finish my pudding,' he declared, and did so. An armchair was set up for him on the lawn and Sir Tatton, then 85 years old, 'followed the progress of the conflagration' as the household staff laboured to rescue the house's many treasures. After the fire, Sledmere was quickly restored and the Sykes family is still in residence. The house is open to the public and music lovers should make sure they visit between 2 and 4 p.m. when the enormous pipe organ is being played.

Across the road from Sledmere House are two remarkable, elaborately detailed, monuments. The **Eleanor Cross** – modelled on those set up by Edward I in memory of his Queen, was erected by Sir Tatton Sykes in 1900; the **Wagoners Memorial** designed by Sir Mark Sykes, commemorates the

1,000-strong company of men he raised from the Wolds during the First World War. Their knowledge of horses was invaluable in their role as members of the Army Service Corps. The finely-carved monument is like a 'storyboard', its panels depicting the Wagoners' varied duties during the war. In the main house itself, a recently re-designed exhibit tells the story of the Wagoners Special Reserve through old photographs, memorabilia and some of the medals they were awarded.

WEST LUTTON
10 miles NW of Driffield off the A64 or B1253

West Lutton church is yet another of the many repaired or restored by Sir Tatton Sykes in this corner of the East Riding. It stands overlooking the village green and pond, its lych gate reached by a tiny bridge.

WHARRAM PERCY
11 miles W of Driffield off the B1248

A minor road off the B1248 leads to one of the most haunting sights in the county – the deserted medieval village of **Wharram Percy** (English Heritage; free). There had been a settlement here for some 5,000 years but by the late 1400s the village stood abandoned. For a while the church continued to serve the surrounding hamlets but in time, that too became a ruin. The manor house of the Percy family who gave the village its name, peasant houses dating back to the 13th century, a corn mill, a

88   THE WOLD COTTAGE

Wold Newton, Driffield

Outstanding country house accommodation set in 300 acres of farmland and surrounding woodland – the perfect tranquil retreat.

see *page 250*

Wharram Percy

POCKLINGTON

14 miles SW of Great Driffield
off the A1079

Set amidst rich agricultural land with the Wolds rising to the east, Pocklington is a lively market town with an unusual layout of twisting alleys running off the marketplace. Its splendid church, mostly 15th century but with fragments of an earlier Norman building, certainly justifies its title as the Cathedral of the Wolds (although strictly speaking Pocklington is just outside the Wolds). William Wilberforce went to the old grammar school here and, a more dubious claim to fame, the last burning of a witch in England took place in Pocklington in 1630.

Founded in Anglo-Saxon times by 'Pocela's people', by the time the *Domesday Book* was compiled Pocklington was recorded as one of the only two boroughs in the East Riding. A market followed in the 13th century, but it was the building in 1815 of a canal linking the town to the River Ouse, and the later arrival of the railway, that set the seal on the town's prosperity.

A popular and unusual attraction in Pocklington is the **Penny Arcadia** housed in the Ritz Cinema in the marketplace. 'Not so much a museum as a fun palace,' it contains a wonderful collection of penny-in-the-slot amusement machines ranging from 'What the Butler Saw' to fortune-telling and pinball machines.

•

The pretty village of Warter, about four miles south of Huggate, is where the 'oldest horse race in the world' has its winning post. The post is inscribed with the date 1519, the year in which the Kipling Cotes Derby was first run. This demanding steeple chase which passes through several parishes is still held annually on the third Thursday in March.

•

---

cemetery complete with exposed skeletons – these sad memorials of a once thriving community stand windswept and desolate. Until fairly recently it was assumed that the villagers had been driven from their homes by the plague but scholars are now certain that the cause was simple economics: the lords of the manor, the Percys, turned their lands from labour-intensive crop cultivation to sheep farming which needed only a handful of shepherds. Unable to find work, the villagers drifted elsewhere.

HUGGATE

10 miles W of Great Driffield off
the B1246 or B1248

Huggate is tucked away deep in the heart of the Wolds with two long-distance walks, the Minster Way and the Wolds Way, skirting it to the north and south. The village clusters around a large green with a well which is claimed to be the deepest in England.

The people of Pocklington have good reason to be grateful to Major P. M. Stewart who, on his death in 1962, bequeathed **Burnby Hall and Gardens** to the town. The eight acres of gardens are world-famous for the rare collection of water-lilies planted in the two large lakes. There are some 50 varieties and in the main flowering season from July to early September they present a dazzling spectacle. The Major and his wife had travelled extensively before settling down at Burnby and there's a small museum in the Hall displaying his collection of sporting trophies.

A mile outside the town is **Kilnwick Percy Hall**, a magnificent Georgian mansion of 1784 built for the Lord of the Manor of Pocklington. It now houses the Madhyamaka Centre, the largest Buddhist settlement in the western world. Visitors can stay in converted stables at the Hall, either to take part in one of the residential courses or to use as a base for exploring the area. There's a modest charge for full board; smoking and drinking alcohol are not allowed.

A few miles to the south of Pocklington is **Londesborough Park,** a 400-acre estate which was once owned by the legendary railway entrepreneur, George Hudson. He had the York to Market Weighton railway diverted here so that he could build himself a comfortable private station. The railway has now disappeared but part of its route is included in the popular long-distance footpath, the Wolds Way.

NUNBURNHOLME

13 miles SW of Great Driffield off the A1079

Named after the Benedictine nuns who first settled here, the village church in the village is well worth a visit as just inside is a 1,000-year-old Saxon cross elaborately carved with arches, animals and representations of the Madonna. It was also here that the famous ornithologist the Reverend Francis Orpen Morris was born. Heavily influenced by the 18th-century naturalist Gilbert White, Morris penned the multi-volumed *History of British Birds*.

GOODMANHAM

14 miles SW of Driffield off the A1079

Goodmanham is always mentioned in accounts of early Christianity in northern England. During Saxon times, according to the Venerable Bede, there was a pagan temple at Goodmanham. In AD 627 its priest, Coifu, was converted to the Christian faith and with his own hands destroyed the heathen shrine. Coifu's conversion so impressed Edwin, King of Northumbria, that he also was baptised and made Christianity the official religion of his kingdom. Other versions of the story attribute King Edwin's conversion to a different cause. They say he was hopelessly enamoured of the beautiful Princess Aethelburh, daughter of the King of Kent. Aethelburh, however, was a Christian and she refused to marry Edwin until he had adopted her faith.

89 THE GAIT INN

Millington, York

Picturesque 16th-century inn in a delightful village setting. Real ales, home-cooked food lunchtimes (Sat-Sun) and evenings (Tues-Sun).

see page 250

90 THE WINDMILL INN

Beverley

Welcoming inn serving all-day drinks, home-made dishes (lunch only) and superb accommodation in late 17th-century buildings close to the Minster.

 see page 251

91 THE CORNER HOUSE

Beverley

Eight real ales and an outstanding selection of traditional and innovative meals expertly prepared and presented.

 see page 251

●

From Beverley, serious walkers might care to follow some or all of the 15 mile Hudson Way, a level route that follows the track of the old railway from Beverley to Market Weighton. The Hudson Way wanders through the Wolds, sometimes deep in a cutting, sometimes high on an embankment, past an old windmill near Etton and through eerily abandoned stations.

●

MARKET WEIGHTON

16 miles SW of Driffield on the A614/A1069

Market Weighton is a busy little town where mellow 18th-century houses cluster around an early Norman church. Buried somewhere in the churchyard is William Bradley who was born at Market Weighton in 1787 and grew up to become the tallest man in England. He stood 7 feet 8 inches high and weighed 27 stones. William made a fortune by travelling the country and placing himself on display. He was even received at Court by George III who, taking a fancy to the giant, gave him a huge gold watch to wear across his chest.

SOUTH DALTON

13 miles SW of Driffield off the B1248

The most prominent church in East Yorkshire, **St Mary's Church**, has a soaring spire more than 200 feet high, an unmistakable landmark for miles around. Built in 1861 by Lord Beaumont Hotham, the church was designed by the famous Victorian architect JL Pearson and the elaborate internal and external decorations are well worth looking at.

BEVERLEY

13 miles S of Driffield on the A1035

'For those who do not know this town, there is a great surprise in store ... Beverley is made for walking and living in.' Such was the considered opinion of the late Poet Laureate, John Betjeman. In medieval times, Beverley was one of England's most prosperous towns and it remains one of the most gracious. Its greatest glory is the **Minster** whose twin towers, built in glowing magnesian limestone, soar above this, the oldest town in East Yorkshire. More than two centuries in the making, from around 1220 to 1450, the Minster provides a textbook demonstration of the evolving architectural styles of those years. Among its many treasures are a superb, fine wood carvings from the Ripon school, and a 1,000 year old *fridstol*, or sanctuary seat. Carved from a single block of stone, the fridstol is a relic from the earlier Saxon church on this site. Under Saxon law, the fridstol provided refuge for any offender who managed to reach it. The canons would then try to resolve the dispute between the fugitive and his pursuer. If after 30 days no solution had been found, the seeker of sanctuary was given safe escort to the county boundary or the nearest port. The custom survived right up until Henry VIII's closure of the monasteries.

Unlike the plain-cut fridstol, the canopy of the 14th-century Percy Shrine is prodigal in its ornamentation – 'the finest piece of work of the finest craftsmen of the finest period in British building.' The behaviour of some visitors to this glorious Shrine was not, it seems, always as reverent as it might have been. When Celia Fiennes toured the Minster in 1697 she recorded that the tomb of 'Great Percy, Earle of Northumberland was a little fallen in and a hole so bigg as many put their hands in and touch'd the body which was much of it entire.' Great Percy's remains are now decently concealed once again.

As well as the incomparable stone carvings on the shrine, the Minster also has a wealth of wonderful carvings in wood. Seek out those representing Stomach Ache, Toothache, Sciatica and Lumbago – four afflictions probably almost as fearsome to medieval people as the Four Riders of the Apocalypse.

Close by is the **North Bar,** the only one of the town's five medieval gatehouses to have survived. Unlike many towns in the Middle Ages, Beverley did not have an encircling wall. Instead, the town fathers had a deep ditch excavated around it so that all goods had to pass through one of the gates and pay a toll. North Bar was built in 1409 and, with headroom of little more than 10 feet, is something of a traffic hazard, albeit a very attractive one. Next door is Bar House, in which Charles I and his sons stayed in the 1630s. Another visitor to the town, famous for very different reasons, was the highwayman Dick Turpin who, in 1739, was brought before a magistrates' hearing conducted at one of the town's inns. That inn has long since gone and its site is now occupied by the Beverley Arms.

St Mary's Church, just across the road from the Beverley Arms, tends to be overshadowed by the glories of Beverley Minster. But this is another superb medieval building, richly endowed with fine

North Bar, Beverley

carvings, many brightly coloured, and striking sculptures. A series of ceiling panels depicts all the Kings of England from Sigebert (AD 623-37) to Henry VI. Originally, four legendary kings were also included, but one of them was replaced in recent times by a portrait of George VI. Lewis Carroll visited St Mary's when he stayed with friends in the town and was very taken with a stone carving of a rabbit – the inspiration, it is

137

92 CROWN & ANCHOR

Tickton, Beverley

Outstanding riverside public house and restaurant found just northeast of Beverley off the A1035.

see page 251

believed, for the March Hare in *Alice in Wonderland*. Certainly the carving bears an uncanny resemblance to Tenniel's famous drawing of the Mad Hatter.

The wide market square in the heart of the town is graced by an elegant **Market Cross,** a circular pillared building rather like a small Greek temple. It bears the arms of Queen Anne in whose reign it was built at the expense of the town's two Members of Parliament. At that time of course parliamentary elections were flagrantly corrupt

but at Beverley the tradition continued longer than in most places – in 1868 the author Anthony Trollope stood as a candidate here but was defeated in what was acknowledged as a breathtakingly fraudulent election.

The Guildhall nearby was built in 1762 and is still used as a courtroom. The impressive courtroom has an ornate plasterwork ceiling on which there is an imposing Royal Coat of Arms and also the familiar figure of Justice holding a pair of scales. Unusually, she is not wearing a blindfold. When an 18th-century town clerk was asked the reason for this departure from tradition, he replied, 'In Beverley, Justice is not blind.'

Just around the corner from the Guildhall was one of the oldest working cinemas in the country. The **Picture Playhouse** was built in 1866 and an inscription on its pediment still advertises its original function as the town's Corn Exchange.

Beverley boasts two separate museums and galleries. The **Beverley Art Gallery** contains an impressive collection of local works including those by Frederick Elwell RA and the **East Yorkshire Regimental Museum** has six rooms of exhibits chronicling the area's long association with the regiment.

SKIDBY

16 miles S of Driffield off the A164

In the 1800s more than 200 windmills were scattered across the Wolds. Today, **Skidby Mill** is the

Skidby Mill

138

only one still grinding grain and producing its own wholemeal flour. Built in 1821, it has three pairs of millstones powered by four 12-metre sails, each weighing more than 1.25 tonnes. Weather permitting, the mill is working every weekend, Bank Holidays and, during the school summer holidays, Wednesday to Sunday.

At the same location is the **Museum of East Riding Rural Life** where the farming year is chronicled using historic implements and fascinating photographs. The displays feature the Thompson family, who owned Skidby Mill for more than a century, and other local characters.

HOLDERNESS

Lordings, there is in Yorkshire, as I guess
A marshy country called Holdernesse.

With these words Chaucer begins the Summoner's story in the *Canterbury Tales*. It's not surprising that this area was then largely marshland since most of the land lies at less than 10 metres above sea level. The name Holderness comes from Viking times: a 'hold' was a man of high rank in the Danelaw, 'ness' has stayed in the language with its meaning of promontory. The precise boundaries of the Land of Holderness are clear enough to the east where it runs to the coast, and to the south where Holderness ends with Yorkshire itself at Spurn Point. They are less well-defined to the north

and west where they run somewhere close to the great crescent of the Wolds. For the purposes of this book, we have taken as the northern limit of Holderness the village of Skipsea, where, as you'll discover in the next entry, some early Norman Lords of Holderness showed a remarkable lack of loyalty to their King.

HORNSEA

14 miles NE of Hull on the B1242/B1244

This small coastal town can boast not only one of the most popular visitor attraction in Humberside, **Freeport Hornsea**, but also Yorkshire's largest freshwater lake, Hornsea Mere. **Hornsea Mere**, two miles long and one mile wide, provides a refuge for over 170 species of birds and a peaceful setting for many varieties of rare flowers. Human visitors are well provided for, too, with facilities for fishing, boating and sailing. Hornsea is also the home of the excellent sands, a church built with cobbles gathered from the shore, well-tended public gardens and a breezy, mile-long promenade all adding to the town's popularity.

The excellent **Hornsea Museum**, established in 1978, is a folk museum that has won numerous national awards over the years as well as being featured several times on television. The museum occupies a Grade II listed building, a former farmhouse where successive generations of the Burn family lived for 300 years up until 1952. Their way of life, the

93 ROWLEY MANOR COUNTRY HOUSE HOTEL

Little Weighton, nr Hull

Magnificent Grade II listed manor house set in 5½ acres of grounds and offering every luxury amid a relaxed and friendly atmosphere.

see page 252

139

94 THE ROSE AND CROWN

Hornsea

Attractive and welcoming pub just a short stroll from the beach at Hornsea.

 see page 253

95 THE MARINE HOTEL

Hornsea

Spacious and welcoming seafront hotel, open every day for ales and food with five comfortable ensuite guest bedrooms.

 see page 254

96 SAL'S CAFÉ AND STEAK HOUSE

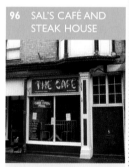

Hornsea

Friendly establishment open daily for breakfast right through to evening, with a menu of steaks and much more.

 see page 254

personalities and characters who influenced the development of the town or found fame in other ways, are explored in meticulously restored rooms brimming with furniture, decorations, utensils and tools of the Victorian period. The kitchen, parlour and bedroom have fascinating displays of authentic contemporary artefacts, and the museum complex also includes a laundry, workshop, blacksmith's shop and a barn stocked with vintage agricultural implements.

In Swallow Cottage next door, children can undergo the Victorian school experience under the tutelage of 'Miss Grim' – writing on slates, having good deportment instilled and, above all, observing the maxim 'Silence is Golden.' The cottage also houses a comprehensive and varied display of early Hornsea pottery, various temporary exhibitions, and, in summer, a refreshment room for visitors. Remarkably, this outstanding museum is staffed entirely by volunteers.

For a satisfying shop-till-you-drop experience, **Hornsea Freeport** – the 'Independent State of Low Prices' – is hard to beat. There are discounts of up to 50 per cent or more on everything from designerwear, childrenswear and sportswear to chinaware, kitchenware and glassware. There are themed leisure attractions and bright, fun-filled play areas to keep the children amused.

Butterfly World is home to more than 200 species of colourful butterflies.

AROUND HORNSEA

ATWICK

2 miles NW of Hornsea on the B1242

Like Hornsea, Atwick once had its own mere. Some years ago, excavations in its dried-up bed revealed fossilised remains of a huge Irish elk and the tusk of an ancient elephant, clear proof of the tropical climate East Yorkshire enjoyed in those far-off days. Atwick is a picturesque village on the coast, just two miles north of Hornsea. It has been a regular winner of local – and, in 1997, county – awards in the Britain in Bloom competition.

SKIPSEA

5 miles NW of Hornsea on the B1242

When William the Conqueror granted Drogo de Bevrere the Lordship of Holderness, Drogo decided to raise his **Castle** on an island in the shallow lake known as Skipsea Mere. Built mostly of timber, the castle had not long been completed when Drogo made the foolish mistake of murdering his wife. In the normal course of events, a Norman lord could murder whomever he wished, but Drogo's action was foolish because his wife was a kinswoman of the Conqueror himself. Drogo was banished and his lands granted to a succession of other royal relatives, most of whom also came to a sticky end after becoming involved in rebellions and treasonable acts. The castle was finally abandoned in the mid-13th century and all that remains now is the great motte, or mound, on which it was built and the earth ramparts surrounding it.

WEST NEWTON

5 miles.S of Hornsea off the B1238

Just outside the village of West Newton is **Burton Constable Hall,** named after Sir John Constable who in 1570 built a stately mansion here which incorporated parts of an even older house, dating back to the reign of King Stephen in the 1100s. The Hall was again remodelled, on Jacobean lines, in the 18th century and contains some fine work by Chippendale, Adam and James Wyatt. In the famous Long Gallery with its 15th-century Flemish stained glass, hangs a remarkable collection of paintings, among them Holbein's portraits of Sir Thomas Cranmer and Sir Thomas More, and Zucchero's Mary, Queen of Scots. Dragons abound in the dazzling Chinese Room, an exercise in oriental exotica that long pre-dates the Prince Regent's similar extravaganza at the Brighton Pavilion. Thomas Chippendale himself designed the fantastical Dragon Chair, fit for a Ming Emperor. Outside, there are extensive parklands designed by Capability Brown, and apparently inspired by the gardens at Versailles. Perhaps it was this connection that motivated the Constable family to suggest loaning the Hall to Louis XVIII of

Skipsea Castle

France during his years of exile after the Revolution. (Louis politely declined the offer, preferring to settle rather closer to London, at Hartwell in Buckinghamshire.) Also in the grounds of the Hall are collections of agricultural machinery, horse-drawn carriages and 18th-century scientific apparatus.

The descendants of the Constable family still bear the title 'Lords of Holderness' and along with it the rights to any flotsam and jetsam washed ashore on the Holderness peninsula. Many years ago, when the late Brigadier Chichester Constable was congratulated on enjoying such a privilege, he retorted, 'I also have to pay for burying, or otherwise disposing of, any whale grounded on the Holderness shore – and it costs me about £20 a time!' The huge bones of one such whale are still on show in the grounds of the Hall.

97 THOMPSON'S TRADITIONAL FISH & CHIPS

Brandesburton, Driffield

Licensed restaurant and takeaway of delicious and fresh fish and traditional meals. New addition to established branch at Wetwang.

see page 255

141

98 WITHERNSEA LIGHTHOUSE

Withernsea

Stunning views can be found at the top of this 120ft lighthouse, built in the late 19th century.

  see page 256

99 THE HOLDERNESS INN

Patrington

Relaxed atmosphere, great food and drink in large and welcoming inn near the coast.

  see page 256

WITHERNSEA

The next place of interest down the Holderness coast is Withernsea. Long, golden sandy beaches stretch for miles both north and south, albeit a mile further inland than they were in the days of William the Conqueror. The old **Lighthouse** is a striking feature of the town and those energetic enough to climb the 127-ft tower are rewarded by some marvellous views from the lamp room. The lighthouse was decommissioned in 1976 and now houses two small museums. One is dedicated to the history of the Royal National Lifeboat Institution; the other to the actress Kay Kendall. Her grandfather helped build the lighthouse in 1892 and was the last coxswain of the deep sea lifeboat. Kay was born in Withernsea and later achieved great success in the London theatre as a sophisticated comedienne but she is probably best remembered for the rousing trumpet solo she delivered in the Ealing Studios hit film *Genevieve*.

South of Withernsea stretches a desolate spit of flat windswept dunes. This is **Spurn Point** which leads to Spurn Head, the narrow hook of ever-shifting sands that curls around the mouth of the Humber estuary. This bleak but curiously invigorating tag end of Yorkshire is nevertheless heavily populated – by hundreds of species of rare and solitary wild fowl, by playful seals, and also by the small contingent of lifeboatmen who operate the only permanently

manned lifeboat station in Britain. Please note that a toll is payable beyond the village of Kilnsea, and there is no car park. Access to Spurn Head is only on foot.

AROUND WITHERNSEA

HALSHAM

4 miles W of Withernsea off the B1362

Halsham was once the seat of the Constable family, Lords of Holderness, before they moved to their new mansion at Burton Constable. On the edge of Halsham village, they left behind their imposing, domed mausoleum built in the late 1700s to house ancestors going back to the 12th century. The mausoleum is not open to the public but is clearly visible from the B1362 Hull to Withernsea road.

PATRINGTON

4 miles SW of Withernsea on the A1033

Shortly after it was built, **St Patrick's Church** at Patrington was dubbed 'Queen of Holderness', and Queen it remains. This sublime church took more than 100 years to build, from around 1310 to 1420, and it is one of the most glorious examples of the eye-pleasing style known as English Decorated. Its spire soars almost 180 feet into the sky making it the most distinctive feature in the flat plains of Holderness. St Patrick's has the presence and proportions of a cathedral although only enjoying the status of a parish church. A parish church,

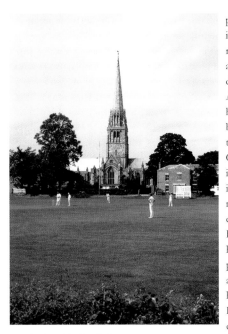

St Patrick's Church, Patrington

place every Wednesday in the square with its row of Georgian shops and early 19th-century dwellings. Nearby, in St Augustine's Gate, is the handsome Town Hall, built in 1692. From time to time, the town's Civic Silver Collection is on display here. It includes the oldest civic mace in the country, dating back to 1415. Hedon Museum (free) has displays of maps, photographs and artefacts relating to the history of Hedon and Holderness; these are changed regularly. Limited opening times.

PAULL
12 miles W of Withernsea off the A1033

Fort Paull's role as a frontier landing and watch point goes back to at least Viking times. Henry VIII built a fortress here in the mid-1500s; a second fort was added at the time of the Napoleonic wars. Charles I based himself at Fort Paull for some time during the Civil War; Winston Churchill visited its anti-aircraft installations during the Second World War.

Today, the spacious 10-acre site offers a wide variety of attractions for all the family. In addition to the historical displays, including rare period and contemporary artillery, there are classic military vehicles, an array of waxwork creations, a

nevertheless, which experts consider among the finest dozen churches in Britain for architectural beauty. Patrington's parish council go further: a notice displayed inside St Patrick's states unequivocally, 'This is England's finest village Church.' Clustering around it, picturesque Dutch-style cottages complete an entrancing picture and just to the east of the village the Dutch theme continues in a fine old windmill.

HEDON
10 miles W of Withernsea off the A1033

Founded around AD 1130 by William le Gros, Lord of Holderness, Hedon quickly became a port and market town of great importance. Its market still takes

100 THE BURNS HEAD INN

Patrington Haven

Excellent pub with home-made food just a few miles from the Humber and Spurn Head.

see page 257

101 COACH AND HORSES

Welwick

Charming inn with delicious home-cooked food and one delightful guest room, close to Spurn Head.

see page 257

parade ground where re-enactments take place, an assault course for youngsters, a Bird of Prey Centre, museum, gift shop, bar and restaurant. The fort is open seven days a week, all year.

SELBY

In 1069 a young monk named Benedict, from Auxerre in France, had a vision. It's not known exactly what the vision was but it inspired him to set sail for York. As his ship was sailing up the Ouse near Selby, three swans flew in formation across its bows. (Three swans, incidentally, still form part of the town's coat of arms.) Interpreting this as a sign of the Holy Trinity, Benedict promptly went ashore and set up a preaching cross under a great oak called the Stirhac. The small religious community he established went from strength to strength, acquiring many grants of land and, in 1100, permission to build a monastery. Over the course of the next 120 years, the great **Selby Abbey** slowly took shape, the massively heavy Norman style of the earlier building gradually modulating into the much more delicate early English style. All of the Abbey was built using a lovely cream-coloured stone.

Over the centuries this sublime church has suffered more than most. During the Civil War it was severely damaged by Cromwell's troops who destroyed many of its statues and smashed much of its stained glass. Then in 1690 the central tower collapsed. For years after that the Abbey was neglected and by the middle of the 18th century a wall had been built across the chancel so that the nave could be used as a warehouse. That wall was removed during a major restoration during the 19th century but in 1906 there was another calamity when a disastrous fire swept through the Abbey. Visiting this serene and peaceful church today it's difficult to believe that it has endured so many misfortunes and yet remains so

Selby Abbey

144

beautiful. Throughout all the Abbey's misfortunes one particular feature survived intact – the famous Washington Window which depicts the coat of arms of John de Washington, Prior of the Abbey around 1415 and a direct ancestor of George Washington. Prominently displayed in this heraldic device is the stars and stripes motif later adapted for the national flag of the United States. Guided tours of the cathedral are available.

Devotees of railway history will want to pay their respects to Selby's old railway station. Built at the incredibly early date of 1834 it is the oldest surviving station in Britain. From Selby the railway track runs straight as a ruler for 18 miles to Hull – the longest such stretch in Britain.

AROUND SELBY

RICCALL

4 miles N of Selby on the A19

The ancient village of Riccall was mentioned in the *Domesday Book* and has a church that was built not long after. The south doorway of the church dates back to about 1160 and its fine details have been well-preserved by a porch added in the 15th century. The village's great moment in history came in 1066 when the gigantic King Harold Hardrada of Norway and Earl Tostig sailed this far up the Ouse with some 300 ships. They had come to claim Northumbria from Tostig's half-brother King Harold of England but they were comprehensively defeated at the

Battle of Stamford Bridge.

Riccall is popular with walkers: from the village you can either go southwards alongside the River Ouse to Selby, or strike northwards towards Bishopthorpe on the outskirts of York following the track of the dismantled York to Selby railway. This latter path is part of the 150-mile-long Trans Pennine Trail linking Liverpool and Hull.

Just to the south of Skipwith, the Yorkshire Wildlife Trust maintains the **Skipwith Common Nature Reserve.** This 500 acres of lowland heath is one of the last such areas remaining in the north of England and is of national importance. The principal interest is the variety of insect and birdlife, but the reserve also contains a number of ancient burial sites.

SOUTH MILFORD

9 miles W of Selby off the A162

About nine miles west of Selby, near the village of South Milford, is the imposing 14th-century **Steeton Hall Gatehouse**, all that remains of a medieval castle once owned by the Fairfax family. A forebear of the famous Cromwellian general is said to have ridden out from here on his way to carry off one of the nuns at Nun Appleton Priory to make her his bride. He was Sir William Fairfax; she was Isabel Thwaites, a wealthy heiress.

SHERBURN-IN-ELMET

10 miles W of Selby on the A162

This attractive village was once the capital of the Celtic Kingdom of Elmete. Well worth visiting is **All**

About three miles northeast of Carlton is the village of Drax which, as well as providing Ian Fleming with a sinister-sounding name for one of the villains in his James Bond thrillers, also provides the National Grid with 10 per cent of all the electricity used in England and Wales. The largest coal-fired power station in Europe, Drax's vast cooling towers dominate the low-lying ground between the rivers Ouse and Aire. Drax power station has found an unusual way of harnessing its waste heat by channelling some of it to a huge complex of glasshouses covering 20 acres; part of the heat goes to specially constructed ponds in which young eels are bred for the export market. Guided tours of the power station are available by prior arrangement.

105 THE PLOUGH INN

Snaith

Spacious, tidy inn with food, drink and accommodation a few miles south of Selby.

 see *page 260*

Saints' Church which stands on a hill to the west and dates from about 1120. Its great glory is the nave with its mighty Norman pillars and arcades. A curiosity here is a 15th-century Janus cross which was discovered in the churchyard during the 1770s. The vicar and churchwarden of the time both claimed it as their own. Unable to resolve their dispute, they had the cross sawn in half: the two beautifully carved segments are displayed on opposite sides of the south aisle.

WEST HADDLESEY

5 miles SW of Selby on the A19

At **Yorkshire Garden World** gardeners will find endless inspiration in its six acres of beautiful display and nursery gardens. Organically grown herbs, heathers, ornamental perennials, wild flowers and climbers are all on sale; the gift shop has a huge variety of home made crafts, herbal products, Leeds pottery and garden products; and the many different gardens include a Heather and Conifer Garden, an Aromatherapy Garden, an Open Air Herb Museum, a Lovers' Garden, and the Hall Owl Maze for children.

CARLTON

6 miles S of Selby on the A1041

A mile or so south of Camblesforth, off the A1041, is **Carlton Towers**, a stately home that should on no account be missed. This extraordinary building, 'something between the Houses of Parliament and St Pancras Station',

was created in the 1870s by two young English eccentrics, Henry, 9th Lord Beaumont, and Edward Welby Pugin, son of the eminent Victorian architect, A.G. Pugin. Together, they transformed a traditional Jacobean house into an exuberant mock medieval fantasy in stone, abounding with turrets, towers, gargoyles and heraldic shields. The richly-decorated High Victorian interior, designed in the manner of medieval banqueting halls, contains a minstrels' gallery and a vast Venetian-style drawing room. Both Beaumont and Pugin died in their forties, both bankrupt. Carlton Towers is now the Yorkshire home of the Duke of Norfolk and is open to the public during the summer months.

In Carlton village the Comus Inn is the only licensed premises in the country to bear that name. It is believed to have been named after the Greek god of sensual pleasure, Comus, the son of Bacchus.

GOOLE

10 miles SE of Selby on the A614

Britain's most inland port, some 50 miles from the sea, Goole lies at the hub of a waterways network that includes the River Ouse, the River Don (known here as the Dutch River), the River Aire and the Aire & Calder Navigation. The **Waterways Museum,** located on the dockside, tells the story of Goole's development as a canal terminus and also as a port connecting to the North Sea. The museum displays model ships and many photographs dating from

1905 to the present day, and visitors can explore an original Humber Keel, *Sobriety*, and watch crafts people at work. There are also occasional short boat trips available.

More of the town's history is in evidence at **Goole Museum & Art Gallery** which displays ship models, marine paintings and a changing programme of exhibitions. Other attractions in the town include its refurbished Victorian Market Hall, open all year Wednesday to Saturday, and a well-equipped Leisure Centre which provides a wide range of facilities for all ages.

HEMINGBROUGH

4 miles E of Selby off the A63

Anyone interested in remarkable churches should seek out **St Mary's Church** at Hemingbrough. Built in a pale rose-coloured brick, it has an extraordinarily lofty and elegant spire soaring 190 feet high and, inside, what is believed to be Britain's oldest misericord. Misericords are hinged wooden seats for the choir which could be folded back when they stood to sing. Medieval woodcarvers delighted in adorning the underside of the seat with intricate carvings. The misericord at Hemingbrough dates back to around 1200.

HOWDEN

9 miles E of Selby on the A63

Despite the fact that its chancel collapsed in 1696 and has not been used for worship ever since, **Howden Minster** is still one of

the largest parish churches in East Yorkshire and also one of its most impressive, cathedral-like in size. From the top of its soaring tower, 135 feet high, there are wonderful views of the surrounding countryside – but it's not for the faint-hearted. The ruined chapter house, lavishly decorated with a wealth of carved mouldings, has been described as one of the most exquisite small buildings in England.

When the medieval Prince-Bishops of Durham held sway over most of northern England,

 106 THE BREWERS ARMS HOTEL

Snaith

Inn with micro-brewery on the premises. Real ales, great food served 12–9 daily, accommodation.

see page 260

 107 THE VIKING HOTEL

Goole

Modern pub found off J36 of the M62. Open all day every day for tasty food and a selection of draught bitters, lagers and more.

see page 260

Howden Minster

108 THE WHITE SWAN

Bubwith, Selby

Quality inn and Indian restaurant found on the A163 east of the A19. Real ales, tasty food and a relaxed and friendly atmosphere.

 see page 261

109 THE STATION HOTEL

Howden

Spacious, well-appointed inn with real ales, home-cooked food and three excellent guest bedrooms.

 see page 261

110 THE ROYAL OAK

Portington, Howden

Destination pub for great food, adjacent to the A614 between Howden and Market Weighton. Friendly, family-run.

 see page 262

111 THE BLACK SWAN

Eastrington

Friendly family-run village pub with home-cooked food weekends and evenings, located a short drive northeast of Howden.

 see page 261

they built a palace at Howden which they used as a pied-à-terre during their semi-royal progresses and as a summer residence. The Hall of that 14th-century palace still stands, although much altered now.

Howden town is a pleasing jumble of narrow, flagged and setted streets with a picturesque stone and brick Market Hall in the marketplace. The celebrated aircraft designer Barnes Wallis knew Howden well: he lived here while working on the R100 airship which was built at Hedon airfield nearby. It made its maiden flight in 1929 and successfully crossed the Atlantic. At the nearby Breighton Aerodrome is the **Real Aeroplane Museum**, which illustrates the history of flight through the work of Yorkshire aviation pioneers.

About four miles northwest of Howden are the striking remains of **Wressle Castle**, built in 1380 for Sir Henry Percy and the only surviving example in East Yorkshire of a medieval fortified house. At the end of the Civil War, three of the castle's sides were pulled down and much of the rest was destroyed by fire in 1796. But two massive towers with walls six feet thick, the hall and kitchens remain. The castle is not open to the public but there are excellent views from the village road and from a footpath that runs alongside the River Derwent. A fine old windmill nearby provides an extra visual bonus.

HULL

During the Second World War Hull was mercilessly battered by the Luftwaffe: 7,000 of its people were killed and 92 per cent of its houses suffered bomb damage. Then in the post-war years its once huge fishing fleet steadily dwindled. But Hull has risen phoenix-like from those ashes and is today the fastest-growing port in England. The port area extends for seven miles along the Humber with 10 miles of quays servicing a constant flow of commercial traffic arriving from, or departing for, every quarter of the globe. Every day, a succession of vehicle ferries link the city to the European gateways of Zeebrugge and Rotterdam. Hull is unmistakably part of Yorkshire but it also has the freewheeling, open-minded character of a cosmopolitan port.

Hull's history as an important port goes back to 1293 when Edward I, travelling north on his way to fight the Scots, stopped off here and immediately recognised the potential of the muddy junction where the River Hull flows into the Humber. The king bought the land from the monks of Meaux Abbey (at the usual royal discount) and the settlement thenceforth was known as 'Kinges town upon Hull'.

The port grew steadily through the centuries and at one time had the largest fishing fleet of any port in the country with more than 300 trawlers on its register. The port's rather primitive facilities were greatly improved by the construction of a state-of-the-art dock in 1778. Now superseded, that dock has been converted into the handsome Queen's Gardens, one of the many attractive open spaces created by this flower-conscious city which also loves lining its streets with trees, setting up fountains here and there, and planting flower beds in any available space. And waymarked walks such as the **Maritime Heritage Trail** and the **Fish Pavement Trail** make the most of the city's dramatic waterfront.

A visit to Hull is an exhilarating experience at any time of the year but especially so in October. Back in the late 1200s the city was granted a charter to hold an autumn fair. This began as a fairly modest cattle and sheep mart but over the centuries it burgeoned into the largest gathering of its kind in Europe. Hull Fair is now a nine day extravaganza occupying a 14-acre

site and offering every imaginable variety of entertainment. That takes care of October, but Hull also hosts an Easter Festival, an International Festival (some 300 events from mid-June to late July), a Jazz on the Waterfront celebration (August), an International Sea Shanty Festival (September) and a Literature Festival in November.

Throughout the rest of the year, Hull's tourism office modestly suggests you explore its 'Marvellous Museums – Fabulous and Free' – a quite remarkable collection of eight historic houses, art galleries and museums. Perhaps the most evocative is the **Wilberforce House Museum** in the old High Street. William Wilberforce was born here in 1759 and, later, it was from here that he and his father lavished thousands of pounds in bribes to get William elected as Hull's Member of Parliament. Nothing unusual about

●

Before leaving the city of Hull, make sure you see two of its more unusual features. Firstly, visitors to Hull soon become aware of its unique public telephones. They are still the traditional, curvy-topped, heavily-barred boxes but with the distinctive difference that Hull's are all painted a gleaming white. What isn't apparent is that by some bureaucratic quirk, Hull remained the only municipally owned telephone company in Britain until it was floated on the Stock Exchange, as Kingston Communications, early in 2000. The sale brought the City Council a huge windfall. The second unusual feature of Hull: in Nelson Street you can avail yourself of award-winning loos. These spotless conveniences, complete with hanging baskets of flowers, have become a tourist attraction in their own right.

●

Hunter Dock Marina, Hull

The Deep in Hull advertises itself as the World's Only Submarium. Its huge main tank contains 2.5 million litres of water, 87 tonnes of salt – and some fearsome Sand Tiger and Leopard sharks. Visitors can walk the ocean floor in the world's deepest viewing tunnel, pilot a submarine in the futuristic research station, Deep Blue One, and ride in the underwater lift surrounded by sharks, rays, potato grouper, golden trevally, Napoleon wrasse, and hundreds of other sea creatures

that kind of corruption at the time, but William then redeemed himself by his resolute opposition to slavery. His campaign took more than 30 years and William was already on his deathbed before a reluctant Parliament finally outlawed the despicable trade. The museum presents a shaming history of the slave trade along with a more uplifting story of Wilberforce's efforts to eliminate it for ever.

Other stars of the 'Magnificent Eight' are **The Ferens Art Gallery** which houses a sumptuous collection of paintings and sculpture that ranges from European Old Masters (including some Canalettos and works by Franz Hals) to challenging contemporary art; the **Hull Maritime Museum** which celebrates seven centuries of Hull's maritime heritage and includes a fine collection of scrimshaw. A more unusual museum is the **Spurn Lightship**. Once stationed on active duty 4.5 miles east of Spurn Point, the 200-ton, 33-metre long craft is now moored in Hull's vibrant Marina. Visitors can explore the 75-year-old vessel with the help of its knowledgeable crew. The city's noisiest museum is the **Streetlife Transport Museum** which traces 200 years of transport history. Visitors are transported back to the days of horse-drawn carriages, steam trains, trams and penny-farthing cycles. There are curiosities such as the 'Velocipede', the Automobile à Vapeur (an early

steam-driven car), and Lady Chesterfield's ornamental sleigh, caparisoned with a swan, rearing unicorn and a panoply of bells to herald her approach.

AROUND HULL

HESSLE

5 miles W of Hull off the A63

At Hessle the River Humber narrows and it was here that the Romans maintained a ferry, the *Transitus Maximus*, a vital link in the route between Lincoln and York. The ferry remained in operation for almost 2000 years until it was replaced in 1981 by the **Humber Bridge** whose mighty pylons soar more than 500 feet above the village.

It is undoubtedly one of the most impressive bridges on earth, and also one of the least used – someone described it as the least likely place in Britain to find a traffic jam. With an overall length of 2,428 yards (2,220m), it is one of the world's longest single-span bridges. For more than a third of a mile only four concrete pillars, two at each end, are saving you from a watery death. From these huge pylons, 510 feet (155m) high, gossamer cables of thin-wired steel support a gently curving roadway. Both sets of pylons rise vertically, but because of the curvature of the earth they actually lean away from each other by several inches. The bridge is particularly striking at night when the vast structure is floodlit.

The great bridge dwarfs Cliff

Mill, built in 1810 to mill the local chalk. It remained wind-driven until 1925 when a gas engine was installed. Although it is no longer working, the mill provides a scenic feature within the **Humber Bridge Country Park**. This well laid out park gives visitors a true back-to-nature tour a short distance from one of modern man's greatest feats of engineering. The former chalk quarry has been attractively landscaped, providing a nature trail, extensive walks through woodlands and meadows, picnic and play areas, and picturesque water features.

WELTON

10 miles W of Hull off the A63

A little further south is the pretty village of Welton where a stream flows past the green, under bridges and into a tree-encircled duck pond. It has a church dating from Norman times which boasts a striking 13th-century doorway and Pre-Raphaelite windows made by William Morris' company of craftsmen. In the graveyard stands a memorial to Jeremiah Found, a resilient local reputed to have outlived eight wives.

The notorious highwayman Dick Turpin was not a local but his villainous, if romantic, career came to an end at Welton village when he was apprehended inside the Green Dragon Inn. Local legend has it that this establishment gave him hospitality before he was taken off to the magistrates at Beverley who committed him to the Assizes at York where he was found guilty and hanged in 1739.

BRANTINGHAM

11 miles W of Hull off the A63

The village of Brantingham, just off the A63, is worth a short diversion to see its remarkable **War Memorial,** once described as 'lovingly awful'. Conceived on a monumental scale, the memorial was built using masonry recycled from Hull's old Guildhall when that was being reconstructed in 1914. Various stone urns placed around the village came from the same source.

NORTH FERRIBY

18 miles SE of Pocklington on the B1231

It was here, in 1946, that some late Bronze Age boats dating from 890 BC to about 590 BC were found on the shore. Made from planks held together with strips of yew, they indicate that travel on the River Humber began much earlier than had been previously thought. A model of the boats can be seen in Hull's Transport and Archaeology Museum.

SOUTH CAVE

14 miles W of Hull off the A63

The village of South Cave is, officially, a town with its very own Town Hall in the marketplace. The name is said to be a corruption of South Cove since the southern part of the parish is set around a backwater of the Humber. The village is separated into two distinct areas by the grounds of the Cave Castle Golf Hotel. This building dates back to Elizabethan times and was once the home of George Washington's great grandfather.

112 THE HALF MOON

Elloughton, Brough

Spacious traditional pub with real ales and excellent home-cooked food at lunch and dinner daily.

    see page 262

113 THE GREEN DRAGON

Welton, Hull

Outstanding inn with fresh, expertly prepared food and luxury accommodation open all day every day.

    see page 263

114 OLIVER'S COFFEE SHOP

Swanland, North Ferriby

Charming place open 9.30–5 daily for a tempting hot and cold snacks or meals, teas, coffees and soft-drinks, and delicious home-made cakes.

    see page 264

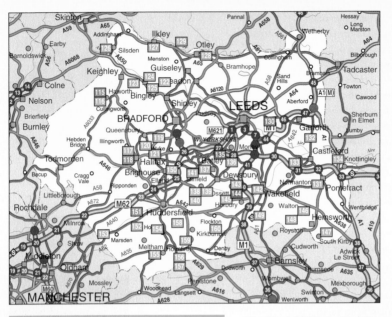

West Yorkshire

'The county of West Yorkshire, while having the scenery of the Pennines, is still dominated by the effects of the Industrial Revolution that turned this region into one of the world's great wool manufacturing areas. The land had been farmed, mainly with sheep, since the Middle Ages and, in order to supplement their wages, the cottagers took to hand loom weaving in a room of their home. However, the advances in technology, beginning in the 18th century, replaced the single man-powered looms with water-powered machinery that was housed in the large mill buildings in the valley bottom and close to the source of power – the fast flowing streams and rivers coming down from the surroundings hills and moors.

During the 19th century there was an explosion of building and the quiet riverside villages grew into towns and the South Pennine textile boom was in full flow. At first the conditions in the mills were grim as, indeed, were the living conditions for the mill workers but, with the reduction in the hours of the working day, people were able to take the opportunity to discover, and in some cases rediscover, the beauty of the surrounding moorland. Not all the villages were completely taken over by the mills and, in many, the old stone built weavers' cottages, with their deep windows to let in light for the worker within, survive.

Although the Yorkshire woollen textile industry is now almost a thing of the past, the heritage of those prosperous days can be seen in almost any town or village of the region. The wealthy mill owners built grand villas for themselves and also contributed to the construction of the marvellous array of opulent civic buildings that are such a feature of West Yorkshire towns. Today, however, many of the mills, which have remained redundant for decades are now being put to other uses while places such as Bradford, Leeds, Huddersfield and Wakefield are finding new industries to take the place of the old. There is a wealth of interesting museums here that concentrate on the wool industry but there are also others such as the National Museum of Photography, Film and Television, in Bradford, that look towards the future. Coal mining, too, was a feature of West Yorkshire and the National Coal Mining Museum, near Wakefield, provides visitors with the opportunity to go down a real mine shaft.

However, despite there being several grand stately homes in the area, such as Temple Newsam near Leeds, East Riddlesden Hall near Bradford and Harewood House, the foremost residence that most people make a pilgrimage to in West Yorkshire is The Parsonage at Howarth. It was here that the Brontë family moved to in 1820 and, surrounded by the wild Pennine landscape, the three sisters, Charlotte, Anne and Emily, became inspired by their surroundings and wrote some of the most famous novels in the English language. Now a museum dedicated to the tragic sisters, this fine Georgian house is a starting point for a 40-mile footpath that takes in many of the places that feature in the Brontë novels.

115 BRONTË PARSONAGE MUSEUM

Haworth

Friendly hosts provide a warm welcome, real ales and a very good variety of food at the **Royal Oak**.

 see page 264

116 THE KINGS ARMS

Haworth

Excellent ales, food and one lovely double room just 500 yards from the famed Brontë parsonage.

 see page 265

BRONTË COUNTRY

This area of West Yorkshire, surrounding the Brontë family home at Haworth, is dominated by the textile towns and villages along the valley bottom and the wild and bleak moorland above. The land has been farmed, mainly with sheep, since the Middle Ages. In order to supplement their wages, the cottagers took to hand loom weaving in a room of their home. The advances in technology, beginning in the 18th century, replaced the single man-powered looms with water-powered machinery that were housed in the large mill buildings in the valley bottom and close to the source of power.

During the 19th century there was an explosion of building and the quiet riverside villages grew into towns; the South Pennine textile boom was in full flow. At first the conditions in the mills were grim as, indeed, were the living conditions for the mill workers but, with the reduction in the hours of the working day, people were able to take the opportunity to discover, and in some cases rediscover, the beauty of the surrounding moorland.

Not all the villages were completely taken over by the mills. In many, the old stone-built weavers cottages, with their deep windows to let in light for the worker within, survive. This, then, was the landscape of the area to which the Brontë family moved in

1820 when their father, Patrick, took up the position of rector of Haworth. Within five years, both Maria Brontë (the mother) and two of the five girls died; the unhealthy climate having begun to take its toll. Though all the remaining children did receive an education it was in a somewhat haphazard way and they spent much of their time with each other isolated at the parsonage. After various attempts at working, generally as teachers, the girls, and their brother Branwell, all returned to the parsonage in the mid-1840s and this is when their writing began in earnest.

HAWORTH

12 miles N of Halifax off the A6033

Once a bleak moorland town in a dramatic setting that fired the romantic imaginations of the Brontë sisters, Haworth has been transformed into a lively, attractive place, with wonderful tea houses, street theatre, and antique and craft shops, very different to how it must have been in the Brontë's days. It was then a thriving industrial town, squalid amidst the smoke from its chimneys, filled with the noise of the clattering looms, which were rarely still. It is worth exploring the ginnels and back roads off the steeply rising high street, to get a feeling of what the place was like in the days of the Brontës.

The Parsonage, built in 1777, is the focus of most Brontë pilgrimages and is now given over to the **Brontë Parsonage Museum**. The Brontë Society has restored the interior to resemble as closely as possible the house in which the sisters lived with their father and brother. There are exhibitions and displays of contemporary material, personal belongings, letters, and portraits, as well as a priceless collection of manuscripts, first editions, and memorabilia in the newer extension.

Taking their inspiration from the surrounding bleak and lonely Haworth Moor and from the stories they made up as children, the three sisters, Anne, Charlotte, and Emily, under male *noms de plume*, all became published authors while Branwell, though by all accounts a scholar, sought refuge in the beer at the local inn. Then the tuberculosis that had attacked the family earlier returned and, one by one, Patrick Brontë's children succumbed to the terrible disease. The story of the Brontë family is one of tragedy but the circumstances of their deaths were all too common in the 19th century and graphically illustrate the harshness of life some 150 years ago.

Many visitors are drawn to the area by the story of the family and the **Brontë Way,** a 40-mile linear footpath with a series of four guided walks, which links the places that provided inspiration to the sisters. The most exhilarating and popular excursion is that to **Top Withins**, a favourite place of Emily's and the inspiration for the 'Wuthering Heights' of the novel. The route also takes into account a great variety of scenery, from wild moorlands to pastoral countryside.

Brontë enthusiasts can also sit in the Black Bull, where Branwell

Worth Valley, Near Haworth

sent himself to an early grave on a mixture of strong Yorkshire ale, opium, and despair (although the last two are not available here these days). The Post Office, from where the sisters sent their manuscripts to London publishers, is still as it was, as is the Sunday School at which they all taught. Sadly, the church which they all attended no longer exists, although Charlotte, Emily, and Branwell (Anne is buried in Scarborough) all lie in a vault in the new church which dates from 1879.

The countryside around Haworth inspires the modern visitor as much as it did the Brontës. This is excellent walking country and it is worth taking a trip through the Penistone Hill Country Park, following the rough track by old moorland farms to the Brontë Falls and stone footbridge. For the energetic, the path eventually leads to the deserted ruins of Top Withins Farm, said to have been the inspiration for the setting of *Wuthering Heights*. It is said that the ghost of Emily Brontë has been

As well as devotees of the Brontë legend, Haworth is popular with steam railway fans. The town is the headquarters of the Keighley & Worth Valley Railway, a thriving volunteer-run railway which serves six stations (most of them gas-lit) in the course of its 4¾-mile length. The railway owns an extensive and varied collection of locomotives and everything combines to re-create the atmosphere of the days of steam. There are daily services during July and August and intermittent services throughout the rest of the year. To listen to the talking timetable, telephone 01535 643629.

155

•

*Outside the town centre
of Keighley is Cliffe
Castle which, despite its
deceptive name, is – in
fact – a grand late-19th-
century mansion
complete with a tower,
battlements, and
parkland, which once
belonged to local mill
owners, the Butterfields.
It now houses Keighley
Museum, which
concentrates on the
fascinating local
topography and geology
of Airedale as well as the
history of the town. Also
housed in the museum is
the hand loom, complete
with unfinished cloth,
that was used by Timmy
Feather, the last hand
loom weaver in England.
Part of the building is
still furnished and
decorated in the lavish
style of the 1880s.*

•

seen walking, with her head bowed, between the Parsonage and Top Withins Farm.

THORNTON

4 miles W of Bradford on the B6145

Thornton is an essential stopping place on the Brontë trail for it was here that the three sisters were born, at No. 74 Market Street, now open to the public as the **Brontë Birthplace**. Their father was the vicar of Thornton and one of the treasures of his parish church is a font, inscribed with the date 1687, in which Charlotte, Emily and Anne were all baptised. Charlotte was only four years old, her two sisters still toddlers, when the family moved a few miles northwest to Haworth where their father had been appointed rector.

KEIGHLEY

10 miles NW of Bradford on the A650

Lying at the junction of the Rivers Worth and Aire, this bustling textile and engineering town, despite its modern redevelopment, still retains a strangely nostalgic air of the Victorian Industrial Revolution. It was that era of rapid growth that created the town seen today, beginning at Low Mill in 1780, when cotton spinning on a factory scale was first introduced. Reminders of hardship endured by the many factory workers of that time can be seen in the labyrinth of ginnels and terraces which lie amid the many elaborately decorated mills. There are delightful carvings and on one early mill chimney are

three heads, one wearing a top hat; in contrast is the classical French-styled **Dalton Mill** in Dalton Lane with its ornate viewing gallery.

The centre of Keighley is dominated by impressive Victorian civic buildings and a beautifully set out covered shopping precinct, where the statue of legendary local giant, Rombald, stands. The parish church, also in the centre, is famous as the site where Patrick Brontë often officiated at marriages. The graveyard contains 15th-century headstones, as well as a crude cross made from four carved heads which is believed to be Saxon in origin. Above the town, by way of escaping the industrial past, one might enjoy a walk in Park Woods, taking the cobbled path to Thwaites Brow, which affords magnificent views of the town below.

To the south of Keighley runs the line of the **Keighley and Worth Valley Railway** to Haworth and Oxenhope. This restored steam railway line, which is run completely by volunteers, passes through some attractive small villages and some notable stations complete with vintage advertising signs, gas lighting and coal fires in the waiting rooms. At Ingrow Station, **The Museum of Rail Travel** contains some fascinating items connected with Victorian travel, among them three small locomotives, coaches in various liveries, the clock from Manchester's Mayfield Station, an interesting collection of posters and other memorabilia from the golden age of steam.

156

HAINWORTH

1 miles SE of Keighley off the A650

The **Worth Way** is an interesting five mile walk from the heart of industrial Keighley to the eastern edge of the Worth Valley at Oxenhope. This landscape has changed little since the time when Mrs Gaskell wrote about the area while visiting Charlotte Brontë in 1856. En route, the Worth Way passes close to the village of Hainworth which stands high on the hillside and commands some grand views of Harden Moor.

RIDDLESDEN

1 mile NE of Keighley off the A629

Parts of **East Riddlesden Hall**, now a National Trust property, date back to Saxon times. The main building, however, was constructed in the 1630s by James Murgatroyd, a wealthy Halifax clothier and merchant. A fine example of a 17th-century manor house, the gabled hall is built of dark stone with mullioned windows, and it retains its original centre hall, superb period fireplaces, oak panelling, and plaster ceilings. The house is furnished in Jacobean style, which is complemented by carved likenesses of Charles Stuart and Henrietta Maria. East Riddlesden Hall also has one of the largest and most impressive timber framed barns in the North of England which now houses a collection of farm waggons and agricultural equipment. The hall is said to

be haunted by the ghost of a lady dressed in blue who wanders along the building's passageways and sets the child's cradle rocking .

OAKWORTH

1 mile N of Haworth on the B6143

Those visiting Oakworth may find its Edwardian station, on the Keighley and Worth Valley Railway line somewhat familiar. In fact, not only did it feature in the classic film *The Railway Children*, but also in episodes of the TV series *Sherlock Holmes*.

STANBURY

4 miles S of Keighley off the B6143

Close to the village lies **Ponden Mill** which was, in the heyday of Yorkshire's textile industry, one of the largest working mills in the country. At the height of production, cloth from Ponden Mill was exported around the world. Though the vast majority of the mills have now closed and the Yorkshire textile industry is

Timber Framed Barns, Riddlesden

157

To the northwest of Hebden Bridge lies the Land Farm Sculpture Garden and Gallery, a delightful woodland garden created over some 30 years from a barren Pennine hillside that faces north and lies some 1,000 feet above sea level. Attached to the house is an art gallery; both are open at weekends and Bank Holiday Mondays from May to the end of August.

virtually a thing of the past, Ponden Mill is still open, this time as a retail centre selling all manner of textiles from home furnishings and linens to country clothing. To round off your visit, have a look in the clog shop where traditional methods of manufacture are still on show.

OXENHOPE

9 miles W of Bradford on the A6033

This village contains more than 70 listed buildings, including a Donkey Bridge, two milestones, a mounting block, a cowshed, and a pigsty. The early farmhouses had narrow mullioned windows which gave maximum light for weaving and some had a door at first-storey level so that the pieces could be taken out. The first mill here was built in 1792 and, during the 19th century, there were up to 20 mills producing worsted.

Many scenes for *The Railway Children* were set here in 1970 using local views and local people. A

station on the Keighley and Worth Valley Railway also serves the village.

HEBDEN BRIDGE

5 miles NW of Halifax on the A646

This mill town is characterised by the stepped formation of its houses which were stacked one on top of the other up the steep sides of the Calder valley. There has been a village here for many years, centred around the crossing-point of the River Calder. When the first bridge was built is not known but as early as the beginning of the 16th century its state of repair was causing concern and, in a style typical of this area of Yorkshire, a stone bridge was erected close by. Found in St George's Square in the heart of the town, the historic **Hebden Bridge Mill** has, for almost 700 years now, been powered by the fast-flowing waters of the River Hebden. For over four centuries this was a manorial corn mill before it was converted into a textile mill that was finally abandoned in the 1950s. Now lovingly restored, the mill is home to various stylish shops, restaurants and craft workshops.

The **Rochdale Canal**, which slices through the town, was completed in 1798. It was constructed to link the Calder and Hebble Navigation with the Bridgewater and Ashton canals from Lancashire. Used by commercial traffic since 1939, the canal has been repaired and sections of it, including that between Hebden Bridge and

First Bridge, Hebden Bridge

Todmorden, are now open to traffic though, now, it consists mainly of pleasure craft. Motor boat cruises are available from the marina.

One of the first purpose-built industrial towns in the world, Hebden Bridge grew rapidly as the demand for textiles boomed. Over the years, the town has seen many changes of fortune and, today, though textiles have now gone, it is known as 'The Great Town for Little Shops', due its diversity of shops and businesses.

HEPTONSTALL

7 miles NW of Halifax off the A646

The village, one of the main tourist centres in Calderdale, overlooks Hebden Bridge and **Hardcastle Crags**. This beautiful wooded valley is protected and cared for by the National Trust and, from the crags, there are several interesting walks along the purpose built footpaths. It is also one of only three places in Britain where two churches occupy the same churchyard. In this case, the original church, which dates from 1256, was struck by lightning in the 1830s and a new church was built next to the ruin.

TODMORDEN

4 miles W of Hebden Bridge on the A646

This is another typical mill town that grew with the expansion of the textile industry. Before the 19th century, Todmorden had been a spartan place with many of the villagers eking out frugal lives by hand loom weaving. Following the building of the first mill here,

Todmorden began to grow and the highly ornate and flamboyant public buildings were, in the main, built by the mill owners. Though many towns which owe their existence to industry also bear the scars, Todmorden has retained all its charm and character and is an excellent place to visit for those interested in architecture. It boasts a magnificent **Town Hall** designed by John Gibson and opened in 1875. One of the finest municipal buildings of its size in the country, the grand old building stands half in Yorkshire and half in Lancashire. So the ornate carving in the pediment represents the farming and iron trades of Yorkshire in the right panel; the cotton trade of Lancashire in the left.

MYTHOLMROYD

5 miles W of Halifax on the A646

Prior to the 1600s, the valley bottom in what is now Mytholmroyd, was marshy and of little use as foundations for a village, though some of the outlying farms in the area date from the late 14th century. However, with the need to build more mills close to a supply of water, the land was improved and Mytholmroyd joined the age of the Industrial Revolution.

Each spring the town is host to the **World Dock Pudding Championships**. Dock Pudding is unique to this corner of the county and is made from the weed *Polygonum Bistorta* or sweet dock (which should never be confused with the larger docks that are

Every year, on Good Friday in Heptonstall, the Paceggers Play takes place in Weavers Square. It's an ancient method of storytelling with actors dressed in elaborate costumes recounting the legend of St George.

117 STUMP CROSS INN

Stump Cross, Halifax

A warm welcome, range of tasty food and drink and quality accommodation in a peaceful hamlet just north of Halifax.

 see page 264

commonly used for easing nettle stings). In spring the plant grows profusely and local people pick it by the bagful. The docks are then mixed with young nettles and other essential ingredients and cooked to produce a green and slimy delicacy the appearance of which is found by many to be rather off-putting. It is usually served with bacon after having been fried in bacon fat and is believed to cure acne and cleanse the blood.

HALIFAX

Halifax boasts one of Yorkshire's most impressive examples of municipal architecture, the glorious 18th-century **Piece Hall**. It possesses a large quadrangle where regular markets are held on Fridays and Saturdays, surrounded by colonnades and balconies behind which are some 40 specialist shops. On Thursdays a flea market is held here and there's a lively and varied programme of events for all the family throughout the season. There's also an art gallery with a varied programme of contemporary exhibitions and workshops, a museum and tea room.

The **Town Hall** is another notable building, designed by Sir Charles Barry, architect of the Houses of Parliament, and there's an attractive Borough Market, constructed in cast iron and glass with an ornate central clock.

In Gibbet Street stands a grisly reminder of the past – a replica of a guillotine, the original blade being kept in the Piece Hall Museum. There are many hidden places in old Halifax to explore: from Shear's Inn, an old weavers' inn near the town centre, one can walk up the cobbled Boy's Lane, very little changed from Victorian times, or trace out the ancient *Magna Via*, a medieval path to the summit of Breacon Hill.

Halifax also boasts the largest parish church in England. Of almost cathedral sized proportions, it dates from the 12th and 13th centuries although most of the present building is from the 1400s. It has a lovely wooden ceiling, constructed in 1635, and visitors should look out for 'Old Tristram', a life-sized wooden effigy of a beggar, reputedly based on a local character. It was designed to serve as the church poor box – and still does.

Right next door to Piece Hall, the **Calderdale Industrial Museum** houses still-working looms and mill machinery, hand textile demonstrations and among the many displays one celebrating the town's greatest contribution to modern travel, the cats-eye! From the Great Wheel to the Spinning Jenny, from mining to moquette,

Gibbet Street, Halifax

from steam engines (in live steam) to toffee, the museum provides a riveting insight into Halifax's industrial heritage.

Situated next to Halifax railway station, **Eureka!** is Britain's first and only interactive museum designed especially for children between three and 12 years old. With more than 400 larger than life exhibits and exciting activities available, Eureka! opens up a fascinating world of hands-on exploration. A team of 'Enablers' help children make the most of their visit; there are regular temporary exhibitions, and the complex includes a café and gift shop.

Now a vibrant complex of businesses, galleries, theatre, café and design and book shops, **Dean Clough** is housed in a magnificent Victorian carpet mill that is a reminder of Halifax's textile heritage. Built between 1840 and 1870 by the Crossley family, this mill was once home to one of the world's leading carpet factories, which ceased production in 1982.

Shibden Hall and Park, about a mile out of town, is somewhere very special that should not be missed. The Old Hall itself lies in a valley on the outskirts of the town and is situated in 90 acres of parkland. The distinctive timber framed house dates from 1420 and has been carefully furnished to reflect the various periods of its history. The 17th-century barn behind the Hall houses a fine collection of horse-drawn vehicles and the original buildings have been transformed into a 19th-century village centre with a pub, estate worker's cottage, saddler's, blacksmith's, wheelwright's and potter's workshop.

Also on the outskirts of the town is the **Bankfield Museum**, the home between 1837 and 1886 of Edward Akroyd, the largest wool manufacturer in Britain. He lavished money and attention on the building, transforming it from a modest town house into a magnificent Italianate mansion with elaborate ceilings, staircases and plasterwork. After his death, his sumptuous home became a museum and now houses an internationally important collection of textiles and costumes from around the world. Contemporary crafts are also featured and the museum hosts an interesting programme of temporary exhibitions, workshops, seminars, master classes and gallery demonstrations. Here, too, is a Toy Gallery, the Duke of Wellington's Regimental Museum and the Marble Gallery that sells contemporary crafts. Surrounding his house, Akroyd built a model village called Akroydon that, with its terraced houses, allotments, park and church was the first 'urban' village. The Bankfield Museum is open all year round from Tuesday to Sunday and on Bank Holiday Mondays.

AROUND HALIFAX

SOWERBY BRIDGE

2 miles SW of Halifax on the A58

Sowerby Bridge has a rather odd connection with the Brontës. For a

118 BANKFIELD MUSEUM

Halifax

Set in a Victorian mill owner's house, there is an important collection of textiles, various objects from around the world plus a programme of exhibitions and activities.

🏛 *see page 266*

119 THE WINDMILL INN

Shelf, Halifax

Superb food is the hallmark here, with fisherman's pie, pork steaks with wild mushroom sauce and more at country inn just outside Bradford.

❚ *see page 266*

120 THE QUEEN VICTORIA

Northowram, Halifax

Delicious Thai and English dishes served every day at lunch and dinner. Real ales, freshly prepared food and genuine hospitality.

❚ *see page 266*

121 THE BROWN HORSE INN

Coley, Halifax

A fantastic menu of traditional and exotic meat, fish, poultry and vegetarian dishes make booking essential at all times at this superb inn.

❚ *see page 267*

while, Branwell Brontë worked as a booking clerk at the railway station here. He was dismissed in March 1842 when discrepancies were found in his accounts. Branwell also worked in the same role at nearby Luddenden Foot where he was a member of the library at the White Swan inn. (At that time, several hostelries provided this amenity for their patrons.) A condition of membership of the library stipulated 'sobriety and decorous conduct' on pain of a fine of 2d (0.8p) for each offence. This requirement must have caused Branwell some difficulty as he was a scandalously heavy drinker.

An important crossing of both the Rivers Ryburn and Calder in medieval times, and possibly as far back as the Roman occupation, Sowerby Bridge first had water-powered mills as early as the 14th century. The mills, first used for grinding corn, moved into textile production and by the 1850s were all steam-driven. **Greenups Mill,** built in 1792, was the first integrated woollen mill in Yorkshire with all the textile processes brought under one roof. Sowerby Bridge also boasted one of the first turnpike roads in Britain, constructed in 1735. Just a short time later the Calder and Hebble Navigation, surveyed by John Smeaton, the designer of the Eddystone Lighthouse, was opened in 1770, followed by the Rochdale Canal in 1804. A reminder of the busy days of the canal is Tuel Lane Lock and Tunnel which joined the two man-made waterways. It re-opened in 1996 and it is a grand

sight to watch the narrowboats negotiating what is the deepest lock in the country.

SHELF

4 miles NE of Halifax on the A6036

At Pepper Hill in Shelf a congregation was established in 1858 as a mission from Halifax. The building was built in 1861 and extensively rebuilt in 1936 after the roof collapsed. It is a simple building befitting its rural setting and has some attractive Art Deco 'Rising Sun' pattern windows dating from the 1930s. At 1,000 feet above sea level, it earns the distinction of being the highest Unitarian Chapel in Britain.

RIPPONDEN

5 miles SW of Halifax on the A58

Ripponden lies in the valley of the Ryburn, a tributary of the Calder. An ancient packhorse bridge crosses the river and, right beside it, the Old Bridge Inn which is one of the oldest inns in Yorkshire. It was already in existence in 1313 and its interior, with its sloping floors and different levels, has been compared to a funfair crazy house.

BRADFORD

Bradford is a city with much to offer the visitor. In terms of numbers, the most popular attraction is undoubtedly the **National Museum of Photography, Film and Television**, which houses IMAX, one of the largest cinema screens in the world. If you suffer from vertigo you'll need to close your eyes as the huge, wrap-around screen shows such heart-stopping scenes as roller-coaster rides and Alpine mountaineering. There's plenty to keep you occupied here for hours – virtual reality exhibits, the Kodak Gallery which leads you on a journey through the history of popular photography, an extensive TV display which ranges from the world's first TV pictures to the very latest, and much, much more. A recent addition is a vast new space presenting world-class exhibitions on photography, film, TV and new media.

Of related interest is Britain's only **Museum of Colour**. 'The World of Colour' gallery looks at the concept of colour, how it is perceived and its importance. Visitors can see how the world looks to other animals, mix coloured lights and experience strange colour illusions. In the 'Colour and Textiles' gallery you can discover the fascinating story of dyeing and textile printing from Ancient Egypt to the present day. Computerised technology allows you to take charge of a dye-making factory and decorate a room. The museum is open Tuesday to Saturday all year round.

Found in Lister Park, the collections at the **Cartwright Hall Art Gallery** reflect the diverse cultural mix that helps to make Bradford the vibrant and unique city it has become in the 21st century. From Victorian paintings and sumptuous Indian silks to the challenges of contemporary art,

this gallery is as interesting and far-reaching as the city itself.

The **Bradford Industrial Museum and Horses at Work** celebrates the city's industrial heritage. It is housed in an original worsted spinning mill complex built in 1875 and re-creates life in Bradford in late Victorian times. Open all year, the museum also offers horse-bus and tram rides, a shire horse centre, a reconstructed mill owner's house and the working men's back to back cottages. The complex also includes a café, shop and picnic area.

Architecturally, the most striking building in Bradford must be **Lister's Mill**. Its huge ornate chimney dominates the city skyline and its claimed that it is wide enough at the top to drive a horse and cart around. The mill fell silent some years ago though its exterior has been cleared up and there are plans to use it to house a museum dedicated to the industry that brought the city its wealth – wool.

A rather quirkier sign of the city's former riches is **Undercliffe Cemetery**. Here the wool barons were buried, each in a more opulent Gothic mausoleum than the last. It is easy to spend an hour here admiring the Victorian funereal art on show with the cityscape laid out before you.

The fact that the city has a **Cathedral** is an indication of its importance. The first evidence of worship on the site is provided by the remains of a Saxon preaching cross. Today the Cathedral contains many items of interest, including

122 OLD GLEN HOUSE

Baildon

Scenic location a short walk from historic Shipley Glen. Real ales, excellent food, cosy ambience.

 see page 267

123 READERS AT ST IVES

Bingley

Superb tea rooms on the St Ives Estate, open daily from 10.30. Tasty dishes using fresh local produce. Speciality teas and coffees.

 see page 267

124 THE BROWN COW

Bingley

Warm and inviting public house with eight real ales and excellent, hearty home-cooked food, open every session and all day Fri-Sun.

 see page 268

125 THE FISHERMAN'S

Dowley Gap, Bingley

Fantastic location overlooking the Leeds-Liverpool Canal. Superb freshly prepared food using local produce.

 see page 268

beautiful stained glass windows, some of which were designed by William Morris, carvings and statuary.

AROUND BRADFORD

SHIPLEY

4 miles N of Bradford on the A6037

Although Shipley town is mainly industrial, **Shipley Glen** is a very popular area for tourists. Within the grounds is a narrow gauge, cable hauled tramway, built in 1895, that carries passengers a quarter of a mile up the side of a steep hill, passing en route through Walker Wood, famous for its bluebells.

SALTAIRE

4 miles NW of Bradford off the A657

Saltaire is the model village created by Titus Salt for the workers at his mill. Salt was a very benevolent employer and determined to provide his workers with everything essential for a decent standard of living. Built between 1851 and 1876, the facilities in the village were designed to cater for all their needs – health, leisure and education, but there were no public houses. The spiritual needs of the work force were attended to by the elegant Congregational church which has been described as the most beautiful Free Church in the north of England.

A statue of Titus Salt stands in nearby Robert's Park (where swearing and gambling were banned) above the figures of a llama and an alpaca whose wool he

imported for spinning in his mills.

The Victoria Boat House was built in 1871 and has been beautifully restored, with an open fire, pianola and wind-up gramophone, all re-creating a traditional parlour atmosphere where you can enjoy cream teas and attend special Victorian Evenings in the dress of that time. Also in Saltaire is the **Museum of Victorian Reed Organs** which has a collection of more than 45 instruments, including harmonicas and an American organ, which are demonstrated from time to time, and some of which are available for visitors to try.

Saltaire isn't completely locked in the past. The former Salt's Mill has been converted into the **1853 David Hockney Gallery** which displays the world's largest collection of paintings by the internationally acclaimed artist who was born in Bradford in 1937.

A couple of miles northeast of Baildon, at Guiseley, is the most famous fish and chip shop in the world, Harry Ramsden's. Harry's career as the world's most successful fish frier began in Bradford where he was the first to offer a sit-down fish and chip meal. He moved to Guiseley in 1928 and the original white-painted wooden hut, 10 feet by 6 feet, in which he started business is still on the site today. The present building holds its place in the *Guinness Book of Records* as the world's busiest fish and chip restaurant, serving nearly one million customers each year.

SILSDEN

11½ miles NW of Bradford on the A6034

This well-contained stone built industrial town, which spreads uphill from the Leeds and Liverpool Canal, owes its development to the textile industry. Rows of terraced cottages and houses lie on the steep hillsides and there is newer housing on the outskirts of the town. It was the birthplace of Augustus Spencer, Principal of the Royal College of Art (1900-20), whose memorial can be seen in the 18th-century parish church.

Outside The King's Arms, in the centre of the village, stands an old mounting block, a survival from the days when this was a coaching and post house inn. The resident ghost probably dates back to that era as well.

ILKLEY

Originally an Iron Age settlement, Ilkley was eventually occupied by the Romans who built a camp here to protect their crossing of the River Wharfe. They named their town *Olicana*, so giving rise to the present name with the addition of the familiar *ley* (Anglo-Saxon for 'pasture'). Behind the medieval church is a grassy mound where a little fort was built and in the town's museum are altars carved in gritstone, dedicated to the Roman gods.

The spring at **White Wells** brought more visitors to the town in the 18th century. A small bath house was built where genteel and elderly patients were encouraged to take a dip in the healing waters of the heather spa. Early Victorian times saw the development of the Hydros – hydropathic treatment hotels – providing hot and cold treatments based on the idea of Dr Preissnitz of Austria who, in 1843, became the director of Britain's first Hydro at nearby Ben Rhydding.

The coming of the railways from Leeds and Bradford in the 1860s and '70s, during a period of growth in the Yorkshire woollen industry, saw the town take on a new role as a fashionable commuter town. Wool manufacturers and their better-paid employees came, not only to enjoy the superb amenities, but to build handsome villas. If Bradford and Leeds were where people made their brass, so it was said at the time, then it was usually at Ilkley that it was spent. Even today, Ilkley sports some remarkable and opulent Victorian architecture as proof of this.

126 THE GROUSE AT SILSDEN

Silsden
Contemporary and stylish restaurant with an excellent menu of Modern English and Continental dishes expertly prepared and presented.

see page 269

Cup and Ring Stone, Ilkley

Ilkley's patrons and well-to-do citizens gave the town a splendid Town Hall, Library, Winter Gardens and King's Hall and a sense of elegance is still present along The Grove. It is still a delight to have morning coffee in the famous Betty's coffee house and discerning shoppers will find a wealth of choice, some in a perfectly preserved Victorian arcade complete with potted palms and balconies.

Between the remains of the Roman fort and the River Wharfe lie the **Riverside Gardens**, a favourite place for a stroll that might lead over a 17th-century packhorse bridge across the river. On the side of this bridge, beside the stone steps, the flood levels of the river have been marked, along with the dates. On the opposite side of the river is The Lido, one of the few surviving outdoor swimming pools in Yorkshire. Its idyllic surroundings and extensive terraces make it a popular place in summer while, next to the

Lido is an indoor pool open all year round. From the Lido a footpath leads up to Middleton Woods, in May a sea of bluebells.

Housed in a building that dates from the 15th, 16th and 17th centuries, complete with mullioned windows, carved beams and an interesting wall privy, the **Manor House Art Gallery and Museum** tells the history of Ilkley from its prehistoric roots through to its development as a Victorian spa town; upstairs is an art gallery hosting a programme of temporary exhibitions throughout the year.

One of the most famous West Yorkshire attractions has to be **Ilkley Moor**, immortalised in the well-known song. Like any of the Yorkshire moors, Ilkley Moor can look inviting and attractive on a sunny day but ominous and forbidding when the weather takes a turn for the worse. The River Wharfe runs along the edge of the moor and through the town of Ilkley which is clustered within a narrow section of the valley in the midst of heather moorland, craggy gritstone and wooded hillside. Few places in the north can equal Ilkley Moor or, more correctly, Rombalds Moor. The moorland, much of it still covered in heather, is also an area of national importance for its archaeology. There is a series of mysteriously marked cup and ring stones dating from the Bronze Age. Almost in the centre of the moor is an ancient stone circle, no doubt a site of some religious importance. Only the keen walker is likely to find these, located high up on the

Medieval Church, Ilkley

166

moor, but there is a fine example of a cup and ring stone in the lower part of St Margaret's churchyard in Queen's Road.

AROUND ILKLEY

ADDINGHAM

3 miles W of Ilkley off the A65

Although Addingham dates back to Saxon times (it was named after a Saxon chieftain, Adda), the village enjoyed its greatest prosperity in the 18th century when no fewer than five water mills lined the banks of the Wharfe. Four of them were textile mills and no longer operate, but the fifth, a timber mill, is still working.

BURLEY IN WHARFEDALE

3 miles SE of Ilkley on the A65

Mentioned in the Anglo-Saxon Chronicle in AD 972 as Burhleg and in the *Domesday Book* as Burghelai, Burley remained a small riverside settlement until the 1790s when the Industrial Revolution reached the village. Many of the terraces of stone-built cottages, designed for the mill workers, have survived and are now highly desirable residences. Burley's population has doubled since the 1920s but the Main Street is still lined with Yorkshire stone cottages and houses, and the surrounding hills frame every view.

OTLEY

5 miles SE of Ilkley on the A660

Although it now forms part of the Leeds Metropolitan District, Otley has retained its distinctive character,

still boasting a busy cobbled marketplace and many little alleyways and courtyards. Each May the Wharfedale Agricultural Show, founded in 1799 and the oldest show of its kind in England, is held in a nearby field.

Even older is Prince Henry's Grammar School, founded in 1602 by James I and named after his eldest son. In front of the building in Manor Square is a statue of Thomas Chippendale, the great furniture maker who was born in Otley in 1718. In 1754 Chippendale published *The Gentleman and Cabinet-Maker's Director*, which was immensely influential in both Britain and the USA. His own workshop produced a comparatively small number of pieces but he gave his name to a style that dominated a generation and is still highly prized.

In addition to the statue on the front of the Grammar School, Otley's most famous son is commemorated by a plaque on the wall of Browns Gallery which records that Thomas Chippendale was born in 1718 in a cottage that stood on this spot.

Otley's parish church dates from Saxon times although the main body was constructed in the 11th century. An unusual memorial, close by, is a stone model of Bramhope Railway Tunnel with its impressive crenellated entrance portals. It was built in the 1830s on the Leeds-Thirsk railway line and more than 30 labourers died during its construction – a tragic loss of life which the model commemorates.

127 THE DALESWAY HOTEL

Ilkley

Excellent pub with nine handsome and elegant guest rooms offering every comfort, set in the heart of Ilkley.

🍴 🛏 *see page 269*

128 THE RING O' BELLS

Newmarket, Otley

Charming small pub with a good selection of thirst-quenchers and a warm and friendly atmosphere.

🍴 *see page 270*

Looking at a map of the area, many people's attention is drawn to the curiously named Cow and Calf Rocks which form a striking moor-edge landmark above Ben Rhydding. The Cow is a great gritstone outcrop concealing an old quarry, popular with climbers, while the free-standing Calf is a giant boulder.

129 THE BLACK HORSE AT ASKWITH

Askwith, Ilkley

Truly excellent food in a picturesque setting just a couple of miles east of Ilkley and northwest of Otley off the A65.

 see page 271

An attractive feature of the town is **The Chevin Forest Park,** a forested ridge above the town which can be reached by a delightful walk that starts in the town. There is also a pleasant walk along the River Wharfe.

BEN RHYDDING

1 mile E of Ilkley off the A65

'A few weeks spent at Ben Rhydding seem to effect a complete change in the system', wrote one Victorian visitor to the spa. 'I have seen delicate women, scarcely able to walk feebly round the garden on their first arrival, become strong enough to walk to the Hunting-tower, a lovely point in the heart of the moor at some distance from the house.'

The original Ben Rhydding Hydropathic Hotel, opened in 1844 by a consortium of Leeds businessmen, was built in the Scottish baronial style so popular at the time. By 1908, interest in hydropathy had declined and the exuberant building became the Ben Rhydding Golf Hotel. Later it was turned into flats but finally demolished in 1955.

Athough the name suggests some Scottish connection – and the surrounding scenery certainly has a Caledonian grandeur – 'Ben Rhydding' is actually derived from nearby Bean Rhydding, or bean clearing.

HAREWOOD

8 miles N of Leeds on the A61

One of the grandest stately homes in the country, **Harewood House** was built at a time when many of the most illustrious names in the

history of English architecture, interior decoration, furniture making and landscape gardening were at the peak of their powers.

For the creation of Harewood in the mid-1700s, Edwin Lascelles was able to employ the dazzling talents of Robert Adam, John Carr, Thomas Chippendale and Capability Brown. Edwin's son, Edward, was one of the first to patronise a young artist named JMW Turner and many of Turner's paintings are still here along with hundreds by other distinguished painters collected by later generations of the family.

Many of the finest of them are displayed in a superb gallery that extends along the whole west end of the house. Among the masterpieces on show are works by Bellini, Titian, Veronese, El Greco and Tintoretto, while family portraits by Reynolds, Hoppner and Gainsborough look down from the silk-covered walls of the opulent drawing rooms. Along with superb gardens, charming walks, a bird garden which is home to some 120 exotic species, an adventure playground, boat trips on the lake, and an extensive events and exhibitions programme, Harewood House is indisputably one of Yorkshire's must-see visitor attractions.

LEEDS

In recent years, the city of Leeds has seen something of a renaissance. Its waterfront, neglected and derelict for so long, is now buzzing with new developments. Abandoned warehouses have been imaginatively transformed into fashionable bars, restaurants and tourist attractions, all less than 15 minutes walk from the shopping centre. Debenhams has recently opened a new flagship store in the heart of the city and other high profile stores are also flocking to the city. Perhaps the most talked about store is Harvey Nichols whose Knightsbridge emporium enjoyed a heightened reputation in the 1990s thanks to the BBC series *Absolutely Fabulous*. In parallel with these developments the Aire and Calder Navigation, which commenced construction in 1704, is being transformed to enable leisure traffic to use the waterway as well as freight.

The city is also a major European cultural centre with its own opera and ballet companies, Northern Ballet Theatre and Opera North, while the West Yorkshire Playhouse, regarded as the 'National Theatre of the North', provides a showcase for classic British and European drama as well as work by new Yorkshire writers. The Leeds International Film Festival, held every October since 1986, has hosted major world premieres for films such as *Brassed Off*.

The **Thackray Medical Museum**, one of the largest museums of its kind in Europe, possesses more than 25,000 extraordinary objects in its collection. They range from a surgical chain saw and Prince

Albert's Medical Chest through to a 17th-century correction frame. Visitors can listen in to the thoughts and feelings of a surgeon, his assistants and Hannah Dyson, an 11-year-old girl whose leg has been crushed in a factory accident, as they prepare for the amputation of Hannah's leg. Or you might prefer to walk through a giant gut in Bodyworks and find out exactly why your tummy rumbles.

Opened by Queen Elizabeth II in 1998, the **Royal Armouries** trace the development of arms and armour from the 5th century BC to modern times. The museum utilises interactive computer displays, videos, films, music and poetry to tell the story of arms and armour in battle, self-defence, sport and fashion. Outside, the Tiltyard features jousting and hunting tournaments daily from April to September, while a bustling Menagerie Court includes displays of falcons, hunting dogs and horses.

To the northwest of the city, **Kirkstall Abbey** is one of the most complete ruins in this part of Yorkshire. Building started in 1152 by the Cistercians and was completed within a generation, so Kirkstall is regarded by many as representing Cistercian architecture at its most monumental. It was executed with typical early Cistercian austerity as can be seen in the simplicity of the outer domestic buildings. The bell tower, a 16th century addition, was in contravention of the rule of the Order that there were to be no

•

Leeds boasts some outstanding galleries and museums. Located right next to the monumental Town Hall, the Leeds City Art Gallery showcases an exceptional collection of Victorian and French Post-Impressionist paintings along with major works by Courbet, Lowry, Sickert, Stanley Spencer and Bridget Riley. Linked to the gallery is the Henry Moore Institute, the first centre in Europe devoted to the display and study of sculpture of all periods. There's also a Craft & Design shop selling cards, jewellery and pottery, and an art library.

•

169

Kirkstall Abbey, Leeds

130 TEMPLE NEWSAM

Leeds

Set in over 1,500 acres of land, this magnificent Tudor-Jacobean house is home to rich collections of works of art, and the superb gardens are a delight.

 see page 270

stone bell towers as they were considered an unnecessary vanity.

A few miles north of Leeds city centre is one of the UK's most popular garden tourist attractions and home to the largest collection of tropical plants outside Kew Gardens – **Tropical World**. Visitors can follow the 'Tropical Trail' into an Amazon rain forest where waterfalls tumble into jungle pools and birds of every hue fly through the trees. There's also a 'Desert World' and a 'Nocturnal House' where fruit bats, monkeys, bush babies and rock cavies reside – animals that can normally only be seen during twilight hours.

A couple of miles southwest of the city is **Temple Newsam House**, often referred to as the 'Hampton Court of the North'. Set in 1,200 acres of parkland (entry to which is free), this Tudor-Jacobean gem boasts extensive collections of decorative arts displayed in their original room settings. Among them is one of the largest collections of Chippendale furniture in the

country. Adjacent to Temple Newsam House is the country's largest approved Rare Breeds Centre – **Home Farm**. Visitors to this working farm will see pigs, goats, horses and poultry alongside interesting displays of vintage farm machinery and past farming methods.

BRAMHAM

8 miles NE of Leeds off the A1

Bramham Park is one of Yorkshire's most exquisite country houses and is special for a number of reasons. The house itself dates from the Queen Anne era. It was built for Robert Benson, Lord Bingley, between 1698 and 1710, and is superbly proportioned in an elegant and restrained classical style. The final effect is more French than English and indeed the gardens were modelled on Louis XIV's Versailles, with ornamental canals and ponds, beech groves, statues, long avenues and an arboretum with an impressive collection of rare and unusual trees. The interior contains elegant furniture and paintings by major artists such as Kneller and Sir Joshua Reynolds.

ABERFORD

13 miles E of Leeds on the B1217

To the southeast of this village lies an elegant Edwardian mansion, **Lotherton Estate and Gardens**, providing a fascinating insight into life in those serene days before the First World War. It was once the home of the Gascoigne family who were local land and coal mine owners. They were also enthusiastic travellers and collectors with a discriminating taste that is evident in the family paintings, furnishings and works of art on display.

The house, gardens and estate were given to the citizens of Leeds in 1968 by Sir Alvary and Lady Gascoigne. Since then their collections have been added to and now include superb 19th- and 20th- century decorative art as well as costume and Oriental art. Other attractions include the Edwardian formal gardens, a walled garden with some quirky spiral topiary, a bird garden with more than 200 species of rare and endangered birds, a 12th-century Chapel of Ease, deer park and café. The estate and gardens are open Tuesday to Sunday and Bank Holiday Mondays March to December.

PONTEFRACT

9 miles SE of Leeds off the M62/A1

Shakespeare alluded to the town in his plays as 'Pomfret' – a place of influence and power, often visited by kings and their retinues. The great shattered towers of **Pontefract Castle** stand on a crag to the east of the town. Built by Ilbert de Lacy in the 11th century, it was one of the most formidable fortresses in Norman England. In medieval times it passed to the House of Lancaster and became a Royal Castle. Richard II was imprisoned here and tragically murdered in its dungeons on the orders of Henry Bolingbroke who then assumed the crown as Henry IV.

The castle was a major Royalist stronghold during the Civil War, after which it was destroyed by Cromwell's troops. Today it remains as a gaunt ruin with only sections of the inner bailey and the lower part of the keep surviving intact. There is an underground chamber, part of the dungeons where prisoners carved their names so that they might not be utterly forgotten. The unfortunate Richard II may have been incarcerated in this very chamber.

Many of the streets of Pontefract evoke memories of its medieval past with names such as Micklegate, Beast Fair, Shoe Market, Salter Row and Ropergate. Modern development has masked much of old Pontefract but there are still many old Georgian buildings and winding streets.

The town's most famous products, of course, are Pontefract Cakes. Liquorice root has been grown here since monastic times and there's even a small planting of liquorice in the local park. The

131 THE LIQUORICE BUSH

Pontefract

Excellent centuries-old pub, pristine and elegant, in the centre of Pontefract. Lunchtime meals, real ales, warm and friendly ambience.

see page 272

Pontefract Castle

132 THE WHITE HORSE

Ledston, Castleford

Outstanding pub, attractive and welcoming inside and out, with a superb selection of ales and expertly prepared meals.

 see page 274

133 THE NEW WHEATSHEAF

Whitwood, Castleford

Great food is the main attraction at this handsome and popular inn just a short drive from Junction 31 or 32 of the M62.

 see page 273

134 THE GOLDEN LION HOTEL

Ferrybridge

Home-cooked food, real ales and comfortable accommodation, found 1 mile north of Pontefract on the B6136.

 see page 274

town celebrates this unique heritage with the five day **Pontefract Liquorice Fayre** in mid-August which includes two days of jousting, archery and battle re-enactments at Pontefract Castle.

ACKWORTH

3 miles S of Pontefract off the A628

This village is home to the famous Ackworth School, founded by the Quakers in 1779 and standing opposite a row of early 19th-century cottages. Outside the village a Plague Stone can still be seen beside the road, where villagers would leave money in exchange for food that was brought here when Ackworth was cut off during an outbreak of the Plague.

SOUTH ELMSAL

7 miles S of Pontefract on the B6474

Now a lively market and shopping area, South Elmsal has maintained its mining heritage, as it remains the home of the Frickley Colliery Brass

Band. Early in the 17th century it was the birthplace of Colonel John Morris, who took Pontefract Castle for the Royalists in 1648 and held on to it for 10 months despite almost overwhelming attacks by Cromwell's troups.

CASTLEFORD

3 miles NW of Pontefract on the A656

It was here at Castleford that the Romans crossed the River Aire and then built a fort to protect this important crossing. Sadly little remains of the settlement that the Romans called 'Legioleum', although archaeological finds from that period can be seen in the town's excellent Castleford Museum Room at the town library. Here, not only are these remains exhibited but there are also displays on the lives of ordinary people in Victorian Castleford.

The home of Allison's flour, which is still stone-ground on the banks of the riever, Castleford was

Castleford Crossing

172

also, in 1898, the birthplace of the internationally-renowned sculptor Henry Moore. One of the most influential artists of the 20th century, the town has honoured its famous son with Moore Square, a fine area of York stone paving with a series of large stone archways that stands close to the place where the family's home once stood – though sadly the house itself was demolished in the 1970s.

BATLEY

6 miles S of Leeds on the A653

This typical industrial town is home to the Bagshaw Museum, housed inside a strangely Gothic residence in Wilton Park. The museum was founded by the Bagshaw family and many of the collections here were gathered by them on their travels, including items brought back from Alaska by Violet Bagshaw in her 100th year! From ancient Egypt to Asia and the Americas, there are all manner of exhibits and they, along with the exotic interior of this Victorian house, make a visit here particularly memorable. Meanwhile, in the park itself there are nature trails and also the Butterfly Conservation Centre, which houses a rich assortment of butterflies, many of which are becoming close to extinction in the wild. The Centre is open from April to September.

Elsewhere in the town there is the Batley Art Gallery, which plays host to a changing programme of exhibitions that, in particular, feature local artists. In the historic Alexandra Mill there is the Skoops

Motor Museum. The collection of cars on display here ranges from a Benz Motor Wagon of 1885 to the latest Ferrari F40. The museum also boasts the only surviving Bramham – chassis number 128. The museum is open Wednesday to Sunday.

BIRSTALL

6 miles SW of Leeds on the A653

This town is home to **Oakwell Hall**, an Elizabethan manor house that dates from 1583 and is one of England's most charming historic houses. Now set out as a 17th-century home, the panelled rooms contain a fine collection of oak furniture, reproduction soft furnishings and items of domestic life. The gardens contain period plants, including culinary and medicinal herbs, while the grounds are now Oakwell Hall Country Park. Charlotte Brontë visited the Hall in the 19th century and it appears as 'Fieldhead' in her novel *Shirley*.

DEWSBURY

8 miles SW of Leeds on the A653

Dewsbury is an extremely old town which once had considerable influence. It has one of the region's oldest town centres with an imposing Town Hall designed by Henry Ashton and George Fox. It also has a number of other notable public and commercial buildings, a substantial shopping area (with some 443,500 square feet of retail floorspace) and a famous open market.

According to legend, **Dewsbury Minster** is situated at the very spot where, in AD 627, St

135 THE OLD VICARAGE HOTEL

Morley, Leeds
Awarded 2 Stars by the AA, elegant former Victorian vicarage in its own well-tended grounds.

 see page 275

136 THE NEW SCARBOROUGH INN

Tingley, Wakefield
Attractive village pub not far from J28 of the M62. Spacious, welcoming, with freshly prepared food and good range of drinks.

 see page 276

137 THE PARK

Batley
Convivial and welcoming pub with food daily, a short walk from the centre of Batley.

 see page 276

138 CAFÉ BOO

Mirfield

The best cup of coffee in town, and breakfast, hot and cold sandwiches and snacks, cakes, tea and more. Friday night tapas bar.

 see *page 276*

139 NOSH! CAFÉ BAR

Mirfield

Hot and cold meals and snacks including roast dinners and buffet lunches in modern café open from 7.30 a.m.

 see *page 278*

140 THE NAVIGATION TAVERN AND THE LOCK RESTAURANT

Mirfield

First-class food, drink and accommodation in spacious and elegant inn set alongside the Calder and Hebble Navigation Canal.

 see *page 277*

141 THE NEW CHARNWOOD

Heckmondwike

Handsome Victorian pub with range of drinks and excellent seasonally changing menu, found just south of Halifax along the River Calder.

 see *page 278*

Paulinus baptised converts to Christianity in the River Calder. The church dates from the 12th century although the tower was erected in 1767 to a design by the eminent York architect, John Carr. The interior has some interesting features, among them fragments of an Anglo-Saxon cross and coffin lids. The Minster is perhaps best known for its custom of tolling the 'Devil's Knell' on Christmas Eve to ward off evil spirits with a bell known as Black Tom. There are Brontë connections here. Patrick Brontë was curate of Dewsbury between 1809-11, and Charlotte taught at Wealds House School nearby. The school was run by a Miss Wooler who later gave her away when she was married.

The **Dewsbury Museum** is dedicated to childhood and, open all year, it takes visitors on a fascinating journey right back to the first decades of the 20th century, as seen through the eyes of a child.

GOMERSAL

8 miles SW of Leeds on the A643

This ancient village, which featured in the *Domesday Book*, is home to another house that featured in Charlotte Brontë's famous novel, *Shirley*. The Red House, which dates back to 1660, was the home of woollen cloth merchants the Taylor family, and the author often came here to see her close friend Mary Taylor in the 1830s. The house

Boer War Memorial, Dewsbury

features as 'Briarmains' in the novel. Today the house is just as the two young Victorian ladies would have remembered it, and it portrays, faithfully, middle-class domestic life of the time. There is an elegant parlour and a stone-floored kitchen while, outside in the restored barn, the Secret's Out Gallery explores the author's connections with the Spen Valley.

WAKEFIELD

One of the oldest towns in Yorkshire, Wakefield stands on a hill guarding an important crossing of the River Calder. Its defensive position has always been important and it was the Battle of Wakefield in 1460, when the Duke of York was defeated, that gave rise to the mocking song *The Grand Old Duke of York*.

Many students of the Robin Hood legends claim that the famous outlaw had his origins in Wakefield. As evidence they cite the Court Rolls in which one Robin Hode is noted as living here in the 14th century with his wife Matilda. Also medieval in origin are the **Wakefield Mystery Plays** which explore Old and New Testament stories in vivid language.

There are four main streets in the city, Westgate, Northgate, Warrengate and Kirkgate, which still preserve the medieval city plan. One of the most striking surviving buildings of that time is the tiny Chantry Chapel on Chantry Bridge which dates from the mid-1300s and is the best of only four such examples of bridge chapels in England. It is believed to have been built by Edward IV to commemorate the brutal murder of his brother Edmund. Grandest of all though is **Wakefield Cathedral** which was begun in Norman times, rebuilt in 1329 and refashioned in 1470 when its magnificent 247-ft high spire – the highest in Yorkshire – was added. The eastern extension was added in 1905 and was considered necessary after the church became a Cathedral in 1888. Other interesting buildings in the town include the stately Town Hall, the huge County Hall, the recently restored Victorian Theatre Royal and many fine Georgian and Regency terraces and squares.

Wakefield's cultural attractions include **Wakefield Art Gallery**, housed in an attractive former Victorian vicarage just a short stroll from the town centre. Collections include many early works by locally born sculptors Henry Moore and Barbara Hepworth along with important work by many other major British modern artists.

Wakefield Museum, located in an 1820s building next to the Town Hall, was originally a music saloon and then a Mechanics' Institute. It now houses collections illustrating the history and archaeology of Wakefield and its people from prehistoric times to the present day. There is also a permanent display of exotic birds and animals garnered by the noted 19th-century traveller, naturalist and eccentric Charles Waterton, who lived at nearby Walton Hall where he created the world's first nature reserve. Also of interest is the **Stephen G Beaumont Museum** which houses an unusual exhibition of medical memorabilia and exhibits telling the story of the local lunatic asylum that was founded in 1818 and only closed in 1995. The museum, which has a scale model of the early 19th-century building, is only open on Wednesdays.

Just south of the city centre stands **Sandal Castle**, a 12th-century motte-and-bailey fortress that was later replaced by a stone structure. It overlooks the site of the Battle of Wakefield in 1460. Such was this castle's importance that Richard III was planning to make Sandal his permanent northern stronghold when he was killed at Bosworth Field. Today all

142 THE QUEENS ARMS

Wakefield

Spacious 18th-century pub with food daily, situated a short drive from Wakefield off the A636.

see page 278

143 THE COCK AND BOTTLE

Ossett

Charming and convivial pub. Draught bitters, lagers and more; food midday to 3 p.m. weekdays/6 p.m. weekends.

see page 280

144 DIMPLE WELL LODGE HOTEL

Ossett

Premier hotel with excellent facilities. Superb dinner menu, ten gracious and elegant guest bedrooms.

 see page 279

145 THE BREWERS PRIDE

Ossett

This friendly Free House has eight real ales (including those from the local Ossett brewery) and is well known for miles around.

see page 280

that remains are ruins as the castle was destroyed by Cromwell's troops after a siege in 1645. From the castle there are magnificent views across the Calder Valley. Discoveries made during recent excavations of the site can be found in Wakefield's new Interpretive Centre.

A visit to the **National Coal Mining Museum** for England at Caphouse Colliery in Overton, a few miles southwest of Wakefield, includes a guided tour 450 feet underground, indoor exhibitions and videos, outdoor machine displays, a working steam winder, train rides and, for children, an adventure playground and some friendly pit ponies.

Over to the southeast from Wakefield, **Nostell Priory** is one of the most popular tourist venues in this area. The word 'priory' is misleading since it evokes the picture of an ecclesiastical

structure. But Nostell is in fact a large Palladian building erected on the site of an old Augustinian priory. It was in 1733 that the owner, Sir Rowland Winn, commissioned James Paine to build a grand mansion here. Paine was only 19 at the time and this was his first major project. Thirty years later, only half the state rooms were constructed and Sir Rowland's son, also named Rowland, engaged an up and coming young designer to complete the decoration. The young man's name was Robert Adam and between 1766 and 1776 his dazzling designs produced an incomparable sequence of interiors.

There was a third man of genius involved in the story of Nostell Priory – the cabinet maker Thomas Chippendale. What is believed to be his 'apprentice piece', made around 1735, is on display here – an extraordinary doll's house six feet high and replete with the

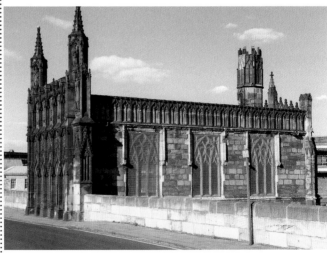

Chantry Chapel on Chantry Bridge, Wakefield

most elaborate detail, every minuscule door, window or desk drawer functioning perfectly. Today, Nostell Priory can boast the most comprehensive collection in the world of Chippendale's work.

AROUND WAKEFIELD

NORMANTON

4 miles E of Wakefield off the A655

A former mining town, Normanton has a spacious park, a moat round a hill where the Romans built a camp, and a large, mostly 15th-century church with a fine 500-year-old font. The stained glass windows here are something of an oddity since none of them originally belonged to the church. They were part of a collection amassed by a 19th-century resident of the town who was himself a glass painter and bequeathed the unrelated pieces to the church. The most striking is a 15th-century *Pietà* in the east window which has been identified as Flemish in origin.

WINTERSETT

6 miles SE of Wakefield off the A638

Found on the historic estate of Walton Hall, once the home of the famous 19th-century naturalist Charles Waterton, is the **Heronry and Waterton Countryside Discovery Centre**, which provides information and exhibitions about the surrounding country park, which includes two reservoirs and woodland that was once part of the ancient Don Forest. The centre is

open Tuesday to Friday and Sundays all year round.

RYHILL

8 miles SE of Wakefield on the B6428

The village of Ryhill is mentioned in the *Domesday Book* as part of land granted to Robert de Lacy by William the Conqueror. Known as Rihella, in 1124 Robert de Lacy transferred lands including Ryhill to Nostell Priory, where it remained in control of the Nostell canons until the Dissolution of the Monasteries in 1654. A prosperous London merchant, Sir Rowland Winn, bought the Nostell estate and Ryhill village; the estate has remained in the hands of the Winn family ever since. Ryhill attracts many visitors for its three beautiful reservoirs - popular for fishing, sailing and birdwatching - for its Heronry Centre and for some famous nature walks.

WOOLLEY

6 miles S of Wakefield off the A61

Despite being surrounded by industrial towns, Woolley has managed to retain its rural air and its old hall, now a course and conference centre, standing on land that was originally enclosed as a hunting park during the reign of Henry VII. Just to the northeast lies **Newmillerdam Country Park and Boathouse** which was, in the 19th century, part of the Chevet Estate and a playground for the local Pilkington family. The boathouse, built in the 1820s, has been restored as a visitors' centre (open Sundays and Bank Holiday

146 THE CATCHPENNY

Fitzwilliam, Pontefract

Charming, comfortable and welcoming pub, recently refurbished, in village off the B6273.

see page 280

147 THE CHURCH HOUSE

South Kirby

Outstanding, well-run pub with great food every day, stone's throw from the village church in charming location midway between Pontefract and Barnsley.

see page 281

148 THE SPORTSMAN INN

Ryhill, Wakefield

Family-run pub with home-cooked food in picturesque village off the B6428/ B6132.

see page 280

149 THE FOX & HOUNDS

Newmillerdam, Wakefield

By the A61 next to Newmillerdam Country Park, excellent ales and food in charming, welcoming pub.

see page 282

150 THE BLACK HORSE INN

Clifton, Brighouse

Superb inn with a distinguished menu, real ales and excellent accommodation, in the heart of Yorkshire yet just a mile from the M62.

  see page 283

Mondays), while the rest of the 240-acre park offers ample opportunity for walking and viewing wildlife at close quarters. Just to the northwest lies Woolley Edge, from where there are wonderful views out across Emley Moor and, on a clear day, all the way to Barnsley. The discovery of a flint axe as well as flints and scrapers from the Iron Age suggest that there have been settlements here since prehistoric times.

HUDDERSFIELD

Huddersfield's earliest roots can be found on the 1,000-ft high Castle Hill which has been occupied as a defence since the Stone Age. Simple tools, flints, bone needles, combs and pottery dating back to 2000 BC have been unearthed here. The much later ramparts of an Iron Age fort, built here around 600 BC

can still be seen. In 1147 the Normans repaired the earthworks and built a motte and bailey castle which was apparently used as a base for hunting. The hill was also used as a beacon when England was threatened by the Spanish Armada, and again during the Napoleonic wars. The lofty Jubilee Tower, built in 1897 to celebrate Queen Victoria's Diamond Jubilee, is the most recent structure on the summit and was funded by public subscription. Inside the tower there's a museum which traces the hill's 4,000 years of history.

With its steep, often cobbled streets, millstone grit cottages and larger Victorian dwellings, Huddersfield has a very distinctive character all of its own. The town flourished in Victorian times and its most impressive buildings date from that era. The stately railway station was designed by James

Castle Hill, Huddersfield

178

Pigott of York and built between 1846-50, to be followed by the Italianate Town Hall.

Back in the town, the **Tolson Memorial Museum** has displays that range from the tools of the earliest settlers in the area to modern day collections contributed by local people. One of the most popular exhibits is the collection of vintage vehicles and motoring memorabilia in the 'Going Places' collection. Other displays trace the story of the Industrial Revolution, so important to the growth of the town, and the political protests it engendered.

Huddersfield Art Gallery holds the Kirklees Collection of British Art covering the last 150 years, with a lively programme of exhibitions that showcase contemporary works from regional, national and international artists.

The town is also home to two canals that helped to link Huddersfield not only with the national canal network but also with other industrial towns. Completed in 1780 and paid for by the Ramsden family, the **Huddersfield Broad Canal** was constructed to link the town with the Calder and Hebble Navigation. The canal's Aspley Basin is today home to a marina. In 1794, work began on the **Huddersfield Narrow Canal**, linking the town with Ashton-under-Lyne. Its centrepiece, the Standedge Tunnel, took 17 years to complete and is the longest, highest and deepest canal tunnel in the country. The **Standedge Visitor Centre** at Marsden houses an exciting and interactive exhibition telling the story of the canal and the tunnel. The surrounding countryside offers a wide range of activities including walking, cycling and fishing, and this area of outstanding natural beauty is also a haven for wildlife.

AROUND HUDDERSFIELD

SCAPEGOAT HILL

3 miles W of Huddersfield off the A62 or A640

About a mile south of the oddly-named Scapegoat Hill the **Colne Valley Museum** is housed in three 19th-century weavers' cottages near the parish church. Visitors can see a loom chamber with working hand looms and a Spinning Jenny; a weavers' living room of 1850 and a gas-lit clogger's shop of 1910. On two weekends a year, a craft weekend is held when many different skills are demonstrated. Light refreshments are available and there's also a museum shop. Run entirely by its members, the museum has featured many times on TV and is open weekends and Bank Holidays throughout the year but party visits can be arranged at other times.

MARSDEN

7 miles SW of Huddersfield on the A62

Situated at the head of the Colne Valley, this village is an historic Trans-Pennine crossing point with the Standedge rail, canal tunnels and a packhorse route that leads out of the valley. It also has strong

151 COLNE VALLEY MUSEUM

Golcar

Set in three 19th century weavers' cottages, the museum offers an insight into the life and work of the time.

🏛 *see page 282*

152 BULLS HEAD

Blackmoorfoot, Linthwaite, Huddersfield

Traditional and welcoming coaching inn found two miles from Meltham, high up in Blackmoorfoot.

🍴 *see page 284*

153 THE GREAT WESTERN INN

Marsden, Huddersfield

Outstanding inn in an outstanding location, amid acres of moorland 8 miles southwest of Huddersfield on the A62.

🍴 *see page 284*

154 THE OLD FARMHOUSE TEA ROOM

Netherton, Huddersfield

Superb tea room restaurant serving brunch, lunch and afternoon tea, with fresh main courses, hot and cold gourmet sandwiches, cakes and ice creams.

 see page 285

links with the Luddites, who were opposed to the changes, particularly in mechanisation, that the Industrial Revolution brought.

Situated above the village is the Marsden Moor Estate (National Trust), a tract of nearly 6,000 acres of Pennine moorland that is full of industrial architecture. Public footpaths criss-cross this land which, as well as providing grazing for sheep, is home to numerous moorland birds including golden plover, grouse, curlew, snipe and twite. Meanwhile, the moorland's deep peat provides a habitat for acid-loving plants and for animals that can survive in this bleak and exposed environment.

ARMITAGE BRIDGE

2½ miles S of Huddersfield on the A616

This village is home to the North Light Gallery that concentrates on hosting major exhibitions of the very best in 20th-century and contemporary art while, throughout the year, the North Light Studio holds classes and a programme of weekend workshops.

HONLEY

3 miles S of Huddersfield off the A616

The centre of this delightful little Pennine village has been designated as a site of historic interest. There are charming terraces of weavers' cottages and lots of interesting alleyways, and the old village stocks still stand in the churchyard of St Mary's. The Coach and Horses Inn has strong connections with the Luddite movement of the early 1800s. It was here, in 1812, that

two Luddites, Benjamin Walker and Thomas Smith, spent the night drinking after murdering a mill owner at nearby Marsden. They were later arrested, convicted and executed at York. Not far from the inn is another interesting feature – an old well dated 1796 whose date stone warns passers-by they will be fined 10 shillings (50p) for 'defouling' the water.

MELTHAM

5 miles S of Huddersfield on the B6107/B6108

A typical Pennine mill town, Meltham is mostly Victorian but with a handsome Georgian parish church dating from 1786 which is challenged in size by the spacious Baptist Chapel, rebuilt in 1864. Only two mills have survived but the Meltham Mills Band, founded in 1845, is still thriving and has won many competitions throughout the country, including the British Championship.

Some customs of the past have also managed to survive. On Collap Monday (the day before Shrove Tuesday) the town's shopkeepers distribute free sweets to children; there is carol singing on Christmas Eve in the centre of the village; and on Whit Monday the different congregations of churches and chapels join in the Whitsuntide Walk around the town accompanied by the brass band.

THONGSBRIDGE

5 miles S of Huddersfield on the A616

Upperthong, Netherthong and Thongsbridge derive the common

element of their names from the Danish word 'thing' meaning an assembly or council. Thongsbridge is set beside a tributary of the River Holme and is very much a part of the *Last of the Summer Wine* country.

HOLMBRIDGE

7 miles S of Huddersfield on the A6024

This charming village stands at the head of a steep-sided valley and enjoys picture postcard views of the Pennines and the Holme valley. There are cottages here dating from the 1700s and the area is known for its unusual style of architecture, four-decker cottages dug into the hillside. The lower cottage is approached from the front, the upper cottage is reached by a steep flight of stone steps leading round the back.

HOLMFIRTH

6 miles S of Huddersfield on the A6024/A635

BBC-TV's longest running situation comedy, *Last of the Summer Wine*, has made the little Pennine town of Holmfirth familiar to viewers around the world. Visitors can enjoy an authentic bacon buttie in the real Sid's Café, gaze at Nora Batty's cottage and sit in the famous pub. The rest of the town offers a network of side lanes, courts and alleyways while the terraces of weavers' cottages are typical of a town famous for its production of wool textiles.

As with so many of these moorland villages, there is a lot of surrounding water and in its time Holmfirth has suffered three major floods. The worse occurred in 1852

155 HERVEY'S WINE BAR

Holmfirth

Tapas and traditional lunches and dinners at this cosy and charming establishment. Good selection of wines, real ales, spirits and lagers.

 see page 285

156 THE WHITE HORSE

Holmfirth

The inn made famous in *Last of the Summer Wine*, with superb accommodation, food and drink amid scenic surroundings.

 see page 286

Holmfirth

157 BUTCHERS ARMS

Hepworth, Holmfirth
Do seek out this marvellous inn with exceptional food, a wide selection of ales and warm and welcoming ambience.

 see page 287

158 THE GOLDEN COCK INN

Farnley Tyas, Huddersfield
Gracious and welcoming inn with first-class, delicious food and real ales, just off the A616 and A629 five miles northeast of Holmfirth.

 see page 288

when the nearby Bilberry Reservoir burst its banks, destroying mills, cottages and farms, and killing 81 people. A pillar near the church records the height the waters reached.

Holmfirth has a lovely Georgian church, built in 1777-8 in neo-classical style to the designs of Joseph Jagger. The gable faces the street and the tower is constructed at the eastern end against a steep hillside.

During the first half of the 20th century a comprehensive range of traditional saucy seaside postcards was produced by Bamforths of Holmfirth. The company also printed hymn sheets and, rather surprisingly, made many early silent movies. Bamforths also owned a cinema in the town which has recently been restored as **Picturedrome**. The re-instated building now hosts a wide range of film events and other entertainment, and also displays a selection of the vintage postcards.

HEPWORTH
7 miles S of Huddersfield on the A616

What is one to make of a village that lies on the River Jordan, has a house that has always been known as Solomon's Temple (although no one knows why), and a parcel of land called Paradise, the only place it is said where fruit trees will grow? There are some other curious names here, including Meal Hill, where the Romans brought their hand-mill stones to grind corn, and **Barracks Fold** where, during the plague, the healthy

barricaded themselves against the infected. There are still some triangular patches of land in the village that are believed to contain the common graves of the plague victims.

FARNLEY TYAS
3 miles SE of Huddersfield off the A626 or A629

Farnley Tyas is another attractive Pennine village with scattered stone farmhouses and barns, and 18th- and 19th-century workers' cottages grouped around the crossroads. It is mentioned in the *Domesday Book* as 'Fereleia': the Tyas part of its name comes from the Le Teyeis family which owned much of the land hereabouts from the 13th century.

DENBY DALE
8 miles SE of Huddersfield on the A635/A636

Denby Dale is, of course, famous for its production of gigantic meat pies. The first of these Desperate Dan-sized dishes was baked in 1788 to celebrate George III's return to sanity; later ones marked the victory of Waterloo and Queen Victoria's Jubilee. The 1928 monster meal was organised to raise funds for the Huddersfield Royal Infirmary but the festivities were almost cancelled when the organisers discovered that a large part of the pie had gone bad. Four barrowloads of stinking meat were secretly spirited away.

Perhaps because of that mishap, no more great pies were attempted until 1964 when it was decided to commemorate the four royal births of that year. On this occasion two walls of Mr Hector Buckley's barn, in which the pie had been baked, had to be demolished to get it out. The most recent pie was made in 2000 as part of the town's Millennium celebrations. It weighed a hearty 12 tonnes.

CLAYTON WEST

8 miles SE of Huddersfield on the A636

A popular attraction at Clayton West is the **Kirklees Light Railway**, a 15" gauge steam railway which runs along the old Lancashire & Yorkshire Clayton West branch line. The track runs through gently rolling farmland for about four miles with a quarter-mile long tunnel adding to the thrill. The large station/visitor centre at Clayton West provides passengers with comfortable, spacious surroundings to await their train or take advantage of the light refreshment café and the souvenir shop. The railway operates daily during the season and every weekend throughout the year. For

train times and other information, telephone 01484 865727.

One of the leading attractions of the area is found about three miles northeast of Clayton West, conveniently close to Junction 38 of the M1. The **Yorkshire Sculpture Park** draws in some 200,000 visitors a year and since you only pay a small charge for parking it represents amazing value for money. Changing exhibitions of sculpture are set in the beautiful 18th-century parkland of Bretton Hall, 200 acres of historic landscape providing a wonderful setting for some of the best sculpture to be seen in Britain today by artists from around the world.

Alongside the programme of indoor and outdoor exhibitions, more permanent features include the YSP collection of works in many different styles (from 19th-century bronzes by Rodin to contemporary sculptures), and a display of monumental bronzes by Henry Moore sited within the adjacent 100-acre Bretton Country Park.

159 THE FARMERS BOY INN & OLD BARN RESTAURANT

Shepley, Huddersfield

A traditional coaching inn with a menu of hearty favourites, real ales and a convivial atmosphere.

🍴 *see page 289*

160 THE WHITE HORSE

Emley, Huddersfield

Friendly inn with good selection of beers and more, in lovely village off the A636, A637 or A629 six miles southeast of Huddersfield.

🍴 *see page 290*

South Yorkshire

'South Yorkshire tends to be overlooked as a tourist venue, but this is a region of great age and antiquity and, in many places, real beauty, both natural and man-made. Sheffield, rightly claims to be England's greenest city, and the wild open spaces of the Pennine moorlands of the Peak District National Park roll right up to its western boundaries.

Sheffield's prosperity is founded on steel and, in particular, cutlery, and though there are few ancient buildings in England's fourth-largest city to explore, there is a wealth of museums and galleries on offer to the visitor. To the north of Sheffield is Barnsley, whose prosperity comes from the rich seams of coal that have been exploited in the local area. Meanwhile, to the east lies Rotherham, where iron ore has been mined and smelted since the 12th century. While its wealth is certainly based upon metal, Rotherham is also the home of Rockingham pottery that was once favoured by royalty.

Further east again is the charming riverside town of Doncaster, which was established by the Romans and today has the air of a pleasant market town. However, this was once one of the country's most important centres of steam locomotive manufacture and it is famous for having created the *Mallard*, which still holds the record for the top speed attained by a steam train. Today, though, Doncaster is best known as the home of the St Leger, Britain's oldest classic horse race.

Elsewhere in the county visitors can discover the delights of Roche Abbey, a 12th-century Cistercian house, Conisbrough Castle, which boasts the oldest stone keep in England, and the faded Victorian grandeur of Brodsworth Hall.

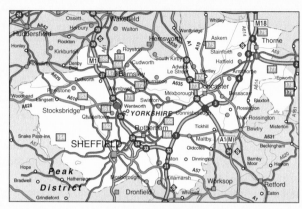

184

SHEFFIELD

In recent years Sheffield has re-invented itself. England's fourth-largest city, it is still busy with its steel, cutlery, engineering and tool-making industries but is also a vibrant, international, multi-cultural city and a world-class centre for sport, headquarters of the government-backed UK Sports Institute and with an impressive array of international venues. There are facilities for ice-skating, dry skiing and two indoor climbing centres. It has also recently overtaken Leeds as the fastest-growing city in Yorkshire, thanks to a forward-looking programme of new housing and public spaces that continue to draw students in their thousands, many of whom choose to stay on in Sheffield after they've finished their studies.

Among the city's many museums is the **Kelham Island Museum** which tells the story of Sheffield in a living museum. Visitors can see the mighty River Don Engine in steam – the most powerful working steam engine in Europe; reconstructed workshops; the 'Little Mesters' working cutler; and craftspeople demonstrating traditional 'Made in Sheffield' skills. For children up to nine years old, 'The Melting Shop' provides an interactive experience where they can 'clock on' to become a piece of steel – including being rolled and hammered!

Sheffield's industrial heritage is celebrated at the **City Museum and Mappin Art Gallery** (free) in

Weston Park. The museum houses the city's collection of cutlery, metalwork, ceramics, coins, archaeology and natural history. The Mappin Art Gallery has a permanent display of Victorian paintings and organises an imaginative programme of temporary exhibitions.

Sheffield has several outstanding galleries devoted to the visual arts. The **Millenium Galleries** have helped to establish the city as a cultural force in the north of England. A remarkable building of white columns and

Sheffield Cathedral

185

•

Sheffield's most picturesque museum is undoubtedly the Bishop's House Museum which dates from around 1500 and is the earliest timber-framed house still standing in the city. Many original features survive and the bedchamber and great parlour are furnished in the style of the home of a prosperous 17th-century yeoman. There are also displays on Sheffield in Tudor and Stuart times, and changing exhibitions on local history themes.

•

161 THE COMMERCIAL INN

Chapeltown, Sheffield

Excellent pub with up to 12 real ales to sup and hearty and freshly prepared food daily.

 see page 290

striking glass arches, it holds four unique galleries that showcase not only Sheffield's impressive metalware collection but also provide space to show the city's wonderful collection of paintings, drawings and natural history exhibits. One gallery hosts visiting installations from the Victoria & Albert museum and other distinguished collections from throughout the country; another features the very best of contemporary design and technology, while a third houses the fascinating collection formed for the people of Sheffield in 1875 by the Victorian artist, critic and sage John Ruskin. It includes paintings, watercolours and drawings, minerals, plaster casts and architectural details, illuminated manuscripts and books.

Nearby, the **Graves Art Gallery** (free) displays a wide-ranging collection of British art, from the 16th century to the present, along with European paintings and a fine collection of watercolours, drawings and prints. One of its major treasures is the Grice Collection of Chinese ivories which forms the centrepiece of a display of non-European artefacts.

Another gallery of interest, the **Site Gallery** (free), is devoted to photographic and new media exhibitions and events. One of the largest contemporary visual art and media centres in the country, the gallery also offers darkroom and digital imaging facilities, as well as photographic and digital courses in the recently created education suite.

The **Traditional Heritage Museum** offers a unique collection of displays on life and work in the city between the 1850s and 1950s while, at the University of Sheffield, the **Turner Museum of Glass** contains over 300 items of contemporary and art glass from Europe and the United States along with a unique collection of over 100 drinking glasses.

A museum of a very different nature is the **Sheffield Bus Museum**, housed in the Tinsley Tram sheds on Sheffield Road. The collection includes many types of bus and other transport-related exhibits such as destination blinds, old timetables and models. The museum also houses the Tinsley Model Railway layout.

Of related interest is the **South Yorkshire Railway** in Meadowbank. As well as displaying more than 60 locomotives, there are vintage carriages and wagons, and a signal box. Plans are under way to run a steam-hauled passenger service on the three-and-a-half miles line from Meadowhall to Chapeltown.

Nor is Sheffield all hustle and bustle. The city's most peaceful spot has to be the **Botanical Gardens** with collections of shrubs, trees and plantings sheltered in an historic landscape first opened in 1836.

AROUND SHEFFIELD

CROSSPOOL

4 miles W of Sheffield on the A57

Intriguingly, it was a fit of pique

that led to the building of **The Bell Hagg Inn**. Back in the 1830s a certain Dr Hodgson offered the vicar of Stannington (a village across the River Rivel from Crosspool) a large donation for the church funds. But Hodgson was well known as a gambler and frequenter of pubs so the vicar declined the generous offer. Incensed by this rebuff, Hodgson bought the land directly opposite the church and built the pub there, a monument to drinking that no one attending Divine Service at Stannington church could possibly overlook. It clings to the cliffside, a defiant piece of architecture obviously intended to make a statement. Amazingly, the pub survived Dr Hodgson and today it's owned and run by John and Genine Chidlaw who offer their customers excellent food, well-maintained ales, varied entertainment and comfortable accommodation.

OUGHTIBRIDGE
5 miles NW of Sheffield on the A6102

This pleasing village is set on the west bank of the River Don looking across to the tree-covered slopes of Wharncliffe Wood. The settlement dates back to Saxon times at least but surprisingly there is no church and no evidence of there ever having been one.

WHARNCLIFFE SIDE
5 miles NW of Sheffield on the A6102

Nestling in the valley below Wharncliffe Crags, Wharncliffe Side is a community of some 2,000 people and a popular location for commuters to Sheffield and Stocksbridge. An old tradition in the village tells of the Dragon of Wantly which lurked in the recesses of the crags and terrorised the local people until a knight by the name of More did battle with the monster and killed it. A cave up on the crags is still called the Dragon's Den and local children experience an enjoyable frisson of terror by shouting into its depths. Another ancient tradition in the village is the Whitsuntide walk when Sunday school children process around Wharncliffe Side stopping at various points to sing hymns.

PENISTONE
15 miles NW of Sheffield on the A628

Perched 700 feet above sea level, Penistone forms a gateway to the Peak District National Park which extends for some 30 miles to the south of the town. Penistone's oldest building is the 15th-century tower of its parish church which overlooks a graveyard in which ancestors of the poet William Wordsworth are buried. Later centuries added an elegant Dissenters' Chapel (in the 1600s) and a graceful Cloth Hall in the 1700s.

RENISHAW
9 miles SE of Sheffield on the A616

This sizeable village gives its name to **Renishaw Hall**, home of Sir Reresby and Lady Sitwell and located about a mile or so to the northwest. The beautiful formal Italian gardens and 300 acres of wooded park are open to visitors, along with a nature trail and a

162 OLD RED LION
Grenoside, Sheffield
Attractive, traditional 18th-century coaching inn with excellent food and drink every day.

 see page 290

163 THE WAGGON & HORSES

Oxspring, Sheffield
Charming 18th-century pub on the edge of the Peak District National Park with excellent food, including special world cuisine nights.

see page 291

164 THE STRINES INN
Bradfield, Sheffield
Fantastic public house with accommodation amidst breathtaking moorland scenery within the Peak District National Park.

 see page 291

About three miles northeast of Wales, at North Aston, is the Tropical Butterfly House, Falconry and Wildlife Centre. Here you can, if you wish, hold a tarantula or fondle a snake. Children can cuddle a bunny or bottle feed a calf. The Centre includes a well-stocked tropical butterfly house, a Bird of Prey centre which has regular flying demonstrations, an Animal Nursery, Farmyard Corner, Nature Trail, children's play area and gift shop.

Sitwell family museum, an art gallery, a display of Fiori de Henriques sculptures in the Georgian stables, and a café. The Hall itself is open to group and connoisseur tours by special arrangement only.

WALES

9 miles SE of Sheffield on the B6059

A mile or so to the west of Wales the **Rother Valley Country Park** provides excellent facilities for water sports including sailing, windsurfing, canoeing and jet skiing, as well as a cable water ski tow. Visitors can hire equipment or use their own, and training courses from beginner to instructor level are available in various water sports. Other attractions include a lakeside golf course, a Craft Centre with craftspeople at work, cycle hire, gift shop, cafeteria – and Playdales, a 'mega play area' for children under 14.

ROTHERHAM

The town's most striking building is undoubtedly the **Church of All Saints**. With its soaring tower, pinnacled buttresses and battlements, and imposing porch, it is one of the finest examples of perpendicular architecture in Yorkshire. It dates mainly from the 15th century although there is evidence of an earlier Saxon church on the site.

A church here was listed in the *Domesday Book* and in 1161 the monks of Rufford Abbey were granted the right to prospect for

and to smelt iron, and to plant an orchard, and from that day industry has existed side by side with agriculture.

Seventy-five per cent of the Borough of Rotherham is actually rural but it was heavy industry that put the town on the map. From the mid-18th century, the Walker Company of Rotherham was famous for cannons, their products serving to lethal effect in the American War of Independence and at the Battle of Trafalgar. They also built bridges, among them Southwark Bridge in London and the bridge at Sunderland. Another famous bridge builder was born here in 1901: Sir Donald Coleman Bailey invented the Bailey Bridge which proved to be of great military value, especially during the Second World War.

The town also had lighter industries. Rockingham Pottery, produced here in the late 18th and early 19th century, is now highly prized by collectors. There's a fine collection at the **Clifton Park Museum,** a stately building whose interior has changed little since it was built in 1783 for the Rotherham ironmaster, Joshua Walker. The most breathtaking piece is the spectacular Rhinoceros Vase which stands almost four feet high. In addition, the museum houses a collection of other Yorkshire pottery, English glass, silver and British oil paintings and watercolours. The grounds around Clifton House form the largest urban park in the Borough which has 10 urban parks altogether, along with three country parks, seven golf courses, 10 swimming pools and a leisure centre.

Another museum of interest is the **York and Lancaster Regimental Museum** in the Central Library. The regiment had strong ties with South Yorkshire, its recruits drawn mainly from Barnsley, Sheffield and Rotherham. The displays include historic uniforms, campaign relics and more than 1,000 medals, among them nine Victoria Cross groups. There are also sections on local militia, rifle volunteers and territorials.

Dramatically set within the former Templeborough steelworks, **Magna** was the UK's first science adventure park. This imaginative exploration of the power of the four natural elements – earth, air, fire and water – offers visitors the opportunity of experiencing the full power of lightning, firing a water cannon, manoeuvring a real JCB digger, getting close to a tornado or blowing up a virtual rock face. In the Living Robots Show predator robots pursue each other in an epic struggle to survive and breed. In the Power Pavilion, after donning overalls and cap for your 'shift', you can shed a few pounds by creating electricity on a giant treadmill, test your strength in a self-lifting chair, attack a target with a giant catapult and discover how much you would weigh on the planets Mars or Jupiter. The site also has a restaurant, cafeteria, picnic areas and shops.

To the northwest of the town, the palatial 18th-century mansion **Wentworth Woodhouse** boasts the longest frontage in England, some 600 feet long. The house is not open to the public but is clearly visible from its Park. Also visible are a number of follies and monuments dating from the 1700s. The most curious of these is the Needle's Eye which consists of a tower with a stone urn on top and is pierced by a carriageway. Legend says it was built in response to a wager by the Marquis of Rockingham, owner of Wentworth Woodhouse, that he could drive through the eye of a needle. One structure which *is* open (on Sunday afternoons during the season), is the Wentworth Mausoleum which was built in 1788 in memory of the 2nd Marquis.

A little further afield, near the village of Maltby, are the dramatic ruins of **Roche Abbey** (English Heritage). The abbey dates from the 12th century and takes its name from the rocky limestone of the riverside site. The majestic remains of this great abbey stand in a landscape fashioned by Capability Brown in the 1770s as part of the grounds of Sandbeck Park, home of the Earls of Scarborough.

Roche Abbey

189

165 THE FULLERTON HOTEL

Thrybergh, Rotherham

Impressive and welcoming inn a few miles northeast of Rotherham off the A630, open daily for great food and drink.

 see page 291

166 THE TRAVELLERS INN

Bramley, Rotherham

Home-cooked food, draught keg ales and a welcoming, friendly atmosphere at inn found on the A631 east of Rotherham.

 see page 292

167 MORNING STAR INN

Barnsley

Handsome 1930s inn with draught keg ales, hot and cold snacks all day long and comfortable accommodation.

 see page 292

AROUND ROTHERHAM

TANKERSLEY

7½ miles N of Sheffield off the A6195

This parish is mentioned in the *Domesday Book*, and the Hall here was used in the now-classic film of the 1970s, *Kes*. During the War of the Roses between the houses of York and Lancaster, Tankersley Park was the site of a battle; it again saw conflict later during the Civil War when the Royalists gained victory over Cromwell's troops. In the 14th-century Church of St Peter there are cannon balls and a bullet found after that battle.

WORTLEY

8 miles NW of Sheffield on the A629

This village's name comes from the Saxon meaning 'clearing for growing vegetables' and archaeological investigations on Wharncliffe Chase have indicated that there was a small British settlement here during the time of the Roman occupation. Mentioned in the *Domesday Book*, although it had declined in importance since the reign of Edward the Confessor, in the late 12th century Cistercian monks began to lay the foundations of the iron industry, and iron-forging began here in the Middle Ages. In the 1700s Sir Thomas Wortley built Wharncliffe Lodge as a hunting lodge and, just over a century later during the Civil War, Sir Francis Whortley raised a private army of 900 to fight for the king's cause.

The ancestral home of the Wortley family, Wortley Hall, was built in the late 1500s on the site of an older residence; over the centuries it has been much altered and even left to decay. Restoration work was carried out in the late 18th and early 19th centuries, and it was also around this time that the landscaping and ornamental planning of the grounds and gardens took place.

Back in the village there are the school and schoolhouse built in 1874 by the Wortley family and only closed in 1993, while the oldest house in the village, Tividale Cottage, was practically rebuilt and certainly modernised in 1983. In the early 1700s this was the home of head-master William Nevison, and the cottage is thought to have been the birthplace of his son, the highwayman John Nevison.

Just outside the village are Top and Low Forge, which are said to have been in operation in the 12th century although the earliest documentation dates from 1567. However, by the 17th century these two forges were working ceaselessly, along with many others in the area and, while Top Forge closed in 1912, Low Forge continued production until 1929.

BARNSLEY

The county town of South Yorkshire, Barnsley stands on the River Dearne and derived its Victorian prosperity from the rich seams of coal hereabouts. It has an appropriately imposing Town Hall although the building is comparatively recent, completed in 1933. Nearby, the **Cooper Gallery** is a lively centre for the arts which hosts a varied programme of exhibitions throughout the year as well as housing a fine permanent collection.

The town's most impressive museum is actually located a few miles to the west, in the village of Cawthorne. **Cannon Hall** is a magnificent 18th-century country house set in formal gardens and historic parkland. It offers unique collections of pottery, furniture, glassware and paintings, along with the 'Charge Gallery' which documents the story of the 13th/18th Royal Hussars.

About a mile to the south of Barnsley is the **Worsbrough Mill Museum and Country Park**. The Grade II listed mill dates from around 1625. A steam mill was added in the 19th century and both have been restored to full working order to form the centrepiece of an industrial museum. Wholemeal flour, ground at the mills, can be bought here. The mill is set within a beautiful 200-acre country park, whose reservoir attracts a great variety of birds including heron.

Another three miles to the southeast, situated in attractive South Yorkshire countryside just off the M1 (J36), the **Elsecar Heritage Centre** is an imaginative science and history centre which is fun and educational for all the family. Visitors can discover hands-on science in the Power House; nostalgic travel on the Elsecar

Steam Railway; the history of South Yorkshire in the Elsecar People exhibition; and interactive multi-media in the Newcomen Beam Engine Centre. The centre is also the base for several working craftspeople who make and sell their products here. Special events include a Friends of Thomas the Tank Engine day.

AROUND BARNSLEY

SILKSTONE
4 miles W of Barnsley off the A628

The travel writer Arthur Mee dubbed Silkstone's parish church 'The Minster of the Moors' and it is indeed a striking building. Parts of the church date back to Norman times but most of it was built during the golden age of English ecclesiastical architecture, the 15th century. Outside, there are graceful flying buttresses and wonderfully weird gargoyles. Inside, the ancient oak roofs sprout floral bosses on moulded beams, and old box-pews and lovely medieval screens all add to the charm.

The old stocks just outside **The Ring o' Bells** are another sign of the antiquity of this former mining village.

THURLSTONE
9 miles SW of Barnsley off the A628

Thurlstone developed when the first settlers realised that the nearby moors provided extensive grazing for sheep and the lime-free waters of the River Don were ideal for the washing of wool. Today the village still has some fine examples of the

168 THE TALBOT INN AND RESTAURANT

Mapplewell, Barnsley

Excellent cuisine with full menu and specials board of meat, fish, poultry and vegetarian dishes expertly prepared and presented.

🍴 *see page 293*

169 THE FULL HOUSE AND SANGDAO'S THAI RESTAURANT

Monk Bretton, Barnsley

Spacious and attractive place with two bars and authentic Thai restaurant (Weds-Sat 6.30-10.30) and traditional Sunday carvery (12-5).

🍴 *see page 294*

170 THE WHARNCLIFFE ARMS

Carlton, Barnsley

Large and impressive pub; hearty and tasty food and drink; on the B6132 a few miles north of Barnsley.

🍴 *see page 295*

171 THE SHIP INN

Elsecar

Just a few steps from the Heritage Centre in Elsecar, a friendly and comfortable pub open every session, all day at weekends.

 see page 295

172 THE DROP INN

Wombwell, Barnsley

Friendly family-run inn with food, drink and comfortable chalet-style accommodation.

 page 295

weavers' cottages which sprang up during the early 19th century, the best of which can be seen on Tenter Hill. Here the finished cloth would have been dried and stretched on 'tenters' – large wooden frames placed outside on the street which gave the road its name.

The village's most famous son was Nicholas Saunderson, born in 1682, who was blinded by smallpox at the age of two. He taught himself to read by passing his fingers over the tombstones in Penistone churchyard – 150 years before the introduction of Braille. Nicholas went on to attend grammar school and rose to become Professor of Mathematics at Cambridge University.

DUNFORD BRIDGE

15 miles SW of Barnsley off the A628

Located just inside the Peak National Park, The Stanhope Arms is very much a hidden place. The hamlet of Dunford Bridge is only shown on very large scale maps but if you are travelling westwards from Barnsley on the A628, after 13 miles or so you will see a sign for the pub off to the right. It's well worth seeking out this grand old inn, originally built in the 1800s as a shooting lodge for the Cannon Hall Estate. It stands beside the entrance to the Woodhead railway tunnel which runs beneath the moors for more than three miles. When the tunnel opened in 1852 it was twice as long as any other in the world. There's an interesting

display of memorabilia regarding the tunnel and the camp built for the Tunnel Tigers (the men who built it), in the snug of the Stanhope Arms.

DONCASTER

The Romans named their riverside settlement beside the River Don *Danum*, and a well-preserved stretch of the road they built here can be seen just west of Adwick le Street. The modern town boasts some impressive buildings, notably the Mansion House built in 1748 and designed by James Paine. The Minster of St George was rebuilt in 1858 by Sir George Gilbert Scott and it's an outstanding example of Gothic revival architecture with its lofty tower, 170 feet high and crowned with pinnacles. The lively shopping centre is enhanced by a stately Corn Exchange building and a market which takes place every Tuesday, Friday and Saturday. Doncaster was once one of the most important centres for the production of steam engines. Thousands were built here, including both the Flying Scotsman and the Mallard. The Mallard still holds the record for the fastest steam train in the world, achieving a top speed of 125mph in July 1938. For a further insight into the history of the town and surrounding area, there is **Doncaster Museum** which contains several exciting and informative exhibitions on the various aspects of natural history,

local history and archaeology.
Housed in the same building is the
**Regimental Museum of the
King's Own Yorkshire Light
Infantry**, which reflects the history
of this famous local regiment.

There is no-one connected
with the racing fraternity who has
not heard of the St Leger, one of
the oldest classic races, which has
been held at Doncaster since 1776.
Doncaster Racecourse provides a
magnet for all horse-racing
enthusiasts and there are a total of
26 meetings each year.

Another three miles or so to
the northwest of Doncaster,
Brodsworth Hall (English
Heritage) is a remarkable example
of a Victorian mansion that has
survived with many of its original
furnishings and decorations intact.
When Charles and Georgiana
Thellusson, their six children and
15 servants moved into the new
hall in 1863 the house must have
seemed the last word in both
grandeur and utility. A gasworks in
the grounds supplied the lighting
and no fewer than eight water
closets were distributed around the
house, although rather surprisingly
only two bathrooms were installed.

More immediately impressive
to visitors were the opulent
furnishings, paintings, statuary and
decoration. The sumptuous
reception rooms have now a rather
faded grandeur and English
Heritage has deliberately left it so,
preserving the patina of time
throughout the house to produce
an interior that is both fascinating

Sandell Park, Doncaster

and evocative. A vanished way of
life is also brought to life in the
huge kitchen and the cluttered
servants wing. The Hall stands in
15 acres of beautifully restored
Victorian gardens, complete with a
summer house in the form of a
classical temple, a target range
where the family practised its
archery, and a pets cemetery where
the family dogs - and a prized
parrot with the unimaginative
name of Polly - were buried
between 1894 and 1988. There is
also a fascinating exhibition
illustrating the family's obsession -
yachting.

•

*On the northwestern
outskirts of Doncaster,
Cusworth Hall is home
to the Museum of South
Yorkshire Life. The Hall
is a splendid Georgian
mansion built in the
1740s and set in a
landscaped park. The
interior features varied
displays on the social
history, industry,
agriculture and transport
in the area.*

•

173 CUSWORTH HALL
TEA ROOM

Cusworth, Doncaster

Cosy, comfortable tea room
serving fresh home-made
meals and cakes.

 see page 296

174 THE DRUM

Bentley, Doncaster

Traditional coaching inn
open all day, every day for
ale. Food at lunch and
dinner Tuesday to Saturday.
Sunday carvery 12-4.

 see page 296

175 THE CROWN
HOTEL

Askern, Doncaster

Exceptional village inn a few
miles north of Doncaster on
the A19.

 see page 296

176 MOORENDS HOTEL

Moorends, nr Doncaster

East of the A614 a short
drive from J6 of the M18.
Open all day. Draught ales,
food, nine guest bedrooms.

 see page 296

AROUND DONCASTER

NORTON

8 miles N of Doncaster off the A19

This sizeable village is located close
to the borders with North and West
Yorkshire and was once busy with
farming, mining and quarrying.
Nowadays it's a peaceful place, a
tranquil base for commuters to
Doncaster and Pontefract. Its most
impressive building is the ancient
parish church of **St Mary
Magdalene** whose splendid 14th-
century west tower is considered by
many to be the finest in Yorkshire.
Once there was also a priory here,
standing beside the River Went, but
now only a fragment of wall
remains. However, the old water
mill has survived.

STAINFORTH

7 miles NE of Doncaster off the A18 or A614

Stainforth was once an important
trading centre and inland port on
the River Don. It also stands on the
banks of the Stainforth & Keadby
Canal which still has a well-
preserved dry dock and a 19th-
century blacksmith's shop. This area
of low, marshy ground was drained
by Dutch engineers in the 1600s to
produce rich, peaty farmland. The
place has retained the air of a quiet
backwater, a little-explored area of
narrow lands and pretty hamlets,
the fields drained by slow-flowing
dykes and canals. The rich peat
resources are commercially
exploited in part but also provide a
congenial home for a great deal of
natural wildlife.

FISHLAKE

10 miles NE of Doncaster off the A614

Set along the banks of the River
Don, which is known here as the
Dutch River, Fishlake is effectively
an island since it is surrounded by
rivers and canals and can only be
entered by crossing a bridge. It's a
charming village with a striking
medieval church famous for its
elaborately carved Norman
doorway, an ancient windmill and a
welcoming traditional inn.

THORNE

10 miles NE of Doncaster on the A614

This ancient market town on the
River Don has been a port since at
least 1500 with ships sailing from
here to York, Hull, London and
Europe. The waterfront was once
busy with boat-builder's yards
where vessels of up to 400 tons
were built. In 1802, Thorne gained
a second waterfront, on the newly
constructed Stainforth & Keadby
Canal which attracted most of the
water traffic from the unpredictable
River Don. As late as 1987 there
were still boat building yards at
work here but in that year they
finally closed and the area is being
carefully developed in a way that
will commemorate the town's
heritage.

BRANTON

4½ miles E of Doncaster off the B1396

Surrounded by agricultural land,
Brockholes Farm has been a
working farm since 1759 and one
where the traditional farming skills
have been passed down from one

generation to the next. Today, at **Brockhole Riding and Visitor Centre**, visitors can see demonstrations of those same skills, such as those carried out by the farrier and the shepherd, as well as seeing many animals associated with traditional free-range farming. There is also a riding centre here that caters for complete beginners through to experienced riders and, along with professional instructors, has a range of horses and ponies to suit all ages and abilities.

FINNINGLEY

7 miles SE of Doncaster on the A614

A unique feature of this pleasant village close to the Nottinghamshire border is its five village greens, the main one having a duck pond complete with weeping willows. Finningley is a living village with a well-used Village Hall, originally a barn but which later served as the village school. Finningley has a beautiful Norman church with a rectors' list dating back to 1293 and a post office which has been in the same family for five generations. The year 2004 saw the opening of the international **Robin Hood Aiport** outside the village, which utilised the runways from the old RAF base, built just before World War II. This has led to increased development and investment in the area while not disturbing Finningley's traditional appeal.

BAWTRY

9 miles SE of Doncaster on the A614

This pleasant little market town stands close to the Nottinghamshire

River Don, Thorne

border and in medieval times it was customary for the Sheriff of South Yorkshire to welcome visiting kings and queens here. In the mid-1500s the then Sheriff, Sir Robert Bowes, accompanied by 200 gentlemen dressed in velvet and 4,000 yeomen on horseback, greeted Henry VIII and – in the name of Yorkshire – presented him with a purse containing the huge sum of £900 in gold.

Today's Bawtry is an upmarket and exciting town with a brand new airport – the Robin Hood Airport, opened in 2004 at nearby Finningley – very good shopping in

177   THE REINDEER

Sandtoft

Superb traditional inn hidden away on the Lincolnshire/Yorkshire border off the A18/A614/ A161.

see page 297

178 THE EPWORTH TAP

Epworth

Stylish bistro, restaurant and wine bar in the heart of Epworth, found 15 minutes from the M180 northeast of Doncaster.

 see page 298

179 WESLEY GUEST HOUSE

Epworth, nr Doncaster

Luxury guest house accommodation in the historic village of Epworth, 15 minutes from the M180.

 see page 299

select boutiques, and an impressive selection of excellent and stylish restaurants. As befits a place that can trace its traditions and heritage back to its days as a bustling 12th-century port on the River Idle with strong connections to the founding fathers of the United States, it has managed to maintain its sense of history and distinct character while keeping up with the times. A happy mix of stunning buildings, small boutiques and sophisticated restaurants, it remains the quintessential English town. Many of the buildings are grand three-storey Georgian affairs that help the town maintain a tranquil and restrained appearance, and shoppers will find everything from clothes and accessories to furniture, soft furnishings and general items for the home. Once a coaching stagepost along the old Great North Road, it continues its proud tradition of offering great food and drink to visitors with a range of elegant eateries that are justly

popular, so that the town has become a regular evening hot spot, particularly at the weekend. The airport has led to increased investment in the area and Bawtry is set to see more changes and improvements in goods and services on offer while maintaining its traditional attractions that make it stand out.

NORTH ANSTON
12 miles S of Doncaster on the A57

This village, separated from its neighbour South Anston by the main road, is home to the **Tropical Butterfly House, Wildlife and Falconry Centre** where not only can visitors see exotic butterflies, birds, snakes and crocodiles in a tropical jungle setting but also enjoy outdoor falconry displays and, at the baby farm animal area, bottle-feed lambs (depending on the season). This centre, open all year, also has a nocturnal reptile room, nature trail and children's outdoor play area.

THORPE SALVIN
14 miles S of Doncaster off the A57

This attractive village is home to the now-ruined Thorpe Salvin Hall, which dates from 1570 and is thought to have been the inspiration for Torquilstone in Sir Walter Scott's *Ivanhoe*.

CADEBY
4 miles SW of Doncaster off the A630

Listed in the *Domesday Book* as 'Catebi', this pleasant little

Thorpe Salvin Hall

village is surrounded on all sides by prime agricultural land. For centuries Cadeby had no church of its own; parishioners had to travel some two miles to the parish church in Sprotbrough. Then in 1856 the owners of the huge Sprotbrough estate, the Copley family, paid for a church to be built in Cadeby. It was designed by Sir George Gilbert Scott, the architect of St Pancras Station in London, and resembles a medieval estate barn with its steeply pitched roofs and lofty south porch. A century and a half later, Cadeby is again without a church since Sir George's attractive church has recently been declared redundant.

Conisbrough Castle

floor chamber where the huge open fireplaces give one a fascinating insight into the lifestyle of Norman times. The castle also offers a visual presentation, a visitor centre and a tea room.

CONISBROUGH

5 miles SW of Doncaster on the A630

The town is best known for the 11th-century **Conisbrough Castle** (English Heritage) which features prominently in one of the most dramatic scenes in Sir Walter Scott's novel *Ivanhoe*. The most impressive medieval building in South Yorkshire, Conisbrough Castle boasts the oldest circular keep in England. Rising some 90 feet and more than 50 feet wide, the keep stands on a man-made hill raised in Saxon times. Six huge buttresses some 6 feet thick support walls that in places are 15 feet deep. Visitors can walk through the remains of several rooms, including the first

SWINTON

8 ½ miles SW of Doncaster on the B6090

This is the town that is home of the world-famous Rockingham porcelain; the story of the amazing small country pottery which grew to become the king's porcelain manufacturer before falling into bankruptcy is told in a special gallery at Clifton Park Museum, Rotherham. However, here in Swinton itself visitors can still see the secluded Swinton Pottery site where, in beautiful surroundings, the Waterloo Kiln (built in 1815) and the Pottery Ponds are the only surviving landmarks of the renowned Rockingham Porcelain works.

Accommodation, Food & Drink and Places of Interest

The establishments featured in this section includes hotels, inns, guest houses, bed & breakfasts, restaurants, cafes, tea and coffee shops, tourist attractions and places to visit. Each establishment has an entry number which can be used to identify its location at the beginning of the relevant county chapter. This section is ordered by county and the page number in the column to to right indicates the first establishment in each county.

In addition full details of all these establishments and many others can be found on the Travel Publishing website - www.travelpublishing.co.uk. This website has a comprehensive database ocovering the whole of Britain and Ireland.

🍴 FOOD & DRINK

2	The Burgoyne Hotel, Reeth
3	The King's Head, Gunnerside
5	The Golden Lion Hotel, Leyburn
6	The Queens Head, Finghall
7	The Three Horseshoes Inn, Wensley
8	Palmer Flatt Hotel, Aysgarth
9	The White Rose Hotel, Askrigg
10	Wilson's, Hawes
11	Beckindales Continental Café, Hawes
13	The Willow, Pateley Bridge
14	Buffers Coffee Shop, Storiths
16	The Blue Bell Inn, Kettlewell
17	The Kings Head, Kettlewell
19	The Royal Shepherd, Skipton
21	The Waterside, Skipton
22	The Dog and Gun Inn, Sutton-in-Craven
23	The Lister Arms Hotel, Malham
24	The Boar's Head Hotel, Long Preston
26	The Lamb and Flag, Ripon
27	Dish's Café Bar & Bistro, Ripon
29	The George and Dragon Inn, Melmerby
30	The Masons Arms, Bishop Monkton
32	Divan Hotel, Thirsk
34	The Vale of York, Carlton Miniott
35	The Dog & Gun, Carlton Miniott
36	The Wellington Heifer, Ainderby Steeple
37	The Waggon and Horses, Bedale
38	Otterington Shorthorn, South Otterington
39	The Moors Tea Room, Danby
40	Castleton Tea Rooms, Castleton
43	The Barn Hotel & Tea Rooms, Hutton-le-Hole
45	The White Horse and Griffin Hotel, Whitby
47	The Khyber Restaurant, Whitby
48	The Bottom House, Whitby
50	Estbek House, Sandsend
51	Bridge Cottage Café Tea Rooms, Sandsend
52	The Wilson Arms, Sneaton
54	The Anvil Inn, Sawdon
56	Victoria Court Bar & Restaurant, Filey
58	The Ship Inn, Muston
59	The Buck Inn, Hunmanby
60	The New Inn, Thornton-le-Dale
61	The Black Swan, Kirkbymoorside
62	The Feathers Hotel, Helmsley
64	The Pheasant at Harome, Harome
67	The Hidden Monkey Tea Rooms, Malton
68	The King's Head, Malton
69	The Queen's Head, Amotherby

70	The Cresswell Arms, Appleton-le-Street
72	The Middleton Arms, North Grimston
75	The Dawnay Arms, Shipton by Beningbrough
76	The College Arms, Linton-on-Ouse
77	The Blue Bell Country Inn, Alne
79	Wombwell Arms, Wass
81	St Vincent Arms, Sutton upon Derwent
82	The White Swan Inn, Wighill
84	The Chestnut Horse, Great Kelk
85	The Buck Hotel, Driffield
86	The Bell in Driffield, Driffield
87	The Bay Horse Inn, Kilham
89	The Gait Inn, Millington
90	The Windmill Inn, Beverley
91	The Corner House, Beverley
92	Crown & Anchor, Tickton
94	The Rose and Crown, Hornsea
95	The Marine Hotel, Hornsea
96	Sal's Café and Steak House, Hornsea
97	Thompson's Traditional Fish & Chips, Brandesburton
99	The Holderness Inn, Patrington
100	The Burns Head Inn, Patrington Haven
101	Coach and Horses, Welwick
102	The New Inn, Barlby
103	The Greyhound Inn, Riccall
104	The Ash Tree Inn & Restaurant, Barkston Ash
105	The Plough Inn, Snaith
106	The Brewers Arms Hotel, Snaith
107	The Viking Hotel, Goole
108	The White Swan, Bubwith
109	The Station Hotel, Howden
110	The Royal Oak, Portington
111	The Black Swan, Eastrington
112	The Half Moon, Elloughton
113	The Green Dragon, Welton
114	Oliver's Coffee Shop, Swanland
116	The Kings Arms, Haworth
117	Stump Cross Inn, Stump Cross
119	The Windmill Inn, Shelf
120	The Queen Victoria, Northowram
121	The Brown Horse Inn, Coley
122	Old Glen House, Baildon
123	Readers at St Ives, Bingley
124	The Brown Cow, Bingley
125	The Fisherman's, Dowley Gap
126	The Grouse at Silsden, Silsden
127	The Dalesway Hotel, Ilkley
128	The Ring O' Bells, Newmarket
129	The Black Horse at Askwith, Askwith
131	The Liquorice Bush, Pontefract
132	The White Horse , Ledston
133	The New Wheatsheaf, Whitwood
134	The Golden Lion Hotel, Ferrybridge
135	The Old Vicarage Hotel, Morley
136	The New Scarborough Inn, Tingley

137	The Park, Batley
138	Café Boo, Mirfield
139	Nosh! Café Bar, Mirfield
140	The Navigation Tavern & The Lock Restaurant, Mirfield
141	The New Charnwood, Heckmondwike
142	The Queens Arms, Wakefield
143	The Cock and Bottle, Ossett
144	Dimple Well Lodge Hotel, Ossett
145	The Brewers Pride, Ossett
146	The Catchpenny, Fitzwilliam
147	The Church House, South Kirby
148	The Sportsman Inn, Ryhill
149	The Fox and Hounds, Newmillerdam
150	The Black Horse Inn, Clifton
152	Bulls Head, Blackmoorfoot
153	The Great Western Inn, Marsden
154	The Old Farmhouse Tea Room, Netherton
155	Hervey's Wine Bar, Holmfirth
156	The White Horse, Holmfirth
157	Butchers Arms, Hepworth
158	The Golden Cock Inn, Farnley Tyas
159	The Farmers Boy Inn & Old Barn Restaurant, Shepley
160	The White Horse, Emley
161	The Commercial Inn, Chapeltown
162	Old Red Lion, Grenoside
163	The Waggon and Horses, Oxspring
164	The Strines Inn, Bradfield Dale
165	The Fullerton Hotel, Thrybergh
166	The Travellers Inn, Bramley
167	Morning Star Inn, Barnsley
168	The Talbot Inn and Restaurant, Mapplewell
169	The Full House and Sangdao's Thai Restaurant, Monk Bretton
170	The Wharncliffe Arms, Carlton
171	The Ship Inn, Elsecar
172	The Drop Inn, Wombwell
173	Cusworth Hall Tea Room, Cusworth
174	The Drum, Bentley
175	The Crown Hotel, Askern
176	Moorends Hotel, Moorends
177	The Reindeer, Sandtoft
178	The Epworth Tap, Epworth

🏨 ACCOMMODATION

2	The Burgoyne Hotel, Reeth
5	The Golden Lion Hotel, Leyburn
6	The Queens Head, Finghall
8	Palmer Flatt Hotel, Aysgarth
9	The White Rose Hotel, Askrigg
13	The Willow, Pateley Bridge
16	The Blue Bell Inn, Kettlewell

198

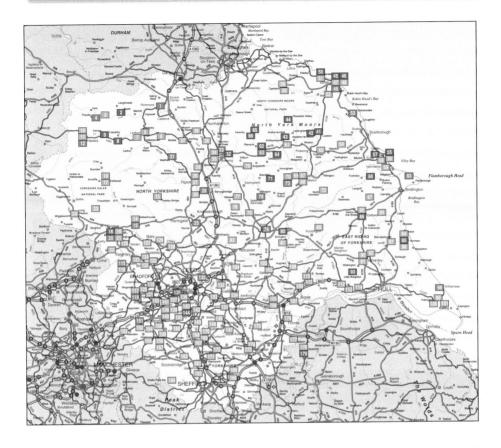

ACCOMMODATION, FOOD & DRINK AND PLACES TO VISIT

1 RICHMONDSHIRE MUSEUM 🏛

Ryders Wynd, Richmond,
North Yorkshire DL10 4JA
☎ 01748 825611

Tucked away down cobbled Ryders Wynd in Richmond is the **Richmondshire Museum**. Run by volunteers, it tells the story of the district from pre historic times. Attractions include the James Herriot vets surgery set from television's *All Creatures Great and Small*, a local chemist's shop and a Dales post office. There is a display about the former lead-mining industry in Swaledale, a transport section which includes a detailed model of Richmond railway station, a reconstruction of a cruck house containing domestic bygones and a gallery devoted to the history of Richmond and its people. Embroidery and a children's corner are among other features. Open daily, 1 lam to 5pm, from Easter to October.

2 THE BURGOYNE HOTEL 🛏

On The Green, Reeth, Nr Richmond,
North Yorkshire DL11 6SN
☎ 01748 884292
e-mail: enquiries@theburgoyne.co.uk
🌐 www.theburgoyne.co.uk

From the impressive ivy-clad stonebuilt exterior to the gracious and welcoming bedrooms and public spaces, **The Burgoyne Hotel** is a superb late-Georgian country house with nine bedrooms and first-class restaurant (open to non-residents by prior booking). The two beautiful drawing rooms are handsomely appointed, while the equally elegant dining room is the place to enjoy hearty breakfasts and first-class dinners created by renowned chef Paul Salonga. The menu changes daily to make use of the freshest local ingredients. Maps and compasses are available for walkers.

4 SWALEDALE WOOLLENS 🏛

Strawbeck, Muker in Swaledale, Richmond,
North Yorkshire DL11 6QG
☎ 01748 886251
e-mail: mail@swaledalewoollens.co.uk
🌐 www.swaledalewoollens.co.uk

For more than 30 years – an occasion marked in 2004 by a visit from HRH The Prince of Wales – **Swaledale Woollens** has been the premier place to buy beautiful and distinctive knitwear and wool. Of the 50-odd recognized breeds of sheep in the UK, Swaledale sheep are among the hardiest, and their wool makes durable, well-insulating clothing that is also lightweight and comfortable.

Swaledale Woollens was established to promote wider use of this excellent wool, and the shop here stocks a small range of natural yarns for those who do their own hand- or machine-knitting, together with a large selection of fantastic jumpers, cardigans, hats, scarves, gloves and more. All garments are made entirely of natural materials – most of the wools are undyed, their patterns created by using various shades of wool from different sheep (Swaledale, Welsh and Wensleydale wool each has its own distinctive colour and particular characteristics). There are also dyed wools in a range of lovely country colours. The shop also has a choice of moccasins, sheepskins, rugs, wallhangings and many more items which make lovely gifts. Open every day.

200

Gunnerside, Richmond,
North Yorkshire DL11 6LD
☎ 01748 886261
e-mail: michaelwatson2@btconnect.com
⊕ www.kingsheadgunnerside.co.uk

The King's Head is a cosy, traditional pub tucked away in the pretty Swaledale village of Gunnerside, located on the B6270 to the west of Reeth.

Owner Mike Watson has been here since 2005; together with his excellent chef and friendly, conscientious staff, he runs a welcoming, comfortable and well-kept pub. The pub began life in the late 1600s as a blacksmith's. The smithy reputedly brewed his own beer as a sideline, and in the 1700s the place became a coaching inn. This Free House is very handsome, with a traditional interior that boasts many original features. Much of its olde-worlde charm remains, the most impressive feature being the superb stone fireplace. The décor and furnishings throughout are cosy and comfortable, enhancing the relaxed atmosphere of the inn. It's a very popular calling place for walkers and those touring the area, and well worth seeking out. Closed on Mondays in winter, it is at other times open every day from midday.

A good place for real ale fans, there are at least two on tap during the winter months, and four in summer. The two regulars are Black Sheep and John Smiths Cask. Of course there are also lagers, cider, stout, a good wine list, select spirits and a good range of soft drinks. Food is served at lunch (12–3) and dinner (6–9), with guests choosing from the menu or daily specials board from a range of tasty dishes. The chef uses the best local produce to create tempting options such as home-made steak-and-ale pie and cottage pie, cumberland sausage, wholetail Whitby scampi, beef curry and Swaledale cheese-stuffed chicken breast. At lunch there are light meals as well as heartier portions available. Booking advised for Saturday evening, Sunday lunchtime and for parties of more than six people. Children welcome. Well-behaved pets welcome. Twice a month there's a fun quiz night held on a Sunday.

5 THE GOLDEN LION HOTEL

Market Place, Leyburn,
North Yorkshire DL8 5AS
☎ 01969 622161   Fax: 01969 623836
e-mail: annegoldenlion@aol.com
🌐 www.thegoldenlion.co.uk

Noted for its fine ensuite accommodation, with a lift to all floors and full disabled facilities, splendid food and a wine cellar to match, **The Golden Lion Hotel** is a true home from home. Owner Anne Wood has been providing the very best in friendly and expert service to all her guests for 22 years. Overlooking Leyburn's huge Market Square at the 'Gateway to Wensleydale', this fine hotel has been dispensing hospitality for over 240 years. Traditional ales are just one of the many draws here, where the accent is firmly on quality home-cooked food served at lunch and dinner. Renowned for its freshly prepared food of local origins, excellent cuisine is served in the 70-seat restaurant, decorated with Dales murals painted by local artist Lynn Foster. The menu offers a good choice of delicious dishes including sirloin steaks, braised lamb steak, local cured gammon, beef-and-ale pie, grilled salmon steak, haddock, scampi, chicken supreme with Stilton and a vegetarian dish of the day. Open all day every day,

there are three real ales (Black Sheep, Theakstons and a rotating guest ale) together with a good complement of lagers, cider, stout, wines, spirits and soft drinks in the oak-panelled bar, where light snacks and cream teas are also available. Special diets are happily catered for, and there is an extensive wine list. The hotel also has banqueting facilities for special occasions or conferences, with space for 80 seated guests or 150 served buffet-style. The 14 tastefully furnished ensuite guest bedrooms all have telephone, TV, radio and tea- and coffee-making facilities, and boast views over Leyburn and across to the racehorse training gallops of Middleham. The Golden Lion is well placed for exploring the Yorkshire Dales and visiting local attractions such as Bolton Castle, Jervaulx Abbey, Masham (with its Brewery Centres) and Richmond. York, Harrogate and Ripon are also within easy reach.

6 THE QUEEN'S HEAD

West Moor Lane, Finghall,
North Yorkshire DL8 5ND
☎ 01677 450259 Fax: 01677 450615
e-mail: info@queenshead-finghall.co.uk
🌐 www.queenshead-finghall.co.uk

The regular ales at the distinctive **Queen's Head** in Finghall are John Smiths, Black Sheep and Theakstons, together with two changing guest ales. Owned and run by Sharon and Peter Farhall, who arrived in 2001 and who have over 30 years' experience in providing great hospitality to all their guests. The Farhalls are ably assisted by head chef Andrew Megson and sous chef John Barley, this superb inn provides wonderful food, drink and accommodation.

The restaurant is open from 8 a.m. for a delicious and hearty breakfast right through to evening meals, with tempting and expertly prepared lunches and afternoon clotted cream teas along the way. The chefs have built up an enviable reputation for the menu, which offers a range of freshly prepared home-cooked dishes to suit all tastes and appetites. Favourites include the hot chicken salad and pork fillets, among many choices from the menu and daily specials

board. Booking is essential at weekends.

New to the inn is quality accommodation in the form of three beautiful and comfortable ensuite guest bedrooms – including a very spacious family room which sleeps six – and also a handsome annexe with three additional guest bedrooms. Occupying a very picturesque setting with magnificent views, particularly to the rear from the deck of the outdoor dining area. The stylish and elegant interior is comfortable and

welcoming, and retains much of its historic charm and character. Dating back in parts to the 14th century, from the rear of the premises guests can see Wyvill Hall – reputedly the fictional home of Toad of Toad Hall.

The quiet village of Finghall is just off the A684 east of Leyburn, making a perfect base from which to explore the many sights and attractions of the region.

Aysgarth, nr Leyburn,
North Yorkshire DL8 3SR
☎ 01969 663228   Fax: 01969 663182

Set in a superb location near the famous Aysgarth Falls, **Palmer Flatt Hotel** is an impressive place open all day for ales, serving great food and providing 12 beautiful and comfortable ensuite guest bedrooms. Licensees Claire and Mark have been at the helm since 2005, with between them 11 years' experience in providing first-class service and hospitality to all their guests.

There are three real ales – Black Sheep, John Smiths Cask and a rotating guest ale – together with a good range of lagers, cider, soft drinks, wines and spirits. Food is served daily at lunch (12–2) and dinner (6– 9) – booking advised for Saturday evening and Sunday lunch. Specialities include the Sunday carvery and local lamb. Locally-sourced produce is used to create all the mouthwatering dishes, with a good variety of starters (home-made chicken liver pate, fresh mussels, pear and watercress salad to name but three) , main courses (Dales beef

fillet, oven-roasted chicken, peppered duck breast, seafood medley and wild mushroom risotto among several other choice dishes) and desserts such as home-made cheesecake, sticky toffee pudding and more. The spacious no-smoking restaurant seats 80 and is very attractively furnished and decorated. Guests can also take their meals in the lounge bars, or in the beautiful garden.

The ambience is always relaxed and welcoming. Standing in four acres of grounds, in the heart of Wensleydale, this tranquil retreat makes an excellent place to use as a base to explore the region. The accommodation is available all year round, with a mixture of

rooms, from singles to family rooms, each individually furnished, gracious and supremely comfortable. Two rooms have four-poster beds. All command panoramic views over the surrounding Dales National Park.

The tariff includes a delicious and hearty breakfast. Handy for the Aysgarth Falls, within the grounds of the hotel, Aysgarth Church, Bolton Castle and superb 'James Herriot country' are all within easy reach. Claire and Mark also run The Kings Head pub in nearby Leyburn – a place for real ale drinkers and lovers of superior food.

9   THE WHITE ROSE HOTEL

Main Street, Askrigg,
North Yorkshire DL8 3HG
☎ 01969 650515   Fax: 01969 650176
e-mail: stay@whiterosehotelaskrigg.co.uk
⊕ www.whiterosehotelaskrigg.co.uk

Superb accommodation and hospitality await guests at **The White Rose Hotel**, an excellent family-run hotel built in 1840 but extensively and tastefully refurbished just a year ago to provide guests with every modern comfort while retaining its original grace and charm. Conveniently located in the heart of the country village of Askrigg, in the Yorkshire Dales National Park. Open all year round, there are 12 outstanding guest bedrooms, all of which are ensuite.

Sightseeing opportunities within a few miles include the magnificent Hardraw Force (England's highest waterfall) and Aysgarth Falls (England's most impressive series of powerful falls) as well as the breathtaking scenery of the region, excellent walking and several of Yorkshire's most impressive and interesting historic sites including Bolton Castle, Middleham Castle, Richmond Castle and the beautiful abbey ruins at Jervaulx, Fountains and Easby Abbeys. Add to this visitor attractions such as the Dales Countryside Museum, Forbidden Corner and Wensleydale Creamery, York, Leeds and Harrogate, and Yorkshire Dales National Park, and it is clear that this is an ideal touring base. The hotel also has a cosy and comfortable bar and characterful restaurant open to non-residents and residents alike. There are always three to four real ales, and a wide range of tasty bar meals and excellent cuisine at lunch (12–2) and dinner (6–9), made with locally-sourced produce. Diners can also take their meals in the lovely conservatory dining area. Among many specialities, there are roast dinners served every day. For a truly relaxing break away from it all, look no further than this superb hotel.

7 THE THREE HORSESHOES INN ¶

Wensley, Leyburn,
North Yorkshire DL8 4HJ
☎ 01969 622327
e-mail: callin@3horseshoeswensley.com
⊕ www.3horseshoeswensley.com

The owners of the charming **Three Horseshoes Inn** in Wensley arrived in June of 2006 and immediately closed the pub for refurbishment. Re-opened on 1st July, it retains its olde-worlde character while now offering guests every modern comfort in stylish and contemporary surroundings. Featuring in the BBC's production

covering life in Wensleydale, aired in August 2006, this fine pub is open all day every day; there are eight hand-pulled ales plus three additional ales from the cask. Four of these come from the inn's own Wensleydale Brewery, in the nearby village of Bellerby. Quality food is served Monday to Saturday.

11 BECKINDALES CONTINENTAL CAFÉ ¶

Burtersett Road, Hawes,
North Yorkshire DL8 3NP
☎ 01969 667784
e-mail: eat@beckingdales.eclipse.co.uk

The home-made specials are justly popular at the excellent **Beckindales Continental Café**, a marvellous place that is bright and spacious, with indoor and outdoor seating in one of the most picturesque villages in the Dales. The menu features a range of delicious sandwiches, soups, salads, toasties, baguettes, paninis and more, together

with mouth-watering cakes, ice-creams and a host of other tempting puddings. To drink there are more than nine different blends of coffee and about 20 teas, including herbal varieties. *Open:* 10 a.m. to 5 p.m. (daily in summer; Friday–Monday in winter).

10 WILSON'S ¶

Market Place, Hawes,
North Yorkshire DL8 3QZ
☎ 01969 667325
e-mail: cmonksfield@hotmail.com

A friendly and family-run establishment in the heart of Hawes, **Wilson's** is the perfect place to stop for a delicious meal while touring the area. Well worth seeking out, this pristine place has a very tasteful décor and relaxed ambience. Open daily 10.30–5 (closed Mondays out of season), the extensive menu of homemade dishes includes specialities

such as steak pie, lasagne, freshly cooked ham, quiches, cakes, scones and much more. Guests choose from the menu and specials board; owners Chris and Christine Monksfield do all the cooking, using only the freshest local produce.

Cosy and comfortable, with seating for 25 indoors and 12 outside, Wilson's is well recommended locally for its tasty home-cooked food. Also available for private parties in the evenings – please ring for details.

12 DALES COUNTRYSIDE MUSEUM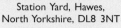

Station Yard, Hawes,
North Yorkshire, DL8 3NT
☎ 01969 666210
e-mail: dcm@yorkshiredales.org.uk
⊕ www.yorkshiredales.org.uk

Visit the **Dales Countryside Museum** and see for yourself how our ancestors survived in this beautiful, but some-times harsh, environment. This award winning museum brings alive the past of the Yorkshire Dales, with interactive exhibits, exciting displays, video and CD Rom. The museum has several galleries, the largest one being in the Victorian goods shed that once housed the goods waiting for collection by the steam engines of the Midland railway. Adjoining the goods shed exhibition hall is the purpose built museum which houses a gift shop and information centre, public toilets, education & study rooms, an outside amphitheatre and the John Baker Exhibition Hall. The Museum's time tunnel will then take you onto the platform of the old station, where a series of railway carriages house the video and artefacts from Dales life throughout the centuries.

The museum showcases local craft workers and craft demonstrations are held throughout the year. For details of opening times, how to get there, exhibitions and events, please telephone the information desk on 01969 667450 or visit the Authority's award winning website. Fully accessible by wheelchair the Dales Countryside Museum is situated in side Station Yard, just off the main A684 at the eastern end of Hawes, Wensleydale. Opening times: 10am until 5pm daily (except Christmas Holidays)

13 THE WILLOW

Park Road, Pateley Bridge, Harrogate,
North Yorkshire HG3 5JS
☎ 01423 711689
⊕ www.nidderdale.co.uk/
willowrestaurant

The Willow is a charming traditional English cottage restaurant and tea room located in one of the prettiest towns in the Dales. The ambience is relaxed and tranquil at this 18th-century oak-beamed cottage, where all food is freshly prepared on the premises using local produce wherever possible. Fully licensed, The Willow offers

everything from morning coffee and afternoon tea to intimate dinners. Booking required on Friday and Saturday evening. There are two comfortable and handsome ensuite guest bedrooms also available.

14 BUFFERS COFFEE SHOP

Back O' Th' Hill Farm, Storiths,
Bolton Abbey, North Yorkshire BD23 6HU
☎ 01756 710253   Fax: 01756 710708
e-mail: bkeith_pam@hotmail.com
⊕ www.bufferscoffeeshop.co.uk

The delightful **Buffers Coffee Shop** is a well-known haven for visitors – and takes its name from its truly amazing collection of model railway and farming memorabilia together with sets of trains, carriages, track, stations and more boxed and available to buy. Upstairs there's an outstanding model rail set laid out to enjoy in the Model Railway Gallery (open Tues–Sun and Bank Hols

10.30–5), while of course, back downstairs you can sample some excellent light snacks, cakes and other home-made treats, all amid colourful surroundings in this converted barn and shippon built in 1633.

15 BOLTON ABBEY

Bolton Abbey Estate Estate Office,
Bolton Abbey, Skipton,
North Yorkshire BD23 6EX
☎ 01756 718009
⊚ www.boltonabbey.com

Bolton Abbey near Skipton is the Yorkshire Estate of the Duke and Duchess of Devonshire. Situated in Wharfedale, in the Yorkshire Dales National Park this historic estate is a magnet for visitors drawn to its breathtaking landscapes and excellent facilities. Visitors have flocked to Bolton Abbey for over one hundred years. On an August Bank Holiday in the 1890's the railway brought 40,000 people to Bolton Abbey; nearly as many people as now visit York in a week. After the First World War visitors arrived by train in their "Sunday Best" with the children carrying buckets, spades and fishing nets. Some fathers never got much further than the Devonshire Arms' Refreshment Room, but many removed their boots and rolled up their trousers to paddle with their children by the sandy river bank. Little has changed over the years; visitors still come to see the landscape that inspired artists like Turner and Landseer, and poets such as Wordsworth.

As the name suggests Bolton Abbey was originally a large monastic Estate, based around the 12th century priory. Legend has it that the Priory was established in 1120 by Cecily de Romille as an expression of her grief following the drowning of her son in the nearby Strid. Today, the ruins of the Priory set in an incomparable position overlooking the river Wharfe will evoke the past glories of the Estate whilst the restored and thriving parish church shows that the Estate is still very much a living community.

16 THE BLUE BELL INN

Kettlewell, Skipton,
North Yorkshire BD23 5QX
☎ 01756 760230
e-mail: info@bluebellinn.co.uk
⊚ www.bluebellinn.co.uk

If you're looking for excellent cask ales, home-cooked food and comfortable accommodation, look no further than the impressive **Blue Bell Inn**. Established in 1680, this traditional inn boasts a lot of character and some very handsome features including the large brickbuilt fireplace and wealth of warm wood panelling. The Blue Bell began life as a coaching inn along the Dales Way, and the route of that famous walk and the popular Inn Way pass directly through Kettlewell, making it an ideal touring base, with numerous other walks, bridleways and mountain biking tracks, limestone cliffs and caves to explore, and pot holes for keen pot-holers.

The four real ales come from the local Copper

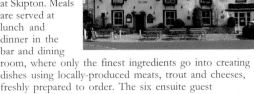

Dragon brewery at Skipton. Meals are served at lunch and dinner in the bar and dining

room, where only the finest ingredients go into creating dishes using locally-produced meats, trout and cheeses, freshly prepared to order. The six ensuite guest bedrooms include a family room; two rooms are on the ground floor and all rooms command marvellous views over the surrounding countryside.

17 THE KINGS HEAD

The Green, Kettlewell, Skipton,
North Yorkshire BD23 5RD
☎ 01756 760242
e-mail: info@kingsheadatkettlewell.co.uk
🌐 www.kingsheadatkettlewell.co.uk

The superb **Kings Head** is a large and impressive inn set in the Yorkshire Dales in the heart of the popular and much-visited village of Kettlewell, 5½ miles northwest of Grassington on the B6160. This handsome premises dates back to the early 18th century, and before becoming an inn it was the village workhouse!

Leaseholders Louise and Russell are now in their third year here, and they have built up an enviable reputation far and wide for their excellent food, drink and accommodation. Popular with locals and tourists alike for their excellent facilities, here you might find walkers, motor-cyclists from this country and abroad, and those touring this beautiful part of the region. A picture-postcard of an inn, it's handsome inside and out, with lots of character and original features including the open fireplace, slab stone floors and more.

Open all day at weekends and for every session weekdays (though closed Monday and Tuesday lunchtimes in the winter months), there are four real ales: Black Sheep and Tetleys are the regulars, alongside two rotating guest ales. Food is served 12–2.30 and 6.30–9 p.m., and it is best to book Friday and Saturday evenings, especially in the summer months. Louise is the cook, preparing all dishes to

order as guests choose off the printed menu or specials board from dishes such as home-made steak-and-ale pie and lamb Henry, most of which are made with locally-sourced produce. This fine inn also boasts four attractive and comfortable ensuite guest bedrooms (three double rooms, one twin), all with first-class amenities. The excellent tariff includes a hearty breakfast. Children welcome. No smoking areas. All major credit cards taken.

18 SKIPTON PARK GUEST'OTEL

2 Salisbury Street, Skipton,
North Yorkshire BD23 1NQ
☎ 01756 700640
e-mail: skiptonpark@btconnect.com
⊕ www.skiptonpark.co.uk

On Salisbury Street in Skipton just a few minutes' walk from the centre of town at the corner of Gargrave Road, **Skipton Park Guest'otel** – combining the best of a hotel and guest house – has been designed for maximum privacy, peace and relaxation. Awarded 4 stars by the RAC and English Tourist Council for guest accommodation, this spacious and impressive property dates back to the 1890s. Skipton Park boasts six luxury ensuite guest bedrooms, including two on the ground floor which are suitable for guests with mobility difficulties. The rooms are spacious and decorated and furnished to a high standard of taste and quality, to ensure guests have a comfortable stay.

Guests can stay on a bed-and-breakfast or dinner, bed and breakfast basis. The special autumn, spring and winter breaks are an attractive option. Here at the Gateway to the Dales, Skipton Park makes an excellent base for exploring Malham Cove, Grassington, Kettlewell, Burnsall and the many sights and attractions of the region, including Skipton itself with its Castle, traditional open-air markets and boat trips along the Leeds & Liverpool Canal. Day trips to Kendal and the Lakes or York, Harrogate or Leeds are also within easy reach. Children welcome. No smoking.

19 THE ROYAL SHEPHERD

Canal Street, Skipton,
North Yorkshire BD23 1LB
☎ 01756 793178

Occupying a superb canalside location, **The Royal Shepherd** is open all day for ales and food. Four real ales include one from the Copper Dragon Brewery in Skipton and rotating guest ales. Home-cooked dishes are the speciality here, and include steak pie and giant Yorkshire pudding with various fillings. Wherever possible, all dishes are made using locally-sourced produce. Meals are served daily – Monday to Saturday from 11 a.m. until 8 p.m., and Sundays from 12 til 6. The outdoor patio area overlooks the canal - just the place to enjoy a relaxing drink or meal on fine days – while the interior offers great comfort in traditional surroundings.

20 THE CRAVEN MUSEUM

Town Hall, High Street, Skipton,
North Yorkshire BD23 1AH
☎ 01756 706407   Fax: 01756 706412
e-mail: museum@cravendc.gov.uk
⊕ www.cravendc.gov.uk

Crammed full of fascinating exhibits, the **Craven Museum** is a great place to explore the history of Skipton and the Craven Dales. The museum displays collections of local history, archaeology, natural history, art and geology in a small but very popular museum situated in the Town Hall at the top of Skipton's busy market place. Temporary exhibitions vary from community projects to items on loan from other museums. Admission is free and the museum is open all year round.

**5 Coach Street, Skipton,
North Yorkshire BD23 1LH
☎ 01756   797797**

Situated in the heart of Skipton and taking its name from its proximity to the Canal Basin, a haven for visitors, **The Waterside** is a café and restaurant of charm and distinction. A superb location to dine and drink, The Waterside is open daily from 8 in the morning until 4 and again from 5 onwards. Attractive and welcoming inside and out, the exterior is an impressive traditional stonebuilt building, while inside all is pristine and spacious, with a simple and tasteful décor that enhances guests' relaxation and comfort.

The daytime menus feature breakfast dishes (served from 8–11.30 a.m.) such as a range of omelettes, full English breakfast, various combinations of hearty steaks, gammon, bacon, sausage, eggs, kippers and more, and hot sandwiches. From 11.30 until 4, the menu boasts main courses including lasagne, steak and mushroom pie, battered haddock, a selection of sandwiches along with vegetarian options and children's meals, supplemented by the daily specials board. Afternoon tea is a real treat, with fresh coffees, tea, hot chocolate, cold drinks, scones and cakes. But it is the evening fare, in particular, that makes The Waterside well worth seeking out, offering the best of Thai and English cuisine. In the evenings the café becomes a full-scale restaurant, seating 48 inside, with room for another 48 outside on the front terrace.

Owners David and Thain Edmonton have been here since August of 2005; Thain is the chef, bringing flair and imagination to the authentic Thai dishes and the more traditional English ones. The evening menu offers everything from a wide selection of tasty Thai starters to main courses featuring chicken, beef, port, duck, lamb, seafood, vegetarian choices and rice and noodle dishes, all expertly prepared and presented. Thain makes use of only the freshest ingredients to create a memorable dining experience, bringing subtle herbs and spices, sauces and traditional Thai

cooking methods to create dishes such as Goong Phao – large Dublin Bay prawns charcoal grilled and served with special chilli sauce – Kaeng Phed Nua – beef in red curry paste with coconut milk, bamboo shoots, red and green peppers and sweet basil leaves – and Yam Woon Sen Gai – a salad of sliced chicken breast with vermicelli noodles. All dishes are mouth-wateringly good and superb value for money. Excellent service is provided by members of the Edmonton family, wearing traditional Thai dress. A licensed premises, guest can enjoy draught beers or wine with their meal.

Colne Road, Malsis, Sutton-in-Craven, Keighley, West Yorkshire BD20 8DS

☎ 01535 633855

e-mail: dogandguninn@btopenworld.com

⊕ www.dogandguninn.net

An outstanding inn that has recently been refurbished, **The Dog and Gun Inn** is an expansive and gracious place to enjoy wonderful ales and fresh delicious food. Situated in the hamlet of Malsis and found adjacent to the Colne-to-Keighley road, this welcoming inn is handsome inside and out, with original features including the large brick- and oak-built fireplaces and beamed ceilings.

Anita and Ross Walker have been tenants here since 2002. Between them they have a wealth of experience: Ross has been a chef for well over 20 years, while Anita has worked in the brewing and licensing trade for more than 25. Open every session and all day in the summer months, there are always five to six real ales – Timothy Taylor brews plus a rotating guest ale. There is also a good range of lagers, wines, spirits, together with cider, stout and soft drinks. Superb food is served daily from midday until 9 p.m.

Locally-sourced produce is used to create delicious dishes including specialities such as charcoal-grilled steaks, home-made steak pie, rack of lamb, poached chicken, curry of the day, pasta, salads and more. The puddings are mouth-watering – be sure to leave room for delights such as home-made bilberry pie, hot chocolate fudge cake and raspberry Pavlova, which can be complemented by a glass of dessert wine such as Muscat de Rivesaltes or Aleatico di Puglia. There are also ports, cognac and armagnac, for an after-dinner tipple, and the wine list is select and impressive. The no-smoking restaurant seats 60, while there is also dining throughout the inn and outside in the handsome garden.

Themed evenings are a regular event – please ring or see the inn's website for more details. Featured in the *CAMRA Guide 2006*, this wonderful pub is well worth seeking out.

23 THE LISTER ARMS HOTEL

**Malham, nr Skipton,
North Yorkshire BD23 4DB
☎ 01729 830330
⊕ www.listerarms.co.uk**

Set in the natural hollow of a valley head, Malham (reached vias the A65 and B6265 from Skipton) boasts some of the finest limestone scenery in Europe. At the heart of this picturesque village, visitors will find the excellent **Lister Arms Hotel**. Brothers Andrew and Jonathan Ditchfield have been at the helm since 1988, and this large and impressive 17th-century purpose-built coaching inn boasts great food, ales and accommodation.

The interior is tasteful and stylish, with polished wood floors, exposed beams and other traditional features happily rubbing shoulders with modern touches such as subtle lighting, clean lines and classic furnishings. In summer there are six real ales, in winter three. Timothy Taylor Landlord and Deuchers IPA are the regulars, with changing guest ales. Draught cider is served all year round. Hearty and tasty meals are served at lunch and dinner. With nine tasteful and comfortable ensuite guest bedrooms and a beautiful and charming self-catering four-bedroom cottage, The Lister Arms makes a perfect base from which to explore the many sights and attractions of this part of North Yorkshire.

24 THE BOAR'S HEAD HOTEL

**9 Main Street, Long Preston, nr Skipton,
North Yorkshire BD23 4ND
☎ 01729 840217
e-mail: ivan-linda@huff.fslife.co.uk
⊕ www.hotelsyorkshiredales.com**

The Boar's Head Hotel in Long Preston, adjacent to the A65 north of Skipton and just 3 miles south of Settle, is a large and impressive public house serving great food, drink and hospitality. Dating back to the 16th century, the interior boasts comfortable seating amid attractive surroundings.

The non-smoking dining room seats 30, while other dining areas include the lovely beer garden. Children are welcome at this friendly pub, where the menu includes traditional favourites, modern dishes and daily specials. Wednesday night is curry night, while on Thursday evenings sirloin steaks are the speciality. The Sunday carvery (also served Bank Holidays) is a sumptuous feast at a very reasonable price. Booking required Friday to Sunday.

There are real ales (Black Sheep and Deuchars) plus a good range of draught keg bitters, lagers, cider, stout, wines, spirits and soft drinks. Licensees Ivan and Linda have been here since 2002, and have over 15 years' experience in the trade. A hub of the community, there's live entertainment every Saturday evening. The accommodation comprises four ensuite guest bedrooms in a range of sizes to suit different tastes and numbers. Each is individually decorated with taste and style, and are very comfortable. A full English breakfast is included in the tariff.

25 MERCER ART GALLERY

Swan Road, Harrogate, HG1 2SA
☎ 01423 556188 Fax: 01423 55613

Situated 100 yards from the entrance to the Valley Gardens and Royal Pump Room Museum, the **Mercer Art Gallery** is home to the district's collection of fine art, which is featured throughout the year as part of an exciting and diverse exhibition programme.

2007 is an exciting year when Harrogate's most famous artist, William Powell Frith, is celebrated with a blockbuster exhibition of works by this great Victorian painter from March to July. This is the first exhibition of his work for over 50 years and the first time over 60 of his paintings, prints and drawings have been brought together.

Other exhibitions include: *Treasures of the Mercer,* a chance to see some highlights from the permanent collection; pastel and charcoal drawings by Knaresborough Castle's 2006 artist in residence, Andrew Cheetham; and art from Turkmenistan.

Watch out for special events and activities for families, adults, and children. Open: Tuesday to Saturday and Bank Holiday Monday 10-5, Sunday 2-5. Admission is free.

26 THE LAMB AND FLAG

**9 High Skellgate, Ripon,
North Yorkshire HG4 1BA**
☎ 01765 602895

Just a minute's walk from the centre of town, **The Lamb and Flag** dates back to the 1820s, when it was known as the Holy Lamb. Open all day, every day for ale, the real ale on tap is John Smiths Cask. Les and Kath are the welcoming hosts; Kath is also an excellent cook who serves up dishes such as home-made steak-and-ale pie and other hearty favourites

at lunchtime only (12–3). Guests can enjoy their pint or food in the handsome traditional bar or lounge of this spacious, welcoming pub, or outside on the lovely patio area or in the secluded beer garden.

27 DISH'S CAFÉ BAR & BISTRO

25 Kirkgate, Ripon,
North Yorkshire HG4 1PB
☎ 01765 602722
e-mail: dishs@hotmail.co.uk
⊕ www.dish25.co.uk

Just steps away from Ripon's wonderful Cathedral, **Dish's Café Bar & Bistro** is a pristine and convivial place to enjoy an excellent meal, drink or snack at lunchtime or dinner. This charming contemporary bistro takes its name from its owner, James Stubley, an experienced professional chef who's nickname, 'Dish', he earned while backpacking round the world gaining knowledge of new flavours and cooking techniques to bring back and use to create the best in good, honest, home-made food.

The menu changes to include the freshest seasonal produce, and features breakfasts made with award-winning sausages and

black pudding, lunches of home-made burgers, and much more – hot, cold, sweet, savoury, it's all home-made and delicious. Open seven days a week from 9.30 to 5 p.m., and in the evenings for private parties.

28 NEWBY HALL AND GARDENS

near Ripon, North Yorkshire HG4 5AE
☎ 0845 4504068
⊕ www.newbyhall.com

Newby Hall and Gardens, near Ripon in North Yorkshire, is one of England's renowned Adam Houses, and home to spectacular treasures and antiques as well as 25 acres of stunning landscaped gardens. Acclaimed as one of the Historic Houses Association's most visited properties, Newby Hall has an enviable position as one of Yorkshire's best-loved historic properties.

Collections inside Newby Hall itself include a set of 18th Century Gobelins tapestries, fine Chippendale furniture, classical statuary and even an unusual selection of European and Far-Eastern chamber pots!

Newby Hall and Gardens remains a firm favourite with families, gardening enthusiasts and heritage lovers who come to experience the many attractions this beautiful estate has to offer.

Newby's miniature railway is ever-popular with children and adults alike, and the Adventure Garden will amuse children for hours. The Sculpture Park takes in many pieces of contemporary work from a variety of artists, all of which are for sale, while the Woodland Walk is a delightful stroll through Bragget Wood and the adjacent orchard.

29 THE GEORGE AND DRAGON INN

Main Street, Melmerby,
North Yorkshire HG4 5HA

☎ 01765 640970

In the mood for a juicy sirloin steak, lamb shank, wholetail Whitby scampi, home-made chilli or curry, aubergine and mozzarella bake or traditional fish and chips? **The George and Dragon Inn** in Melmerby, west off the A1 or A61 (Ripon–Thirsk road), is the place to find. This handsome and welcoming inn began life as a row of cottages and the oldest part dates back to the late 1700s.

Owners Linda and Phil have been here since 2005, offering first-class service and hospitality to all their guests. Open every session (all day in the summer months), there are four real ales including Marston Moor Matchlock Mild and rotating guest ales. Linda is a super cook, serving up tasty food at lunch (12–2.30) and dinner (6–9). This fine inn also boasts three cosy and comfortable ensuite guest bedrooms. An ideal base from which to explore this beautiful part of North Yorkshire, the rooms have excellent facilities.

30 THE MASONS ARMS

St John's Road, Bishop Monkton,
Harrogate, North Yorkshire HG3 3QU

☎ 01765 676631

⊞ www.bishopmonkton.co.uk

Here in the picturesque village of Bishop Monkton, found off the A61 south of Ripon, **The Masons Arms** sits across the road from the village stream in a truly picture-postcard setting. Dating back to the mid-18th century, this fine inn is run by Gary and Halyely, who between them have some 25 years' experience in providing excellent beer, food and hospitality.

Open every session and all day in the summer months, there are three real ales including Tetley Bitter and rotating guest ales from local breweries, together with a very good selection of lagers, wines, spirits,

cider, stout and soft drinks. Tasty meals are served at lunch every day

except Tuesday and evenings Monday and Wednesday to Saturday. The interior is spacious with traditional features including a handsome brickbuilt fireplace and cosy corners, while there's also a pleasant seating area to the front with picnic tables and umbrellas for days when the weather is fine.

31 THEAKSTON BREWERY & VISITOR CENTRE

Masham, Ripon,
North Yorkshire HG4 4EN
☎ 01765 680000
🌐 www.theakstons.co.uk

For beer drinkers, the first place to visit in the Yorkshire Dales is the home of the legendary 'Old Peculier', the **Theakston Brewery**. Robert Theakston began brewing 170 years ago at the Black Bull Inn in 1827. Forty eight years later, his son Thomas built the famous brewery on Masham's Paradise Fields, where it stands today.

Most of the original equipment is still in use today, and with a trained tour guide, visitors can follow the entire brewing process, from selecting the ingredients to filling the casks.

Meet the people behind the beer, ask questions or simply soak up the atmosphere of the brewer's art. Watch one of only seven brewery coopers in England crafting the wooden casks that Theakston's still use for supplying local pubs. After the tour, visitors are invited to the Visitor Centre Bar, where they can enjoy real British beer by a roaring log fire. The admission price includes a complimentary half pint of beer, from a comprehensive selection of Theakston ales, including Old Peculier and Theakston Cool Cask - you'll be spoilt for choice.

32 DIVAN HOTEL

Sutton Road, Thirsk,
North Yorkshire YO7 2ER
☎ 01845 522293   Fax: 01845 574735
e-mail: info@divanhotel.co.uk
🌐 www.divanhotel.co.uk

Family-run by Helen Green and her family, **Divan Hotel** is a stylish and elegant place in the heart of Thirsk. Open all day every day for ale, John Smiths Smooth is complemented by a good range of lagers, cider, stout, wines, spirits and soft drinks. Tasty, expertly prepared food is served every day at lunch and dinner – booking advised at all times and essential at weekends at

this justly renowned eatery, where the menu and daily specials are created using the freshest locally sourced ingredients. Accommodation comprises 12 superior ensuite guest bedrooms including four ground-floor rooms.

33 THE WORLD OF JAMES HERRIOT

23 Kirkgate, Thirsk, N. Yorkshire YO7 IPL
☎ 01845 524234 Fax: 01845 525333
e-mail: jamesherriot@hambleton.co.uk
⊕ www.worldofjamesherriot.org

Celebrating the world's most famous veterinary surgeon, **The World of James Herriot** opened in the spring of 1999 and since then has welcomed more than 200,000 visitors. The attraction occupies the original house, now a Grade II listed building, in which James Herriot lived and worked. The house has been lovingly restored to how it was in the 1940s and '50s with many original pieces of furniture donated by the author's family. After passing through the famous red door, visitors enter the dining room which doubled as the practice office. Then on to the cosy family room where you'll hear James' favourite music – Bing Crosby – playing. Further down the corridor is the practice dispensary where he would make up his prescriptions. Next door is the small surgery where James would treat domestic

animals. At the heart of the house is the large kitchen, the hub of family life.

The garden has also been taken back to the 1950s, re-creating a typical English cottage garden complete with a small vegetable plot. A further exhibit concentrates on the film and TV adaptations of James Herriot's bestselling books – here you'll find the original Austin 7 tourer car, three studio sets from *All Creatures Great and Small*, and some original 1970s cameras and equipment.

34 THE VALE OF YORK

Carlton Road, Carlton Miniott, Thirsk, North Yorkshire YO7 4LX
☎ 01845 523161 Fax: 01845 527222
e-mail: terry.bainbridge2@virgin.net

Licensees Terry and Melody Bainbridge have been at the helm of **The Vale of York**, once known as the Station Hotel, since 2001. Open all day every day for ale, there are four real ales – John Smiths, Samuel Smiths, Black Sheep and Timothy Taylor Landlord – together with a choice of lagers, cider, stout, wines, spirits and soft drinks.

The à la carte menu is available Monday to Saturday (12–2pm, early doors menu from 5.30pm–7pm and evening meals from 7pm to 9pm.) and for the justly popular Sunday carvery (booking advised). The accommodation is available all year round, with 12 ensuite guest bedrooms, five of which are on the

ground floor. Guests can stay on a room-only or bed-and-breakfast basis. Located just a couple of miles from Thirsk and nine miles from Northallerton, the inn makes a very good base from which to explore the Dales and the North York Moors National Park as well as Thirsk, Catterick and the breathtaking scenery and picturesque villages of the region.

35 THE DOG & GUN

Carlton Miniott, Thirsk,
North Yorkshire YO7 4NJ
☎ 01845 522150
e-mail: barrierobinson555@hotmail.com

Found in the village of Carlton Miniott, two miles southwest of Thirsk off the A61, **The Dog & Gun** boasts a warm and friendly atmosphere, excellent real ales and great food. Oak beams, open fires and traditional comforts aplenty can be found here. Brothers Barrie and Robert have been here as leaseholders since 2002.

Open every session weekdays and all day at weekends, there are no fewer than six real ales including regulars John Smiths, Theakstons, Deuchers IPA and Timothy Taylor Landlord, plus rotating guest ales. Twice a year, in February and October, the inn hosts a beer festival, during which there are an extra 20 real ales to sample. Held over the first weekend (Friday to Sunday) of the month, these twice-yearly festivals include a hog roast and family fun day. At this superb inn, food is served

at lunch (12–2) and dinner (6–9) (no food Sunday or Monday evening). The restaurant seats 48, the bar area 40; booking required at all times. Guests choose from the menu or specials board from a range of tempting dishes created by qualified chefs. The Sunday carvery offers a choice of four meats and vegetarian option. Home-made dishes feature on the menu, with steak-and-Guinness pie just one of the hearty favourites, together with an excellent baby lamb and many other choices of daily specials. Guests can enjoy their meal in the huge conservatory-style restaurant.

The real stars here are the staff – friendly, helpful, offering a high standard of service and hospitality. There are smoking and no-smoking areas, a lovely beer garden and ample parking. Families are more than welcome – there's a separate children's menu available. The Sunday quiz night and occasional live music add to this pub's many attractions, and its setting within a few miles of Thirsk, Sion Hill, Sutton Bank, Ripon, Northallerton and Rievaulx Abbey, to name just a few, make it an ideal place to stop for an enjoyable relaxed meal or drink while touring the area.

Ainderby Steeple, Northallerton,
North Yorkshire DL7 9PU

☎ 01609 775542 Fax: 01609 761683

e-mail: thewellingtonheifer@yahoo.co.uk

The Wellington Heifer is family-run by the Mathers family, with professional chef Stuart at the helm, ably assisted by his mother, father, local artist Denise (whose works are on display to good effect), and fellow chef Sophie. This fine inn is open every session serving Black Sheep, Tetleys, the occasional guest ale and a full compliment of lagers, spirits, cider, stout, wines and soft drinks.

The food is superb here, served every day at lunch (12–2) and dinner (6–9). The menu and specials board provide a range of tasty dishes freshly cooked to order, including roast of the day with all the trimmings. Spacious and handsome, this picture-postcard inn is reached via the A684 east of Northallerton, and is located near the church in the lovely village of Ainderby Steeple, with scenic views over the surrounding open countryside. A former coaching inn dating back to the early 1700s and full of character and atmosphere, the interior comprises a bar, no-smoking lounge and no-smoking restaurant.

Throughout, the inn is handsomely decorated and furnished, with exposed brickwork, open fires and other attractive features that enhance the inn's convivial and homely ambience. The restaurant area is elegant and tasteful, light and airy with warm yellow walls, adorned with some of Denise's artwork, exposed beamwork and stylish and attractive seating. For a truly delightful dining experience, look no further. Accommodation's also on hand at this superior inn in two ensuite guest bedrooms available all year round. Ainderby Steeple makes an ideal base from which to explore sights and attractions including Northallerton, Thirsk, Fountains Abbey, Ripon, Thorp Perrow Arboretum and the North York Moors National Park.

37 THE WAGGON AND HORSES

20 Market Place, Bedale,
North Yorkshire DL8 1EQ
☎ 01677 424333   Fax: 01677 425235

A handsome and welcoming 16th-century coaching inn, The impressive **Waggon and Horses** is run by David and Christine Hooley, who bring a wealth of experience to the venture, serving up excellent real ales and hearty food every day from midday to 8 p.m. There's also accommodation in three spacious and attractive ensuite guest bedrooms, both large enough to serve as family rooms. Looking onto the main street in the historic market town of Bedale, it makes an excellent place to enjoy a relaxed drink or meal or to use as a touring base.

HIDDEN PLACES GUIDES

Explore Britain and Ireland with *Hidden Places* guides - a fascinating series of national and local travel guides.

Packed with easy to read information on hundreds of places of interest as well as places to stay, eat and drink.

Available from both high street and internet booksellers

For more information on the full range of *Hidden Places* guides and other titles published by Travel Publishing visit our website on

www.travelpublishing.co.uk or ask for our leaflet by phoning **0118-981-7777** or emailing **info@travelpublishing.co.uk**

38 OTTERINGTON SHORTHORN

South Otterington, Northallerton,
North Yorkshire DL7 9HP
☎ 01609 773816

Freshly prepared, locally sourced food at lunch and evening are the bywords at **Otterington Shorthorn**, an excellent traditional country pub with a welcoming atmosphere. Dating back to the mid-18th century, this former coaching inn lies in the village of South Otterington, adjacent to the A167 just a few miles south of Northallerton. Open Monday evening, Tuesday to Sunday and Bank Holidays, it is open every session weekdays and all days at weekends.

There are three real ales together with a selection of lagers, cider, stout, wines, spirits and soft drinks. Food is served at lunch (Tuesday to Saturday and Bank Holidays 12–2, Sundays 12–4) and evenings (Monday to Wednesday 7–9.30, Thursday to Saturday 5–9.30, Sundays 7–9) in the superb

restaurant. Booking advised at this justly popular place, known particularly for its excellent fish dishes and serving an impressive range of daily specials all expertly prepared by the chef. The inn also boasts excellent accommodation in four guest bedrooms housed in a separate building to the rear of the main premises.

Lodge Lane, Danby,
North Yorkshire YO21 2NB
☎ 01287 660362

The evocative name of **The Moors Tea Room** says it all: picture a charming, pristine tea room set amid some breathtaking North Yorkshire Moors scenery, and this is indeed what awaits you at this excellent establishment. Situated adjacent to the Moors Visitor Centre, it's the perfect place to enjoy a relaxing cuppa and some excellent food while you soak up the marvellous atmosphere.

This handsome building is tastefully decorated and furnished in colours, fabrics and furnishings that ensure a cosy, homely feel and great comfort. Choose from a menu of home-made dishes using the best of locally-sourced produce. Yorkshire ham is one speciality, and a small sample from the menu includes tempting items such as sandwiches filled with free-range chicken and tarragon mayonnaise, dry-cured bacon with free-range fried egg, fresh prawns, goat's cheese with caramelised peppers, together with specials including Yorkshire three-cheese Ploughman's, choice of hearty soups, or prawn, red pepper and tomato frittata. The cakes are nothing short of out of this world - well worth the trip to Danby on their own - and there's a special children's menu with favourites such as macaroni cheese with garlic bread, boiled egg and soldiers, tuna, egg or ham and cheese sandwiches, and more. To drink, there's a comprehensive range of beverages including coffees, teas, fruit juice, milk and soft drinks.

There's room for 40 indoors and another 32 outside on the patio - booking advised for larger parties and on Bank Holidays at this popular and welcoming place. Danby makes a nice stopping-off point while touring the many sights and attractions of the region. Open: Daily April to November from 10 in the morning until 5 in the afternoon, and from 11 til 4 at other times of the year - but please note that from November 2006 until April 2007 the tea room will be closed while the Visitor Centre is being refurbished. Children welcome. No smoking indoors.

40 CASTLETON TEA ROOMS ||

2 Station Road, Castleton, Whitby,
North Yorkshire YO21 2EG
☎ 01287 660135

Castleton Tea Rooms is a family-run business with Angela and Steven at the helm, ably assisted by Angela's mum Jeanette. Open all year round (except Christmas Day, Boxing Day and New Year's Day), this excellent establishment serves up delicious cakes, snacks and full meals . Everything here is home-made, with a very good range of dishes including all-day breakfasts, sandwiches, hot and cold snacks and tempting afternoon teas. The home-made scones are a particular treat, but all dishes here are worth sampling, as they are made using the freshest locally-sourced ingredients, expertly prepared and presented.

41 RECTORY FARM HOUSE ⊢⊣

Levisham, Pickering,
North Yorkshire YO18 7NL
☎ 01751 460304
e-mail: heather@levisham.com
⊕ www.levisham.com

Rectory Farm House Bed and Breakfast and Holiday Cottages are situated in Levisham, a picturesque village with manicured greens, that is set in the heart of the North Yorkshire Moor National Park above a quiet wooded valley. The North Yorkshire Steam Railway runs below

Levisham and from here you can catch the train to enjoy a journey to 'Heartbeat' country and Whitby. A superb location for walking, touring or just relaxing. The coast, (Whitby, Scarborough, Filey), stately homes and many quaint market towns, (Helmsley, Malton, Pickering), are within easy driving distance.

Rectory Farm House is an 18th century property with tastefully furnished rooms with the little extra touches such as bathrobes and fresh flowers. Enjoy afternoon tea (with homebaking) and relax in the guests lounge with its log fires for chilly evenings. Local produce and vegetables from the garden are used for the freshly prepared evening meals that are available, or there are good pubs nearby.

Primrose and Cowslip holiday cottages have been transformed from a traditional stone barn and granary but still retain original features, with spacious sitting rooms and 2 bedrooms (1 double and 1 twin) and fully equipped kitchens. Both cottages are fully centrally heated making winter breaks warm and cosy. Short breaks and B&B terms available in the cottages. Prices and further deatuils on request.

223

42 MANOR FARM COTTAGES

Newton upon Rawcliffe, Pickering,
North Yorkshire YO18 8QA

☎ 01284 763568

e-mail: mpennock@ukonline.co.uk

🌐 www.members.aol.com/
ManorfarmNewton

Newton upon Rawcliffe is an unspoilt, picturesque village situated north of Pickering in the North York Moors National Park. Here you will find three distinctive stonebuilt self-catering cottages set in **Manor Farm**. All three are available all year round and date from the 17th to 19th centuries. All enjoy onsite parking and are tasteful and welcoming, pristine and with great charm.

Short breaks are available out of season at The Granary (sleeps 4-5) and Gateside (sleeps 5-6), while weekly bookings are provided at The Dairy House (sleeps 6). All boast unique features – The Granary's spring garden, The Dairy House's galleried sitting room, Gateside's exposed beamwork are just a few examples of the many touches that make the cottages cosy and welcoming – and fully fitted kitchens, spacious living rooms and a wealth of warm, natural woods. Children are welcome. The surrounding area is very scenic, renowned for its wildflowers and within easy reach of the wonderful North Yorkshire Moors Railway. ETC 3-4 Star.

43 THE BARN HOTEL & TEA ROOMS

Hutton-le-Hole,
York YO62 6UA

☎ 01751 417311

e-mail: bookings@thebarnhotel.info

🌐 www.thebarnhotel.info

Situated right next door to the well-known Ryedale Folk Museum, in the picturesque village of Hutton-le-Hole on the edge of the North York Moors National Park, **The Barn Hotel & Tea Rooms** have earned an enviable reputation for excellent accommodation and as a charming place to stop for a cuppa and something tasty to eat. Owned by Brian and Janet Thomson, who are wonderful hosts, there are seven tastefully decorated and

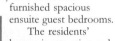

furnished spacious ensuite guest bedrooms. The residents' lounge is attractive and welcoming, with open fire for cool evenings, and the licensed tea rooms (open daily mid-March to mid-November 10.30–5) serve wines and beers as well as a range of teas

and coffees, homemade cakes, puddings, bread and both snacks (soups, sandwiches, pates and more) and substantial meals such as Sunday roasts, all delicious and prepared by Janet using the freshest local produce where possible.

44 THE ORANGE TREE

Rosedale East, Rosedale Abbey, nr
Pickering, North Yorkshire YO18 8RH
☎ 01751 417219
e-mail: relax@theorangetree.com
⊕ www.theorangetree.com

The Orange Tree is unique in its commitment to relaxation. This very special seven-bedroomed licensed guesthouse occupies a secluded and peaceful location a couple of miles north of Rosedale Abbey and just seven miles north of the A170 between Pickering and Kirkbymoorside. The Orange Tree is surrounded by superb walking country, where you can work up a good appetite to increase your enjoyment of the delicious home cooking on offer.

Two of the rooms are on the ground floor; all are elegant and tastefully decorated and furnished. In the specially-designed loft, relaxation treatments such as aromatherapy massage, reflexology and gentle movement classes are provided, and there's also a sauna and a top of the range hot tub in the garden, to help ease away the tensions of everyday life. Guests' complete relaxation is assured at this wonderful rural retreat. Full details of the special breaks available can be found on their website. Bespoke breaks to suit every occasion are also available by arrangement.

45 THE WHITE HORSE AND GRIFFIN HOTEL

Church Street, Whitby,
North Yorkshire YO22 4BH
☎ 01947 604857/825026
Fax: 01947 604857
e-mail: info@whitehorseandgriffin.co.uk
⊕ www.whitehorseandgriffin.co.uk
www.whitehorsecottages.co.uk

Part of Whitby's history, **The White Horse and Griffin Hotel** first opened its doors back in 1681. A proud tradition of service and quality continues today, as owner Stewart Perkins - who bought the hotel when it had been derelict for nearly 50 years, then spent 10 years tastefully restoring it to its original glory (so expertly and accurately done that it has been used as a location for films including the BBC's *David Copperfield*). Guests can't fail to be impressed by the quality of the surroundings, comfort of the accommodation and warmth of the ambience here.

Stewart's wife June and her team look after the restaurants, guest bedrooms and cottages that make up the many enticements of The White Horse and Griffin. The restaurants serve up expertly prepared dishes cooked to order by chefs who use only the freshest ingredients to create an excellent choice of dishes to please every palate.

The hotel has 10 ensuite rooms, bed-and-breakfast accommodation is available at Marstall's Country House, and there are four superb cottages sleeping between 2 and 8 guests.

46 THE GALLERY GUEST HOUSE

17 John Street, Whitby,
North Yorkshire YO21 3ET
☎ 01947 600321
e-mail:
peter@galleryguesthouse.wanadoo.co.uk

Located in the centre of Whitby, **The Gallery Guest House** is the home of Peter and Sandra, excellent hosts who have been offering first-class B&B accommodation since 2000. The house was built in 1858 and is a charming and homely place to use as a touring base. A display of theatre programmes lining the staircase walls gives this charming guest house its name. Open all year round, there are four attractive and very comfortable double ensuite rooms and one single room with private bath. All rooms boast the very best facilities, including DVD players - with a library of DVDs available to borrow. The breakfasts are hearty and delicious.

47 THE KHYBER RESTAURANT

Khyber Pass, Whitby,
North Yorkshire YO21 3PZ
☎ 01947 603500
⊕ www.thekhyberwhitby.co.uk

The **Khyber Restaurant** occupies a superb setting overlooking the harbour and West Beach in Whitby. This airy, spacious and modern restaurant has a very attractive décor, with polished wood floors, large windows and traditional booths for dining. The menu is excellent, with a superb range of freshly caught fish, meats, salads and vegetarian choices as well as sandwiches and snacks. The grilled Yorkshire ham is also well worth sampling, as is the steak pie made with 100% prime beef. Hearty breakfasts are served til midday and there's a separate children's menu. Open: April to October 10.30 - 5 (to 8.45 in peak season; early season closed Mondays).

48 THE BOTTOM HOUSE

7/9 Green Lane, Whitby,
North Yorkshire YO22 4EH
☎ 01947 602413

Close to the harbour on the edge of the town centre in Whitby, **The Bottom House** is a friendly and popular family-run pub with food that is open all day every day. The two real ales here are John Smiths Cask and Theakstons Best, together with a good choice of lagers, wines, spirits and soft drinks. The big draw here is the food; locals and visitors alike rave over the excellent choice of freshly prepared dishes served daily from midday until 5 p.m. (to 7 p.m. during the summer months). Live music Saturday nights from 9.30 p.m.

49 WHITBY MUSEUM

Pannett Park, Whitby,
North Yorkshire YO21 1RE
☎ 01947 602908
⊕ www.whitby-museum.org.uk

In **Whitby Museum** there are worlds to explore from geology to jet carving, from birdlife to bygones, costumes to clocks and from Whitby Abbey to a pirate's pigtail. Ships and men from Whitby travelled the globe, fishing for whales in the Arctic, fighting the African slave trade and exploring the south seas with Captain Cook. In the Museum are many of the treasures they brought back. Whitby jet jewellery was especially popular under Queen Victoria, and jet was also used for miniature carvings. Founded in 1823 to display local Jurassic fossils, this amazing 'Cabinet of Curiosities' still retains its Victorian atmosphere.

50 ESTBEK HOUSE

East Row, Sandsend, nr Whitby,
North Yorkshire YO21 3SU
☎ 01947 893424 Fax: 01947 893625
e-mail: reservations@estbekhouse.co.uk
🌐 www.estbekhouse.co.uk

On the edge of the North Yorkshire Moors coastline, with the Cleveland Way in front and the National Park boundary to the rear, **Estbek House** enjoys a glorious setting in one of England's prettiest villages. The house is Georgian, built around 1750, and hands-on owners David Cross and Tim Lawrence have made it one of the finest restaurants with rooms in the whole county.

The food here is absolutely outstanding, with chef James and his team combining skill and flair at the highest level and putting their personal stamp on every dish. Estbek's signature dish, and its most popular fish dish, is fillet of fresh local halibut, pan-seared and served with a wine sauce or a crab and crayfish sauce. The seafood selection, usually including snapper, sea bass, red mullet and Nile perch, served with a King scallop on a bed of crayfish tails, is a dish fit for a king, and other options – the list is long and mouthwatering! – include a classic steak au poivre, seared duck fillet with a honeyed cherry reduction, and superb

vegetarian dishes such as a trio of spiced bean cakes or couscous stuffed mixed vegetables.

They're as passionate at Estbek about wine as about food, and the selection includes a connoisseur list and a range of excellent quality wines by the glass. There are two dining areas – one in bistro style, the other more traditional, just right for a romantic candlelit dinner. The guest accommodation at the house is also top-class, comprising three doubles and a twin, all with flat-screen TV, CD player, alarm clock, hairdryer, tea & coffee making facilities and a complimentary bathroom guest pack. The double rooms have en suite showers, while the twin is fitted with a whirlpool spa bath. Each room has pictures by local artists, most of local scenes.

The house was built for the manager of the local alum works that once dominated the coastline, producing a substance that was more valuable than gold; its main use was for fixing colours in fabrics. Sandsend nestles between the coast and the Mulgrave Woods, with glorious sandy beaches only 10 yards away and the two fantastic Mulgrave castles a short walk away. It stands on the A174 a short drive or a pleasant walk along the beach to Whitby.

51 BRIDGE COTTAGE CAFÉ TEA ROOMS ¶

East Row, Sandsend, Whitby,
North Yorkshire YO21 3SU
☎ 01947 893111
e-mail: info@bridgecottagecafe.com
⊕ www.bridgecottagecafe.com

Bridge Cottage Café Tea Rooms occupies an historic 16th-century cottage by the sea and boasts delightful walled gardens. The perfect retreat in which to enjoy fresh home-made food and a selection of drinks, it is set in an outstanding location with views to the beach and sea. Owners Allie and Tim have been here since 2005; Allie has over 20 years' experience in catering, and it shows: her menu is simply superb, as are the daily specials.

Just a few examples from the extensive menu include breakfast dishes (served until 11.30 a.m.), fresh seafood and fish dishes such as grilled haddock, Whitby wholetail scampi and Whitby kippers, lime and coriander chicken, quesadillas, a choice of hearty salads and more, together with a range of

fresh sandwiches and, from 2.30 - 4.30, traditional afternoon tea with home-made cakes, scones and more. Cosy and comfortable, there's room for 45 inside and another 50 outside in the gardens. Open Wednesday to Sunday from 9 a.m. to 5 p.m. (to 7 p.m. during the summer holidays), this lovely establishment has won an award as one of the top ten places for children in the Northeast, and boasts a special children's menu, high chairs, colouring books and more to keep little diners happy.

52 THE WILSON ARMS ¶

Beacon Way, Sneaton, Whitby,
North Yorkshire YO22 5HS
☎ 01947 602552
e-mail: enquiries@thewilsonarms.co.uk
⊕ www.thewilsonarms.co.uk

In a superb location just a few miles' drive from Whitby and close to the coast, **The Wilson Arms** has recently been refurbished to a very high standard. A Grade II listed building dating back to the early 1700s, the inn has plenty of character.

This Free House has three real ales – John Smiths, Black Sheep and a changing guest ale – together with a good selection of lagers, cider, stout, wines, spirits and soft drinks. Open every evening for dinner, 6.30-11, and for lunch Friday to Sunday, booking required for Friday and Saturday evenings and Sunday lunchtime. Locally-sourced produce is used to create tasty and filling dishes. This fine inn also boasts six attractive and comfortable guest bedrooms. Guests can stay on a B&B or Dinner, B&B basis.

53 STAINTONDALE SHIRE HORSE FARM

Staintondale, Scarborough,
North Yorkshire YO13 0EY
☎ 01723 870458
⊕ www.shirehorsefarm.co.uk

If you are a smitten horse and pony lover, enjoy the countryside and a happy relaxing environment - this is the place for you. In total there are 18 horses and ponies, from tiny Shetlands to massive Shire Horses. In between, a variety of all shapes and sizes. A Shire stallion called Mascot is the oldest at 22 and like many of the others he was born at the farm. In his younger days he could jump a five bar gate!

It really is about family fun and you can enjoy watching various live shows with both the Shires and the ponies. A pair of matched Shetlands are harnessed to a wagonette and the highlight of the day is possibly the fun and photo Western show. Tony Jenkins, the owner, has a magnificent golden Palomino which he has trained to be a western horse. He has a stunning silver mounted saddle and matching bridle. He also does a few tricks and can see-saw on a rocking bridge.

The farm is idyllicly set in 40 acres of North Yorks National Park coastline and offers excellent facilities for a truly relaxing day out. There are picnic and play areas in safe amenity enclosures and some pretty farm walks to elevated fields where you can enjoy the magnificent coastal and sea views. Seats are provided and at various points you can access the horses in their natural environment.

A timeless flagged floor café and gift shop complete the picture, with tea made from the farm's own fresh spring water. Open Sunday, Tuesday, Wednesday, Friday and Bank Holiday Mondays from mid May to mid September.

54 THE ANVIL INN

Sawdon, Scarborough,
North Yorkshire YO13 9DY
☎ 01723 859896
⊕ www.theanvilinnsawdon.co.uk

The Anvil Inn is a traditional stonebuilt inn with real atmosphere and great food, drink and hospitality on offer. Restored in 1986, this former blacksmith's forge is open every session for ale, Tuesday to Sunday (except Boxing Day), and Black Sheep is the real ale here. Booking advised for meals (served from 12-2 and 6.30-9 Tuesday to Saturday, 12-3 Sundays) at this popular place where the

freshest locally-sourced ingredients are used to create tempting and hearty dishes for the menu and daily specials board. Adjacent to this fine inn there's a self-catering cottage available all year round.

55 HALLAM GUEST HOUSE

5 Station Road, Filey,
North Yorkshire YO14 9AR
☎ 01723 514677
e-mail: john@hallamgh.freeserve.co.uk
⊕ www.hallamguesthouse.co.uk

Just a short walk from the seafront in Filey, **Hallam Guest House** is a real home from home. This handsome Victorian property is owned and run by Sandra and John Simpson, who for over 12 years have been providing first-class service and hospitality to all their guests. Open all year, this licensed guest house has five attractive and welcoming guest bedrooms,

including spacious family room, available on a B&B or Dinner, B&B basis. Breakfasts are hearty and delicious, preparing guests for a day's sightseeing or exploring in the region.

56 VICTORIA COURT BAR AND RESTAURANT

The Crescent, Filey,
North Yorkshire YO14 9JF
☎ 01723 513237

For truly outstanding dining at lunch or dinner, **Victoria Court Bar and Restaurant** is located on The Crescent in Filey, overlooking the shore. This family-run establishment has been offering first-class hospitality for over 20 years. The superb freshly cooked food is guaranteed to suit every taste. Open all year round for lunch and dinner, the restaurant is stylish and spacious.

The Bell family boast two professional chefs, father-and-son team Robert and Richard, and they create and prepare a menu and daily specials with imagination and flair. Speciality dishes include roast loin of pork, steaks and freshly-caught fish dishes. Lunch is served 11.30-2, while dinner is from 6.30-9.30 p.m. Booking is advised at all times at weekends and during school holidays.

The premises are licensed, so guests who simply want to enjoy a relaxing drink amid picturesque and convivial surroundings can choose from a selection of draught keg ales, bottled beers, lagers, wines, spirits, soft drinks or coffee or tea.

57 LINGHOLM COURT HOLIDAY COTTAGES

Lingholm Farm, Lingholm Lane, Lebberston,
Scarborough, North Yorkshire YO11 3PG
☎ 01723 586365 Fax: 01723 585838
e-mail: info@lingholm.co.uk
⊕ www.lingholm.co.uk

Top-of-the-range self-catering is available at **Lingholm Court**, reached by taking the Lebberston turning off the A165. By following the road over the level crossing and continuing into the countryside, Lingholm Court will be found at the end of this road. Set within a 1,200-acre farm, there are four outstanding cottages providing superb accommodation. Available all year round, with shorter breaks out of season, three cottages sleep four, and one sleeps six.

Awarded 4 Stars by the ETC, these converted farm buildings are charming and comfortable, with fully-equipped kitchens, spacious and attractive bedrooms and marvellous views over the surrounding open countryside. Located just

5 miles from Scarborough and 3½ miles from Filey, the cottages make a perfect base from which to explore the area and enjoy the North Yorkshire coast. All bed linen, towels, tea towels and eco-friendly cleaning materials provided.

58 THE SHIP INN

**West Street, Muston, Filey,
North Yorkshire YO14 0ER
☎ 01723 515185**

The village of Muston is found just off the A165 a short drive from Filey. Here you will find the lovely **Ship Inn**, a large and pristine establishment with many original features. The interior is comfortable and spacious, ensuring guests' every comfort.

Open all day every day, this excellent traditional inn has two changing guest ales, so there's always a new real ale to try. Leaseholder Jackie Cook and her friendly, efficient staff offer all their guests first-class service and hospitality. Food is served Tuesday to Sunday and Bank Holidays at lunch (12-2) and dinner (5-9), with plenty of dishes to tempt every palate, all using locally-sourced produce and freshly produced to order. The no-smoking dining room seats 35. Children are welcome. To the rear there's also a superb beer garden with a very good children's play area.

59 THE BUCK INN

**8 Bridlington Street, Hunmanby, Filey,
North Yorkshire YO14 0JR
☎ 01723 891559**

The Buck Inn is a large and distinctive traditional inn situated in the village of Hunmanby, a short drive from the coast and the resorts of Filey, Bridlington and Scarborough. Set in the heart of the village, the inn dates to the early 1800s. Open all day, every day, there's a regular real ale plus occasional guest ale, along with a very good selection

of draught keg bitters, lagers, wines, spirits and soft drinks. Great food is served Tuesday to Saturday 12-2 and 6-8, Sundays 12-3 and 6-8, made with locally-sourced produce and freshly cooked to order.

60 THE NEW INN

**The Square, Thornton-le-Dale,
North Yorkshire YO18 7LF
☎ 01751 474226
e-mail: terryandjo1@btconnect.com
⊕ www.the-new-inn.com**

Guests are assured a warm welcome and genuine hospitality at **The New Inn**. Just a few miles southeast of Pickering on the A170, original features here include exposed beamwork and open fires. The good selection of ales includes Theakstons Best and two rotating guest ales. Home-cooked food is prepared by chef Peter, who boasts over 35 years

experience and who uses fresh local produce to create a selection of delicious dishes. Booking required Friday and Saturday evening and Sunday lunchtime. The accommodation comprises six ensuite guest bedrooms, available all year round.

11 Market Place, Kirkbymoorside,
North Yorkshire YO62 6AA
☎ 01751 431305

There's a cosy, friendly atmosphere at **The Black Swan** in Kirkbymoorside, just 5½ miles northeast of Helmsley on the A170. Comfortable and welcoming, the lounge is the place to enjoy something from the fully-stocked bar, which offers a good selection of real ales, lagers, spirits and fine wines. The menu comprises a tempting choice of hot and cold home-cooked dishes served at both lunchtime and evening.

The beer garden is very attractive, and there's a good-sized car park for guests. Family-run by Andrew, Tracy, Stephen and Lyn since April of 2006, this fine inn is pristine and due, within the lifetime of this edition, for a tasteful and sensitive refurbishment, so that the best of its traditional 17th-century features remain while providing guests with every modern comfort. Tracy and Lyn look after the food – and what great food it is: the extensive menu features classic favourites such as steak and ale pie, roast of the day and haddock, sharing space with venison burgers, sweet and sour chicken and vegetable lasagne. Everything is cooked and prepared on the premises using the freshest local produce - one speciality is the supremely tasty range of sausages, all locally produced.

Andrew and Stephen look after the well-kept ales and wine cellar. There are always four real ales, the regulars being Timothy Taylor Landlord and Black Sheep, with rotating Yorkshire guest ales. The inn is open Tuesday to Sunday all day, and Monday evenings. Food is served Tuesday to Saturday 12–2 and 5.30–8.30, Sundays 12.30–5.30. One unique feature of The Black Swan is that it's the only premises in Kirkbymoorside, a charming and ancient market town with many fine Georgian houses, where guests can sit outside to the front of the inn and enjoy their drink or meal.

62 THE FEATHERS HOTEL

Market Place, Helmsley, York,
North Yorkshire YO62 5BH
☎ 01439 770275
⊕ www.feathershotelhelmsley.co.uk

Taste and elegance are the bywords at **The Feathers Hotel** in Helmsley, a gracious and impressive place offering the best in food, drink and accommodation. Dating back to the 15th century, it began life as two distinct buildings that were later joined into one.

Set in the heart of the picturesque market town of Helmsley, where it overlooks the market square, the hotel retains much of its original character and charm while offering the most up-to-date comforts to all its guests. The ambience is always warm, friendly and relaxed. The décor is just one of many draws here, as the hotel houses one of the finest collections of Mouseman furniture in the nation, including the bar top in the famous Pickwick Bar – the largest single piece of oak that the Mouseman ever worked upon. Mouseman was the sobriquet of Robert Thompson, the famous craftsman who would add the distinctive 'signature' of a crouching mouse to all his work.

There's something to quench every thirst in the bar, from real ales and a very good wine list to lagers, spirits, cider, stout and soft drinks. And to eat? The Feathers enjoys an enviable reputation for serving up hearty portions of fresh, quality local produce, expertly prepared and presented. Meals are served in the (no-smoking) Feversham Lounge, a spacious, tasteful and attractive room where you can dine in comfort. The accommodation at this fine hotel is simply superb, with 16 en suite guest bedrooms furnished with understated elegance. Some rooms feature four-poster beds.

233

63 DUNCOMBE PARK 🏛

Helmsley, York YO62 5EB
☎ 01439 772625

A girls' school for 60 years, this Baroque mansion built in 1713 is now the family home of Lord & Lady Feversham. The restored principal rooms are typical of a late 19th century "grand interior", and the landscaped "green garden" with its temples and terraces, has been described as 'the supreme masterpiece of the art of the landscape gardener'. The National Nature Reserve within over 400 acres of rolling Parkland is a delight to explore. End a  perfect day with a visit to the Parkland Centre Tearoom & Shop, taste the delights of homemade food and browse at your leisure the unusual hand made crafts made in Yorkshire.

HIDDEN PLACES GUIDES

Explore Britain and Ireland with *Hidden Places* guides - a fascinating series of national and local travel guides.

Packed with easy to read information on hundreds of places of interest as well as places to stay, eat and drink.

Available from both high street and internet booksellers

For more information on the full range of *Hidden Places* guides and other titles published by Travel Publishing visit our website on

www.travelpublishing.co.uk
or ask for our leaflet by phoning
0118-981-7777 or emailing
info@travelpublishing.co.uk

64 THE PHEASANT AT HAROME

Harome, Helmsley,
North Yorkshire YO62 5JG
☎ 01439 771241
Fax: 01439 771744

The Pheasant Hotel began life as the village blacksmith's, two cottages and shop, renovated and extended to create this attractive and very comfortable country house hotel. There are 15 ensuite guest bedrooms complete with every modern comfort and amenity, available on a dinner, bed and breakfast basis. All rooms face south or southwest, some overlooking the village pond and mill stream, others looking out over the hotel's courtyard and charming walled garden.

Cosy comforts include the intimate oak-beamed bar, spacious drawing room and handsome dining room. Luxury is provided in the shape of the superb indoor heated swimming pool, lovely conservatory dining room  and scenic gardens overlooking the village pond. Meals are created using the freshest local produce including local poultry, game and fish, Yorkshire lamb and Helmsley beef. Booking advised at all times for non-residents. Located fewer than three miles from Helmsley, it is a wonderful rural retreat and an excellent touring base. Riding available in Helmsley, as is golf at reduced rates for guests at the 18-hole course at Kirkbymoorside.

65 LASKILL GRANGE

Hawnby, North Yorkshire YO62 5NB
☎ 01439 798268   Fax: 01439 772003
e-mail: suesmith@laskillfarm.fsnet.co.uk
⊕ www.laskillgrange.co.uk

The outstanding **Laskill Grange** offers truly idyllic holiday accommodation. This charming, warm country farmhouse is set on a 600-acre farm with its own natural spring water. This peaceful rural retreat is reached by taking the B1257 out of Helmsley to reach the village of Hawnby. At the gracious and elegant farmhouse, Laskill Farm, bed and breakfast accommodation comprises three doubles, two twins and one single guest bedrooms, all ensuite. Every room has fine traditional features, complemented by elegant and stylish décor and furnishings that ensure guests' every comfort. All rooms are lovingly cared for and well equipped.

The guests' lounge boasts an open fire, while the superb grounds include a lovely garden with lake, stream and summerhouse. The Grange also offers excellent self-catering accommodation in five superior barn conversions. Reached just across a courtyard from the main farmhouse, The Forge sleeps six, The Granary sleeps four to six,

The Smithy and Coach House sleep four while Bridge Cottage sleeps two. The Coach House is suitable for guests with disabilities. All boast handsome and welcoming traditional features such as stone fireplaces and exposed oak beams, complemented by every modern convenience such as the well-fitted kitchens, fully equipped with cooker, microwave, dishwasher and washing machine.

Outside there is a barbecue area, patio and a shared garden activity area. Guests are welcome to enjoy free fishing along the nearby River Seph. All fuel, power, linen and towels are included in the tariff. Pets are allowed in some of the cottages. An ideal base from which to discover the countless delights of North Yorkshire – a region of dramatic moorland, spectacular scenery, hidden dales, pretty villages and stunning coastline, there are lots of places of historical interest and stately homes nearby, including Rievaulx Abbey, Nunnington Hall, Castle Howard, Mount Grace Priory, Byland Abbey, Ryedale Folk Museum, York, Beverley and the delights of the Heritage Coast, all within easy reach. The Grange and surrounding area is also a walker's paradise, with lots of excellent eating places locally. Awarded 4 Diamonds by the AA.

66 THE HAWNBY HOTEL

Hawnby, Helmsley,
North Yorkshire YO62 5QS
☎ 01439 798202 Fax: 01439 798344
e-mail: info@hawnbyhotel.co.uk
⊕ www.hawnbyhotel.co.uk

Set in the heart of the North Yorkshire Moors National Park, one of the most beautiful parts of Yorkshire, **The Hawnby Hotel** is a welcoming and appealing hotel in a peaceful rural setting reached via the B1257 from Helmsley. A former drovers' inn dating back to the early 19th century, this fine hotel offers excellent food and accommodation. The arrival of head chef Neil Haughley, with 20 years of experience, has heralded a fantastic new menu which guests can enjoy in the handsome, no-smoking restaurant or in the delightful, well-kept gardens. Booking is advised at weekends.

Open all year round, the hotel boasts nine superb en suite guest bedrooms, six of which are located in the main building,

while the other three are within the tastefully refurbished stables opposite. Awarded 4 Diamonds by the ETC, the hotel makes an excellent base from which to explore not just the great outdoors – there's outstanding hiking, walking, cycling and riding nearby – but also the many historic attractions of the region.

67 THE HIDDEN MONKEY TEA ROOMS

34 The Market Place, Malton,
North Yorkshire YO17 7LW
☎ 01653 694982

Located in the centre of Malton, **The Hidden Monkey Tea Rooms** is a charming place to stop for excellent refreshments while exploring the town and surrounding region. A bright and cosy front area looks out over the Market square, while there's also a dining area and upstairs seating. A mouthwatering range of home-made cakes, soups (home-made daily), sandwiches, hot and cold snacks and meals from the menu and specials board are served Monday to Saturday 9 a.m. to 5 p.m. Booking advised for Saturday lunchtime. Children welcome. No smoking.

68 THE KING'S HEAD

5 Market Place, Malton,
North Yorkshire YO17 7LP
☎ 01653   692289

The impressive **King's Head** dates to the mid-1700s and began life as a coaching inn. Standing in the centre of Malton looking into the Market Place, the inn has recently been refurbished to offer guests comfort amid handsome and welcoming surroundings. Open all day, every day (except Christmas Day), there's a very good selection of draught keg ales including Boddingtons, John Smiths Smooth, Carling, Fosters and more. Tasty food is served daily from midday until 7 p.m. The excellent main meal deal offers two meals for £5. Licensees Luke and Danielle plan to provide quality accommodation here soon - please ring for details.

High Street, Amotherby, nr Malton,
North Yorkshire YO17 6TL
☎ 01653 693630   Fax: 01653 699447
e-mail: qhamotherby@aol.com

Situated in the tranquil village of Amotherby, just a couple of miles northwest of Malton off the B1257, **The Queen's Head** is a spacious and welcoming Free House with elegant restaurant. Owners Jon and Mandy Woollen have been here for five years, bringing a wealth of experience and expertise to the job of providing top-quality food, drink and service to all their customers. Superbly appointed, the décor and furnishings are modern, stylish and elegant.

The inn is renowned far and wide for its restaurant, now newly refurbished to provide every comfort. In charming and convivial surroundings in this spacious restaurant (seating 85), guests can enjoy a range of traditional Cantonese dishes, all expertly prepared and presented. All dishes use the freshest locally-sourced ingredients. The restaurant is open from 5 until 11 p.m. seven nights a week; booking required at weekends. A takeaway

service is also available. The inn stocks three well-kept real ales – Tetleys, a Copper Dragon brew and a rotating guest ale - together with a very good selection of wines, spirits, lagers, cider, stout and soft drinks.

The beer garden is a welcoming place to enjoy excellent food and drink on fine days – and during the lifetime of this edition will include a state-of-the-art children's play area. The inn is completely accessible to guests with disabilities, and prides itself, justifiably, on its 'green' policy: geothermic energy is used to heat the premises, and solar energy to heat the water. They also recycle wherever possible. For anyone seeking good food, good drink and a relaxed, friendly and informal ambience, The Queen's Head is well worth seeking out!

Appleton-le-Street, Malton,
North Yorkshire YO17 6PG
☎ 01653 693647   Fax: 01653 698471

Situated in Appleton-le-Street, on the B1257 a couple of miles west of Malton, **The Cresswell Arms** dates back to the late 1800s and began life with a blacksmiths to one side and a butcher shop to the other, all now incorporated within the main, spacious and impressive building of this fine inn.

It is run by Liz Gibson, who has been leaseholder for five years and is ably assisted by Debbie, who looks after front of house, and by excellent chef Steve, who together with Liz ensures the quality, freshness and preparation of the delicious food served at lunch and dinner daily (Monday to Saturday 12–2 and 6.30–9 and Sundays 12–2 and 6.30–8.30).

The inn boasts two dining areas, one completely new that seats 50 and the other seating 24. Both areas are welcoming and tastefully decorated and

furnished, with warm woods, bright and pristine paintwork and individual touches that make them homely and very attractive. Guests choose from the menu and, at weekends, the tasty specials. Using meat and produce sourced locally to guarantee quality and freshness, booking is advised at all times but particularly at weekends at this justly popular inn, renowned for its food. Both dining areas are no-smoking.

To drink there are two real ales – John Smiths and a changing guest ale – together with a full complement of lagers, cider,

stout, wines, spirits and soft drinks. To the rear of the building are the accommodation units: 10 comfortable and handsomely appointed guest bedrooms, all designed with guests' every comfort and convenience in mind. Eight rooms are on the ground floor, a mixture of spacious twins and doubles; one room has been specially adapted for guests with disabilities. Each room is individually decorated and furnished to the highest standard.

71 CHURCH FARM

Scackleton, nr Hovingham,
North Yorkshire YO62 4NB
☎ 01653 628403
e-mail: cynthia.firby@btinternet.com

This hidden gem, once found, is the kind of place you'll want to return to time and time again. **Church Farm** is set in the village of Scackleton, just a couple of miles southwest of Hovingham off the B1363 or B1257. A working farm surrounded by hundreds of acres of picturesque countryside, this magnificent home amid well-kept, eye-catching gardens has been providing superb bed-and-breakfast accommodation since 1992.

Open all year round (bar Christmas and New Year), there are three delightful guest bedrooms. Comfortable and well appointed, each room commands marvellous views over the fields and woods and to the moors beyond. Downstairs is the gracious guests' lounge with exposed pine beams and open fire. Home cooking is the order of the day here: owner Cynthia's hearty farmhouse breakfast sets guests up for a day's walking or exploring York (just 14 miles away), the North York Moors and the coast.

72 THE MIDDLETON ARMS

Main Street, North Grimston, Malton,
North Yorkshire YO17 8AX
☎ 01944 768255
e-mail: info@middletonarms.com
⊕ www.middletonarms.com

A large, traditional and welcoming coaching inn dating back to the 1700s, **The Middleton Arms** is set in the village of North Grimston, found on the B1248 southeast of Malton. Roz and Lofty are your hosts; they arrived here in January of 2006 and bring a wealth of experienced in the trade to providing first-class ales, food and accommodation. The interior is pristine and charming, with highly polished floors, floral curtains and a tasteful décor. The ambience is always relaxed and friendly. Open every session weekdays and all day at weekends in the summer months, there are always two or three real ales, with Timothy Taylor Landlord and Tetleys the regulars here. Quality food is served daily at lunch (12–2.30) and dinner (6.30–9), and the inn boasts two dining areas. The main

restaurant seats 44, while the lounge bar seats 24. Both areas are

no-smoking. There's also a spacious beer garden to the rear of the inn. Guests choose from the menu or daily specials board from a range of dishes expertly prepared by the inn's qualified chefs. Booking advised for Saturday evenings. Upstairs, there are three comfortable and attractive letting rooms available for bed-and-breakfast accommodation, and the inn makes a very good base from which to explore the many sights and attractions of the region.

73 CASTLE HOWARD

York, North Yorkshire YO60 7DA
☎ 01653 648444
e-mail: house@castlehoward.co.uk
🌐 www.castlehoward.co.uk

Castle Howard, winner of York Tourism Bureau's 'Out of Town Attraction of the Year' award, is now so much more than a magnificent 18th century house with extensive collections and breathtaking grounds featuring temples, lakes and fountains. Historical characters, such as the original architect, Sir John Vanbrugh and the 6th Countess, Lady Georgina provide a first person observation of what life was like at Castle Howard. Other characters include Widow Etty, whose husband was killed in an accident during the construction of Castle Howard; the 18th century Governess awaiting the next generation, busying herself with the tutorage of the young visitors; the 5th Earl's Butler, who is a fountain of knowledge and good sense - just what is needed to curb the rash spending of the Earl; the School Mistress, helping to run the school relocated to Castle Howard during the Second World War, who can be spotted covering 'indecent' statues and ensuring the girls do not run down the corridors.

The range of tours around the house and gardens are very popular and include restoration and renovation; the great fire of 1940; the haunts of *Brideshead Revisited*; the history of the Roses and many more. There are various places to stop and enjoy refreshments and a plant centre and tree nursery, both open for sales to the public. A varied programme of events takes places throughout the year, including the Proms Spectacular and Archaeology Weekends.

Open daily between February and November, a land-train is available to transport visitors from the car park to the house and there is disabled access to many parts.

74 JORVIK VIKING CENTRE

Coppergate, York,
North Yorkshire YO1 9WT
☎ 01904 543402

The world famous **JORVIK** centre in York transports visitors back in time to experience the sights, sounds and - perhaps most famously - the smells of 10th century York. Over 20 years of archaeological research led to the new re-creation of Viking Age York in JORVIK, which re-opened to wide acclaim in April 2001. The new JORVIK now presents a far broader view and more detailed depiction of life in the Viking Age. Visitors to the centre are shown that, in AD 975, York was a bustling commercial centre where 10,000 people lived and worked. Travelling in state-of-the-art time capsules, visitors are carried past and through two storey dwellings, enjoying views over backyards and rooftops, and even glimpsing the Viking Age equivalent of today's Minster.

February 2002 saw the launch of the new 'Viking Voyagers' exhibition. Visitors can get the low-down on all aspects of sea-faring from trading in the Far East and raiding in the North East, to life on board and the technicalities of mastering the ocean waves. The year-long exhibition features hands-on activities, artefacts and new academic research around the theme of Viking ships and is not to be missed.

18 years after it first opened, JORVIK still retains its status as one of the world's icon attractions and its many superb qualities make it an enduring favourite with children and adults alike.

Main Street, Shipton by Beningbrough,
York, North Yorkshire YO30 1AB

☎ 01904 470334

⊕ www.thedawnayarms.co.uk

Situated in the quiet and friendly village of Shipton by Beningbrough on the A19 near York, **The Dawnay Arms** is one of the most attractive and welcoming village inns in the Vale of York. This spacious and handsome traditional inn has recently undergone a tasteful refurbishment to keep all of its 18th-century charm while offering every modern comfort. The décor, tables, chairs and carpets are all new, and the renovation incorporated a formerly unused room that is now part of the main front bar/lounge area and also no-smoking.

Garry and Pamela Carter became the landlords here in November of 2002, and are proud to uphold the inn's longstanding reputation for good, traditional home-cooked food in a relaxing atmosphere. The Dawnay Arms has a wide selection of soft drinks, spirits, wines and ales including hand-pulled ales, as well as an extensive menu. Guests can dine indoors in a selection of rooms or enjoy the fresh air in the lovely beer garden when the weather allows. Closed Monday and Tuesday lunchtimes, the inn is open all other sessions and all day on Sunday, and food is served Wednesday to Friday 12-2

and 5.30-9, Saturday 12-2 and 6-9, and Sundays 12-8. Chef Gareth creates wonderful dishes using the freshest locally-sourced ingredients. The Early Bird specials are served Monday to Friday from 5.30 to 6.45. Booking at this justly popular eatery is required Friday to Sunday and at all times for parties of more than six.

Despite lying almost two miles apart, the alliance of Shipton and Beningbrough is steeped in history, and stems from the fact that Shipton was once part of the Beningbrough Estate, first owned by the Bourdner family and later by the Dawnay family. It only gained

its independence in 1917, when the Beningbrough Estate was broken up. The village of Shipton is mentioned in the *Domesday Book*. Shipton, Overton and Beningbrough were, by all accounts, very popular settlements in the 16th and 17th centuries, part of the Royal Forest of Galtres, where English monarchs loved to hunt. The Dawnay Arms inn began life as The Bay Horse and was originally built in 1730. It became The Dawnay Arms in the mid-19th century, named for the Lord of the Manor Payan Dawnay; the family Coat of Arms can be seen over the door.

Main Street, Linton-on-Ouse, York,
North Yorkshire YO30 2AY
☎ 01347 848823

Located in the picturesque village of Linton-on-Ouse, found off the A19 a short distance northwest of York, **The College Arms** is a well-recommended pub and restaurant popular with locals and visitors from much further afield. Dating back to the 1700s, the inn was owned by University College, Oxford, which is how it comes by its name. Closed Monday to Thursday lunchtimes, it's open every evening through the week and all day Friday, Saturday, Sunday and Bank Holidays.

Owners Peter and Jacqui have been here since 1999, offering first-class hospitality, food and drink to all their guests. There are two real ales - John Smiths Cask and a changing guest ale - together with a good selection of wines, spirits, soft drinks, lagers and more. The décor boasts a wealth of traditional features and the atmosphere is always relaxed and comfortable. Housed within the pub is the excellent 'Saffron Spice', the evocative name of the superb Indian restaurant where chef and host Shabba creates a wide choice of tempting dishes. Food is served from 5.30 to 10.30 daily (later on Friday and Saturday), and at Sunday lunchtime from midday until 6 p.m. On Sundays, for a fixed price you can eat as much as you like. Booking required for Friday and Saturday.

The menu incorporates both traditional and more innovative Indian cuisine, including dishes such as chicken makhani (marinated in ginger, garlic and home-made yoghurt), jalfrezie dishes, bhunas, massala meals, tikka, tandoori and balti dishes and much more, all expertly prepared to order. Ranging in spiciness from korma dishes to vindaloo, there's something to tempt every palate, and this excellent restaurant is well worth seeking out. Linton-on-Ouse is a good stopping point while touring the Vale of York, an area rich in natural beauty with some lovely stately homes, major centres at York and Leeds, and a range of outdoor pursuits including good walking and cycling.

77 THE BLUE BELL COUNTRY INN

Main Street, Alne, York,
North Yorkshire YO61 IRR

☎ 01347 838331

🌐 www.bluebellalne.co.uk

Just 11 miles northwest of York off the A19, in the quiet and secluded village of Alne set alongside the River Kyle, **The Blue Bell Country Inn** is a fine place to enjoy great food, drink and hospitality. Run by Michael and Annette Anson with help from their son David, who runs the bar, this one-time country farmhouse is a hostelry upholding the best traditions of English country pubs.

Cheerful and welcoming inside and out, there are well-kept gardens to the front and rear, and an air of warm hospitality throughout. Lots of style and class are in evidence in the handsome lounge, bar and restaurant. Here guests will find a choice of at least three real ales (John Smiths, Black Sheep and Timothy Taylor Landlord) and a good selection of wines together with lagers, cider, stout, spirits and soft drinks – something, in fact, to quench every thirst. Food is available at lunchtime Wednesday to Saturday and Bank Holiday Mondays (11.30–2), from midday to 8 p.m. Sundays, and at dinner Monday to Saturday. Both Michael and Annette cook – Michael does the superb main courses such as beef stroganoff, roast duckling, vegetable and cheese Wellington, seared venison and pheasant and the justly popular fish and seafood dishes, which include sea bass, salmon, lemon sole, lobster, king prawn and monk fish, while Annette creates the starters and the tempting range of sweets.

Together they have earned the inn a fine reputation for fresh, delicious food, and have made this a destination pub for great meals. The outstanding Stables Restaurant has original features such as the low-beamed ceiling. Guests can also dine in the cosy lounge. Booking is advised at weekends. Children welcome. During the lifetime of this edition, bed-and-breakfast accommodation will become available at the inn – please telephone or visit the inn's website for more details.

78 SUTTON PARK 🏛

Sutton-on-the-Forest York
North Yorkshire YO6 1DP
☎ 01347 810249
e-mail: info@statelyhome.co.uk
🌐 www.suttonpark.co.uk

Sutton Park is a charming lived-in house, built of mellow brick in 1730 by Thomas Atkinson. The house contains beautiful eighteenth century furniture, paintings mostly from Buckingham House, now Buckingham Palace, and an important collection of porcelain. Magnificent plaster-work by Cortese is also in evidence.

The House is a fine example of early Georgian architecture overlooking beautiful parkland. It is filled with a rich collection of 18th century treasures all put together with great style to make a most grand but inviting lived-in stately home.

Silver Gilt winner 2005 Yorkshire in Bloom for Best Tourist & Visitor Attraction, the gardens attract visitors from both home and abroad and have been featured in many prestigious publications. Herbaceous and rose borders are full of rare and interesting plants, laid out with great care over the past forty years.

In the grounds are a walled pond garden, Edwardian fernery, Georgian Icehouse, Woodland Walks and Children's Adventure Playground.

79 WOMBWELL ARMS 🍴

Wass, North Yorkshire YO61 4BE
☎ 01347 868280   Fax: 01347 868039
e-mail:
wykes@thewombwellarms.wanadoo.co.uk
🌐 www.thewombwellarms.co.uk

At the foot of the scenic Hambleton Hills, the **Wombwell Arms** is a country Free House and inn dating back to the 18th century and providing real ales, an extensive wine list, hearty and delicious meals and excellent accommodation. Owners Steve and Mary Wykes have been here since 2004, and are friendly and welcoming hosts.

There are always a minimum of two real ales – Black Sheep and Timothy Taylor Landlord – together with an occasional guest ale and a selection of lagers, select wines, soft drinks, spirits, cider and stout served in two characterful bars. Food is served at lunch and dinner daily in the two restaurants, which boast traditional features including the exposed beamwork and seat 45 guests – booking required for Friday and Saturday evenings and Sunday lunchtime for the menu that makes best use of the freshest Yorkshire produce. There are two double ensuite rooms within the inn and an adjacent cottage that offers a ground-floor double and spacious family room, available all year round.

81 ST VINCENT ARMS

Main Street, Sutton upon Derwent, York,
North Yorkshire YO41 4BN

☎ 01904 608349

⊕ www.stvincentarms.co.uk

An outstanding property situated in Sutton upon Derwent found southeast of York off the A1079, the **St Vincent Arms** is owned and personally run by six members of the Hopwood family, who have been here at this gracious and welcoming inn since 1990.

Open every session, one big draw here are the nine real ales, which include selections from all round the country – Timothy Taylor Landlord, London Pride, John Smiths, Charles Wells Bombardier, York Terrier, Old Mill St George's, Fullers Porter and ESB, to name but a few. This astonishing choice of ales is complemented by an equally good range of lagers, wines, spirits and soft drinks as well as cider and stout. Winner of CAMRA's Pub of the Year award not once but twice in the past four years, the Hopwoods know their ales and are proud to carry on a long tradition of serving up the finest ones to their guests.

The food here is no less a draw, served daily at lunch (12–2) and dinner (7–9.30). The no-smoking restaurant seats 60 diners; booking required for Friday, Saturday and Sunday. The menu and specials board offer an excellent range of fresh home-cooked dishes, all expertly prepared and presented. A short sampling from a typical day's specials board includes trio of crevettes, smoked salmon and samphire, aubergine and tomato bake, chicken liver pâté, east coast lobster, pan-fried Dover sole, rib-eye steak or lamb curry. The atmosphere here is always convivial and welcoming. For its drink, food and relaxed, friendly ambience, this fine pub is well worth seeking out.

Kexby, York YO41 5LQ
☎ 01904 489368

Located adjacent to the main A1079, east of York, the village of Kexby is an ideal place to use as a base while touring in the region, and **Ivy House Farm** is the perfect choice for a home from home. It is owned by Kathleen Daniel, who has lived here for 50 years and provided excellent bed and breakfast accommodation for 30 of them. Set in a 132-acre working farm, there are three comfortable and welcoming guest bedrooms (two ensuite,

one with private bath) available all year round except at Christmas. The tariff includes a hearty and delicious Yorkshire farmhouse breakfast. Children welcome.

HIDDEN PLACES GUIDES

Explore Britain and Ireland with *Hidden Places* guides - a fascinating series of national and local travel guides.

Packed with easy to read information on hundreds of places of interest as well as places to stay, eat and drink.

Available from both high street and internet booksellers

For more information on the full range of *Hidden Places* guides and other titles published by Travel Publishing visit our website on

www.travelpublishing.co.uk
or ask for our leaflet by phoning
**0118-981-7777 or emailing
info@travelpublishing.co.uk**

RSPB North of England Office,
4 Benton Terrace, Sandyford Road,
Newcastle upon Tyne NE2 1QU
☎ 01912 813366

The chalk cliffs at Bempton form part of England's largest seabird colony between Flamborough Head and Bempton. Over 200,000 seabirds breed on the reserve alone. As well as managing reserves such as this the RSPB also works for the better protection of the marine environment.

For much of the year, the cliffs at Bempton are relatively quiet, but during the breeding season, between April and August, they are crammed with birds. The spectacle, noise, activity and smell all contribute to an overwhelming and memorable experience. As many seabird colonies are on remote islands Bempton offers a rare opportunity to watch breeding seabirds at close quarters.

Both puffins and gannets breed at Bempton. About 2,000 pairs of puffins return to the cliffs to breed and each pair lays a single egg in a crevice in the rock face. Between May and the end of July they regularly visit their young with small fish but by August, the young puffins have left the cliffs to spend the winter on the North Sea. Bempton has the largest mainland gannet colony (gannetry) in Britain. Over 2,500 pairs nest on the cliffs and can be seen here from January to November, but are most active between April and August when they are breeding. They will travel up to 60 miles to find food. When fishing, gannets can dive from heights of up to 130 feet, entering the water at up to 60 mph.

Six other species of seabirds nest at Bempton Cliffs. Kittiwakes are the most numerous, with 45,000 pairs packed onto the cliffs. Guillemots and razorbills also nest on the narrow cliff ledges. Look out for the distinctive gliding flight of fulmars around the cliffs, and herring gulls and a few shags also nest on the cliffs.

82 THE WHITE SWAN INN

Main Street, Wighill, Tadcaster,
North Yorkshire LS24 8BQ
☎ 01937 832217

Wighill is an ancient settlement on the West Yorkshire/North Yorkshire border, which has seen its fair share of history, growing to a peak population of 280 in the mid-19th century and now boasting about 208 inhabitants. Peaceful and picturesque, it has a very nice village church. A short drive north of Tadcaster in this charming village of Wighill,

The White Swan Inn is a distinctive 18th-century inn that was once also the village blacksmith's. Set back slightly from the road with a gravel driveway and patio seating area to the front, it is tasteful and welcoming throughout. This family-run pub is in the capable hands of father-and-son team Steve and Carl Lofthouse, who took over in April of 2006 and have already attracted favourable attention from locals and visitors alike for the handsome premises, comfortable ambience and superb food and drink. Steve has over four years' experience in catering, and this shows in the care and attention he pays to making sure all guests receive excellent service and hospitality.

Open all day every day for ale, the three regulars are Theakstons, Timothy Taylor Landlord and Old Speckled Hen, together with a good choice of lagers, cider, stout, spirits, soft drinks and wine list. There are two separate dining areas (both no smoking) that seat up to 40 guests in total. There is also additional seating in the lovely beer garden to the rear and the patio area to the front of the inn. Food is served at lunch and dinner every day. The varied menu includes house specialities such as lamb shank, steaks and more, while the Sunday roast (served 12–4 p.m.) has attracted rave reviews.

84 THE CHESTNUT HORSE

Main Street, Great Kelk, Driffield,
East Yorkshire YO25 8HN
☎ 01262 488263

A quality hidden public house well worth seeking out to enjoy, **The Chestnut Horse** is found in the picturesque hamlet of Great Kelk, located off the A614 or A165 between Driffield and Bridlington. Once known as The Board, the inn dates back to 1793 and in its long history has served as a mortuary and counting house. Open every evening and all day Sundays, there are always two to four real ales (Samuel Smiths is the regular) plus two draught Belgian beers and a good selection of other thirst-quenchers including soft drinks, wines and spirits.

Food is served during opening times and from midday on Sundays (booking required Saturday

evenings) with superb chef-prepared dishes using local produce, such as prime steaks, fish pie, steak-and-mushroom pie, traditional Hungarian goulash, lamb cutlets, grilled trout and more. The interior is spacious and welcoming, and there's also a secluded and lovely beer garden to the rear of this excellent inn.

85 THE BUCK HOTEL

1 Market Place, Driffield,
East Yorkshire YO25 6AP
☎ 01377 253748

Situated in the heart of Driffield on the main road of the town, **The Buck Hotel** is a really impressive inn with great food, drink and accommodation. Open all day every day, there is one real ale (John Smiths Cask) together with a full selection of lagers, cider, stout, wines, spirits and a good choice of soft drinks. Tenant Graham Frazer is a convivial

and welcoming host who doubles as chef, creating excellent and hearty dishes Tuesday to Sunday lunchtime (11.30-2.30). His roasts and steak pies are justly popular. The accommodation comprises five comfortable bedrooms available all year round.

87 THE BAY HORSE INN

Middle Street, Kilham, Driffield,
East Yorkshire YO25 4RL
☎ 01262 420220

Standing in the village of Kilham, a few miles northeast of Driffield found off the A614 or B1249, **The Bay Horse Inn** is a very impressive, spacious and pristine place with great food, drink and hospitality. The interior is very attractive, with a tasteful décor and furnishings that ensure guests' comfort. Open every session weekdays and all day at weekends and Bank Holidays, there's a good selection

of ales and food served Friday to Sunday evenings 6–9.30 and also for Sunday lunch (12–1.30), with a full menu and specials board of home-made dishes such as steak and ale pie, all made using local produce.

248

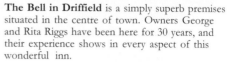

Market Place, Driffield,
East Yorkshire YO25 6AN
☎ 01377 256661   Fax: 01377 253228
e-mail: bell@bestwestern.co.uk
🌐 www.thebellindriffield.co.uk

The Bell in Driffield is a simply superb premises situated in the centre of town. Owners George and Rita Riggs have been here for 30 years, and their experience shows in every aspect of this wonderful inn.

The handsome and comfortable dining room is open for everything from morning coffee (9.30-11.30), lunch (12-1.30) and afternoon teas (2-4.30) through to dinner and bar meals (served 7-9.30). With main courses such as broiled salmon fillet, lamb cutlets, oven-roasted breast of duckling, leek and cheddar tartlets and a selection of steaks, there's something delicious to satisfy every appetite. The excellent Sunday lunch is worth a special visit, with a selection of meals including grilled plaice, roast sirloin of beef, duckling or pork with all the trimmings, and vegetarian options such as spinach and ricotta cannelloni or spicy mushroom stroganoff. And don't forget to leave room for dessert, which includes mouthwatering choices such as vanilla cheesecake, dark chocolate cup, sticky toffee pudding and raspberry Pavlova. All dishes are

expertly prepared using the freshest locally-sourced ingredients.

The accommodation, available all year round except at Christmas, comprises 16 luxurious and individually designed and decorated rooms, all ensuite and some located on the ground floor. Guests can stay on a B&B or dinner and B&B basis, and The Bell has been awarded a rating of 3 Stars for accommodation by the ETC. No children under the age of 16.

All this and we've not even mentioned the outstanding extra facilities, which include the

on-site Driffield Spa where guests can relax, unwind and indulge in the spa and saunarium, with a selection of water, heat, massage and steam treatments, physioacoustic chair (which helps to alleviate back pain and stress, reduce high blood pressure and ease the symptoms of arthritis), floatation chamber and more. There's a range of spa days on offer or guests can create their own tailor-made package. Open: Monday to Friday 9 a.m.-9.30 p.m, Saturday and Sunday 10-5. There's also a first-class gym with state-of-the-art facilities, swimming pool, jacuzzi and squash court.

88 THE WOLD COTTAGE ⊨

Wold Newton, Driffield,
East Yorkshire YO25 3HL
☎ 01262 470696
e-mail: katrina@woldcottage.com
⊕ www.woldcottage.com

Once a gentleman's country retreat, **The Wold Cottage** is a spacious Georgian farmhouse set in 300 acres of its own grounds. Peace and tranquillity are assured at this marvellous traditional farmhouse, surrounded by scenic countryside with views of new and mature woodlands and, further afield, the delights of the East coast, Bempton Cliffs, historic houses, the North Yorkshire Moors and the charming towns of Beverley and York.

A friendly family atmosphere pervades this charming home, where there are five ensuite guest bedrooms, each individually decorated and furnished, and two self-catering cottages sleeping four to six people. A real hidden gem, it's been awarded a 5 Star Gold Award rating – justly deserved for the high standard of the facilities and hospitality on hand here. The guests' sitting room is cosy and comfortable, while breakfast offers the traditional full English breakfast as well as a good and varied selection of cereals, yoghurt, fruits, croissants and home-made jams. Katrina is an accomplished cook who has worked with the *Ready, Steady, Cook* team! Evening meals by prior arrangement. For a relaxing and memorable break, look no further.

89 THE GAIT INN ⧪

Millington, York YO42 1TX
☎ 01759 302045

The picturesque **Gait Inn** and its village setting in Millington is a must for visitors and locals alike. Owner Stuart Stephenson is a one-time farmer who, with his wife Helen, took the helm here in August of 2005. They've built a real success here with their excellent food, drink and hospitality. The venue helps, too – a lovely 16th-century establishment that oozes character and charm.

Open every evening and Saturday and Sunday lunchtimes, real ales include John Smiths Cask, Theakstons, Best, Tetleys, Black Sheep and a changing guest ale. Delicious home-cooked food is served Tuesday to Sunday evenings 7–9 p.m. and weekends from 12–2.30. Booking required for Friday and

Saturday evening and Sunday lunch. Home-made dishes are

the speciality here, with the home-made steak pie highly recommended. The produce is all sourced locally and Helen does most of the cooking. The interior is spacious and welcoming, with a handsome traditional décor, while there's also a large and well-kept beer garden to the rear of the pub. Children welcome.

90 THE WINDMILL INN

53 Lairgate, Beverley,
East Yorkshire HU17 8ET
☎ 01482 862817   Fax: 01482 870741

Just a short walk from the famous Minster, **The Windmill Inn** is a comfortable and friendly inn family-run by the Wilkinsons for the past 30 years. Formerly a row of cottages dating back to the late 17th, this handsome inn provides a range of keg bitters and a good selection of draught lagers, as well as quality traditional meals at lunchtime (11.30–2). Produce is sourced locally and home-made dishes are the speciality here. There are 19 en suite bedrooms, six of which are located on the ground floor. Most are located in a purpose-built annex and all offer a very high standard of quality and comfort.

91 THE CORNER HOUSE

2-4 Norwood, Beverley,
East Yorkshire HU17 9ET
☎ 01482 882652 Fax: 01482 880110

Set in the centre of the charming and picturesque town of Beverley, **The Corner House** has been offering first-class food and drink for hundreds of years. Leaseholders Ann-Marie and Peter and manager Howard take pride in upholding this fine tradition of quality and service. Warm and welcoming, this convivial inn boasts no fewer than eight real ales, together with delicious meals every day – lunch Monday to Friday 12-2, Saturday 1-6 and Sunday 1-4, evening meals Monday to Friday 5-8, and weekend breakfasts 10-1. The menus offer a staggering choice of

expertly prepared dishes such as a range of pies, warm salads, sausages and bubble and quack (made with Gressingham duck breast).

92 CROWN & ANCHOR

Weel Road, Tickton, Beverley,
East Yorkshire HU17 9RY
☎ 01964 542816   Fax: 01964 543271
e-mail: crownandanchor@hotmail.co.uk

Occupying an outstanding location adjacent to the River Hull in the peaceful village of Tickton, found off the A1035 a couple of miles northeast of Beverley, the **Crown & Anchor** pub is a superb place offering great food, drink and hospitality. Leaseholder Gary Newborn has been at the helm here since 2004, bringing over 30 years' experience in the trade.

Open every session weekdays and all day Saturday and Sunday, there are two real ales (Riddings Bitter and Marstons Pedigree) plus the occasional guest ale, together with a good selection of lagers, cider, stout, wines, spirits and soft drinks. Tasty fresh-cooked food is available every day at lunch (Mon to Sat 12-2, Sunday

12-3) and dinner (Mon-Sat 5-9, Sunday 4-8). Specialities include home-made steak pie, chicken curry and fish and chips. Tea-time specials are available from 5-7.30 p.m. daily.

93 ROWLEY MANOR COUNTRY HOUSE HOTEL

Rowley Road, Little Weighton, nr Hull,
East Yorkshire   HU20 3XR
☎ 01482 848248   Fax: 01482 849900
e-mail: info@rowleymanor.com
🌐 www.rowleymanor.comk

An outstanding property set in 5½ acres within 35 acres of parkland, **Rowley Manor Country House Hotel** is a magnificent country house hotel open all year round. Owners Amanda and Brian Hewitt-Jones have been here since December of 2005, and

bring a wealth of experience to offering all their guests the best in comfort and quality.

The history here makes for interesting reading, as it began life as the rectory of Saint Peter's Church – it is said there has been a church on this site since 1150 – built in 1621. Seventeen years later the rector, Revd Ezekiel Rogers, set sail with some 20 of his parishioners and their families to the New World, establishing the settlement of Rowley in what is now the state of Massachusetts. Rowley

Manor remained the parish rectory until 1928, when the estate was purchased by a local shipping magnate who modernised the house and commissioned the superb pine panelling that graces the study, carved by the renowned artist Grinling Gibbons. After the owner's death in1969 the Manor was transformed into a hotel, which today offers all guests a country house welcome as well as excellent food and service.

The menus are simply superb, with all home-made dishes and locally-sourced fresh ingredients combined by the accomplished

chef to create tempting and satisfying dishes such as oven-roasted guinea fowl, fillet of seabass, Gressingham duck, corn-fed chicken and slow-braised lamb. The desserts are of a similar high standard. Meals are served to residents and non-residents alike at dinner in the spacious and exquisitely appointed dining room; booking advised for Sunday lunch. The 16 guest bedrooms are decorated with taste and style, and include rooms with four-poster beds. Peace and relaxation are assured at this stylish and comfortable country house hotel.

94 THE ROSE AND CROWN

33 Market Place, Hornsea,
East Riding of Yorkshire HU18 1AN
☎ 01964 535756

Situated in the heart of Hornsea just a short stroll from the beach and coastline, **The Rose and Crown** has a distinctive gabled exterior, making it look medieval, though in fact it is a relatively modern pub, dating back to the early 1900s.

Occupying the site of an earlier public house, this fine inn offers all guests a comfortable and pleasant rest-stop in which to enjoy a drink or meal while touring in the area. Leaseholders Lisa Jane and Matthew have been here since January of 2006. It's their first venture into the licensing trade together, though Matthew brings 12 years' experience of providing first-class service and hospitality. Very popular with locals and a must for visitors, the interior of this warm and welcoming pub is very comfortable and enhances the pub's relaxed and welcoming ambience. There's also a very pleasant outside patio area, just the place to enjoy a drink on fine days.

Open all day, every day, there are three real ales here – Marstons Pedigree and two rotating guest ales – together with a good selection of lagers, wines, spirits and soft drinks. Excellent food is served Friday, Saturday and Sunday lunchtimes (12–3), from November - February on Sunday only, with a menu of hot and cold dishes prepared by Lisa Jane, who's an accomplished cook. Everything from sandwiches to roast dinners is available, and all use the freshest ingredients, locally sourced wherever possible. This fine pub makes a very good place to stop for a relaxing drink or lunch while touring in Hornsea and around the many sights and attractions of Yorkshire's East Riding.

95 THE MARINE HOTEL

Seafront, Hornsea,
East Riding of Yorkshire HU18 1NJ
☎ 01964 532183

Overlooking the sea at Hornsea, the welcoming **Marine Hotel** has great food, drink and accommodation. Open all day every day for ales, food is served from midday until 9 p.m., with a menu of hearty favourites such as succulent steaks, speciality grills, all-day breakfast, roast chicken, salads, sandwiches, light bites and more. This fine hotel also boasts five comfortable ensuite guest bedrooms, available  all year round. Guests can stay on a room-only or B&B basis. Just a short walk from the beach, the hotel makes an excellent base from which to explore the coast and inland region of the East Riding.

Looking for:

- *Places to Visit?*
- *Places to Stay?*
- *Places to Eat & Drink?*
- *Places to Shop?*

COUNTRY LIVING MAGAZINE **RURAL GUIDES**

HIDDEN INNS

HIDDEN PLACES

COUNTRY **Pubs & Inns**

off the **motorway** 3rd edition

www.travelpublishing.co.uk

96 SAL'S CAFÉ AND STEAK HOUSE

8A Newbegin, Hornsea,
East Yorkshire HU18 1AG
☎ 01964 537973

A warm welcome is assured at **Sal's Café and Steak House**, situated in the heart of Hornsea. Sally Cooper has owned and run this excellent place for three years; ably assisted by Lisa, Ruth, Wendy and Matthew, she provides first-class service and friendly hospitality to all her customers.

Open seven days a week from 9 a.m. weekdays and 10 a.m. at weekends, guests choose from a menu of tempting delights – but if what you want is not on the menu and they have the ingredients in stock, they'll make it for you. The all-day breakfasts and roast dinners (available every day) are extremely popular. From 7 p.m. there's a special evening menu featuring fantastic steak dishes among many other choices which make use of the freshest local produce. Bookings are accepted for the evenings and it is licensed for diners. Closed Sunday and Monday evenings. Children welcome.

97 THOMPSON'S TRADITIONAL FISH & CHIPS

89 Main Street, Brandesburton, Driffield,
East Yorkshire YO25 8RGH
☎ 01964 542349   Fax: 01964 541300

In the village of Brandesburton, found off the A165 northeast of Beverley, Deborah and Polat Akcicek are the proud owners of the distinctive and excellent **Thompson's Traditional Fish & Chips**, which enjoys a well-earned reputation for quality and follows the success of their flagship chippie in Wetwang, on the A166 east of Driffield. People drive for miles to sample the delights of the menu here, where there's seating for 30 to the front of the shop.

At Brandesburton, in addition to the takeaway there's a very good fully-licensed restaurant serving famous fish and chips together with a range of home-made meals and traditional Sunday lunches. The restaurant has a handsome interior with pine furniture, and is fully air conditioned.

Open daily from 11.30 a.m. (midday on Sundays) until 8.30 (Monday and Tuesday), 9 (Wednesday, Thursday and Sunday) or 9.30 (Friday and Saturday), with last orders in the restaurant half an hour before closing, the menu of starters, main courses and snacks includes tasty home-made dishes such as steak pie, fisherman's pie, vegetarian meals, steaks, salads

and light bites. The menu also includes children's choices – pizza, fish tiddlers, fish fingers, sausages, chicken nuggets served with chips, beans or peas – and special senior citizen deals for one, two or three courses. Booking advised.

At both Brandesburton and Wetwang, the extensive takeaway menu boasts the full range of chip shop favourites including fresh haddock and cod (caught in Icelandic waters and brought to Bridlington), scampi, fish cakes and patties together with chicken, beef, sausage meals and pies. The Wetwang branch of this fine establishment, on the Main Street there, has been established for many years – indeed, its success encouraged Polat and Debbie to open the new one here in Brandesburton.

255

98 WITHERNSEA LIGHTHOUSE

Hull Road, Withernsea,
East Yorkshire HU19 2DY
☎ 01964 614834

Withemsea Lighthouse was erected in 1892/93 by Trinity House taking about 18 months to build. The decision to construct a Lighthouse was a result of the numerous losses of sailing ships during the 19th century, when coal was shipped from Newcastle to Hull and many vessels failed to complete their voyage safely. Probably the most significant loss was the grounding of the new fishing smack "Genesta" when the Captain froze to death in the rigging. Shortly afterwards construction commenced.

The Lighthouse which has always been painted white in accordance with tradition, is of brick and concrete, with octagonal walls some 5ft thick, tapering to 2ft, making it architecturally unusual in Britain. Its' overall height is given as 120ft, or 127ft above mean high water. The light is reached by means of a 144-step spiral staircase and the original lamp was housed within an octagonal revolving lens, taking 24 seconds for a complete turn. In 1936 the clockwork mechanism was removed and the lamp was electrified, increasing the range on a clear night to 17 miles.

With the technical improvements in modem navigational aids the light was finally extinguished on 1st July 1976 and the lens removed. It had first shone every night for 82 years except during the blackouts in World Wars I and 2.

The base of the lighthouse features many exhibits of the ships, wrecks and coastguards of the area, as well as photographs of Withersea in the Victorian and Edwardian eras. The views from the lamproom are breathtaking and non-climbers are treated to views of the town and coastline. Refreshments and souvenirs are on sale.

99 THE HOLDERNESS INN

9 High Street, Patrington, Hull,
East Yorkshire HU12 0PL
☎ 01964 630091

David and Andrea Hackney offer all their guests a warm welcome at The Holderness Inn, a spacious and convivial pub with great food and drink. The traditional interior will please real pub lovers, while the menu has something to tempt every appetite. Food is served Tuesday to Sunday from midday to 8 p.m. Home-made pies include steak and ale or chicken and mushroom, while there are also hearty favourites such as steaks, honey-and-mustard chicken, fish and seafood dishes and much more.

Open all day every day for ale, there's Tetleys Cask and a good range of lagers, wines, spirits and soft drinks. Located just 17 miles east of Hull on the B1445,

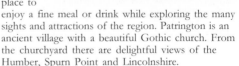

the inn is handy for visiting the coast and makes the perfect place to

enjoy a fine meal or drink while exploring the many sights and attractions of the region. Patrington is an ancient village with a beautiful Gothic church. From the churchyard there are delightful views of the Humber, Spurn Point and Lincolnshire.

100 THE BURNS HEAD INN

Patrington Haven,
East Yorkshire HU12 0QJ
☎ 01964 630530
e-mail: burns.head@ntl.com

The Burns Head Inn is an excellent Free House and restaurant found at Patrington Haven, equidistant from Hull and Withernsea off the A1033. The décor and interior of this large and impressive inn are traditional and cosy, with exposed beams and other original features adding to the warm and welcoming atmosphere. Owners Marlene and Dennis Wicks have been here since 1988, and their experience as friendly hosts shows in the excellent service and hospitality they provide all their guests.

Open lunchtime and evenings Monday to Thursday, and all day Friday to Sunday, there's one real ale (John Smiths Cask) plus lagers, cider, stout, wines, spirits and soft drinks – something to please every palate. Food is served from 12–2 and 6–9; guests can dine in the restaurant or, if they prefer, in the lounge, public bar areas or outside in the handsome garden area complete with ornamental pond (fenced off for safety). The home-made curries are a popular choice here, as are the home-made chips, paninis and special two-main-courses for 7-pounds deals.

101 COACH AND HORSES

Main Street, Welwick,
East Yorkshire HU12 0RY
☎ 01964 630503

Welwick is a peaceful village found on the B1445, southeast of Patrington towards Easington and Spurn Head. Here you will find the **Coach and Horses**, a cosy and very quaint inn boasting draught keg bitters and a full selection of lagers, wines, spirits and soft drinks. Excellent food is served each day from opening, with a menu and daily specials including home-made steak and ale

pie, giant Yorkshire puds with locally-produced sausages. This charming place also has one guest room available all year round. The inn is open Monday to Thursday from 5 p.m., Friday from 4 p.m., Saturday from 1 p.m. and Sunday from midday.

102 THE NEW INN

Howden Road, Barlby, Selby,
North Yorkshire YO8 5JE
☎ 01757 702349
e-mail: thenewinnbarbly@tiscali.co.uk

The lovely village of Barlby can be found off the A19 just a short drive from the centre of Selby. Here, the New Inn offers excellent food, drink and hospitality. Colin and Gillian Deakin arrived here in 2002 and, through hard work and dedication, have made

the inn a real success story. Open all day, every day for ale, there's food Tuesday/Wednesday 5-8, Thursday/Friday 5-9, Saturday 12-9 and Sundays 12-3, then light bites from 4-7. Locally-sourced produce is used to create home-made and home-cooked dishes – even real hand-made chips!

257

103 THE GREYHOUND INN

82 Main Street, Riccall,
North Yorkshire YO19 6TE
☎ 01757 249101
e-mail:
bobowens@greyhound1.wanadoo.co.uk

Four miles north of Selby off the A19 you'll find **The Greyhound Inn**, a pristine and welcoming pub in the heart of the ancient village of Riccall. This convivial family-run village pub dates back to the late 1800s. The interior is charming, while outside there's a superb beer garden.

Open every session weekdays, and all day from Friday to Sunday, the pub boasts quality ales (including John Smiths and Timothy Taylor Landlord) together with a good range of lagers, cider, stout, wines, spirits and soft drinks. Relaxed and warm, the ambience is always a draw here, making the inn popular with locals and visitors alike – many of whom are in the region to enjoy the attractions of River Ouse walking, the Trans Pennine Trail, Skipwith Common Nature Reserve, Selby, York and the surrounding area. The Sunday carvery (served 12-2) is justly

popular, with several roasts and all the trimmings. Booking advised. Leaseholders Bob, Chris and Anne, offer all their guests a warm welcome.

104 THE ASH TREE INN & RESTAURANT

London Road, Barkston Ash, Tadcaster,
North Yorkshire LS24 9PP
☎ 01937 557247   Fax: 01937 558182
e-mail: nfo@ashtreeinn.com
🌐 www.ashtreeinn.com

The Ash Tree Inn & Restaurant is an 18th-century gem built adjacent to the ancient Towton battleground and set in the rural area of Barkston Ash, a very pleasant village located adjacent to the A162 south of Tadcaster. The pub offers traditional food and beers in an unspoilt and welcoming environment, making for a very convenient place to relax and enjoy some real ales or to sample the traditional and specialist foods as it's just 30 minutes from York and Leeds, 5 minutes from the A64 and 10 minutes from the A1.

This fine traditional inn boasts no fewer than four real ales, including John Smiths Cask and Black Sheep. Alan and Gill Phillips are your friendly hosts; they have over 16 years' experience in the trade and this shows in the high quality of service and hospitality they offer every guest. Alan prides himself on ensuring that he serves quality beers and real ales, along with a selection of over 50 different shorts and spirits. Winner of the Yorkshire Food Pub of the Year and complimented in the press with the praise 'the

food is designer but the prices are not', the Phillips cater for intimate celebrations, business lunches and traditional family meals. The 50-seat restaurant offers both quality and service that will exceed your expectations. All food is prepared from fresh produce. Booking is advised at all times if you would like to dine in the restaurant, though the full menu is also offered throughout the bar and in superbly maintained garden and patio area - the perfect place to enjoy the summer weather and the breathtaking Yorkshire country air. There is also an ornamental pond stocked full of goldfish and Koi carp (and separately fenced off so that it is safe for young children).

With up to 40 main courses on the standard menu, there are also daily specials offering extra specialist options. Any of the dishes can be tailored to suit guests' taste, so there's no need to hesitate to ask if you prefer something a little different. Food is served Monday to Thursday 11.30-2 and 6-9, Friday and Saturday 11.30-2 and 6-9.30, and Sunday 12-4 for traditional Sunday lunch, then 4-8 p.m. for the main menus. Just a few examples of chefs Elaine and Robert's expert creations include home-made steak pie, fisherman's platter, mixed grill, prime fillet steak, broccoli and cream cheese bake and beef lasagne. The tasty chef's special sauces to garnish your steak include red wine, wild mushroom, Stilton and garlic - all mouthwatering and delicious.

105 THE PLOUGH INN

Shearburn Terrace, Snaith,
East Yorkshire DN14 9JJ
☎ 01405 860751

Situated in the heart of Snaith, found where the A645 meets the A1041 and a short drive from J35 of the M62, **The Plough Inn** dates back to the early 1800s. A smithy once stood to the rear of the inn, where you will now find a spacious beer garden. Leaseholders Chris and Paul have been here since December 2005; it's their first venture into the licensing trade (though Chris has experience in the entertainment business) and they bring a lot of enthusiasm to the task.

The interior boasts traditional features such as the huge brickbuilt fireplace and exposed beams, and has a warm and friendly atmosphere. Pristine and

welcoming, this fine pub is open all day, with two real ales (John Smiths and Tetleys) and a full range of other thirst quenchers: lagers, cider, stout, wines, spirits and soft drinks. Food is served at lunch and teatime, with a menu of hearty favourites cooked to order. This sturdy inn also has four guest bedrooms, with more becoming available within the lifetime of this book.

106 THE BREWERS ARMS HOTEL

Pontefract Road, Snaith,
East Yorkshire DN14 9JS
☎ 01405 862404   Fax: 01405 862397

The superb **Brewers Arms Hotel** in Snaith is worth seeking out. Owned by the Old Mill Brewery, located to the rear of the hotel, this impressive inn has both a long and proud history and a bright future. Manager and chef Bob Johnston has a real success on his hands. Open all day every day for ale, there are four real ales

from the inn's own brewery, together with a good range of lagers, cider, stout, soft drinks, wines and spirits. Delicious food is served 12–9 daily. The inn also boasts 14 excellent ensuite guest bedrooms.

107 THE VIKING HOTEL

Western Road, Goole,
East Yorkshire DN14 6RG
☎ 01405 721821   Fax: 01405 763611
e-mail: vikingshotel@btconnect.com

Situated at the edge of Goole, found off the M62, **The Viking Hotel** has recently been refurbished and is spacious and modern. Open all day, every day, this friendly pub serves up a selection of up to four draught keg bitters, four draught lagers, draught cider and stout, and a good choice of wines, spirits and soft drinks.

Food is served Monday to Saturday midday to 8.30 p.m. and Sunday 12-7 (with carvery from 12-3). The delicious food includes dishes such as steaks, grills, fish and seafood, Indian and Chinese options, light bites, burgers, baguettes and much more. Booking advised Sunday lunchtime.

108 THE WHITE SWAN

9 Main Street, Bubwith, York,
North Yorkshire YO8 6LT
☎ 01757 288209

Located in the village of Bubwith, found on the A163 east of the A19 and towards the A614, **The White Swan** is a handsome and impressive public house open all sessions weekdays and throughout the day at weekends. Real ales include Theakstons, John Smiths and changing guest ales. Recently refurbished and redecorated inside and out, the inn is pristine and welcoming.

The 'New Himalayan' is the name of the excellent Indian restaurant and takeaway housed within the main building, open every day from 5.30 to 10.30 for an excellent choice of traditional dishes and chef's specials using the freshest ingredients. The seafood specials are a particular treat, and the restaurant is also renowned for its curry dishes – from mild korma meals to super-spicy vindaloos and dupiazas, there's something to tempt every palate. The ambience is always friendly and relaxed at this traditional village pub.

109 THE STATION HOTEL

4 Bridgegate, Howden,
East Yorkshire DN14 7AB
☎ 01430 431301

The Station Hotel in Howden began life in the 1800s, when it was known as The Black Bull. Today it maintains its long tradition of offering first-class food, drink and accommodation to weary travellers (or anyone fancying a relaxing pint or meal in convivial and very pleasant surroundings!). Alan Lewis (who's known as 'Taffy') is the new leaseholder here, but he has many years' experience in the trade. Open from 4 p.m. weekdays and all day at weekends, the real ales here are John Smiths and a rotating guest ale. The accommodation is excellent: three comfortable, handsome rooms, each with its own luxury bathroom and shower.

111 THE BLACK SWAN

High Street, Eastrington,
East Yorkshire DN14 7PR
☎ 01430 410339

Found off the A614 a short drive northeast of Howden, **The Black Swan** is traditional in all the best senses of the word. This is a friendly family-run village pub with Debbie and Gary your hosts, ably assisted by Lauren, Lewis and also Debbie's mum, Elaine, an expert in the kitchen who does most of the cooking. Open Monday to Thursday from 4

p.m., and all day at weekends, there are two real ales – John Smiths and Tetleys – together with a selection of soft drinks, lagers, cider, stout, wines and spirits. Food is served every evening (5–8 p.m.) and also during the day on Saturday (1–6) and Sunday (1–3).

261

110 THE ROYAL OAK

Holme Road, A614, Portington, Howden,
East Yorkshire DN14 7NA
☎ 01430 430563   Fax: 01430 430420
e-mail: theroyaloakfoggs@aol.com

Standing adjacent to the A614 between Howden and Holme-on-Spalding-Moor, **The Royal Oak** is a picturesque and impressive place. This friendly, family-run inn has Douglas and Elaine Smith at the helm, ably assisted by their sons Darren and Timothy and daughter Katy. The family have been in the pub trade for nearly 15 years, and it's experience that shows in the high standard of service they provide.

This Free House serves up great food, drink and lashings of hospitality, with real ales (Black Sheep plus two rotating guest ales), an excellent menu and a convivial and welcoming ambience. Food is served Monday and Tuesday 5-9, Wednesday to Friday 12–2 and 5–9, weekends and Bank Holidays 12–9. Booking required Friday, Saturday and Sunday. Visitors come from miles around just for the food – and it's a journey well worth making!

112 THE HALF MOON

61 Main Street, Elloughton, Brough,
East Yorkshire HU15 1HU
☎ 01482 667362

A quality public house, **The Half Moon** is situated in the village of Elloughton, found a short drive off the A63. Family-run by Nick and Edna, their son Colin and his partner Celi, all locally born and bred, this convivial pub dates back to 1929. The interior provides traditional comforts, while outside there's a large and pleasant beer garden. Open every session and all day on Sundays, there's a minimum of three real ales, usually including Timothy Taylor Landlord, John Smiths Cask and Tetley Bitter.

Excellent food is served at lunchtime (12–2 Monday to Saturday) and dinner (6–9.30 Monday to Thursday; 6–10 Friday and Saturday) and on Sundays from midday until 9 p.m. There's room for up to 50 diners but booking is advised at weekends and for

parties of more than six. Guests choose from the printed menu or several daily specials boards, including those for starters, sweets and light lunches. Home cooking is the rule, with locally-sourced produce wherever possible used to create a range of tempting dishes such as steaks, pan-fried lemon swordfish, pork and chive sausages, lamb jalfrezi, mixed grills and fried haddock. The early evening meals (6–7 p.m.) offer a two-for-one deal on main meals.

Cowgate, Welton, Hull,
East Yorkshire HU15 1NB
☎ 01482 666700 Fax: 01482 667808
e-mail:
greendragon.welton@pathfinderpubs.co.uk
🌐 www.pathfinderpubs.co.uk

The superb **Green Dragon** is a gracious and elegant 17th-century inn set in the picturesque village of Welton. Just five miles west of Hull (reached via the A63), it's an ideal location for exploring the coast or Yorkshire Wolds. Licensees George Robertson and Mark Ayling took over in 2005, though they bring a wealth of prior experience in the trade – in George's case some 20 years of providing first-class service and hospitality to guests.

Open all day, every day for ale, there are four rotating real ales to choose from, together with a very good selection of lagers, cider, stout, wines, spirits and soft drinks – something to quench every thirst. A Pathfinder pub (their motto, 'Strive, Thrive, Enjoy'), it's friendly and homely, with an extensive menu that includes classic dishes such as 'local catches' – haddock, sea bass, Whitby scampi and more – house

favourites like chargrilled sausages, lamb shank, chef's curry of the day and daily pie choice, together with light bites, salads, sandwiches and a selection of hot and cold snacks. There are also a range of vegetarian choices, pasta dishes and much more. Food is served every day from midday until 10 p.m. All of the food is fresh and home-made, using the best local produce to create tempting meals at lunch and dinner. On Sundays there's a choice of three roasts for Sunday lunchtime. Booking is advised at all times.

The 4-Star ETC rated accommodation

comprises 11 ensuite guest bedrooms that are the height of luxury, with king-sized beds, power shower and bath, complementary bathrobes, free wireless broadband access, iron and ironing board, LCD television with Freeview, hair dryer and, of course, tea- and coffee-making facilities as standard, all for very reasonable rates. The accommodation is available all year round. Some of the rooms are set in the main building, others housed in the refurbished barn/outbuildings to the rear of the property. The tariff includes a hearty and delicious breakfast.

114 OLIVER'S COFFEE SHOP ⚟

3 West End, Swanland, North Ferriby, East
Yorkshire HU14 3QP
☎ 01482 633008
e-mail:
burnettcatering@burnett414.karoo.co.uk

Just a short drive off the main A63, **Oliver's Coffee Shop** is a handsome and spacious brickbuilt establishment with an attractive and welcoming décor and excellent range of delicious meals, home-baked treats and hot and cold drinks. Open seven days a week, 9.30–5, guests choose from the printed menu or changing daily specials board from a wide selection of expertly prepared dishes. Everything from snacks to main meals such as steak pie, broccoli bake, lasagne and salads feature on the menu, and the home-made cakes are well worth leaving room for! Booking advised at all times.

115 BRONTË PARSONAGE MUSEUM 🏛

Haworth, Keighley,
West Yorkshire BD22 8DR
☎ 01535 642323
⊕ www.bronte.pig.uk

Charlotte, Emily and Anne Brontë, were the authors of some of the greatest books in the English language. Haworth Parsonage was their much loved home and *Jane Eyre*, *Wuthering Heights* and *The Tenant of Wildfell Hall* were all written here. Set between the village of Haworth and the wild moorland beyond, this Georgian house still retains the atmosphere of the Brontës time. The rooms they used are filled with their furniture, clothes and personal possessions. Here you can marvel at the handwriting in their tiny manuscript books, admire Charlotte's wedding bonnet and imagine meeting Emily's pets from her wonderfully lifelike drawings.

117 STUMP CROSS INN ⚟

Godley Lane, Stump Cross, Halifax,
West Yorkshire HX3 7AY
☎ 01422 321066   Fax: 01422 354571

A spacious and impressive licensed inn and restaurant with accommodation, the **Stump Cross Inn** nestles in the charming hamlet of Stump Cross, just a mile or so from the centre of Halifax on the A6036 towards Bradford. With over 40 years in the licensing trade, leaseholder Richard – ably assisted by his daughter Rebecca – offers first-class food, drink and hospitality.

Built in 1900 on the site of an earlier inn, it's open all day, every day for ale. The lunchtime and evening menus (Monday to Friday 12–2.30 and 5.30–8.45, Saturday 12–2.30 and 5.30–8, Sundays 12–3.30) offer an excellent range of tasty dishes, including early-bird specials (5.30–7.30 p.m.) and the tempting carvery with one, two or three courses served Thursday to Saturday. Booking advised for Friday and Saturday, and essential on Sundays.

Traditional and comfortable throughout, the inn boasts nine handsome and welcoming guest bedrooms upstairs, with a range of double, twin and triple rooms.

116 THE KINGS ARMS

2 Church Street, Haworth,
West Yorkshire BD22 8DR
☎ 01535 647302
e-mail: kingsarmshawarth@hotmail.com
🌐 www.kingsarmshawarth.co.uk

In the heart of famous Howarth, **The Kings Arms** is an impressive and venerable stonebuilt building in keeping with the wonderful local church and Brontë parsonage. Dating back to the 17th century it has always been an inn, and today keeps up its long and fine tradition for offering great food, drink and hospitality.

The pub boasts a long and interesting history. The private rooms upstairs were once used as the Manorial Courts, while the cellar once served as the local mortuary! Comfortable, cosy and welcoming, the interior décor and furnishings enhance the marvellous ambience at this fine pub. Open all day every day, there are always three to four real ales on tap, including Tetleys, Black Sheep and changing guest ales, as well as draught-kept cider, lager and stout, wines, spirits and soft drinks. Well known for its excellent food, served Mon-Sat 12-8,

Sun 12-5, diners can choose from the menus or specials board from a range of both traditional and more innovative dishes such as prawns Creole, porcini ravioli, expertly-cooked steaks, burgers, baked salmon fillet, Cumberland sausage and much more – just the thing to keep you going while you're exploring the many sights and attractions of the area – expertly prepared by the chef using the freshest locally-sourced produce. The Duke's Bistro seats 24; guests can also dine in other areas of the pub, or in the beer garden on fine days.

The accommodation comprises one attractive and comfortable double ensuite guest bedroom, available all year round. Licensees Kevin and Susan Duke have been here since 1999, bringing 25 years' experience in the trade. Ably assisted by their son Michael, they offer all their guests the finest service and hospitality.

265

118 BANKFIELD MUSEUM 🏛

Akroyd Park Boothtown Road
Halifax HX3 6HG
☎ 01422 354823 / 352334
e-mail:
bankfield.museum@calderdale.gov.uk

Set in a wonderful Victorian millowner's house, Bankfield has a growing reputation as a centre for textiles and contemporary craft. With its internationally important collection of textiles, weird and wonderful objects from around the world, plus commissions by leading makers and a varied programme of exhibtitions and activities, there is much to see and enjoy. Don't miss the Toy Gallery; the Duke of Wellington's Regimental Museum and the Marble Gallery, a new selling space for contemporary craft. Open: Tuesday to Saturday 10am

- 5pm. Sundays 2pm - 5pm Bank Holiday Mondays 10am - 5pm. Free admission.

119 THE WINDMILL INN ¶

17 Stanage Lane, Shelf, Halifax,
West Yorkshire HX3 7PR
☎ 01274 679027

Found in the village of Shelf, just off the A6036 in the countryside near Bradford, **The Windmill Inn** is a friendly inn with well-kept ales, great food and genuine hospitality. Leaseholders Jennifer and David have made the place a popular destination for Jennifer's delicious home-cooked food – served Tuesday to Sunday at lunch and dinner –

and the range of real ales. Speciality dishes include Lamb Henry and chicken tikka – all dishes use locally-sourced ingredients, and there is always a selection of two-course special offers. This comfortable inn boasts a lovely conservatory and well-tended beer garden, including a superb children's play area.

120 THE QUEEN VICTORIA ¶

10–12 Victoria Place, Northowram,
Halifax, West Yorkshire HX3 7HY
☎ 01422 202952

Just two miles northeast of Halifax on the A6036 is the village of Northowram – worth seeking out for the excellent **Queen Victoria** pub and restaurant.

Open all day, every day for ale, there are always three real ales – Timothy Taylor Landlord, Black Sheep and a changing guest ale – together with a selection of lagers, cider, stout, wines, spirits and soft drinks. The interior of this supremely comfortable inn is cosy and warm, with a wealth of handsome burnished wood panelling, tasteful paintings and prints adorning the walls and a gleaming bar.

The big draw here in addition to the great ales and

friendly hospitality, offered by Wan and daughter Golf, is the fantastic Bangkok Kitchen restaurant, where the freshest ingredients are used to create authentic Thai dishes with delicious choices such as a range of curries, stir-fries, salads and rice and noodle dishes, together with traditional English meals including mixed grills, steaks and haddock. The daytime menu (Monday to Saturday midday to 6 p.m.) features beef stew, lamb hot pot and steak-and-ale casserole. The Sunday roasts are a particular treat.

121 THE BROWN HORSE INN

Denholmegate Road, Coley, Halifax,
West Yorkshire HX3 7SD
☎ 01422 202112
e-mail: yvonne@brownhorse.co.uk
⊕ www.westyorkshirepubs.com

In the hamlet of Coley, found off the A58 or A6036, **The Brown Horse Inn** is a hidden gem well worth seeking out. Run by sister and brother team Yvonne and Philip, this excellent premises is open all day, every day with four tip-top choices of ale: John Smiths, Ruddles, Black Sheep and Timothy Taylor Landlord. Dating back to 1856, this welcoming and traditional inn also boasts superb food at lunch (daily) and dinner (Monday to Friday), with a range of expertly prepared traditional dishes – fish is a speciality – together with exotic choices such as emu, crocodile and kangaroo! Booking required at all times at this justly popular place.

123 READERS AT ST IVES

St Ives Estate, Harden Road, Bingley,
West Yorkshire BD16 1AT
☎ 01274 515887
e-mail:
readers_digestibles@blueyonder.co.uk

Superb tea rooms and more, **Readers at St Ives** is found within the St Ives Estate (which includes a golf club) on the B6429 out of Bingley towards Harden. Open seven days a week from 10.30 am (til 4 pm Sun-Thurs and until 8pm Fri and Sat), it serves a range of teas, coffees and excellent food made using locally-sourced produce. A traditional tea rooms providing traditional and international cuisine, this charming place makes an excellent place to stop for refreshment while touring the area. Owner Julia Reader also runs another tea rooms at Mercury Quays in Shipley, with the same high standard of service and quality.

122 OLD GLEN HOUSE

Prod Lane, Baildon,
West Yorkshire BD17 5BN
☎ 01274 589325
e-mail: oldglenhouse@aol.com

Occupying a secluded countryside setting yet just a short walk from historic Shipley Glen, **Old Glen House** is an outstanding pub with real ales, home-cooked food and a wonderful ambience. Inglenook fires, stone walls and exposed beams enhance the cosiness of the place, which began life as a farm and was later (ironically enough) a Temperance hotel. Open all day every day, there are two rotating guest ales together with a full complement of alcoholic and alcohol-free beverages.

Superb food is served at lunchtime (Mon-Fri 12-2.30, Sat 12-3, Sun 12-5.30) and dinner (Weds-Sat 5.30-9.30). Booking advised at all times. The menu changes monthly to make use of the freshest seasonal meats and produce. The chefs' specialities include mouthwatering freshly caught fish, lamb dishes,

steaks and much more. On the last Thursday of the month gourmet themed evenings are held – please ring for details. Winner in 2006 of the prize for Best Pub in Yorkshire and Humberside (beating out competition from 1400 other pubs), this excellent place is well worth seeking out.

124 THE BROWN COW ❚❚

Ireland Bridge, Bingley,
West Yorkshire BD16 2QX
☎ 01274 564345
e-mail: joanne.thirkell@btconnect.com

The Brown Cow is a superb public house. This picture-postcard pub has a warm and inviting interior with attractive décor and comfortable furnishings. Reached by turning left from the centre of Bingley onto the B6429 (Harden Road) and found immediately over the first bridge on your left, the pub dates back to the 1600s and is the perfect place to enjoy a relaxing drink or meal.

Open every session weekdays and all day Friday to Sunday, there are no fewer than eight real ales – the full range of Timothy Taylor brews are here – together with something to quench every thirst, with premium draught and bottled lagers, wines, spirits and soft drinks. Food is served Monday to Friday 12-2 and 6-9, and Saturday and Sunday midday until 9 p.m. Booking is advised Friday to Sunday. The menu and specials board feature a full range of chef-prepared dishes using locally-sourced produce. Tasty specialities include Timothy Taylor steak-and-ale pie and the chicken and tiger prawn sizzler. Hosts Joanne and Dave and their friendly, helpful staff provide first-class service and hospitality.

125 THE FISHERMAN'S ❚❚

Dowley Gap, Bingley,
West Yorkshire BD16 1TS
☎ 01274 561697

The Fisherman's is the place for some of the best food on the Leeds-Liverpool Canal. Occupying a superb scenic location a short drive from the centre of Bingley, this excellent public house is run by Bob and Jeanette Halliday, who together have 35 years' experience in providing first-class service and hospitality to their guests. Open all day every day, there's a changing real ale to enjoy together with a full range of lagers, bitter, cider, spirits, wines and soft drinks. Quality food is served daily at lunch and dinner and local produce is used to create a fantastic range of light bites, snacks, main courses, burgers, salads, sizzling platters and more, all expertly prepared and presented.

HIDDEN PLACES GUIDES

Explore Britain and Ireland with *Hidden Places* guides - a fascinating series of national and local travel guides.

Packed with easy to read information on hundreds of places of interest as well as places to stay, eat and drink.

Available from both high street and internet booksellers

For more information on the full range of *Hidden Places* guides and other titles published by Travel Publishing visit our website on

www.travelpublishing.co.uk
or ask for our leaflet by phoning
0118-981-7777 or emailing
info@travelpublishing.co.uk

126 THE GROUSE AT SILSDEN

Keighley Road, Silsden,
West Yorkshire BD20 0EH
☎ 01535 657788   Fax: 01535 655742

The Grouse at Silsden is a stylish and modern restaurant with an excellent lunchtime and evening menu. The accent is firmly on the best of contemporary English and European cooking, with tempting dishes such as home-made salmon and haddock fishcake, Italian salad with cannelini and borlotti beans, albacore tuna, pasta, onion, pepper and olive oil, fish and chips made with Taylors beer batter and home-made chips, Gressingham duck, roast rack of lamb, Nidderdale chicken and chargrilled marinated pork fillet kebab with couscous.

Meat and game dishes are very popular in season, as are the fresh fish dishes. And don't forget to leave room for the mouth-watering puddings, which include fresh raspberry Pavlova and chocolate and brandy truffle torte. *Open:* Lunch (Weds–Sat 12–2, Sun 12–3) and dinner (Tues–Fri 6–9.30, Sat 6–10). Booking required Friday and Saturday evenings and Sunday lunchtime.

127 THE DALESWAY HOTEL

1 Leeds Road, Ilkley,
West Yorkshire LS29 8DH
☎ 01943 605438
e-mail: daleswayhotel@hotmail.co.uk
⊚ www.hotelilkley.co.uk

A must for visitors to this very popular area, **The Dalesway Hotel** is set in the centre of Ilkley. A traditional pub with guest rooms, it was recently refurbished and now offers the best of classic style and elegance with every modern comfort and convenience.

The two real ales on tap are Tetleys and Timothy Taylor Landlord, together with a full range of lagers, bitter, cider, stout, wines, spirits and soft drinks. Tempting food is served daily at lunch and dinner – there's plenty of choice and local produce is used wherever possible. It's the accommodation here that is truly outstanding, with nine beautifully and comfortably furnished and decorated rooms available all year round. A great place to use as a base while exploring this scenic and historic area, this fine hotel offers the perfect home from home.

Newmarket, Otley,
West Yorkshire LS21 3AE
☎ 01943 463711

In the heart of Otley yet hidden away in Newmarket, **The Ring O' Bells** is a cosy and charming early 19th-century inn that once formed part of a brewery. What this intimate pub lacks in size it makes up for in character and hospitality, with a convivial ambience and welcoming, traditional décor.

Leaseholders Kim and Eddie make all their guests feel very welcome, serving up one real ale (Tetleys) alongside a selection of keg draught lagers, cider and stout, wines, spirits and soft drinks. During the lifetime of this edition they hope to serve Sunday lunches and all-days sandwiches, but at present the

pub serves drinks only. The Ring O' Bells makes an ideal place to stop for some refreshment while exploring the region, with delights such as Chevin Forest Park, Otley's cobbled marketplace and the many sights and attractions of Leeds and Bradford, just a few miles south.

Temple Newsam Road, off Selby Road
Leeds LS15 0AE
☎ 0113 264 5535
e-mail: temple.newsam@leeds.gov.uk
⊕ www.leeds.gov.uk/templenewsam

Temple Newsam is one of the great historic estates in England. Set within over 1500 acres of parkland, woodland and farmland landscaped by Capability Brown in the 18th century, it is a magnificent Tudor–Jacobean mansion. Famous as the birthplace of Lord Darnley and home to the Ingram family for over 300 years, the mansion houses rich collections of works of art. The garden is renowned for its Rhododendron and Azalea walk and features the National Plant Collections of Delphinium, Phlox and Aster novi–belgii. Europe's largest working Rare Breeds Farm, with over 400 animals, is set within the original estate Home Farm.

Temple Newsam hosts many events each year from music festivals to funfairs and there are regular family activities, demonstrations, guided walks or tours taking place throughout the year.

Temple Newsam is managed and maintained by the Parks and Countryside and Museums and Galleries Sections of Learning and Leisure, Leeds City Council.

129 THE BLACK HORSE AT ASKWITH

Askwith, Ilkley, West Yorkshire LS21 2JQ
☎ 01943 461074   Fax: 01943 851332

The Black Horse is a simply outstanding place set in the picturesque village of Askwith, found high up off the A65 between Ilkley and Otley. Dating back to 1860, this fine inn commands magnificent views over the surrounding countryside. This distinctive pub is pristine and comfortable.

Leaseholder Paul Spencer was brought up in the licensing trade, though this is his and his wife Carol's first venture as licensees. They have been here since 2005 and have already built up an enviable reputation for superb food and ales.

The restaurant seats 100, with extra seating available on the spacious outdoor patio. All but one small dining area is non-smoking. The restaurant is open at lunch (12–2 Monday to Saturday, 12–4 Sundays) and dinner (Tuesday to

Saturday 6–9 p.m.). Booking is essential for the fantastic Sunday carvery, and is also advisable for Friday and Saturday evenings to avoid disappointment.

Guests choose off the printed menu and blackboard specials from an extensive range of dishes with the best of traditional and modern influences and inspiration: traditional fishcakes sit alongside spring rolls, seafood pancakes, smoked salmon and prawn parcels, deep-fried whitebait and Greek beef stifado, among many other tempting dishes. There are also delicious summer salads and a choice of at least four vegetarian dishes. All produce used is sourced locally and all dishes are home-made, freshly cooked and expertly prepared and presented.

Askwith is a very pretty village worth exploring in its own right, plus there's some great walking in the area, over the open moorland from Brick House or Blubberhouses, for example, and this excellent pub makes a perfect place to reward yourself with a truly special pint and meal.

Market Place, Pontefract,
West Yorkshire WF8 IAX

☎ 01977 600863   Fax: 01977 780071

e-mail: theliquoricebush@wanadoo.co.uk

Situated in the heart of Pontefract, in the Market Place, **The Liquorice Bush** takes its charming name from the popular annual Liquorice Fair held in the town every July, and from the long associations the town has with liquorice, being a centre of production for hundreds of years.

Dating back many hundreds of years itself, the inn has always maintained a strong reputation for hospitality. Recently refurbished, the décor and furnishings are very attractive and comfortable, enhancing the pub's welcoming ambience. Warm woods, exposed beams – the best of traditional and modern comforts meet here in this truly excellent pub. Three real ales are on tap – Black Sheep, Timothy Taylor Landlord and a rotating guest ale – together with a choice of lagers, ciders, stouts, wines, spirits and soft drinks.

Experienced licensees Shaun and Gill White took over at this fine inn in February of 2003. They bring a wealth of experience to offering great hospitality and a high standard of service and quality to all their guests. Food is available at lunchtime Monday to Saturday (11-2.30), as well as on select Sundays such as race days and during the annual Liquorice Festival. Guests choose from a menu packed with delicious fresh snacks and full meals, all making use of local produce. Special food deals include two main courses for a discount price, and various drink promotions.

Well worth seeking out while touring the region, this delightful pub is a relaxing and welcoming place to enjoy a hearty pint or meal. Children welcome.

133 THE NEW WHEATSHEAF

Altofts Lane, Whitwood, Castleford,
West Yorkshire WF10 5QB
☎ 01977 553052   Fax: 01977 519001
e-mail: info@wheatsheaf.com
🌐 www.wheatsheaf.com

Whether you're hungry for a carvery, tasty bar meal or a full à la carte experience, **The New Wheatsheaf** at Whitwood, Castleford located just a short drive form the M62 at Junction 31 is the perfect place to stop and enjoy an expertly prepared and delicious meal.

The popular pub and restaurant has been owned by the Ackroyd family for over 20 years. Open every day and all day Sundays, this spacious and very comfortable inn has one real ale (John Smiths Cask) together with a very good choice of keg beers, lagers, cider, stout, wines, spirits and soft drinks.

The big draw here though is the food. You can choose from a wide range of freshly prepared bar meals in the bar lounge which is fully air conditioned.

Always popular on the bar menu is the Steak and Kidney pie and a wide choice of daily specials accompanied by a selection of self service vegetables.

Lunch is served Monday to Saturday 12pm-2pm, evenings 5.30-9pm and Sunday 12pm-8pm. The non-smoking air conditioned restaurant seats 110 and serves an evening carvery or you can choose from the à la carte menu which includes the "Wheatie Steak" a one pound sirloin steak with all the trimmings. Vegetarians are well catered for with a menu that serves dishes such as nut cutlets, pastas and bakes. There is also a children's menu to keep the little ones happy. Delicious cold desserts, home made sponge puddings and apple pies are a real treat if you can manage them.

The restaurant is open Monday to Friday 7pm to 9.30pm, Saturday sitting times are 6.30pm, 7.30pm and 8.30pm. On Sundays there is a traditional three course lunch served between 12pm and 3pm in the restaurant. While enjoying the meal, guests are also sure to enjoy the relaxing ambience and tasteful surroundings, as the inn is decorated and furnished with understated elegance and style

30 Main Street, Ledston, Castleford,
West Yorkshire WF10 2AB
☎ 01977 553069

The lovely village of Ledston is found 1½ miles east off the A656, north of Castleford. Here thirsty travellers have been coming to enjoy the fine drink and food available at **The White Horse**, an institution dating back to the 17th century. Known locally as Mary Carr's, this outstanding premises boasts a fantastic outdoor floral display. The interior is equally impressive.

Open all day, every day, there are two real ales (Black Sheep and Speckled Hen) together with a good range of keg bitters, lager, cider, stout, wines, spirits and soft drinks. Truly excellent food is available Monday to Thursday 12-2.15 and 5.30-9, Friday to

Sunday 12-9, with a varied menu of dishes using the

freshest local produce including the local butchers. Guests can dine throughout the pub or outside in the two superb patio areas festooned with flowers. Food-themed evenings include Steak Night (Tues), Fish Night (Weds) and specially-priced deals including a complementary bottle of wine.

1 The Square, Ferrybridge,
West Yorkshire WF11 8ND
☎ 01977 673527
e-mail: goldenlionhotel@yahoo.co.uk

A warm welcome is always assured from Tom, Jan, son Danny and daughter Charlotte at **The Golden Lion Hotel,** open all day every day.
Delicious, home-cooked food is served lunch and evenings at this friendly, 18th century riverside Inn.

The Sunday Carvery is not to be missed; offering choice of roasts with real Yorkshire pudding! Watch boats sail along the River Aire from the beer garden, enjoy organised entertainment evenings, and/or have a private party in the function room. Located just a few minutes from the M62 and A1 - stop off on your travels, or linger a little longer and stay in one of the eight guest bedrooms.

135 THE OLD VICARAGE HOTEL

Bruntcliffe Road, Morley, Leeds,
West Yorkshire LS27 0JZ
☎ 0113 253 2174   Fax: 0113 253 3549
e-mail: sales@oldvicaragehotel.co.uk
🌐 www.oldvicaragehotel.co.uk

The Old Vicarage Hotel stands in Bruntcliffe Road in Morley. A short drive from the M62, it's a friendly, family-run premises with owner Khurram Shabir at the helm. As its name suggests, the hotel began life as the vicarage for next-door St Andrew's Church. It was built in 1893, and incorporates a more recent purpose-built extension in keeping with the original style and character of the main house. The hotel sits in one-and-a-half acres of its own well-tended grounds.

Open all year round, there are 25 ensuite letting rooms of differing sizes and styles. Doubles, twins, family rooms – there's something to cater for all tastes and requirements. The guest bedrooms, dining room and guests' sitting rooms are a happy marriage of traditional touches, such as the handsome fireplaces, and modern comforts, with beautiful antiques and also every up-to-date facility. Guests can come on a B&B or dinner, B&B basis. During the lifetime of this book there will be a handsome new restaurant on the premises; meanwhile there's quality food available for residents (and non-residents by arrangement). Licensed for residents and diners only, there are drinks served in the dining room and also the guests' 'honesty bar', where you help yourself and just make a note of what you've had. There's also another, no-smoking, guests' sitting room on the ground floor.

The atmosphere is always relaxed and welcoming, and this fine hotel has been awarded 2 Stars by the AA. To reach The Old Vicarage, leave the M62 at Junction 27, following signs for the A650. Turn right at the roundabout onto the A650, signposted Wakefield. Go through two sets of traffic lights and past the petrol station (on your left). The hotel is the next left just before St Andrew's Church.

136 THE NEW SCARBOROUGH INN

43 Dewsbury Road, Tingley, Wakefield,
West Yorkshire WF3 1LH
☎ 0113 253 4762

The New Scarborough Inn stands in the village of Tingley, in Dewsbury Road close to Junction 28 of the M62. Built around 1920, it's a spacious and welcoming inn, cosy and comfortable inside and with an attractive beer garden outside.

Leaseholders Clare and Jason have been here since 2005. It's their first venture into the licensing trade, but they already have a real success on their hands. They've built up the reputation and the inn is popular with visitors and locals alike. Open Monday to Thursday from tea-time, and Friday to Sunday all day, there are two real ales (Tetley and Black Sheep) together with a good choice of lagers, cider, stout, wines, spirits and soft drinks. Tasty food is served Friday and Saturday midday to 2.30 and 5–7.30, and Sundays 12–3. Clare does the cooking using the freshest local produce; guests choose from the menu or specials board from a full range of delicious dishes.

137 THE PARK

Bradford Road, Batley,
West Yorkshire WF17 8HG
☎ 01924 475289

A short walk from the centre of Batley, **The Park** is a large and popular pub open all day every day. Excellent food is served daily, with freshly prepared dishes using the best local produce. The Sunday lunch is justly popular. The pub also boasts a good range of draught keg bitters, lagers and other thirst-quenchers including wines, spirits and soft drinks. The large function room is available for hire, and there's weekly entertainment Thursday nights from 8 p.m., with live music. The interior is cosy and comfortable, while outside there's an outstanding children's play area. Tenants Denis and Annie and their friendly staff offer all their guests a warm welcome and great hospitality.

138 CAFÉ BOO

156 Huddersfield Road, Mirfield,
West Yorkshire WF14 8AN
☎ 01924 499494
🌐 www.cafeboo.co.uk

Open Monday to Saturday 9.30-4, and for tapas every Friday evening 5.30-10.30 p.m., the marvellous fully licensed **Café Boo** is a stylish and relaxed place, with downstair and upstair seating and free car parking opposite. There is an excellent range of home-cooked dishes. A small sample from the menu includes all-day breakfast, hot paninis, fresh-cut sandwiches with the filling of your choice, home made soup, delicious cakes, scones and more. To drink, there's the best cup of coffee for miles around, together with teas, hot chocolate and a range of cold drinks. On Friday nights the tapas selection includes olives, meatballs, deep-fried brie, smoked mackerel, garlic mushrooms, salad, chicken and more.

140 THE NAVIGATION TAVERN & THE LOCK RESTAURANT

6 Station Road, Mirfield,
West Yorkshire WF14 8NL
☎ 01924 492476   Fax: 01924 499110

Set alongside the Calder and Hebble Navigation Canal in Mirfield, just a few miles northeast of Huddersfield, the outstanding **Navigation Tavern and Lock Restaurant** offers the very best in ale, food, accommodation and hospitality. Owner Kevin O'Donnell has been here eight years; ably assisted by Christine and sons Jamie and Steven.

This popular premises dates back around 180 years. Spacious and attractive, it combines the best of traditional and modern comforts. The décor enhances the inn's warm and welcoming ambience, with a stylish dining room with polished wood floors and elegant seating, and a handsome and welcoming bar area. Open all day every day, there are five real ales – John Smiths, Theakstons Olde Peculiar, XB, Best and a rotating guest ale – together with a full complement of lagers, cider, stout, wines, spirits and soft drinks. The

service is always friendly and efficient. Superb food is served Tuesday to Saturday 12-2.30 and 6-9.30, and Sundays 12-4. The lovely Lock Restaurant seats 54 and is no-smoking throughout. Guests choose from the menu and specials board for a selection of tempting and hearty dishes expertly prepared using locally-sourced produce. The traditional Sunday lunch offers a choice of meats with all the trimmings, or vegetarian option.

The accommodation here is also excellent, with five attractive and comfortable ensuite guest bedrooms available all year round. All rooms are doubles or twins; a chairlift can help guests with limited mobility. Guests stay on a room-only or B&B basis, and the inn makes a very good base from which to explore the Yorkshire moors and many historic and cultural sights and attractions of the region.

139 NOSH! CAFÉ BAR ¶

188 Huddersfield Road, Mirfield,
West Yorkshire WF14 8AT
☎ 01924 480174
⊕ www.noshcafe.co.uk

For a tasty bite to eat in or take away, **Nosh!
Café Bar** is the place to look for. This
relaxed, informal café serves up everything
from hot meals, roast dinners and buffet
lunches to freshly cut sandwiches, kids'
dishes and cappuccinos. Outside catering is
also available. Bright and friendly, it's set on
Mirfield's main street and is open Monday-
Friday from 7.30-2.30, Saturdays 8-1. Owner
Joanne Clayton uses only the freshest
ingredients to create some outstanding
dishes, including
her all-day
breakfasts and
home-made pies.
A good choice
of hot and cold
drinks ensures
you'll come away
well-fed and
satisfied.

141 THE NEW CHARNWOOD ¶

4 Westgate, Heckmondwike,
West Yorkshire WF16 0EH
☎ 01924 406512
⊕ www.thenewcharnwood.co.uk

The New Charnwood is a wonderful place
to relax in comfortable surroundings and
enjoy contemporary English food and drink.
The menus change seasonally and lighter
lunches include paninis and fresh
sandwiches on granary baton or white
teacake with a range of fillings such as bacon,
brie and cranberry, and mozzarella, pesto and
roasted peppers. Mouth-watering main
courses such as bangers and mash, beef
stroganoff,
whole seabass
and pork
medallions are
bound to please
every palate.
Owner Terry is
a chef with over
10 years'
experience and

together with his partner Pauline he offers
first-class service and friendly hospitality.

142 THE QUEENS ARMS ¶

Denby Dale Road, Wakefield,
West Yorkshire WF2 8ED
☎ 01924 202141

A top-of-the-range public house located a short
drive from Wakefield along the Denby Dale Road
(A636), **The Queens Arms** dates back to the 1700s
and began life as a coaching inn called The White
House. Experienced licensees Neil and Geoff took over in February of 2006, though they have
been in the trade since 1999.

Open all day every day, there are draught keg ales,
lagers, wine, soft drinks, spirits and more behind the
bar, together with delicious food served daily. Monday
to Saturday (12-2.15 and 5-8) and Sundays (12-3.30), the

professional
chef
prepares an
excellent
range of
dishes for
the menu
and daily
specials

board. Popular dishes include the steaks, mixed grills
and home-made pies, and there are also several very
good vegetarian options. Booking advised on Sundays.
Spacious and attractive, the interior is traditional and
comfortable, while outside there's a very pleasant and
picturesque beer garden.

144 DIMPLE WELL LODGE HOTEL

The Green, Ossett,
West Yorkshire WF5 8JX
☎ 01924 264352   Fax: 01924 274024
e-mail: thedimplewell@btconnect.com
🌐 www.dimple-well-lodge-hotel.co.uk

One of the premier places to dine, stay or hold a celebration, **Dimple Well Lodge Hotel** is a gracious and elegant place standing in its own manicured grounds. The premises date back some 175 years and began life as a private residence known as 'The Cottage' – a bit of a misnomer, as this is an expansive and impressive property.

Owned and personally run by Susan and Enzo Sechi since December 2005, this marvellous hotel offers all the first-class service and amenities of a much larger hotel as well as the personal attention of a much more intimate setting. It comes well recommended by locals and visitors alike for the hospitality, facilities and especially the cuisine. Enzo is a professional chef who has been cooking since he was a small boy. Food is served Monday to Saturday evenings from 5.30 to 9 p.m. Early Bird Specials are available 5.30-7. Booking is advised at all times at this justly popular eatery. Enzo is a simply superb chef, creating a menu of traditional and modern English dishes with a subtle

Mediterranean influence. A small sample from the extensive menu, which changes with the seasons to make use of the freshest produce, includes main courses such as slow-roasted lamb shank with rosemary essence, pan-fried sea bass with fresh mussels, herbs and basil oil, and fresh tagliatelle with summer vegetables and pesto.Food can also be served at lunchtime by appointment for two or more.

The ten superb ensuite guest bedrooms come in a mixture of sizes to suit every guest. Guests stay on a B&B or Dinner, B&B basis. A very popular venue for weddings and private parties, it is licensed for residents and diners only. Children welcome.

143 THE COCK AND BOTTLE

7 Bank Street, Ossett, Wakefield,
West Yorkshire WF5 8PS
☎ 01924 273208

Situated in the heart of Ossett, **The Cock and Bottle** is a warm and welcoming family-run pub, with leaseholders Simon and Kath assisted by Simon's mum, Kate. Open all day every day, there is a good selection of draught keg bitters, lagers, cider, stout and wines, spirits and soft drinks. During the lifetime of this edition there are plans to have some real ales as well. Food is served from opening time until 3 p.m. weekdays and until 6 p.m. at weekends. The menu offers a good choice of home-cooked dishes; on Sundays the lunch includes three roasts with all the trimmings.

145 THE BREWERS PRIDE

Low Mill Road, Healey Road, Ossett,
West Yorkshire WF5 8ND
☎ 01924 273865
e-mail: sally@brewers-pride.co.uk
⊕ www.brewers-pride.co.uk

Renowned for the range of quality real ales, super food and excellent entertainment, **The Brewers Pride**, tucked away in Healey Road in Ossett, is a fine pub worth seeking out. Licensee Sally Hastewell has been here eight years and runs this popular Free House, which has no fewer than eight real ales to sample and enjoy, changing regularly but always including some brews from Red Lion Ales (the local Ossett brewery). Tempting home-cooked food is served Monday to Saturday 12-2, and there are food-themed evenings every Wednesday night (steak night, curry night, home-made pies night).

146 THE CATCHPENNY

Lane Ends, Fitzwilliam, Pontefract,
West Yorkshire WF9 5NJ
☎ 01977 611984

The Catchpenny is located in the village of Fitzwilliam, off the B6273 southwest of Pontefract and northwest of Hemsworth. A charming pub dating back to the early 1800s, it is run by Christopher and Nicola, who arrived in 2006 and, with great zeal and dedication, refurbished the place from top to bottom. Open all day, every day for ale, there's a premium real ale, a session real ale and a rotating guest ale. The menu in the large and stylish restaurant has a good selection of traditional Yorkshire dishes, expertly prepared using the freshest ingredients by professional chefs.

148 THE SPORTSMAN INN

124 Station Road, Ryhill, Wakefield,
West Yorkshire WF4 2BZ
☎ 01226 722797

An intricate part of village life since 1822, the friendly **Sportsman Inn** has an enviable reputation for its traditional home-cooked food and warm hospitality. The village of Ryhill is famed for its wonderful walks, and most people start their explorations of the area at The Sportsman. This excellent family-run pub with Vanessa Robinson and her mother Dagmar at the helm for the past 10 years is popular with locals and with visitors from many miles around who come to sample the selection of ales and great food. The outstanding menu of freshly cooked dishes using the best local produce is served Tuesday to Sunday 12-3 and Monday to Friday 5-9.30. Booking advised Fridays and Sundays.

147 THE CHURCH HOUSE

Barnsley Road, South Kirby,
West Yorkshire WF9 3LA
☎ 01977 651560

The Church House takes its name from its proximity to the village church, just across the road. Large and sturdy, this pristine brickbuilt pub has stood here only since 1971, a few yards away from where an earlier village pub once stood.

This handsome and welcoming pub in the heart of South Kirkby – located a few miles northeast of Barnsley off the A638/A639 – is well worth seeking out for its excellent food, drink and atmosphere. Local couple Robert and Anne-Marie McKeegan took over here in 2005. Robert has been in the trade since 1990 and through their hard work they have made this a very popular place to enjoy a drink, dine and be entertained. Open all day, every day, there is one changing guest ale to enjoy, together with a full range of lagers, cider, stout, wines, spirits and soft drinks.

Excellent, delicious food is served Monday to Saturday midday until 9 p.m., and Sundays midday until 5. Robert is the chef, and guests choose from a menu of hearty dishes such as steaks, full rack of ribs, Whitby scampi, fisherman's salad and chicken curry. All produce is purchased locally wherever possible. Popular dishes include the braised steak and traditional Sunday roasts (the latter served between midday and 2 p.m.) The no-smoking restaurant seats 44, with room for another 36 diners throughout the pub. Between 12 and 8 p.m. Monday to Saturday, there's a truly special offer of two main courses for £7.

Children are welcome, and there's a large and well-kept beer garden and children's play area to the side of the pub. Sunday nights there's a fun quiz held from 9 p.m.

281

149 THE FOX AND HOUNDS

672 Barnsley Road, Newmillerdam,
Wakefield, West Yorkshire WF2 6QQ
☎ 01924 255474

Located opposite Newmillerdam Country Park adjacent to the A61, **The Fox and Hounds** is an outstanding pub dating back to the early 1800s. Kath Conway, the licensee, has been here since early in 2006; it's her first venture into the licensing trade and she's got a real success on her hands. The furniture and décor are superb, and the inn is open all day, every day.

There are two real ales – John Smiths Cask and a rotating guest ale – together with a full complement of lagers, spirits, wines and non-alcoholic drinks. Excellent food is served every day from 10.30 in the morning until 9 at night. The menu and specials boards (including special kids' board) provides a selection of tasty dishes to

choose from, made with locally-sourced produce. Barbecues are held a couple of times a week, weather permitting. Children welcome. Private parties happily catered for, for up to 100 guests.

151 COLNE VALLEY MUSEUM 🏛

Cliffe Ash, Golcar,
Huddersfield, HD7 4PY
☎ 01484 659762

Three nineteenth-century weavers' cottages near Golcar Parish Church are the home of the museum. See the life and work of the 19th century in restored period rooms – the loom chamber with working hand looms and a Spinning Jenny, the weaver's living room of 1850 and a gas-lit clogger's shop of 1910. The museum is run entirely by its members. On two weekends a year a craft and working weekend is held when there are many different crafts being demonstrated. The museum has featured on TV and is recommended by the Good Museum Guide Open: Sat, Sun and Bank holidays 2pm-5pm except Christmas and New Year. Facilities for schools. Shop and light refreshments. Admission Charge.

HIDDEN PLACES GUIDES

Explore Britain and Ireland with *Hidden Places* guides - a fascinating series of national and local travel guides.

Packed with easy to read information on hundreds of places of interest as well as places to stay, eat and drink.

Available from both high street and internet booksellers

For more information on the full range of *Hidden Places* guides and other titles published by Travel Publishing visit our website on

www.travelpublishing.co.uk or ask for our leaflet by phoning **0118-981-7777** or emailing **info@travelpublishing.co.uk**

150 THE BLACK HORSE INN

Clifton, Brighouse,
West Yorkshire HD6 4HJ
☎ 01484 713862   Fax: 01484 400582
e-mail: mail@blackhorseclifton.co.uk
🌐 www.blackhorseclifton.co.uk

Quality shines through at **The Black Horse Inn**, distinguished in so many respects: location, standard of accommodation, the excellence of the food and the genuine warmth of the hospitality on offer. Set in the tranquil village of Clifton, just a mile from the M62 at Junction 25, this traditional inn makes an ideal base from which to explore the many scenic and historic sights and attractions of the region, from York, beautiful rural villages and the wealth of country houses, gracious parks and other beauty spots to Leeds, Bradford and Huddersfield fewer than 20 minutes away.

The inn has been family-run for over 60 years. Jane, now at the helm, was born here; she and her husband Andrew have been providing all their customers with the best in quality and service for over seven years. The inn itself dates back more than 350 years, and boasts a number of charming original features while also providing every modern comfort. Open all day, every day for ale,

the real ales on tap are Black Sheep, Timothy Taylor Landlord and a rotating guest ale.

Excellent food is served daily from midday until 9.30 p.m., with two separate elegant and tastefully decorated restaurants and the bar area where guests can enjoy a selection of tempting dishes. Booking is advised at all times, but particularly at weekends. The menu changes with the seasons to make the most of the freshest local produce, with something for every palate and including mouthwatering choices such as grilled lobster, local steak and Black Sheep ale pie, hearty steaks, slow-braised Welsh lamb, warm salad of Toulouse sausage, chicken and vanilla poached pear, and wild mushroom risotto.

The separate function room seats 60 or accommodates 100 for a buffet, and there's a very pleasant courtyard to the rear of the inn. Open all year round for accommodation, there are 21 comfortable and attractive ensuite guest bedrooms, some of which are located on the ground floor, making them easily accessible to guests with disabilities. The rooms come in a range of sizes including family rooms, and guests can stay on a B&B or dinner, B&B basis.

152 BULLS HEAD ᵧ

Blackmoorfoot, Linthwaite, Huddersfield,
West Yorkshire HD7 5TR
☎ 01484 842715   Fax: 01484 844158
e-mail: clarkevvy@btinternet.com

Set high up in Blackmoorfoot, looking down towards Linthwaite and the A62, the **Bulls Head** began life as a coaching inn back in the mid-1700s. This fine establishment is open all day, every day for ale, with three real ales on tap – Theakstons, Marstons Pedigree and a rotating guest ale – together with a good complement of lagers, cider, stout, wines, spirits and soft drinks.

Welcoming and relaxed, the inn is family run by Michelle and Kevin, ably assisted by Kevin's son Owen, who offer first-class service and hospitality to all their guests. Great food is served daily at lunch and dinner (Mon-Fri 12-2.15 and 5-8.30, Sat 12-4.30 and 5-

8.30, Sun 12-6) with a wide choice of tempting and hearty dishes using locally-sourced meat and produce. Booking required at weekends. The speciality here is called 'A Load of Bull' and features a giant square Yorkshire pudding filled with delicious roast beef. The traditional Sunday lunch boasts a choice of meats with all the trimmings.

153 THE GREAT WESTERN INN ᵧ

Manchester Road, Marsden, Huddersfield,
West Yorkshire HD7 6NL
☎ 01484 844315   Fax: 01484 846360
e-mail: enquiries@greatwesterninn.co.uk

Alex and Rachel offer all their guests a warm welcome at **The Great Western Inn**, an outstanding place in an outstanding location. Situated on the A62 a mile or so southwest of Marsden, the inn is surrounded by thousands of acres of moorlands looking over and towards both Wessenden and Saddleworth Moor. This family-run Free House dates back to 1838, and began life as a coaching inn. Closed Mondays except Bank Holidays, the inn is open every other session weekdays and all day Saturday and Sundays.

There are always at least three real ales (Black Sheep, Timothy Taylor Golden Best and Timothy Taylor Best are the regulars here) as well as a good choice of lagers, cider, stout, wines, spirits and soft drinks. Rachel does all the cooking, creating mouthwatering dishes in portions so generous they

have to be seen to be believed. Dishes change with the seasons but are served at lunch (12-2.30) and dinner (5-9); pensioners' specials are available Tuesday to Friday lunchtime. All produce is locally sourced; specials include the fresh fish every Friday, bought that morning at the fish market. On Sunday there are no fewer than 12 main courses to choose from. Booking advised at weekends. It's also worth asking about the campsite available locally - please ring for details if you're thinking of stopping in this beautiful part of the world.

154 THE OLD FARMHOUSE TEA ROOM

Netherton Moor Road, Netherton,
Huddersfield, West Yorkshire HD4 7LE
☎ 01484 668949   Fax: 01484 668940

Much more than the standard tea room awaits visitors to **The Old Farmhouse Tea Room**. 'Food that soothes' could well be the byword here, where the surprisingly extensive menus guarantee a marvellous brunch, lunch or tea-time treat. Situated within the grounds of the well-known Hinchliffe's Farm Shop, just a short distance from the centre of Netherton, this charming and welcoming establishment is open Tuesday to Saturday 9–5 and Sundays 10–4, accommodating 56 indoors and another 36 on the outside decking area.

Locally-sourced produce is used to create superb home-cooked meals, sandwiches and a mouthwatering range of cakes. For brunch why not try the home-made sausages and free-range eggs? In the afternoons traditional cream teas with hand-baked scones, cakes and biscuits are complemented by a selection of home-made ice creams, gourmet sandwiches, fresh salads and main courses including king prawns in garlic butter, pan-fried monkfish, slow-cooked chicken or open beef pie, all delicious. Fully licensed, meals can be accompanied by wine or bottled beers, fizzy drinks or fresh juices as well, of course, by a full range of teas and coffees.

155 HERVEY'S WINE BAR

Norridge Bottom, Holmfirth,
West Yorkshire HD9 7BB
☎ 01484 686925
e-mail: jon@herveys.co.uk
⊕ www.herveys.co.uk

One of Holmfirth's hidden treasures, **Hervey's Wine Bar** is a charming place – the light and airy interior is very homely and welcoming, with the Aga and copper pots open to view in one corner, pale wood dining tables and a cream-and-green décor. Run by Jon and Hazel Shaw, who are friendly hosts offering first-class service and hospitality, Hervey's is open throughout the day Tuesday to Sunday and Bank Holidays.

There are four real ales – including three from the Copper Dragon brewery at Skipton and a rotating guest ale – together with a good selection of lagers, spirits and superior wines. The range of tasty tapas includes spare ribs, steak sandwich, hearty salads, hummous with pitta

bread, seafood paella and much more, while the lunchtime and evening menu and specials board offer

locally-sourced produce home-cooked and prepared by Hazel, an accomplished cook. Booking advised Friday and Saturday. Well worth seeking out, this excellent place is close to the post office and found off the Huddersfield Road and Station Road in the heart of Holmfirth.

156 THE WHITE HORSE

Scholes Road, Jackson Bridge, Holmfirth,
West Yorkshire HD9 1LY
☎ 01484 683940 Mob: 07731 136058
e-mail: janicegraydon@tiscali.co.uk
⊕ www.thewhitehorsejacksonbridge.co.uk

You may recognise **The White Horse** from *Last of the Summer Wine*, as it featured as the place where the three main characters did their drinking. One area of the pub is dedicated to the series, with many photos on display. Open every day, there are two real ales –

Tetleys Cask and a rotating guest ale – together with a good range of lagers, cider, stout, wines, spirits and soft drinks, all served with a smile by leaseholders Janice and Mark, ably assisted by their son Peter.

Janice does the cooking, creating mouthwatering dishes. The Sunday roast is justly popular. The interior is spacious and welcoming, while there's also a charming hidden beer garden

and a seating area just across from the inn looking down onto the river. Accommodation is provided in five ensuite rooms available all year round, each recently refurbished with taste and style. Two of the rooms are housed in an adjacent building with its own private entrance, and the tariff includes a hearty and delicious breakfast. The magnificent surrounding countryside makes this a wonderful place to enjoy a few days' peace and relaxation.

HIDDEN PLACES GUIDES

Explore Britain and Ireland with *Hidden Places* guides - a fascinating series of national and local travel guides.

Packed with easy to read information on hundreds of places of interest as well as places to stay, eat and drink.

Available from both high street and internet booksellers

For more information on the full range of *Hidden Places* guides and other titles published by Travel Publishing visit our website on

www.travelpublishing.co.uk or ask for our leaflet by phoning **0118-981-7777** or emailing **info@travelpublishing.co.uk**

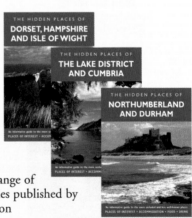

THE HIDDEN PLACES OF
DORSET, HAMPSHIRE AND ISLE OF WIGHT

THE HIDDEN PLACES OF
THE LAKE DISTRICT AND CUMBRIA

THE HIDDEN PLACES OF
NORTHUMBERLAND AND DURHAM

157 BUTCHERS ARMS

38 Towngate, Hepworth, Holmfirth,
West Yorkshire HD9 1TE
☎ 01484 682857

Set in the pretty and tranquil village of Hepworth, found about four miles from Holmfirth high up off the A616, the **Butchers Arms** is an excellent pub dating back in parts to the 1500s. Michael Bell first came here as the chef back in 2001; like many of his customers he fell in love with the village and the inn and, together with his wife Sally, became the leaseholder three years ago.

Large and impressive, this traditional inn stands apart from the rest by virtue of the excellent service Michael, Sally and their team provide, and the range of food and drink on offer - all served up with lashings of sincere Yorkshire hospitality. The opening hours are seasonal, the pub being closed for lunch in winter but open in summer, and always open every evening and all day at weekends and on Bank Holidays.

This fine inn boasts no fewer than 4-6 real ales. The regulars are Black Sheep and two ales from the Ossett Brewery, together with rotating guest ales. As befits a pub as distinguished as this one, there's a very good selection of lagers, keg beers, cider, stout, wines, spirits and soft drinks. And to eat? Delicious food is served 12.30 to 2.30 and Monday to Saturday evenings from 6 to 9.30 p.m. The no-smoking restaurant seats 60, and there's room for another 40 diners in the bar areas. When the weather is fine, guests can enjoy their drink or meal on the terrace patio or in the attractive beer garden. The menu offers a variety of Modern English dishes using the freshest local produce. All dishes are home-made and home-cooked. Booking is essential at all times, as the excellence of the food has earned the inn a reputation far and wide.

Occasional evening entertainment includes live music, usually on Sunday evenings, and there's a fun quiz every Wednesday from about 9 p.m. If you're looking for accommodation in the area, which is well worth a few days' exploration, the inn has links with several excellent local bed-and-breakfast establishments.

287

2 The Village, Farnley Tyas, Huddersfield,
West Yorkshire HD4 6UD
☎ 01484 666644 Fax: 01484 668937
e-mail:
thegoldencockinn@btopenworld.com

The historic village of Farnley Tyas is located just two miles east of Honley off the A616 or A629, part of an area once owned by the Earl of Dartmouth. The excellent **Golden Cock Inn** was, even then, a well-known feature, and proudly displayed on the wall of the inn is its full and colourful history. Records of 1821 name the first listed licensee, but the inn is much older than that.

As part of its role as the centre of village life, the inn once played host to the three-day 'Rent Dinners', where local tenants would come to pay their half-yearly rent and be given dinner, one day set aside for smaller landholders and the other two for farmers with larger holdings. Today the host is Stephen Watkins, who has been here since 2001 and takes justified pride in upholding the long tradition of hospitality and service at the inn.

Open all day, every day, there are three real ales - Tetleys, Black Sheep and Timothy Taylor Landlord - together with a full range of lagers, wines, soft drinks, spirits, cider and stout. It is for the fine food that people come from far and wide to visit the inn, served Monday to Thursday 12-3 and 6-9, Friday and Saturday 12-3 and 6-9.30, and Sundays and Bank Holidays 12-9, with a traditional Sunday lunch (offering a choice of five starters, five main courses and five desserts) from 12-4 and then the full main menu from 4-9. The printed menu and specials board provide a full complement of delicious dishes created with the freshest local produce, with a huge selection of tempting choices such as soy-glazed tuna steak, pork spare ribs, roasted salmon, king scallops, pan-fried seabass, cannelloni pasta stuffed with ricotta, lamb rump, spicy nut roast and venison steak, as well as a good choice of steaks and grills, all expertly prepared and presented. Guests dine in the handsome and spacious dining room, which seats 45, or can take advantage on fine days of the lovely decking area to the rear of the inn.

Self-catering accommodation is available in the village; please ring for details.

44 Marsh Lane, Shepley, Huddersfield, West
Yorkshire HD8 8AP
☎ 01484 605941/605355
e-mail: oldbarnshepley@aol.co.uk
🌐 www.oldbarnshepley.com

The Farmers Boy Inn and Old Barn Restaurant is situated in the lovely village of Shepley, found off the A636 or A629. It began life as a coaching inn with adjacent blacksmith's, and dates back to the late 1700s. Open all day, every day for ale, there are three on tap – Tetleys, Black Sheep and a rotating guest ale – as well as a selection of thirst-quenchers including lagers, cider, stout, wines, spirits and soft drinks.

Well worth seeking out for the delicious food, tasty meals are served Wednesday – Friday 12–2.30 and 6–9.30, Saturdays 6–10 p.m. and Sundays 12 – 5. The menu and daily specials board feature classic

dishes such as sirloin steaks, grilled gammon, halibut and

whole sea bass, and homemade lasagne, together with a selection of hot and cold sandwiches, hearty salads, burgers, vegetarian dishes and more. The best, freshest local produce is used to create these dishes. Booking advised, particularly at weekends.

289

160 THE WHITE HORSE ¶

2 Chapel Lane, Emley, Huddersfield,
West Yorkshire HD8 9SP
☎ 01924 840937

The **White Horse** is a spacious and friendly inn set in the picturesque village of Emley southeast of Huddersfield. Run by Shirley Mallinson, who was born in the village and is the daughter of a local farmer, the inn is situated on what was once a drovers' road and began life as a coaching inn back in the early 1800s.

John Smiths Cask and a rotating guest ale are here for real ale-lovers, while there's a good

selection of lagers, cider, stout, wines, spirits and soft drinks. Open Monday and Tuesday from 4 p.m., and all day the rest of the week, good food is served at Sunday lunchtime (12-2.30) and on Steak Night (Tues from 7-9 p.m.) when all meals are served with a complimentary bottle of wine.

162 OLD RED LION ¶

210 Main Street, Grenoside, Sheffield,
South Yorkshire S35 8PR
☎ 0114 246 7383

The **Old Red Lion** can be found in the older part of the north Sheffield suburb of Grenoside, off the A61. A one-time coaching inn dating back to the late 1700s, this distinctive pub serves up excellent food and drink every day. Tetleys is the regular real ale here, complemented by a rotating guest ale.

Mother and daughter team Jacquie and Katie are excellent hosts, and this family-friendly pub has excellent

food at lunch (12-3 daily) and dinner (5-8 Monday to Saturday). Guests choose from the menu or specials board for a selection of home-cooked dishes using locally-sourced produce. Hot baguettes, steak-and-ale pie and the traditional Sunday lunch are particularly popular favourites.

161 THE COMMERCIAL INN ¶

107 Station Road, Chapeltown, Sheffield,
South Yorkshire S35 2XF
☎ 0114 246 9066

Renowned throughout this quiet part of the outskirts of Sheffield and beyond for the quality ale and food served here, **The Commercial Inn** is a distinctive pub dating back to the 1880s. Leaseholders Paul and Kate have been at the helm since 1993, serving up great food, drink and hospitality.

There are no fewer than 8 real ales – and usually more like 10 or 12 – at this friendly and welcoming place. Regulars include Wentworth Pale Ale (known as 'Whopper'), Oatmeal Stout, Needles Eye and Wards. The others change regularly, and the pub has been known to get through 10 to 12 different real ales a

week. Hearty and delicious food is served Monday to

Saturday 12-2.30 and 6-9, and Sunday lunchtime. Booking advised for Sunday lunch.

Twice a year (over the last weekends in May and November) the pub hosts a beer festival featuring up to 30 real ales to sample.

290

163 THE WAGGON AND HORSES

Sheffield Road, Oxspring, Sheffield,
South Yorkshire S36 8YQ
☎ 01226 763259
e-mail: thewaggon-horses@hotmail.com
⊕ www.thewaggon-oxspring.co.uk

The village of Oxspring is found just off the A629, a couple of miles from Penistone at the edge of the Peak District National Park. This late 18th-century pub began life as a coaching inn; today the premises are stylish and full of character. Well known both locally and further afield for its excellent food and hospitality, the inn is open all day every day.

There are two real ales – Tetleys and Timothy Taylor Landlord – and a full selection of lagers, wines, spirits, soft drinks and more. Locally-sourced produce is used to create tempting dishes at lunch and dinner. Sunday lunch is justly popular; booking advised. Once a month the cuisines of Italy, France, Mexico, India or China are featured, with a special menu of authentic dishes. And if you're celebrating a birthday, given two days' notice the chefs can prepare a complementary birthday cake for you and your dining companions.

164 THE STRINES INN

Bradfield Dale, Sheffield,
South Yorkshire S6 6JE
☎ 0114 285 1247

Heading northwest out of Sheffield towards the Peak District, you will come across the superb **Strines Inn**, a hidden gem found a couple of miles off the A57 just within the Peak District National Park. Dating back to the 16th century, this inn is brimming with character and is open every session weekdays and all day at weekends in winter, and all day every day Easter to the end of October. There are always two to four real ales here, with Marstons Pedigree the regular. Delicious home-cooked food is served daily. The accommodation is simply outstanding, with three ensuite guest bedrooms, all with four-poster beds and marvellous scenic views in every direction.

165 THE FULLERTON HOTEL

Vale Road, Thrybergh, Rotherham,
South Yorkshire S65 4DD
☎ 01709 850435

The village of Thrybergh is found off the A630 a few miles northeast of Rotherham. At the heart of the local community, visitors are very welcome to the impressive **Fullerton Hotel**. This friendly place is open all day every day, there's a range of draught keg lagers, cider and stout, together with wines, spirits and soft drinks. The Fullerton Hotel also has a large secure beer garden and childrens play area.

166 THE TRAVELLERS INN

Bawtry Road, Bramley, Rotherham,
South Yorkshire S66 2TS
☎ 01709 540550
e-mail: travellersinns66@aol.com

Bramley is situated on the A631, a very short distance from J1 of the M18 east of Rotherham. Here can be found the convivial **Travellers Inn**, a former coaching inn dating back to 1826. Leaseholders Anne and Andrew have been here since 2003 and, through hard work and dedication, have turned it into a very popular venue, especially for food.

With excellent décor and furnishings throughout and offering first-class hospitality, the inn is open all day every day. Draught keg ales include Stones, Carling, Kronenberg, Fosters, Strongbow and Guinness. To eat, there's a superb Sunday carvery with a choice of five meats and all the trimmings served up from midday to 6 p.m., and the rest of the week tasty meals are available at lunch (12-2) and dinner (5-8.30). As an extra treat, the inn is open Saturday mornings from 10 a.m. til midday for hearty breakfasts. Home-cooked dishes are the speciality here, and there are always special offers.

167 MORNING STAR INN

Dobie Street, Barnsley,
South Yorkshire S70 4JH
☎ 01226 284436

Morning Star Inn is a large and imposing brickbuilt inn occupying a quiet street off the A61 a short drive out of Barnsley on the Sheffield road. Dating back to the 1930s, it is run by Martine and Gary, who have been here since June of 2006. Martine is Barnsley born and bred, and though it's her and Gary's first venture into the licensing trade, they bring a wealth of enthusiasm and have already built up a loyal following, thanks to their excellent food, drink and accommodation.

Open all day, every day, the keg draught ales include Thwaites Smooth and Thwaites Daniels. Hot and cold snacks are available throughout opening hours; at the time of writing, Sunday lunches were planned for the near future. The accommodation comprises two comfortable double rooms. Traditional and cosy inside, there's also a spacious beer garden – just the place to enjoy a relaxing drink on fine days.

168 THE TALBOT INN AND RESTAURANT

Towngate, Mapplewell, Barnsley,
South Yorkshire S75 6AS
☎ 01226 382593/385629
e-mail: thetalbotinn@aol.com

An outstanding property, **The Talbot Inn and Restaurant** dates to the late 19th century. Celebrating its 22nd anniversary in 2006, this outstanding place is renowned for miles around for the quality of the food, drink and hospitality.

Back then, current owner Michael Millas' mother and father Hazel and Leon took over. Leon was a supremely talented chef who passed his skills on to Michael, now a top-class chef in his own right. Together with his wife Raminta, Michael offers the very best in quality and service to all his guests.

Open all day every day for ale, there are two rotating guest ales, changed monthly, together with a full range of lagers, bitters, wines, spirits, soft drinks, cider and stout. Superb cuisine is served daily –

Monday to Saturday 11.30–2 and 6.30–10 and Sundays from midday to 9 p.m. The restaurant is located upstairs, and is intimate and brimming with character, with exposed beams, part-stone walls and other charming features. The excellent menu includes chef's specials such as beef stroganoff, roast duckling, beef Wellington and lamb cutlets, fish dishes of trout, sea bass, cod, halibut and salmon, vegetarian options including spinach and ricotta cannelloni, farfalle gratin and broccoli & cream cheese bake, and choices from the grill – fillet, sirloin, rump and T-bone steaks, mixed grill and gammon ham. All main meals are served with the chef's choice of vegetables and potatoes of the day, or a full salad, and all produce is sourced locally. For those preferring just a light snack, hot and cold bar meals are served downstairs in the main bar, with a selection of daily changing specials.

And for those also touring in the Holmfirth area, 17 years ago the Millas family bought and took over the running of the well-known Foxhouse Inn and Restaurant on Penistone Road. Much larger than The Talbot, it has the same excellent ambience, quality food and well-kept ales.

Rotherham Road, Monk Bretton, Barnsley,
South Yorkshire S71 2NW
☎ 01226 284503 Fax: 01226 243803
e-mail: lewismanda@aol.com

Monk Bretton is found less than a mile from the centre of Barnsley, not far from J37 of the M1. This part of South Yorkshire is well worth seeking out to find **The Full House and Sangdao's Thai Restaurant**, a superb bar and restaurant. Spacious and attractive, the interior boasts three distinct areas: the Legends Bar, the lounge bar and, of course, the Thai restaurant. The Legends Bar is adorned with pictures of well-known sportsmen and –women born in the region. Open every evening weekdays from 5 p.m., and from midday at weekends, there are three real ales on tap – John Smiths Cask is the regular, together with two rotating guest ales. To complement this there are also a very good choice of lagers, wines, spirits and cider, stout and soft drinks.

Authentic Thai cuisine is served in the restaurant and in the two bars from Wednesday to Saturday between 6.30 and 10.30 p.m. The restaurant is tastefully decorated and comfortably furnished, and seats 80 guests. All dishes make use of the freshest locally-sourced produce wherever possible, to create a range of meat, fish, poultry and vegetarian dishes expertly prepared. Booking required for Friday and Saturday evenings. On Sundays there's a tasty Carvery served 12–5 p.m., with a choice of meats and all the trimmings. Children welcome. No smoking in the restaurant.

The entertainment on hand is a real draw here, with a quiz night every Tuesday from 9.30 p.m. (complete with free bar snacks), live cabaret on Thursdays from 9, Friday's 'Golden Oldies' night with music and disco, themed 60s, 70s and 80s nights on Saturdays, and Sunday night games such as bingo, quiz and more. There's also a pool table on the premises, for anyone who fancies a game.

170 THE WHARNCLIFFE ARMS

Fishdam Lane, Carlton, Barnsley,
South Yorkshire S71 3HF
☎ 01226 722483
e-mail: cheryalanburton@yahoo.co.uk

Cheryl and Alan Burton took over as leaseholders at the impressive **Wharncliffe Arms** in June 2006; Alan has been in the trade for over seven years, but this is their first venture together into running a pub. Open every session weekdays and all day Fri-Sun (and all day every day in summer), there is one real ale (Black Sheep) though more are planned for the future. Tasty, hearty food is available at lunch and dinner Tuesday to Saturday 12-2 and 6-9, Sundays and Bank Holiday Mondays 12-9. Cheryl does the cooking

using the freshest ingredients; the menu changes regularly to match what is in season and at its tastiest.

171 THE SHIP INN

Wath Road, Elsecar, Barnsley,
South Yorkshire S74 8HJ
☎ 01226 742289

Nearly opposite the Elsecar Heritage Centre in the historic village of Elsecar, 8½ miles northeast of Barnsley off the B6097, **The Ship Inn** is a welcoming pub run by friendly tenants Sharon and Wally. Open every session weekdays and all day Saturday and Sunday,

the keg ales served include John Smiths Smooth, Magnet and Stones. The interior has recently been redecorated and is tasteful and cosy. Food is available from opening time; diners choose from the menu and specials board for a range of tasty chef-prepared and hearty traditional dishes. The large beer garden has a very good children's play area.

172 THE DROP INN

19 Providence Street, Low Valley,
Wombwell, Barnsley,
South Yorkshire S73 8AN
☎ 01226 751092

The Drop Inn is a friendly family-run place with great food, drink and accommodation. Found off the main A635 between Darfield and the centre of Wombwell, this convivial and welcoming inn dates back to the late 19th century. Kath and Melvyn Wright, ably assisted by daughter Rebecca, son Nick and son-in-law Andrew, offer first-class service and hospitality to all their guests. Closed Mondays until 5 p.m. and Saturdays until 7, it is open all other sessions and all day on Sundays.

A good selection of draught keg bitters, lagers, cider, stout, wines, spirits and soft drinks ensures something to please every thirsty punter. Tasty, fresh food is served Tuesday to Friday 12-2 and 5-8.30, and Sundays 12-3. The menu offers hearty favourites such as giant Yorkshire puddings filled with beef, chilli con carne, chicken and mushroom, steak and kidney and other fillings, freshly made hot and cold sandwiches and more. The chalet-style accommodation adjacent to the inn features two bedrooms and bath per chalet, available all year round.

173 CUSWORTH HALL TEA ROOM ¶

Cusworth Lane, Cusworth, Doncaster,
South Yorkshire DN5 7TU
☎ 01302 390959
◉ www.cusworthtearoom.co.uk

In the grounds of Cusworth Hall, an 18th-century country house on the outskirts of Doncaster and home of the Museum of South Yorkshire Life (closed for refurbishment until March 2007), the excellent **Cusworth Hall Tea Room** is open Tuesday to Sunday from 10 a.m. to 4 p.m. (when the Hall re-opens the tea room will be open seven days a week). Guests

choose from a menu and specials board for a range of delicious home-made hot and cold meals, cakes and more, made with the best of local produce. This cosy and charming place is also available for private parties in the evening – please ring for details.

174 THE DRUM ¶

Watch House Lane, Bentley, Doncaster,
South Yorkshire DN5 9NA
☎ 01302 874488

Situated in Bentley, a short drive from the centre of Doncaster, **The Drum** is a friendly former coaching inn dating back to 1830. Handsome and comfortable inside and out, it's open all day, every day for ale. Food is served Tuesday to Saturday at lunch and dinner, and for Sunday roasts (12-4). Booking advised on Sundays. The chef creates a range of delicious home-made

dishes. There's a large beer garden to the rear with children's play area. Leaseholders Barbara and Terry have been here a year, though Barbara was born and bred in Bentley and is a font of knowledge on the sights and attractions of the local area.

175 THE CROWN HOTEL ¶

High Street, Askern, Doncaster,
South Yorkshire DN6 0AV
☎ 01302 708548

The Crown Hotel boasts a long and proud history of offering excellent drink, accommodation and hospitality to all its guests. This expansive, impressive hotel dates back to the late 1700s. Recently refurbished with great taste and style, it maintains all its original charm while providing guests with every modern comfort. Very popular with locals and visitors alike, there are keg draught ales (Stones and Worthington) plus a good selection

of lagers, cider and stout on draught. No food is served at present, though leaseholder Susan Mawdsley has plans to serve bar meals within the lifetime of this edition. The four guest bedrooms are available all year round.

176 MOORENDS HOTEL ¶

46 Marshland Road, Moorends,
Doncaster, South Yorkshire DN8 4SU
☎ 01405 812170

Known locally as 'Uncle Arthur's' or just 'Uncs', **Moorends Hotel** is a popular pub and hotel with food and drink served all day. Julie and Ivor are your hosts; they arrived here in 2005 and, through hard work and dedication, have made the hotel a very welcoming and popular place. Built as a hostelry for local pitworkers back in the 1930s, this hotel – located north

of Thorne just a few miles from J6 of the M18 and east of the A614 – is open all day every day and serves popular draught keg ales and home-cooked bar snacks and meals. There are also nine guest bedrooms available on a room-only or bed-and-breakfast basis.

177 THE REINDEER

**Thorne Road, Sandtoft,
North Lincolnshire DN8 5SZ
☎ 01724 710774**

Superb, outstanding, excellent – just a few words used to describe **The Reindeer**, an inn with great food, drink and hospitality. Hidden away in the hamlet of Sandtoft in North Lincolnshire, just a stone's throw from the Yorkshire border and found off either the A18, A614 or A161, it is run with aplomb by recent arrivals Jill and Terry. They arrived here in May of 2006; their zeal and enthusiasm have kept the old customers loyal while attracting many happy new ones.

The premises date back to the late 1700s (when the inn was known as The Stag), and the interior of this spacious, traditional inn features exposed beams, open fireplace and other charming and cosy original elements which add to the inn's warm and welcoming ambience. Open every session Monday to Thursday, and all day Friday to Sunday, the inn serves up a good selection of ales, lagers, wines, spirits, soft drinks and more. Food is available Monday, Wednesday, Friday and at weekends at lunch (12–2) and dinner (6–9). Plans are afoot to extend these hours. Jill does the cooking, creating a good range of tempting dishes for the changing menu and specials board, all using the best and freshest local produce.

Guests can dine in the no-smoking restaurant, which seats 50, or in the bar areas or outdoors on fine days in the enclosed beer garden, which also has a play area. Booking advised at weekends. During the lifetime of this edition Jill and Terry hope to be able to provide first-class accommodation as well, as Sandtoft would make an excellent touring base – please ring for further details.

178 THE EPWORTH TAP

9–11 Market Place, Epworth, Doncaster,
South Yorkshire DN9 1EU
☎ 01427 873333

Just a short drive from the Yorkshire border in Lincolnshire, **The Epworth Tap** is a superb and highly recommended restaurant, bistro and wine bar in the heart of the village. Owners Steve and Sarah Ward arrived in 2004 and have a real success on their hands, with an enviable reputation for service, hospitality, the wine list and excellent menu.

Open Wednesday to Saturday from 10.30 a.m. for morning coffee, bistro service 11.30-2 and evenings from 7 p.m. (also open Sundays for traditional lunch from 12-2), booking is advised at all times. The Mediterranean-influenced menu includes delicious fresh fish dishes, duck breast with balsamic beetroot and blue cheese salad, rack of lamb,

steaks, soups, vegetable dishes and much more, all freshly prepared. This homely, welcoming place is well worth seeking out.

179 WESLEY GUEST HOUSE

16 Queen Street, Epworth, Doncaster,
South Yorkshire DN9 1HG
☎ 01427 874512   Fax: 01427 874592
e-mail: enquiries@wesleyguesthouse.com
🌐 www.wesleyguesthouse.com

Wesley Guest House is one of the very best bed-and-breakfast guest houses for miles around, with ratings of 4 Diamonds from the English Tourist Council, AA and the RAC. This magnificent property dates back over 400 years and combines the finest original features with every modern comfort and convenience.

Entered through gates, to ensure privacy, no luxury is overlooked in any detail. Located along the A161, near the Yorkshire/Lincolnshire border, this simply elegant guest house occupies a setting that offers guests both the pleasures of the countryside and the convenience of being near many of the region's most bustling towns, historic attractions and places of interest, as well as the vibrant cities of York and Lincoln. The town of Epworth itself has been a focus of celebrations marking the birth of John Wesley, founder of Methodism, who was born here in 1703. Owner Graham Wilson has had the pleasure of living here since 1948; three years ago, in 2003, he decided to offer top-of-the-range bed-and-breakfast accommodation as well.

There are four ensuite guest bedrooms – one on the ground floor – each individually decorated and furnished with taste and guests' comfort in mind. Breakfast is a hearty and delicious affair, and special diets or requests are cheerfully catered for. Evening meals are also available by arrangement. There's some nice walking in the area, and an outstanding rear garden to wander about it if you desire. Leisure facilities within the house include the snooker room. Recently awarded a 'Quality in Tourism' award, this excellent guest house is well worth seeking out.

Tourist Information Centres

AYSGARTH FALLS
Aysgarth Falls National Park Centre
Aysgarth Falls
Leyburn
North Yorkshire DL8 3TH
Tel No: 01969 662910
Fax: 01969 662919
e-mail: aysgarth@ytbtic.co.uk

BARNSLEY
Cooper Gallery
Church Street
Barnsley
South Yorkshire S70 2AH
Tel No: 01226 206757
Fax: 01226 206757
e-mail: barnsley@ytbtic.co.uk

BATLEY
The Mill Discount Department Store
Bradford Road
Batley
Yorkshire WF17 5LZ
Tel No: 01924 426670
Fax: 01924 446096
e-mail: batley@ytbtic.co.uk

BEVERLEY
34 Butcher Row
Beverley
East Yorkshire HU17 0AB
Tel No: 01482 867430
Fax: 01482 391674
e-mail: beverley.tic@eastriding.gov.uk

BRADFORD
City Hall
Bradford
West Yorkshire BD1 1HY
Tel No: 01274 433678
Fax: 01274 739067
e-mail: tourist.information@bradford.gov.uk

BRIDLINGTON
25 Prince Street
Bridlington
East Riding of Yorkshire YO15 2NP
Tel No: 01262 673474
Fax: 01262 401797
e-mail: bridlington.tic@eastriding.gov.uk

BRIGG
The Buttercross
Market Place
Brigg
North Lincolnshire DN20 8ER
Tel No: 01652 657053
Fax: 01652 657053
e-mail: brigg.tic@northlincs.gov.uk

CLEETHORPES
42-43 Alexandra Road
Cleethorpes
North East Lincolnshire DN35 8LE
Tel No: 01472 323111
Fax: 01472 323112
e-mail: cleetic@nelc.gov.uk

DANBY
The Moors Centre
Danby Lodge
Lodge Lane
Danby, Whitby
North Yorkshire YO21 2NB
Tel No: 01439 772737
Fax: 01287 660308
e-mail: moorscentre@northyorkmoors-npa.gov.uk

DONCASTER
38-40 High Street
Doncaster
South Yorkshire DN1 1DE
Tel No: 01302 734309
Fax: 01302 735385
e-mail: tourist.information@doncaster.gov.uk

DONCASTER
38-40 High Street
Doncaster
South Yorkshire DN1 1DE
Tel No: 01302 734309
Fax: 01302 735385
e-mail: tourist.information@doncaster.gov.uk

GRASSINGTON
National Park Centre
Colvend, Hebden Road
Grassington
North Yorkshire BD23 5LB
Tel No: 01756 752774
Fax: 01756 753358
e-mail: grassington@ytbtic.co.uk

GUISBOROUGH
Priory Grounds
Church Street
Guisborough TS14 6HG
Tel No: 01287 633801
Fax: 01287 633801
e-mail: guisborough_tic@redcar-cleveland.gov.uk

HALIFAX VISITOR CENTRE & ART GALLERY
Piece Hall
Halifax
West Yorkshire HX1 1RE
Tel No: 01422 368725
Fax: 01422 354264
e-mail: halifax@ytbtic.co.uk

HARROGATE

Royal Baths, Crescent Road
Harrogate
North Yorkshire HG1 2RR
Tel No: 01423 537300
Fax: 01423 537305
e-mail: tic@harrogate.gov.uk

HAWES

Dales Countryside Museum, Station Yard
Hawes
North Yorkshire DL8 3NT
Tel No: 01969 666210
Fax: 01969 666239
e-mail: hawes@ytbtic.co.uk

HAWORTH

2/4 West Lane
Haworth, Near Keighley
West Yorkshire BD22 8EF
Tel No: 01535 642329
Fax: 01535 647721
e-mail: haworth@ytbtic.co.uk

HEBDEN BRIDGE

Visitor and Canal Centre, New Road
Hebden Bridge
West Yorkshire HX7 8AF
Tel No: 01422 843831
Fax: 01422 845266
e-mail: hebdenbridge@ytbtic.co.uk

HELMSLEY

The Visitor Centre, Helmsley Castle
Castlegate, Helmsley
North Yorkshire YO62 5AB
Tel No: 01439 770173
Fax: 01439 771116
e-mail: helmsley@ytbtic.co.uk

HOLMFIRTH

49-51 Huddersfield Road
Holmfirth
West Yorkshire HD9 3JP
Tel No: 01484 222444
Fax: 01484 222445
e-mail: holmfirth.tic@kirklees.gov.uk

HORNSEA

120 Newbegin
Hornsea
East Yorkshire HU18 1PB
Tel No: 01964 536404
Fax: 01964 536404
e-mail: hornsea.tic@eastriding.gov.uk

HORTON-IN-RIBBLESDALE

Pen-y-ghent Cafe
Horton-in-Ribblesdale
Settle
North Yorkshire BD24 0HE
Tel No: 01729 860333
Fax: 01729 860333
e-mail: horton@ytbtic.co.uk

HUDDERSFIELD

3 Albion Street
Huddersfield
West Yorkshire HD1 2NW
Tel No: 01484 223200
Fax: 01484 223202
e-mail: huddersfield.tic@kirklees.gov.uk

HULL

1 Paragon Street
Hull
East Yorkshire HU1 3NA
Tel No: 01482 223559
Fax: 01482 613959
e-mail: tourist.information@hullcc.gov.uk

HUMBER BRIDGE

North Bank Viewing Area
Ferriby Road
Hessle
East Yorkshire HU13 0LN
Tel No: 01482 640852
Fax: 01482 640852
e-mail: humberbridge.tic@eastriding.gov.uk

ILKLEY

Town Hall
Station Rd
Ilkley
West Yorkshire LS29 8HB
Tel No: 01943 602319
Fax: 01943 436235
e-mail: ilkley@ytbtic.c.uk

INGLETON

The Community Centre Car Park
Ingleton
North Yorkshire LA6 3HG
Tel No: 015242 41049
Fax: 015242 41701
e-mail: ingleton@ytbtic.co.uk

KNARESBOROUGH

9 Castle Courtyard
Market Place
Knaresborough
North Yorkshire HG5 8AE
Tel No: 0845 3890177
Fax: 01423 866886
e-mail: kntic@harrogate.gov.uk

LEEDS

Gateway Yorkshire, PO Box 244
The Arcade, City Station
Leeds
West Yorkshire LS1 1PL
Tel No: 0113 242 5242
Fax: 0113 246 8246
e-mail: tourinfo@leeds.gov.uk

LEEMING BAR

The Yorkshire Maid, The Great North Road
Leeming Bar, Bedale
North Yorkshire DL8 1DT
Tel No: 01677 424262
Fax: 01677 423069
e-mail: leeming@ytbtic.co.uk

LEYBURN

4 Central Chambers, Railway Street
Leyburn
North Yorkshire DL8 5BB
Tel No: 01969 623069
Fax: 01969 622833
e-mail: leyburn@ytbtic.co.uk

MALHAM

National Park Centre, Malham
Skipton
North Yorkshire BD23 4DA
Tel No: 01969 652380
Fax: 01969 652389
e-mail: malham@ytbtic.co.uk

MALTON

58 Market Place
Malton
North Yorkshire YO17 7LW
Tel No: 01653 600048
Fax: 01653 698374
e-mail: maltontic@btconnect.com

OTLEY

Otley Library & Tourist Information
Nelson Street, Otley
West Yorkshire LS21 1EZ
Tel No: 01943 462485
Fax: 01943 466675
e-mail: otleytic@leedslearning.net

PATELEY BRIDGE

18 High Street
Pateley Bridge
North Yorkshire HG3 5AW
Tel No: 0845 3890179
Fax: 01423 711147
e-mail: pbtic@harrogate.gov.uk

PICKERING

Ropery House, The Ropery
Pickering
North Yorkshire YO18 8DY
Tel No: 01751 473791
Fax: 01751 473487
e-mail: pickering@ytbtic.co.uk

REDCAR

West Terrace
Esplanade
Redcar
Cleveland TS10 3AE
Tel No: 01642 471921
Fax: 01642 471921
e-mail: redcar_tic@redcar-cleveland.gov.uk

REETH

Hudson House, The Green
Reeth
Richmond
North Yorkshire DL11 6TB
Tel No: 01748 884059
Fax: 01748 880012
e-mail: reeth@ytbtic.co.uk

RICHMOND

Friary Gardens, Victoria Road
Richmond
North Yorkshire DL10 4AJ
Tel No: 01748 850252
Fax: 01748 825994
e-mail: richmond@ytbtic.co.uk

RIPON

Minster Road
Ripon
North Yorkshire HG4 1QT
Tel No: 0845 3890178
Fax: 01765 604625
e-mail: ripontic@harrogate.gov.uk

ROTHERHAM VISITOR CENTRE

40 Bridgegate, Rotherham
South Yorkshire S60 1PQ
Tel No: 01709 835904
Fax: 01709 336888
e-mail: tic@rotherham.gov.uk

SALTBURN BY SEA

3 Station Buildings, Station Square
Saltburn-by-Sea
Cleveland TS12 1AQ
Tel No: 01287 622422
Fax: 01287 625074
e-mail: saltburn_tic@redcar-cleveland.gov.uk

SCARBOROUGH

Brunswick Shopping Centre, Westborough
Scarborough
North Yorkshire YO11 1UE
Tel No: 01723 383636
Fax: 01723 507302
e-mail: tourismbureau@scarborough.gov.uk

SCARBOROUGH (HARBOURSIDE)

Harbourside TIC, Sandside
Scarborough
North Yorkshire YO11 1PP
Tel No: Operated by: Scarborough TIC
Fax: 01723 507302
e-mail: harboursidetic@scarborough.gov.uk

SCUNTHORPE

North Lincolnshire Central Library
Carlton Street
Scunthorpe
North Lincolnshire DN15 6TX
Tel No: 01724 297354
Fax: 01724 859737
e-mail: brigg.tic@northlincs.gov.uk

SELBY

Visitor Information Centre
52 Micklegate
Selby
North Yorkshire YO8 4EQ
Tel No: 01757 212181
Fax: 01757 705396
e-mail: selby@ytbtic.co.uk

SETTLE

Town Hall
Cheapside
Settle
North Yorkshire BD24 9EJ
Tel No: 01729 825192
Fax: 01729 824381
e-mail: settle@ytbtic.co.uk

SHEFFIELD

Tourist Information Centre
12 Norfolk Row
Sheffield
Souith Yorkshire
Tel No: 0114 2211900
Fax: 0114 281 4042
e-mail: visitor@sheffield.gov.uk

SKIPTON

35 Coach Street
Skipton
North Yorkshire BD23 1LQ
Tel No: 01756 792809
Fax: 01756 700709
e-mail: skipton@ytbtic.co.uk

SUTTON BANK

Sutton Bank Visitor Centre
Sutton Bank
Thirsk
North Yorkshire YO7 2EH
Tel No: 01845 597426
Fax: 01845 597174
e-mail: suttonbank@ytbtic.co.uk

THIRSK

Thirsk Tourist Information Centre
49 Market Place
Thirsk
North Yorkshire YO7 1HA
Tel No: 01845 522755
Fax: 01845 526230
e-mail: thirsktic@hambleton.gov.uk

TODMORDEN

15 Burnley Road
Todmorden
West Yorkshire OL14 7BU
Tel No: 01706 818181
Fax: 01706 818181
e-mail: todmorden@ytbtic.co.uk

WAKEFIELD

9 The Bull Ring
Wakefield
West Yorkshire WF1 1HB
Tel No: 0845 601 8353
Fax: 01924 305775
e-mail: tic@wakefield.gov.uk

WETHERBY

Wetherby Library & Tourist Information Centre
17 Westgate
Wetherby
West Yorkshire LS22 6LL
Tel No: 01937 582151
Fax: 01937 586964
e-mail: wetherbytic@leedslearning.net

WHITBY

Langborne Road
Whitby
North Yorkshire YO21 1YN
Tel No: 01723 383637
Fax: 01947 606137
e-mail: whitbytic@scarborough.gov.uk

WITHERNSEA

131 Queen Street
Withernsea
East Yorkshire HU19 2DJ
Tel No: 01964 615683
Fax: 01964 615683
e-mail: withernsea.tic@eastriding.gov.uk

YORK (DE GREY ROOMS)

The De Grey Rooms
Exhibition Square
York
North Yorkshire YO1 7HB
Tel No: 01904 550099
Fax: 01904 550098
e-mail: tourism@yorkvic.co.uk

YORK (RAILWAY STATION)

Outer Concourse
Railway Station
Station Road
York
North Yorkshire YO24 1AY
Tel No: 01904 550099
Fax: 01904 550098
e-mail: tourism@yorkvic.co.uk

Towns, Villages and Places of Interest

Y

310

TRAVEL PUBLISHING ORDER FORM

To order any of our publications just fill in the payment details below and complete the order form. For orders of less than 4 copies please add £1.00 per book for postage and packing. Orders over 4 copies are P & P free.

Name:

Address:

Tel no:

Please Complete Either:

I enclose a cheque for £ _____ made payable to Travel Publishing Ltd

Or:

Card No: **Expiry Date:**

Signature:

Please either send, telephone, fax or e-mail your order to:

Travel Publishing Ltd, 7a Apollo House, Calleva Park, Aldermaston, Berkshire RG7 8TN

Tel: 0118 981 7777   Fax: 0118 940 8428   e-mail: info@travelpublishing.co.uk

	Price	Quantity		Price	Quantity
HIDDEN PLACES REGIONAL TITLES			**COUNTRY PUBS AND INNS**		
Comwall	£8.99	....	Cornwall	£5.99	....
Devon	£8.99	....	Devon	£7.99	....
Dorset, Hants & Isle of Wight	£8.99	....	Sussex	£5.99	....
East Anglia	£8.99	....	Wales	£8.99	....
Lake District & Cumbria	£8.99	....	Yorkshire	£7.99	....
Northumberland & Durham	£8.99	....			
Peak District	£8.99	....	**COUNTRY LIVING RURAL GUIDES**		
Yorkshire	£8.99	....	East Anglia	£10.99	....
			Heart of England	£10.99	....
HIDDEN PLACES NATIONAL TITLES			Ireland	£11.99	....
England	£11.99	....	North East	£10.99	....
Ireland	£11.99	....	North West	£10.99	....
Scotland	£11.99	....	Scotland	£11.99	....
Wales	£11.99	....	South of England	£10.99	....
			South East of England	£10.99	....
HIDDEN INNS TITLES			Wales	£11.99	....
East Anglia	£7.99	....	West Country	£10.99	....
Heart of England	£7.99	....			
South	£7.99	....			
South East	£7.99	....	**TOTAL QUANTITY:**		
West Country	£7.99	....	**POST & PACKING:**		
OTHER TITLES					
Off the Motorway	£11.99	....	**TOTAL VALUE:**		

VISIT THE TRAVEL PUBLISHING WEBSITE

Looking for:

- *Places to Visit?*
- *Places to Stay?*
- *Places to Eat & Drink?*
- *Places to Shop?*

Then why not visit the Travel Publishing website...

- Informative pages on places to visit, stay, eat, drink and shop throughout the British Isles.

- Detailed information on Travel Publishing's wide range of national and regional travel guides.

www.travelpublishing.co.uk

HIDDEN PLACES GUIDES

Explore Britain and Ireland with *Hidden Places* guides - a fascinating series of national and local travel guides.

Packed with easy to read information on hundreds of places of interest as well as places to stay, eat and drink.

Available from both high street and internet booksellers

For more information on the full range of *Hidden Places* guides and other titles published by Travel Publishing visit our website on

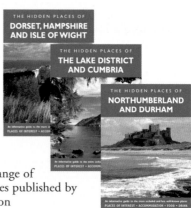

www.travelpublishing.co.uk
or ask for our leaflet by phoning **0118-981-7777** or
emailing **info@travelpublishing.co.uk**

READER REACTION FORM

The *Travel Publishing* research team would like to receive reader's comments on any visitor attractions or places reviewed in the book and also recommendations for suitable entries to be included in the next edition. This will help ensure that the *Country Living series of Guides* continues to provide its readers with useful information on the more interesting, unusual or unique features of each attraction or place ensuring that their visit to the local area is an enjoyable and stimulating experience. To provide your comments or recommendations would you please complete the forms below and overleaf as indicated and send to:

**The Research Department, Travel Publishing Ltd,
7a Apollo House, Calleva Park, Aldermaston, Reading, RG7 8TN.**

Your Name:

Your Address:

Your Telephone Number:

Please tick as appropriate:

Comments ☐   Recommendation ☐

Name of Establishment:

Address:

Telephone Number:

Name of Contact:

READER REACTION FORM

COMMENT OR REASON FOR RECOMMENDATION:

....
....
....
....
....
....
....
....
....
....
....
....
....
....
....
....
....
....
....

Index of Advertisers

315

INDEX OF ADVERTISERS

PLACES OF INTEREST

316